Travel
North
Carolina

TRAVEL NORTH

CAROLYN
SAKOWSKI

ANNE HOLCOMB WATERS

SUE CLARK

DEB BALDWIN

CAROLINA

Going Native in the Old North State

BY THE STAFF OF JOHN F. BLAIR, PUBLISHER

ED SOUTHERN

SUNNY SMITH NELSON

JOHN F. BLAIR, PUBLISHER
WINSTON-SALEM, NORTH CAROLINA

Published by John F. Blair, Publisher

*The paper in this book meets the guidelines
for permanence and durability of the
Committee on Production Guidelines for
Book Longevity of the Council on Library Resources.*

Library of Congress Cataloging-in-Publication Data

Travel North Carolina: going native in the Old North State /
by the staff of John F. Blair, Publisher.
p.   cm.
Includes index.
ISBN 0-89587-232-3 (alk. paper)
1. North Carolina—Guidebooks.   I. John F. Blair, Publisher.

F252.3.T73 2001
917.5604'44—dc21   2001016188

Design by Debra Long Hampton

*We lovingly dedicate this book to
Steve Kirk, Debbie Hampton, Margaret Couch,
Jackie Whitman, and Heath Simpson.
Without them, this book would not be possible.*

Contents

Acknowledgments

Sunny Smith Nelson would like to thank Quinn Capps of the Outer Banks Visitors Bureau; Carl Blake of the Elizabeth City/Pasquotank County Tourism Board; Nancy Nicholls of the Chowan County Tourism Development Authority; Ann T. Byrum of Historic Edenton State Historic Site; Courtney Morris of the Historic Bath Visitor Center; Lloyd D. Childers, light keeper of the Currituck Beach Lighthouse; Laura Catoe and Laura Dunn of Roanoke Island Festival Park; Daryl Law of the North Carolina Aquarium on Roanoke Island; Larissa Brown with *The Lost Colony*; Robert Woody at the Cape Hatteras Lighthouse; Carl Bornfriend of the Frisco Native American Museum and Natural History Center; Penny Leary-Smith of the Dismal Swamp Canal Welcome Center; Karen Hayes of Somerset Place State Historic Site; and Mariann Dellerba of the North Carolina Division of Tourism, Film, and Sports Development.

Anne Holcomb Waters would like to extend her heartfelt thanks to all the terrific people at the convention and visitors' bureaus and chambers of commerce from Cape Lookout to Sunset Beach. Among them are Connie Nelson, Susie Vann, Janis Williams, and Mitzi York. A special thanks also goes to informants Neva Bridges and Doug Wolfe, two excellent booksellers, and to Mariann Dellerba of the North Carolina Division of Tourism, Film, and Sports Development. And finally, I would like to thank my wonderful traveling companions—my husband, Andrew, and my mom, Carroll Holcomb.

Deb Baldwin would like to thank Bruce Daws at Fayetteville City Hall; the staff at the Fayetteville Department of Tourism; the staff at the Fort Bragg Welcome Center; Margaret Skinner at the Carolina Inn; Andy Martin at Residence Inn by Marriott in Southern Pines; Mariann Dellerba of the North Carolina Division of Tourism, Film, and Sports Development; David Perry at the University of North Carolina Press; Jerry Carroll in the North Carolina Room at the Forsyth County Public Library; and the folks at Cape Fear Regional Theatre.

Ed Southern would like to thank Jennifer Couch with the Winston-Salem Convention and Visitors' Bureau; Molly Yarbrough with Winston-Salem Events; David Hampton with Wachovia Bank; Steve Kirk of John F. Blair; and Bob Southern, Lynn Southern, and Courtney Southern for their insiders' knowledge.

Carolyn Sakowski would like to thank the following people for their assistance: Bob Choate of the Alleghany County Chamber of Commerce and his wife, Mary; Carolyn Howser of the Boone Convention and Visitors Bureau; Jill Hatfield of High Country Host; Veronica Williams of the High Point Convention and Visitors Bureau; Adriene Heffner of the Greensboro Area Convention and Visitors Bureau; Shannon Harding at the Yancey County Chamber of Commerce; and Linda Medford at the Mitchell County Chamber of Commerce.

Sue Clark would like to thank Father Cecil Tice of St. Lawrence Basilica in Asheville; David Tomsky of the Grove Park Inn and Spa in Asheville; Guy and Hylah Smalley of Mountain Creek Bed-and-Breakfast in Waynesville; Mariann Dellerba of the North Carolina Division of Tourism, Film, and Sports Development; Barbara O'Neil of Biltmore Estate in Asheville; and Chris, Chad, and Ben Clark, the world's best traveling companions—I'd go anywhere with you guys!

All of the authors would like to thank our intern, Erin Styers, for her help with the appendix. We would also like to thank James Cockerham, the owner of the fabulous Thunderbird used on the book's cover, and Martin Tucker, who brought order out of chaos when he photographed the cover.

Introduction

Who better to publish a travel guide to North Carolina than the staff of a North Carolina publisher? As the staff of John F. Blair, Publisher, planned its future publication projects, we asked ourselves that very question. We looked around and realized that, collectively, we were in a better position to write about our home state than some guy from New York City who popped in for one weekend and recorded his snap judgments.

When we decided to undertake this project, we also decided that we wanted the guide to reflect our individual personalities. That's why you may notice distinct styles for each section.

Here's a brief look at who we are:

Sunny Smith Nelson is the author of the sections on the Outer Banks and the Albemarle region. She was born and raised in Winston-Salem, where her family has resided for over 200 years as members of the Moravian Church. While earning her degree in international studies from the University of North Carolina at Chapel Hill, she imagined herself leaving North Carolina to lead a life of glamour and mystery as a world traveler. Instead, she returned to Winston-Salem because the rent was cheaper. Now working as the Internet marketing director for John F. Blair, she realizes that you sometimes don't know how good you've got it until someone (like your husband from New York) reminds you. She's a born-again North Carolina enthusiast.

Anne Holcomb Waters wrote the sections on the Neuse River region and the Cape Fear coast. In January 1996, she moved to North Carolina to work as John F. Blair's publicity director, but she first visited the state—and fell under its spell—in the 1980s. In the years since her arrival, she has had the pleasure of visiting North Carolina's lower coast on numerous occasions—as a tour guide for her Arkansas relatives, on Blair staff retreats, and for her own pleasure. She holds a degree in ancient Greek from Randolph-Macon Woman's College in Lynchburg, Virginia, where she was introduced to the shag. She and her husband, Andrew, live in Winston-Salem with their three cats and their dog, Doc.

Deb Baldwin was born, raised, and educated in North Carolina. Several lifetimes later, following a life in the theater, a role as editor of a Caribbean newspaper, and work in book publishing, she is the graphic designer at the North Carolina School of the Arts, located in Winston-Salem. After climbing the Andes, cruising the Baltic Sea, cavorting in the Caribbean, and careening across the United States in a convertible, she still considers Chapel Hill to be the ultimate destination.

Ed Southern is a natural to write the Charlotte and Winston-Salem sections, having spent most of his adult life moving back and forth between the two. He was born in Winston-Salem, spent his early childhood there, came back to go to Wake Forest University, and has now come back for good (he hopes) to raise his children. In between, he lived for five years in Charlotte, where his mother and his wife were both raised. He holds a degree in political philosophy and has written extensively for newspapers and literary magazines.

Carolyn Sakowski wrote the sections for Greensboro, High Point, and the High Country. She was born in North Carolina and has lived in the state for 42 years. She grew up in Morganton, graduated from Queens College in Charlotte with a B.A. in history, and got an M.A. in history from Appalachian State University in Boone. She and her husband have an Avery County farm, which he inherited from his grandfather. That's where they escape to mow the fields most weekends in the summer and fall. She is also the author of *Touring the Western North Carolina Backroads* and *Touring the East Tennessee Backroads*.

Sue Clark is a native of Detroit. In March of her senior year at Oakland University in Rochester, Michigan, her father sent her pictures of dogwood trees in bloom. That was enough to entice her to move south. She's been here almost 20 years and considers herself one of North Carolina's biggest fans. Sue has a B.A. in American history with a minor in English from Oakland University. She has worked for John F. Blair for over 10 year; she is director of customer service. Sue is married and has two sons. The Clark family loves to travel and especially enjoys camping in the mountains. Sue's hobbies include cooking (she's also Blair's food editor), needlework, and singing. Yankee by birth, Southern by choice, Sue plans to call North Carolina home for the rest of her life.

When discussing a format for the book, we decided that we didn't want an inclusive listing of every accommodation in each city. If you want that kind of list, we've provided contact information for local convention and visitor bureaus. What we tried to do was avoid the chains, unless there was something unique about a particular chain hotel or motel. We looked for locally owned, one-of-a-kind places that visitors might be unaware of. We did the same thing when choosing restaurants. We tried to find the places that the locals would put on their list if you asked them for the best places in town to eat. We couldn't include them all, but we tried to offer a variety of cuisines and price ranges. We didn't charge any establishment a fee to be included in this book. Although our choices were subjective, we wanted to approach these places just like regular visitors would.

Because prices for both food and lodging fluctuate, we've simply categorized each establishment as Deluxe, Expensive, Moderate, or Inexpensive, based on the scales below.

For accommodations, the breakdown is

Deluxe—Over $125 for a double room
Expensive—$95 to $125
Moderate—$60 to $95
Inexpensive—Under $60 (There aren't many of these left!)

Prices often vary according to the season. For example, you might find some good bargains on the coast if you decide to vacation there in the late fall or winter. In the mountains, the bargains come after the summer and October fall foliage seasons but before the ski season.

For restaurants, the breakdown is

Expensive—Over $18 for most entrées
Moderate—$10 to $18
Inexpensive—Under $10

We worked on our individual sections for over a year. All things considered, it's been a good project for us. Although each of us came to our section with some previous knowledge of the area we were writing about, we all learned even more about our home state. Each of us is proud to be from North Carolina, and we're glad that we can share our enthusiasm with you.

Carolyn Sakowski
President, John F. Blair, Publisher

THE COAST

The Outer Banks

Northern Banks and Beaches

Roanoke Island

Bodie Island

Hatteras Island

Ocracoke Island

A lifelong resident of North Carolina, I was in my mid-20s and on my honeymoon before I ever visited the Outer Banks. I never visited as a child because, I suspect, my parents thought there wasn't much there that would interest someone my age. Their image of the Outer Banks was a six-hour drive from where we lived to small, thin islands offering nothing but sand, surf, and wind. My then-fiancé (and now husband), a transplant from New York who had visited the Banks many times since attending the University of North Carolina at Chapel Hill, told me stories about the long, sandy beaches where one could sit in silence and hear nothing but nature around you, about the oyster and steam-bar restaurants where you could go in to get a bite to eat and end up making friends with the bartender and the person sitting next to you, and about sand dunes as big as houses, where hang gliders with colorful wings would take flight and hover over the waves. We decided to take our honeymoon there because of the things he had told me about—the peace, the friendliness, and the beauty of the Banks.

Our time at the Banks was a whirlwind. We climbed lighthouses, went to see the oldest outdoor drama in the United States, climbed aboard a 69-foot reproduction of one of the ships the Roanoke Island colonists sailed, kayaked in Shallowbag Bay, heard an afternoon jazz concert, walked where the first English child born in the New World probably took her first steps, climbed a sand dune to visit the memorial to the first men in flight, walked through the sand and sea grass of wildlife refuges, strolled the docks of marinas, and stopped by many a restaurant to make friends with other diners and the staff. I was happily surprised to discover that there is much to see and do on the Outer Banks. Most importantly, I discovered that the Outer Banks can be whatever you want them to be—the quiet, wind-swept dunes of my parents' imaginations or the friendly, outgoing, and active vacation spot I found while staying there.

Just the Facts

There are two main roads on the Outer Banks, U.S. 158 (also known as the Croatan Highway) and N.C. 12 (also known as Virginia Dare Trail or the Beach Road). The two parallel one another in the northern section of the Outer Banks. Note that local directions from these roads are customarily given by milepost, rather than by street number. Milepost 1 is in Kitty Hawk and Milepost 16 is in Nags Head.

To reach the Banks from the north, follow either U.S. 17 or V.A. 168 to U.S. 158. Take U.S. 158 East across the Wright Brothers Memorial Bridge over Currituck Sound. To reach the northern communities of Duck, Sanderling, and Corolla, turn left on N.C. 12. To go south toward Kitty Hawk, Kill

Devil Hills, and Nags Head, turn right on either of the two main roads.

From the south, you can take either a land or a water route. Via land, take U.S. 264 East to U.S. 64 East, which will lead you through Roanoke Island to Bodie Island. For a scenic trip, the ferry system is the way to go. The Swan Quarter ferry and the Cedar Island ferry both take travelers to Ocracoke Island, the southernmost island in the Outer Banks. Either ferry ride takes about two and a half hours. Reservations are required in the summer and are advisable year-round. To contact the Swan Quarter ferry office, call 800-773-1094; to contact the Cedar Island ferry office, call 800-856-0343. From Ocracoke, travelers can take the free, 40-minute ferry ride to Hatteras Island to gain access to the rest of the Outer Banks; no reservations are required for the Hatteras ferry.

From central North Carolina, U.S. 64 leads directly across Roanoke Island to Nags Head. From there, travelers turn left on either U.S. 158 or N.C. 12 to head up the coast toward Kill Devil Hills and points north or turn right on N.C. 12 to head south toward Hatteras Island.

The Dare County Regional Airport is located on Airport Road in Manteo. It has runways 3,290 feet and 4,300 feet in length. Fuel and services are offered 24 hours a day, but the airport is open to local charters only. For information, call 252-473-2600. Cars and limousine rentals are available at the airport.

Limited taxi and limousine services are available on the Outer Banks, but you'll find that the best way to explore the area is to drive, bike, or walk.

One of the best sources of information about the area is the Outer Banks Visitors Bureau, 704 U.S. 64/U.S. 264, P.O. Box 399, Manteo, N.C. 27954 (800-446-6262 or 252-473-2138). You can visit their website at www.outerbanks.org to learn about the history, culture, and folklore of the area.

The Aycock Brown Welcome Center, located at Mile-post 1.5 on U.S. 158 in Kitty Hawk, includes a theater, a brochure gazebo, and 17 state-of-the-art displays. Its hours are from 8:30 A.M. to 5 P.M.; later hours are offered in the summer.

The visitor center on the northern end of Roanoke Island is open from 10 A.M. to 6 P.M. from mid-March to November.

Another visitor center is located at the entrance to Cape Hatteras National Seashore at Whalebone Junction, near the intersection of U.S. 64, U.S. 158, and N.C. 12. It is open daily from 9 A.M. to 5 P.M. from mid-March to November.

by Sunny Smith Nelson

PHOTOGRAPH USED IN THE BACKGROUND ON PAGE 3—

Nags Head
COURTESY OF NORTH CAROLINA DIVISION OF TOURISM, FILM AND SPORTS DEVELOPMENT

Nags Head Beach
COURTESY OF OUTER BANKS VISITORS BUREAU

NORTHERN BANKS AND BEACHES

by Sunny Smith Nelson

*D*epending on your perspective, N.C. 12, the main artery on the Outer Banks, either gets its start or meets its end in the northern Banks and beaches. This makes it a great jumping-off point or a good destination as it traverses sand dunes, sea grass, and ocean inlets cut by hurricanes to take you over a peninsula, across two islands, and through 400 years of history. This northern frontier stretches from Corolla to Nags Head. Here, you'll discover the northernmost lighthouse on the Banks, the tallest sand dune on the East Coast, and the spot where man first took flight. Or you can just relax in your lounge chair and watch the day pass by. The northern Banks and beaches offer some of the least and some of the most developed seashore on the Outer Banks. Visitors thus have the opportunity to be alone or in the middle of everything.

Things To Do

HISTORIC PLACES, GARDENS, AND TOURS

- **Currituck Beach Lighthouse**, located off of N.C. 12 in Corolla, is the northernmost lighthouse on the Outer Banks. This was the last major brick lighthouse built on the Outer Banks. Its approximately 1,000,000 bricks were left unpainted to distinguish it from its famous counterparts. Begun in 1873 and completed two years later, it served the 40-mile area of dark coastline between Cape Henry Lighthouse to the north and Bodie Island Lighthouse to the south. The 162-foot Currituck Beach Lighthouse had a light visible at 18 nautical miles. Before the advent of electricity, it was powered by a mineral-oil lamp that consisted of five concentric wicks, the largest of which was four inches in diameter. The lighthouse keeper was required to physically move the huge lens every two and a half hours to keep the light flashing. Cranking by hand the weights that were suspended from a line beneath the lantern, he moved the light much in the way a grandfather clock's gears turn to make the hour chime. The beam flooded the night sky for three seconds before fading to black for 17 seconds. This not only warned passing ships of the treacherous coastline but allowed them to decipher where they were on their journey as well.

The lighthouse is still a navigational tool for sailors today, emitting its beam from dusk until dawn, though the keeper doesn't have to crank the lens nowadays. Visitors are invited to climb the 214 steps to the top, weather permitting. An interpretive guide is on hand to share facts about the lighthouse.

Also on the grounds is the lighthouse keepers' home. Shipped by barge to the Banks already precut and labeled for easy assembly, the Victorian "stick style" dwelling was completed in 1876. Two keepers and their families moved in to share the duplex. Visitors are not allowed to tour the home, as it is undergoing restoration by Outer Banks Conservationists, Inc.

Other structures on the property include cisterns for catching rainwater for household use, an outhouse, a chapel, and a schoolhouse. A museum shop is located in a second lighthouse keeper's home, built in

1870 at Long Point Lighthouse Station on Currituck Sound and shipped to its current location in 1920.

No keepers have lived here since the light was automated in 1939.

Currituck Beach Lighthouse and the museum shop are open daily from 10 A.M. to 6 P.M. from April to November. An admission fee is charged. Children must be at least four years old to climb the lighthouse. For information, call 252-453-4939, or visit their website at www.currituckbeachlight.com.

■ *The Whalehead Club* is located within walking distance of Currituck Beach Lighthouse. Completed in 1925 after three years and $383,000 in construction costs, it was for a time a private residence called Corolla Island, the first home on the Outer Banks to have a basement, an elevator, and a swimming pool.

The local legend surrounding that stunning home reads like a romance novel. Edward Collings Knight, Jr., a wealthy executive with the Pennsylvania Railroad and the American Sugar Refinery, married a beautiful, talented French huntress by the name of Marie Louise LeBel. Marie loved vacationing in what was one of the best duck- and waterfowl-hunting spots in the world (Currituck is Indian for "Land of the Wild Goose"), but when she tried to join a local hunt club, she was turned down due to her gender. So Marie convinced Edward to build her a home that would eclipse any hunt club on the Outer Banks.

Visitors to their dinner parties found numbered and signed Tiffany lighting fixtures, custom-made dining-room table and chairs with a signature water lily design carved into the wood, and door handles and hinges molded to look like water lily buds. Five chimneys, a large library, cork floors, corduroy walls, copper shingles, and pink tiles on the walls of the kitchen were other features of the lavish home.

Though the Whalehead Club fell into disrepair after the Knights' tenure, it was bought by Currituck County in 1992 and is currently being restored to its original grandeur. Plans are for the Whalehead Club to serve as the Currituck Wildlife Museum when the work is completed. The main house, the original boathouse, and the pedestrian footbridge are all listed on the National Register of Historic Homes. Tours are being conducted while restoration is under way. They are given daily from 10 A.M. to 6 P.M. An admission fee is charged for visitors age eight and up. For information, call 252-453-9040, or visit their website at www.whaleheadclub.com.

■ While on the grounds of Currituck Beach Lighthouse and the Whalehead Club, you may spot one of the *wild ponies of Corolla*. These ponies are said to be descendants of mustangs that survived the wreck of a Spanish galleon and swam ashore on the Outer Banks. Efforts are under way to protect them, as their numbers have dwindled greatly because of local development.

■ *Wright Brothers National Memorial*, located at Milepost 8 on U.S. 158 in Kill Devil Hills, honors a moment that changed history.

Orville and Wilbur Wright, bicycle shop owners from Dayton, Ohio, had dreams of flying while they worked on their spokes and gears. They began pursuing their dream in earnest in 1899, when Wilbur wrote to the Smithsonian Institution asking for information on flight. Then the brothers set out to find out for themselves how to fly. For three years, they tested various gliders in and around Kitty Hawk and Kill Devil Hills. They also built a wind tunnel back in Ohio to learn the aerodynamics that would enable them to get off the ground. As Wilbur once said, "It is possible to fly without motors, but not without knowledge and skill."

It was December 14, 1903, when the brothers were ready to test a powered machine. They flipped a coin to see who would fly first; Wilbur won. He eased himself into the plane and took off from the launching rail, but the plane climbed too steeply and stalled. For three days, they repaired the plane. On the morning of December 17, they once again took their 40-foot, 605-pound *Flyer* into the sand. Amid 27-mile-per-hour wind gusts, Orville took flight for the first time, staying aloft for 12 seconds and 120 feet. The brothers took turns flying after that. The fourth and final flight—by Wilbur—was the most successful, lasting 59 seconds and covering 852 feet. After that, a gust of wind overturned the plane and damaged it beyond repair.

The visitor center, administered by the National Park Service, is the first stop at Wright Brothers National Memorial. It contains full-scale reproductions of one of the brothers' gliders and the famous *Flyer* that made the first flight. Interpretive talks are given in the center. The gift shop on

Wright Brothers National Memorial
COURTESY OF OUTER BANKS VISITORS BUREAU

the premises offers books and memorabilia.

Guests can see how the brothers lived and worked by visiting the reconstructed camp buildings on the grounds. Near the camp buildings are markers commemorating the takeoff and landing points of the first four flights.

The centerpiece of the memorial, however, is the 60-foot granite monument atop the 90-foot Big Kill Devil Hill, from which the brothers launched hundreds of glider flights before they ever built their first powered machine. Visitors can walk to the top of the hill and gaze down upon the entire site. There are bronze busts of the Wrights on one side of the monument.

The National Park Service has scheduled several celebrations to mark the 100th anniversary of the first powered flights; the festivities are to culminate on December 17, 2003.

The memorial is open daily except for Christmas. An admission fee is charged. For information, call 252-441-7430.

■ *Colington Island*, just south of Wright Brothers National Memorial, is the site of the first permanent settlement on the Outer Banks. Accessible by Colington Road off U.S. 158, the island features several seafood shops and campgrounds and offers visitors a nice photographic opportunity in a relatively undeveloped area of the Banks.

Museums and Science Centers

■ *Coastal Engineering Research Center*, located on the beach in Duck, is the home of the Waterways Experiment Center, administered by the United States Army Corps of Engineers. Waves, wind, currents, and tides are monitored and recorded at this site. Tours are given Monday through Friday at 10 A.M. from mid-June to August. There is no admission fee.

Special Shopping

The northern Banks and beaches are home to an ever-growing arts community. More than 20 galleries are located between Duck and Nags Head alone. Gallery Row in Nags Head features some of the best in the state.

■ Perhaps the best known of the bunch is *Glenn Eure's Ghost Fleet Gallery* (252-441-6584) at Milepost 10.5 in Nags Head. Offerings here range from gallery showings to poetry readings and guest lectures.

■ *Seaside Art Gallery* (252-441-5418) is located at Milepost 11 on N.C. 12 in Nags Head. You may be surprised at this beach gallery's assortment of works by Picasso, Dali, and Chagall.

▪ Another site you should plan to visit is *Lighthouse Gallery and Gifts* (800-579-2827), located at 301 East Driftwood Street in Nags Head. This gallery offers original works of art, memorabilia, and books pertaining to the area. Authors occasionally stop by to autograph their books and chat with patrons.

▪ *Morales Art Gallery* boasts three locations, at Milepost 10.5 on East Gallery Row in Nags Head (252-441-6484), at Milepost 4.5 in Kitty Hawk (252-255-2036), and at Scarborough Faire in Duck (800-635-6035 or 252-261-7190). All three locations offer original art, limited-edition prints, sculpture, and pottery.

RECREATION

Swimming, fishing, kayaking, windsurfing, parasailing, surfing, water-skiing—the northern Banks and beaches are the place to be for recreation. Watersports are the pastime of choice here. Thanks to the bounty of water, there are countless ways to keep wet. But please note that not all the beaches in this area have lifeguards. And since this area's currents and tides have sunk over 1,500 ships and given it the infamous nickname "Graveyard of the Atlantic," be sure to keep your wits about you while enjoying all the amusements the sea has to offer.

▪ *Kitty Hawk Sports*, the area's largest sports retailer, has locations covering the Outer Banks. Everything from swimwear to stunt kites to surfboards to kayaking gear is offered at its various stores in Corolla (252-453-4999 or 252-453-6900), Duck (252-261-8770), Kitty Hawk (252-261-0145), and Nags Head (252-441-6800 or 252-441-2756). Windsurfing and sailing lessons are available, as is sailing, windsurfing, and kayaking rental equipment. If you can't buy it at one of these stores, then you probably won't find it anywhere.

▪ If fishing is your sport of choice, you will be pleased to see the several piers and marinas dotting the Banks. Indeed, the area is known as the

"Billfish Capital of the World." **Kitty Hawk Pier** (252-441-7494) is open year-round. It offers a lighted fishing area and a restaurant open at 6 A.M. for breakfast. **Nags Head Fishing Pier** (252-441-5141) is also open year-round. Fishermen not getting any bites here have the opportunity to amuse themselves in the game room and arcade. Fees are charged to fish or just to watch others reel in their catch; passes for the week or season are available.

If you're feeling waterlogged, you'll be happy to note that there are plenty of recreational opportunities to be had on land, too.

■ The **Nags Head Woods Preserve**, a 1,100-acre maritime forest managed by the Nature Conservancy, is located on the western shores of Nags Head on Ocean Acre Drive, off U.S. 158. Here, you can see creatures ranging from egrets to turtles to spotted deer. If you're lucky—or unlucky, depending on how you look at it—you may even spot an alligator. The Outer Banks are the northern limit of the American alligator's habitat, and the gators here are a bit smaller than their Florida counterparts. They are probably more afraid of you than you are of them, so you shouldn't worry about having to avoid them. But if you do go in search of them, remember that they are protected by the Endangered Species Act. The preserve offers walking trails and a visitor center, where you can sign up for summer canoe trips and other nature programs. It is open Monday through Friday from 10 A.M. to 3 P.M.; admission is free. For information, call 252-441-2525.

■ **Jockey's Ridge State Park**, located off U.S. 158 in Nags Head, is a 414-acre park that boasts the tallest sand dune on the East Coast; it stands around 140 feet high. Originally used as a horse-racing track at the beginning of the 20th century, this land is now most famous for its kite-flying and hang-gliding opportunities. It was on dunes like these that the Wright brothers learned to fly; on a clear day, you can even see Wright Brothers Memorial. The trails leading up the sand dunes offer a view of the entire width of Nags Head all the way from Roanoke Sound to the Atlantic Ocean. It's this unbeatable panorama that draws so many people to the "Sunset on the Ridge" program that park rangers present around 8

A family at Jockey's Ridge State Park
COURTESY OF OUTER BANKS VISITORS BUREAU

P.M. Friday and Saturday evenings during the summer. Visitors can bring a picnic dinner and enjoy the sunset as they learn how the dunes were formed and the complete story behind the ridge's name. The park offers picnic facilities, restrooms, and a visitor center. The hours vary according to the season, so be sure to call before you visit. Admission is free. For information, call 252-441-7132, or try their website at www.ncsparks.net.

- Getting out of the sand and onto the greens is also possible on the Banks. There are some very impressive golf courses in the area. Kitty Hawk offers **Bermuda Greens** (252-261-0101), at the intersection of U.S. 158 and N.C. 12; **The Promenade** (252-261-4900), at Milepost 1 on U.S. 158; and **Sea Scape Golf Club** (252-261-2158), on U.S. 158. **Nags Head Golf Links** (252-441-8073) is just down the road. Be sure to call for reservations at these courses.

- Camping opportunities abound on the northern Banks. Among the best campgrounds are **Adventure Bound Camp and Kayak Center** (252-255-1130) in Kitty Hawk, **Kitty Hawk Trailer Park** (252-261-2636) in Kitty Hawk, **Colington Park Campground** (252-441-6128) in Kill Devil Hills, and **Joe and Kay's Campground** (252-441-6128) in Kill Devil Hills.

SEASONAL EVENTS

The Outer Banks prides itself on its good-time atmosphere, so the abundance of festivals and celebrations throughout the year comes as no surprise. As you may guess, many center around the area's greatest asset—the water. From seafood feasts to sailing regattas, the Outer Banks knows how to throw a good party.

■ The **North Beach Seafood Festival**, held in Duck every November, includes a craft show, live entertainment, and, of course, lots of steamed, fried, boiled, broiled, and poached seafood. For information, call 252-261-3901.

■ A **Stunt-Kite Competition** is held every October at the best kite-flying spot on earth, Jockey's Ridge State Park. December brings a lit **Stunt-Kite Show** at the park. Hot apple cider, cookies, and Christmas carols add to the holiday mood. For information, call 800-334-4777 or 252-441-4124.

■ **Wacky Watermelon Weekend and Windsurfing Regatta** is held in Nags Head in August. Practice up on your watermelon-eating skills so you can participate in the contests, but remember not to spit the seeds when the Watermelon Queen makes her appearance. You might also try the watermelon bowling event. For information, call 800-948-0759 or 252-441-6800.

Places to Stay

The northern Banks and beaches offer a wide range of places to stay, from charming bed-and-breakfasts to steadfast, reliable chains. Families, honeymooners, and salty old fishermen alike will be able to find the place that fits them best. You'll find that Corolla, Duck, Sanderling, Southern Shores, and Kitty Hawk have much to offer in the way of cottages and bed-and-breakfasts. Kill Devil Hills and Nags Head are where you'll find the majority of hotels and motels.

There are two very pronounced seasons on the Banks; lodgings are very crowded in the summer and nearly uninhabited in the winter. Rates for the same accommodation can differ by as much as $500 between the peak season and the off-season. Minimum stays may be required at some places. Be sure to call well in advance to book your perfect spot. Two good resources to check before booking are the Outer Banks Visitors Bureau's website (www.outerbanks.org) and the Outer Banks Chamber of Commerce's website (www.outerbankschamber.com).

RESORTS, HOTELS, AND MOTELS

▪ *The Sanderling Inn*. Deluxe. 1461 Duck Road, Duck (800-701-4111 or 252-261-4111; www.sanderlinginn.com). One of the most posh places to stay on the Outer Banks, the Sanderling Inn has 94 rooms and four three- and four-bedroom villas. The inn offers all the amenities you'd expect, from wet bars to private porches to a bottle of wine to welcome you upon arrival. The spa is the big attraction here. Guests are also pampered by the pool, the health club, the tennis courts, the sun deck, and the private beach. A complimentary breakfast buffet and afternoon tea are served daily. If you decide to stay here, you should definitely look into the adjoining Sanderling Inn Restaurant.

▪ *Best Western Ocean Reef Suites*. Expensive/Moderate. Milepost 8.5, Kill Devil Hills (800-528-1234 or 252-441-1611). One of the few all-suites hotels on the Outer Banks, the Best Western features 70 suites. All of the rooms are oceanfront and offer two double beds, a living room with a seating group and a double-sized Murphy bed, and a kitchen with a range, a refrigerator, and cookware. Guests enjoy the health club, the Jacuzzi, the outdoor pool, and the restaurant.

■*Quality Inn—John Yancey*. Expensive/Moderate. Milepost 10, Kill Devil Hills (800-592-6239 or 252-441-7141; www.johnyancey-nagshead.com). This oceanfront hotel features 107 guest rooms, all of which have televisions and refrigerators. Some rooms have hot tubs, king-sized beds, fully equipped kitchens, or VCRs with movies. A large heated pool, a playground, and a picnic area are on the grounds.

■ *Quality Inn—Sea Oatel*. Expensive/Moderate. Milepost 16.5, Nags Head (800-440-4386 or 252-441-7191). This oceanfront hotel has 111 rooms, many of which offer a balcony overlooking the beach. All the usual amenities can be found here, including cable television, refrigerators, and microwaves. A continental breakfast is provided. Kids will like the outdoor pool, the volleyball court, and the playground. Sportsmen will like the golf packages that are sold here and the hotel's proximity to a pier. Tickets to *The Lost Colony* outdoor drama are sold here as well.

■ *Ramada Inn*. Expensive/Moderate. Milepost 9.5, Kill Devil Hills (800-635-1824 or 252-441-2151; www.ddltech.com/ramada). This hotel's 172 rooms offer private balconies, microwaves, refrigerators, coffee makers, and cable television. Guests can enjoy dinner in the hotel's restaurant or take in the ocean view from the deck bar. Nice touches include bedtime mints and beach towels at the front desk.

INNS AND BED-AND-BREAKFASTS

■*Advice 5¢*. Deluxe. Scarborough Lane, Duck (800-238-4235 or 252-255-1050). This intimate and friendly inn is close to area shops and restaurants, making an evening stroll for ice cream a pleasure to look forward to each day. Featuring four guest rooms and suites, all with private baths, this inn gives visitors a home-away-from-home feeling. A swimming pool, tennis courts, and a private walkway to the beach are available. Morning tea, coffee, and continental breakfast are provided, as is a unique afternoon tea.

- **Bald View Bed-and-Breakfast**. Deluxe/Expensive. 3807 Elijah Baum Road, Kitty Hawk (252-255-2829; www.baldview.com). Bordering 11 acres of Kitty Hawk Sound and a maritime forest, this bed-and-breakfast offers a respite from the busy pace of the northern Banks and beaches. The four guest rooms offer private baths and televisions, but the best feature is perhaps the spectacular view of the sound. The ocean is only five minutes away, too, affording another opportunity to get wet. A complimentary breakfast is offered every morning. A weekly wine-and-cheese night gives guests a chance to mingle and make new friends.

- **Cypress House**. Deluxe/Expensive. Milepost 8, N.C. 12, Kill Devil Hills (800-554-2764 or 252-441-6127; www.cypresshouseinn.com). This down-to-earth bed-and-breakfast was built in the 1940s as a private hunting and fishing lodge. It now houses six guest rooms with cypress interiors and private bathrooms and features a wonderful wraparound porch where guests can relax and mingle in the morning as they enjoy their home-made breakfast or take in the sun with their afternoon tea.

- **First Colony Inn**. Deluxe/Expensive. Milepost 16, U.S. 158, Nags Head (800-368-9390 or 252-441-2343; www.firstcolonyinn.com). One of the largest inns in Nags Head, First Colony Inn is listed on the National Register of Historic Places. Its 26 guest rooms and four efficiencies have been given a Four-Diamond rating by AAA. Each unique room is aptly appointed with English antiques. Some feature a wet bar, a kitchenette, a whirlpool tub, a sitting room, or a private screened porch. Guests are invited to enjoy a few quiet moments reading in the library or taking in the salty air and the beautiful sunset from the inn's gazebo on the dunes. A continental breakfast buffet is served daily in the inn's breakfast room or can be brought to your room atop a silver tray.

Places to Eat

The restaurants along the northern Banks offer far more than the normal beach fare of fried seafood. You'll find an eclectic blend of Caribbean, Italian, French, Southwestern, and vegetarian cuisine. Everything from elegant "wine dinners" to burgers and fries are available. Most local restaurants are accepting of casual, neat beach attire. If you're unsure of the dress code at your chosen eatery, check ahead just to be safe. During the busy summer season, you can expect a wait for dinner almost anyplace you go; reservations are usually not accepted. Just relax, take a seat, and people-watch as you enjoy the smells coming from the kitchen.

■ **Elizabeth's Café and Winery**. Expensive. Scarborough Faire, Duck (252-261-6145). Voted one of the top 100 restaurants of the 20th century by the International Restaurant and Hospitality Rating Bureau, Elizabeth's serves up haute cuisine without the attitude or the price. Guests order international cuisine from a prix fixe menu that changes nightly. A wine dinner is also available, allowing you to share in Elizabeth's special wines, given an Award of Excellence from *Wine Spectator* magazine. Dinner is served daily.

■ **Port O' Call Restaurant and Saloon**. Expensive/Moderate. Milepost 8.5, Kill Devil Hills (252-441-7484). Feeding locals and tourists alike for 35 years, this restaurant is an Outer Banks landmark. The plush Victorian atmosphere is unique, to say the least—velvet settees, Tiffany lamps, and copious artwork adorn the restaurant. The menu brags that it's the most extensive on the beach, featuring seafood seven ways, from baked to blackened to broiled to grilled to sautéed to steamed to fried. Black Angus beef, chicken, pasta, soups, and salads round out the menu. You can await your table by whiling away the time in the Gaslight Saloon, or retreat there after dinner for a nightcap and to catch the live entertainment. A gift shop in the restaurant features jewelry, nautical items, collector dolls, local and national artists's work, and Tiffany- and Victorian-style lamps. Dinner is served daily March through December. A Sunday brunch buffet is also offered.

■ **Sanderling Inn Restaurant**. Expensive/Moderate. Next to the Sanderling Inn in Duck (252-261-4111 or 252-449-6654). This restaurant features traditional and coastal Southern cuisine prepared with some of the finest and freshest ingredients available in the area. The menu changes regularly to take advantage of what the season has to offer. No matter what time of year, though, you're guaranteed to be welcomed by freshly baked bread and pastries. Housed in what used to be the Caffey's Inlet Lifesaving Station and decorated with memorabilia from times gone by, the restaurant gives a sense of what the area used to be like before it became a tourist destination. An outside pavilion open on weekdays offers a casual dining experience. From the pavilion, guests can watch the sun set over the sound and take in the cool ocean breezes. Reservations are recommended. Lunch, dinner, and a three-course Sunday brunch are offered year-round.

▪ **Black Pelican Seafood Company.** Moderate. Milepost 4, Kitty Hawk (252-261-3171). Black Pelican is housed in the 120-plus-year-old former lifesaving station and telegraph office where Orville and Wilbur Wright sent out the news of their first flight to the world. Diners can enjoy wood-fired oven pizzas or what the restaurant is named for, the fresh local seafood and raw bar. An on-site gift shop offers Wright brothers memorabilia. Lunch and dinner are served daily year-round.

▪ **Madison's Café and Lounge.** Moderate. Sea Holly Square, Beach Road, Kill Devil Hills (252-449-2244). Madison's motto is "New York fare with Outer Banks flair." You'll find excellent pastas, steaks, and seafood here, but the sandwich menu is truly something to behold. Reubens, Philly cheese steaks, and other delights bring a taste of home to visitors from above the Mason-Dixon line. Be sure to save room for the cappuccino and the mouth-watering desserts. The bar stays open late and often offers live entertainment. Lunch and dinner are served daily year-round.

▪ **Quagmire's Oceanfront Bar and Restaurant.** Moderate. Milepost 7.5, Kill Devil Hills (252-441-9188). This is the place to go to watch the moon rise over the Atlantic Ocean and listen to a live band on the outdoor deck. You can enjoy simple bar food with your locally brewed beer, or you can go for one of the generous Mexican- and Caribbean-influenced entrées if you're hungry for an entire meal. Lunch and dinner are served daily April through November.

▪ **The Rundown Café.** Moderate. Milepost 1, Kitty Hawk (252-255-0026). Housed in a structure made to look like a Caribbean beach house, the Rundown Café offers a menu heavy on fresh ingredients and local seafood with an island flair. The entrées range from Jerk chicken to fish tacos to seasoned shrimp. Vegetarian dishes include the deliciously spicy Thai noodles. Among the desserts are chocolate peanut butter pie and—what else?— Key lime pie. The restaurant is open daily for lunch and dinner year-round.

▪ **RV's Restaurant**. Moderate. Milepost 16.5, Nags Head (252-441-4963). Located on the sound at the end of the bypass connecting Manteo and Nags Head, RV's features a great view of the water separating Roanoke Island from the northern Banks. Steaks and seafood are the specialties here, but you'll find chicken and pasta dishes as well. A lounge and full bar serve up a variety of appetizers while you're waiting for your table. RV's is open from February through November for lunch and dinner.

▪ **Awful Arthur's Oyster Bar**. Moderate/Inexpensive. Milepost 6, Kill Devil Hills (252-441-5955). Awful Arthur's is a casual hangout where you can get a dozen oysters at the steam bar or an entire meal in the adjoining restaurant. The local seafood, steaks, chicken, and pasta served here can be washed down with an assortment of beers. Awful Arthur's T-shirts, a favorite of locals and frat guys, are sold in the neighboring gift shop. Lunch and dinner are offered daily year-round.

▪ **Sam and Omie's**. Moderate/Inexpensive. Milepost 16.5, Nags Head (252-441-7366). Breakfast is the specialty here, as evidenced by the special "Omie-lettes" on the menu. This is also a nice place to select a quick yet satisfying lunch from among the restaurant's "Samiches." You can't go wrong with one of the salads, the she-crab soup, the steamed local seafood, or the homemade desserts, either. Sam and Omie's is open daily from March through November for breakfast, lunch, and dinner.

Commercial Fishing
COURTESY OF OUTER BANKS VISITORS BUREAU

ROANOKE ISLAND

Surrounded by the waters of Roanoke Sound and Croatan Sound, Roanoke Island claims the honor of being the birthplace of English America. More than 400 years ago, intrepid explorers discovered this "goodliest land under the cope of heaven" and convinced Queen Elizabeth I to send settlers here to claim the land for England. Several attempts to settle the area were made—including one that saw the birth of the first English child on American soil—but none succeeded. Roanoke Island owes its heritage to this group of brave souls who gave up everything to seek out new opportunities and a new life in a strange land.

Manteo, named for one of the friendly Indians who helped the colonists, is the largest town on Roanoke Island. It prides itself on being a "walkable community." It is here that you will find the majority of shopping and dining opportunities on the island. Plan on spending a morning exploring the many different shops on the waterfront, taking breakfast at one of the coffee shops, browsing the history section of the local bookstore, checking out the kayaking and windsurfing gear at one of the outdoor shops, and feeding the sociable sea gulls that fly over Shallowbag Bay. You'll have chances to explore local history at Roanoke Island Festival Park and *The Lost Colony* outdoor drama as well.

Wanchese, to the south, is the other town on the island. It is much sleepier than Manteo. Also named for one of the Native Americans who assisted the colonists, Wanchese is a fishing village. More than 20 million pounds of fish are caught here every year, making this a fun place to watch boats and fishermen depart or later return with their catch. Wanchese is worth the drive just to see what the Outer Banks without the crowds is like.

Roanoke Island is considered by many to be the heart of Outer Banks art and culture. You won't find any major beaches here. Instead, it's the plays, museums, living-history exhibits, gardens, concerts, and ballets that keep people coming to this small island between the mainland and the barrier islands.

JUST THE FACTS

From the north or the northern Banks, take U.S. 64/U.S. 264 West over the Washington Baum Bridge. From the mainland, take U.S. 64/U.S. 264 East over the William B. Umstead Memorial Bridge.

The Dare County Regional Airport is on Airport Road in Manteo. Its two runways are 3,290 feet and 4,300 feet in length. Fuel and services are offered 24 hours a day, but the airport is open to local charters only. For information, call 252-473-2600. Car and limousine rentals are available at the airport.

Limited taxi and limousine services are offered on the Outer Banks, but you'll find that the best way to explore the area is to drive, bike, or walk.

Many different services offer information about the Outer Banks. One of the best is the Outer Banks Visitors Bureau, 704 U.S. 64/U.S. 264, P.O. Box 399, Manteo, N.C. 27954 (800-446-6262 or 252-473-2138). You can visit their website at www.outerbanks.org to learn about the history, culture, and folklore of the area; a useful page on the website lists the rates and availability of rental units in the area. The town of Manteo has its own website at www.townofmanteo.com.

Things to Do

Visitors who want to see and do it all may be interested in the special-attractions passes, which offer a discount for admission to the island's highlights. The Roanoke Island Attractions Pass offers savings on admission to Roanoke Island Festival Park and the Elizabethan Gardens at Fort Raleigh National Historic Site. Passes can be purchased year-round at the Aycock Brown Welcome Center in Kitty Hawk, at Roanoke Island Festival Park, at the Elizabethan Gardens, and at the Outer Banks Visitors Bureau office in Manteo. The Roanoke Island Queen's Pass includes discounts on admission to the same attractions and provides further savings on admission to the North Carolina Aquarium on Roanoke Island and *The Lost Colony*.

HISTORIC PLACES, GARDENS, AND TOURS

■ **Fort Raleigh National Historic Site**, located off U.S. 64/U.S. 264 at the northern end of the island, allows visitors to step back in time to see how the area looked over 300 years ago to the newly arrived English colonists. You can walk in the footsteps of those who attempted to tame this wild island and disappeared without a trace. A visitor center administered by the National Park Service tells the story of the first colonists on Roanoke Island.

The English tried to settle the area many times, beginning in 1585 under the direction of Richard Grenville, a cousin of Sir Walter Raleigh, who was a leader in the move to explore the New World. Grenville led 600 men to found the first colony. He left a group of them under the direction of Ralph Lane to build fortifications while he returned to England. Relations with the natives soon turned sour, however, and when Sir Francis Drake and his men visited the colony on their way home from Florida, the first colonists took advantage of the opportunity and returned to England.

Undeterred, Grenville came back a short time later with two years' worth of supplies and a smaller, more reliable group of settlers. Before returning to England, he gave the settlers strict instructions about establishing fortifications. It was this group of men who built what is now known as Fort Raleigh.

The appointed governor of the area, John White, came by boat in 1587 with a number of other colonists to assume his duties and further build the colony. He was undoubtedly shocked to find all of the men missing and only one skeleton inhabiting the fort.

Despite the thousands of miles of ocean between him and Mother England and the many travel-weary wards in his care, the governor set about reestablishing the colony. White's colonists were families who had a vested interest in making the settlement permanent, in order to provide a better life for their loved ones. Included was White's own daughter, pregnant at the time with the now-famous Virginia Dare, the first English child born in the New World. Unfortunately, the colonists soon discovered that they were unable to live completely off the land, which was much different from their native home. The governor was thus forced to sail back to England for more provisions.

The romance and mystery of the story enter here. War was raging between England and Spain when White arrived home, and the Spanish Armada ensured that it wasn't until 1590 that he was able to return to the colony. Sailing back into the familiar bay, he was once again shocked to find Fort Raleigh uninhabited. At the entrance, he discovered the word CROATOAN carved on a post, but there was no cross with it—the colonists' agreed-upon signal of danger. Before he was able to search the nearby islands, Governor White was forced to return to England. To this day, no one knows what happened to the colonists of Roanoke Island. Many theories abound as to their fate, but nothing has ever been proved.

The earth embankments at Fort Raleigh, restored in 1950, are much as they were when the colonists lived on Roanoke Island. The Lindsay Warren Visitor Center exhibits relics from the era of Governor White and Virginia Dare and offers maps of the area, books on the Lost Colony, and a 17-minute film on the history of Roanoke Island. The Waterside Theatre on the grounds of Fort Raleigh National Historic Site is the home of *The Lost Colony* outdoor drama during the summer. The site is open daily from 9 A.M. to 6 P.M. from June to the end of August; the hours during the rest of the year are 9 A.M. to 5 P.M. Admission to the site is free, though a fee is charged to see *The Lost Colony*. For information, call 252-473-5772, or visit their website at www.nps.gov/fora.

Elizabethan Gardens

▪ The ***Elizabethan Gardens*** are adjacent to the Waterside Theatre in the heart of Fort Raleigh National Historic Site. Created in 1951 by the Garden Club of North Carolina, the 10-acre gardens are a memorial to America's first English colonists. Designed by M. Umberto Innocenti and Richard Webel to bloom year-round, the gardens feature plants native to the Outer Banks. Visitors enjoy an array of flowering shrubs, trees, plants, and herbs along the property's winding paths. Among the several gardens here are the formal Queen's Rose Garden (which features the "Lost Colony Rose"), the Shakespearean Herb Garden, and the Great Lawn.

The centerpiece may well be the 15th-century Italian fountain, pool, and balustrade in the Sunken Garden, given by John Hay Whitney, a former ambassador to Great Britain. Visitors can stop here to smell the flowers and listen to the gurgling fountain.

Situated next to Roanoke Sound is a 16th-century gazebo made of daub siding and thatched roofing. This area is said to be where the English flag was first raised in the New World.

The gardens are open daily year-round except for Christmas. Extended hours are offered during the summer. Admission is charged for adults and children ages six to 17. For information, call 252-473-3234, or visit their website at www.outerbanks.org.

▪ Like Fort Raleigh National Historic Site, ***Roanoke Island Festival Park*** is dedicated to re-creating the history of the early colonists. This living-history theme park is located on Ice Plant Island in Shallowbag Bay across from downtown Manteo.

Your first stop upon entering the visitor center will be the 8,500-square-foot Roanoke Adventure Museum, which features paintings, artifacts, relics, and interactive exhibits on the important figures and events in Roanoke Island's history. One of the best exhibits is the Civil War cannon found underwater off the island; it was so well packed with firing material that the gunpowder was still dry, meaning that the cannon was still ready for action. A Native American village, a Civil War encampment, a pirate ship, a duck blind, and a 1950s general store are among the other exhibits. Children love the area where they can dress up in swashbuckling buccaneer and dainty m'lady costumes. Actors in period costume are spread throughout the park to share stories of pioneering on Roanoke Island. Inquisitive children and adults can find out what it was like to survive in the hot, swampy, buggy conditions without any of the conveniences we depend upon today. The Native Americans' story is shared as well. A 50-minute film entitled *The Legend of Two-Path* tells what the people already settled on Roanoke Island thought of the new "settlers" who appeared in 1585. Outside the museum are several trails leading to different exhibits, including a settlement site featuring historically costumed soldiers who share what the settlers did for shelter, food, and protection.

The most impressive feature of Roanoke Island Festival Park is perhaps the 69-foot *Elizabeth II*. An authentic representation of the 16th-century *Elizabeth*, one of seven merchant ships used to sail to the new colony, the *Elizabeth II* was built to commemorate the New World's quadricentennial. Interpretive guides on the three-mast, "50-tunne" Elizabethan ship share stories of what it was like to cross the Atlantic and become one of the first to settle the New World.

The famed North Carolina School of the Arts offers special dance, theater, drama, and musical performances in the park during the summer. Summer Scenes is a seven-week series of performances by some of the art world's brightest up-and-coming stars. Past performances have included *A Midsummer Night's Dream, Cinderella,* and the musical *She Loves Me*. Three performances are generally given each day. The morning offering includes puppet shows and fairy and folk tales as part of the Children's Series or master ballet and jazz dance classes. The afternoon performance is often a concert of chamber or jazz music in the 50-seat auditorium on the premises. The evening performances—dance, musical

Elizabeth II

concerts, and dramas presented in the outdoor pavilion—are perhaps the highlight of the series. Admission to Summer Scenes is free with admission to the park, though making a donation is a good way to ensure performances for the next year. Preregistration is required for the dance classes.

Roanoke Island Festival Park is open year-round. Hours vary seasonally. Admission is charged for adults and students; children age five and under are admitted free. For information, call 252-475-1506 or 252-475-1500, or visit their website at www.roanokeisland.com.

MUSEUMS AND SCIENCE CENTERS

■ The *North Carolina Aquarium on Roanoke Island*, tucked away down the long and winding Airport Road off U.S. 64, recently underwent a more than two-year renovation. Now doubled in size to 68,000 square feet, the aquarium dramatizes the "Waters of the Outer Banks" through its freshwater and saltwater galleries. Creatures from North Carolina's rivers, marshes, sounds, and reefs are all highlighted.

The first stop inside the aquarium is the open-air, natural-habitat atrium. Lined with real trees and topped with a huge skylight, the habitat gives a sense of the North Carolina wetlands. Wood ducks,

river otters, and alligators all inhabit this area. Watch out for the mists that spray periodically to keep the "wetlands" wet!

The centerpiece of the aquarium is definitely the 285,000-gallon "Graveyard of the Atlantic" ocean tank, the largest in the state. Inside it are the skeletal remains of a 53-foot, re-created USS *Monitor* shipwreck, a one-third-scale replica of the famed Civil War ship now lying off Cape Hatteras. Created by a team of movie-set designers in Wilmington, the replica is covered with fiberglass orange, pink, and yellow corals, sponges, and sea fans. The fish swimming inside the tank sometimes confuse the replica with the real thing and try to take a nip out of it. The sharks gliding stealthily by the 35-foot-long, five-and-a-half-inch-thick viewing window steal the show. Custom-made in Japan and set into place with a crane, the window wraps overhead, so viewers get a sense of actually being in the water with the ship, sharks, and other ocean creatures.

The aquarium's Discovery Gallery gives kids a chance to touch skates, rays, sea stars, crabs, urchins, and other invertebrates. Charts and graphics on the walls tell about the evolution and characteristics of each animal.

A theater and gift shop round out the aquarium.

The aquarium is open daily year-round except for Thanksgiving, Christmas, and New Year's. A modest fee is charged for adults; children six and under and Aquarium Society members are admitted free. For information, call 800-832-FISH or 252-473-3493, or visit their website at www.ncaquariums.com.

- The *North Carolina Maritime Museum*, located on the Manteo waterfront in the George Washington Creef Boatshop, is a repository of information on the long seafaring history of the Outer Banks. Visitors can learn the art of boat restoration and construction from the curator and volunteers who work here. For information, call 252-475-1750.

SPECIAL SHOPPING

Downtown Manteo offers an array of browsing choices, from shops selling outdoor gear or local artwork to a unique independently owned bookstore. It's easy to spend a few leisurely hours wandering the shops and soaking up the culture.

- A shopping experience not to be missed is the *Christmas Shop and Island Gallery*, located off U.S. 64 next to the Weeping Radish Brewery and Bavarian Restaurant. Built in 1967, the Christmas Shop and Island Gallery is comprised of six buildings, 33 rooms, and 20,000 square feet of local artisans' work, antiques, and—you guessed it—Christmas ornaments. The shops are open daily except for Christmas and New Year's; seasonal hours are in effect. Call 800-470-2838 or 252-473-2838 for more information.

For more information on local businesses, check out the Roanoke Island Business Association's website at www.roanoke-island.com.

RECREATION

- The *Downeast Rover*, a reproduction of a 19th-century topsail schooner, is berthed on the Manteo waterfront by the Tranquil House Inn. The *Rover* offers daytime and sunset cruises. Sailors aboard the 55-foot boat can see Roanoke Island from a completely different perspective and get a close look at the local wildlife, including dolphins, ospreys, and herons. They can help trim the sails, take control of the helm for a moment, and discover what the waters of Roanoke Sound have to offer.

Below decks are a restroom, a lounge, and a ship's store. Be sure to check availability and departure time for the date you're interested in. Reservations are recommended. For more information, call 252-473-4866, or visit their website at www.DowneastRover.com.

▪ *Alligator River National Wildlife Refuge*, located on U.S. 64/U.S. 264 on the Dare County mainland, is comprised of more than 150,000 acres of wild wetland separating the mainland from the Outer Banks. The Alligator River—actually a small sound—is part of the larger Albemarle Sound, one of the most important waterways in the state. Snaking from Alligator Lake in the Dismal Swamp to Albemarle Sound, the Alligator River is said to have received its name from the area's first settlers, who encountered quite a few of those stealthy, beady-eyed creatures. Little did those pioneers know that they were lucky—or unlucky, as the case may be—to have stumbled into the northernmost habitat of the American alligator. Wildlife specialists say the alligators in the Alligator River are smaller than their counterparts in Florida and Georgia, but that fact probably wouldn't have provided much comfort to the first men and women crossing these waters.

Besides alligators, visitors to the refuge will also find black bears, bobcats, bald eagles, white-tailed deer, and red wolves. The red wolf faced extinction as recently as 1996, but thanks to a reintroduction project, the numbers are growing today. All along the highway in the refuge, you'll see red wolf crossing signs, so take care to share the road with these shy creatures.

Admission to the refuge is free. Visitors can take advantage of hiking and wildlife trails, observation platforms, and fishing areas. Kayaking and canoeing are permitted; a guided canoe tour is available for a fee. For more information, call 252-473-1131, or visit their website at www.outer-banks.com/alligator-river.

▪ *Kitty Hawk Sports* offers kayak ecotours led by trained guides. One of the best tours starts in Manteo and heads through Shallowbag Bay into the maritime forest. Kayakers learn useful information about local flora and fauna—like how to distinguish between bug-repellent plants and poison ivy. Call 252-441-6800 for information.

Kayaking
COURTESY OF OUTER BANKS VISITORS BUREAU

▪ Those interested in camping on Roanoke Island might try **Cypress Cove Campground** (252-473-5231; www.outerbankscamping.com). Located on U.S. 64 within a 15-minute drive of all the island's major attractions, it offers 42 RV sites and 20 tent sites. Electrical hookups, hot showers, a camp store, a laundry room, picnic tables, and a dump station are provided. Kids love the playground, the batting cage, and the stocked fishing pond. One-, two-, and three-bedroom efficiencies are available for rent.

SEASONAL EVENTS

▪ First performed in 1937, **The Lost Colony** is the oldest outdoor drama in the United States. Over 3 million theatergoers have witnessed the passion and mystery surrounding the British colonists lost to the wilderness of Roanoke Island. Performed on the grounds of Fort Raleigh National Historic Site at the Waterside Theatre overlooking Roanoke Sound, *The Lost Colony* tells the story of Governor John White; his daughter, Eleanor Dare; her daughter, Virginia Dare, the first English child born in America; and the native Algonquin Indians. The production includes dance, song, fights, and fireworks. Guests witness how Sir Walter Raleigh convinced Queen Elizabeth I to support a settlement in the New World, yet how he was denied the chance to participate in building the colony; how the colonists became friends with the natives yet later lost their allegiance; and how they came to the conclusion that they could no longer survive

Cast of The Lost Colony
COURTESY OF RAY MATTHEWS

at Fort Raleigh. Of course, you'll have to attend a performance to see what Pulitzer Prize–winning playwright Paul Green imagined to be the fate of the colonists.

If you're planning an evening at Waterside Theatre, you'll be well advised to buy your tickets in advance and to bring a healthy supply of bug repellant. If you come prepared, you'll be justly rewarded with a tale of love, loss, and heroic courage.

The Lost Colony is performed Monday through Saturday at 8:30 P.M. from mid-June to late August. On Mondays, children are admitted for half price. Refunds are not given in case of cancellations due to bad weather, though guests are allowed to exchange their tickets for another night's performance. For more information, call 800-488-5012 or 252-473-3414, or visit their website at www.thelostcolony.org. To request advance tickets, write *The Lost Colony*, 1409 U.S. 64/U.S. 264, Manteo, N.C. 27954.

■ **Elizabeth R**, a one-woman show about the thoughts, aspirations, loves, and fears of Queen Elizabeth I, is performed at the Elizabethan Gardens on Tuesday afternoons during the summer. Seating is on the lawn, so blankets and lawn chairs are recommended. To reserve tickets, call 252-473-1061; tickets can also be purchased at the gardens.

The several seasonal festivals held on Roanoke Island are not to be missed if you're in town on the dates they're offered.

■ The **Dare Day Festival** is held annually the first Saturday in June in downtown Manteo. It honors the memory of Virginia Dare and the other Lost Colonists of Roanoke Island. The festival features all-day entertainment, arts and crafts, food, dance, and live music. Call 252-473-1101 for more information.

■ The **New World Festival of the Arts**, held the third week in August on the Manteo waterfront, highlights dozens of local artisans and their work. You can purchase unique paintings, jewelry, crafts, and pottery or just enjoy taking in the culture by the bay. Call 252-473-2838 for more information.

■ The **Herbert Hoover Birthday Celebration**, held on August 10 and sponsored by **Manteo Booksellers**, honors the birthday of our nation's 31st president. This is a quirky way to enjoy a day of book signings, live music, trivia, and birthday cake. Call 252-473-1221 for more information.

■ The **Weeping Radish Oktoberfest**, held in September at the Weeping Radish Brewery and Restaurant on U.S. 64/U.S. 264, features traditional German dishes, Oktoberfest beer, an oompah band, and dancing. For information, call 252-473-1157, or visit the Weeping Radish's website at www.weepingradish.com.

■ The **Lighting of the Town Tree** and the annual **Christmas Parade** are offered the first Friday and Saturday of December, respectively. Guests enjoy Christmas carols, a yule log, floats, and an appearance by Santa. Call 252-473-1101 (ext. 319) for more information.

Places to Stay

Roanoke Island is noted for its array of unique inns and bed-and-breakfasts. If you're looking for the tried and true chains, you may need to try up the road in Nags Head or Kitty Hawk. Rates vary seasonally.

RESORTS, HOTELS, AND MOTELS

- **Elizabethan Inn**. Expensive/Moderate/Inexpensive. 814 U.S. 64, P.O. Box 549, Manteo (800-346-2466 or 252-473-2101; www.elizabethaninn.com). This 80-room, five efficiency Tudor-style motel, located close to all of Roanoke Island's cultural offerings, boasts a wide range of amenities. Guests can enjoy an indoor heated pool, an outdoor pool, a racquetball court, a whirlpool, and a sauna. Complimentary bicycles are available for trips to the Manteo waterfront, Roanoke Island Festival Park, the newly renovated aquarium, and Fort Raleigh National Historic Site. Complimentary breakfast is offered. The on-site restaurant is an option for dinner during the summer. Children stay free in their parents' rooms.

- **Duke of Dare Motor Lodge**. Moderate/Inexpensive. 100 U.S. 64/U.S. 264, Manteo (252-473-2175). This no-frills, 57-room motel offers the basics for a reasonable price. The Duke of Dare has been owned and operated by the same family for over 25 years. It features televisions, phones, and an outdoor pool.

INNS AND BED-AND-BREAKFASTS

- **The White Doe Inn Bed-and-Breakfast**. Deluxe. 319 Sir Walter Raleigh Street, Manteo (800-473-6091 or 252-473-9851; www.whitedoeinn.com). Built in 1898, the White Doe underwent renovations in 1994. It is now a Three-Diamond, three-story, eight-room Queen Anne–style inn. Each of the rooms is individually decorated with antiques and features amenities ranging from four-poster carved rice beds to private whirlpools to stained-glass windows to chandeliers. A full three-course gourmet breakfast, afternoon tea, and bicycles are some of the extras provided for guests. The wraparound porch is the perfect place to read a book, take in the breeze off the water, and enjoy a lazy afternoon. A chef is available to prepare intimate dinners or gourmet picnic baskets to take on your explorations.

▪ *Roanoke Island Inn.* Deluxe/Expensive. 305 Fernando Street, Manteo (877-473-5511 or 252-473-5511). Built in the 1860s for the current innkeeper's great-great-grandmother, the Roanoke Island Inn grew steadily throughout the 20th century to accommodate the growing family and guests who stayed here. Renovated in 1982 and expanded in 1990, this inn offers eight guest rooms, most of which have a view of the nearby bay. Continental breakfast and all the beverages you care to drink are on the house. The inn is generally open from Easter to Thanksgiving, though the owners charmingly advertise their season as ranging from "Easter 'til we're tired."

▪ *Tranquil House Inn.* Deluxe/Expensive. 405 Queen Elizabeth Street, Manteo (800-458-7069 or 252-473-1404; www.1587.com). Guests staying here enjoy being in the middle of everything. The Tranquil House is located on the Shallowbag Bay waterfront in downtown Manteo. The majority of its 25 individually decorated rooms boast a view of the water. This turn-of-the-20th-century reproduction offers suites with sitting rooms, an upstairs porch with rocking chairs, evening wine and cheese, and complimentary continental breakfast. One of the best restaurants in the Outer Banks, 1587, sits conveniently next door.

▪ *Island House of Wanchese.* Expensive/Moderate. 104 Old Wharf Road, P.O. Box 341, Wanchese (252-473-5619; www.bbonline.com/nc/islandhouse/). Located away from the hustle and bustle of downtown Manteo in the quiet fishing village of Wanchese, this is the place to truly get away from it all. The four rooms have private baths, antique furnishings, Oriental rugs, televisions, and radios. Guests enjoy the turn-down service at night and are welcomed in the morning with a home-cooked breakfast. A hot tub on the screened porch, beach chairs, beach towels, beach showers, bicycles, and a freezer for your catch all make this seem like a home away from home. The inn is open year-round. Special discounts are available for senior citizens, honeymooners, and midweek and off-season stays.

- **Scarborough House Inn**. Moderate/Inexpensive. 323 Fernando Street, P.O. Box 1310, Manteo (252-473-3849; www.bbonline.com.nc/scarborough). The keepers of this inn are as local as they come. The Scarboroughs boast lineages on both sides extending as far back as pre–Revolutionary War times. The photos of ancestors that decorate the walls of the five guest rooms chronicle the story of Roanoke Island and the Outer Banks for close to a century. The rooms include antique beds covered with handmade spreads, gleaming pine floors, and antiques, as well as modern amenities like refrigerators, microwaves, coffee makers, and televisions. Continental breakfast is included in the price of your stay.

Places to Eat

Though there are not as many restaurants on Roanoke Island as on the northern Banks, you'll find good variety and tasty food. As you might expect, seafood is available at just about every restaurant and is as fresh as it comes. Those who don't care for seafood will be able to find plenty to satisfy them as well.

- **1587**. Expensive. Queen Elizabeth Street at the Tranquil House Inn, Manteo (252-473-1587; www.1587.com). Named for the year the Lost Colonists arrived on Roanoke Island, this restaurant is one of the most sophisticated on the Banks. The cuisine at 1587 changes seasonally to reflect the local bounty. The chefs blend herbs grown in the restaurant's own garden with free-range chicken, certified Angus beef, and seafood from the Atlantic to create their unique dishes. Guests can enjoy the breeze off Shallowbag Bay and listen to the water lapping against the docks as they enjoy their evening meal. Dinner is served nightly from February through December.

Queen Anne's Revenge. Expensive/Moderate. Old Wharf Road, Wanchese (252-473-5466). Queen Anne's is a nice place to get away from it all and enjoy a fine meal. Its location in Wanchese is to the restaurant's advantage when it comes to seafood dishes. Queen Anne's is also renowned for its homemade bouillabaisse and handmade fettuccine. Desserts prepared on-site by the chefs round out a menu that is high on fresh Outer Banks ingredients. Dinner is served Wednesday through Sunday.

Clara's Seafood Grill. Moderate. Queen Elizabeth Street, Manteo (252-473-1727). This restaurant affords a lovely view of Shallowbag Bay, a casual atmosphere, and a large menu. Diners will find the tried-and-true fried seafood they expect at the beach, yet healthy grilled and steamed dishes are served here, too. This is a great place to catch lunch while trekking through downtown Manteo. Recommended dishes include the oyster po'boy sandwich, the carved roast beef sandwich au jus, and the tuna steak. Lunch and dinner are served daily from March to January.

Fisherman's Wharf. Moderate. N.C. 345 South, Wanchese (252-473-5205). Located over the Wanchese Fish Company near the tip of the island, this place offers bounteous portions and the freshest catch short of reeling in your own. An elevator makes Fisherman's Wharf accessible to those unable to climb stairs. Try to get a window seat so you can watch hardworking local fishermen bring in their catch and greedy sea gulls fight for the scraps. Lunch and dinner are served daily from April through November.

Hurricane Mo's Restaurant and Raw Bar. Moderate. At Pirate's Cove Marina on the Manteo–Nags Head Causeway, P.O. Box 2240, Manteo (252-473-2266). Located at the point where Roanoke Island and Nags Head meet, this casual yet elegant restaurant is a wonderful place to get a plate of oysters on the half shell and a cold beer and watch the boats come in. Fishermen and families alike are welcome here, and the service is gracious and helpful. Among the favorites are the very generous Cajun-fried mahi-mahi étouffée and the lobster pasta with sun-dried tomatoes, roasted garlic, and artichoke cream sauce. Lunch and dinner are served daily from April through November.

- **Weeping Radish Brewery and Bavarian Restaurant**. Moderate/Inexpensive. U.S. 64/U.S. 264 next to the Island Gallery and Christmas Shop, Manteo (252-473-1157; www.weepingradish.com). For a unique dining experience on the Outer Banks, the Weeping Radish is the place to go. It is named after the radish typically served alongside beer in Bavaria. The radish is spiral cut, salted, and folded back together; the salt draws the water out of the radish and gives it the appearance of weeping. At this restaurant, you'll find dishes you'd expect in Germany—sausages, cabbage dishes, potato cakes, and even pretzels. Beer is the Weeping Radish's claim to fame, though. It is one of just a few breweries in the country using the 1516 German Reinheitsgebot, or purity law. Only four ingredients—water, hops, malt, and yeast—go into the beer, which is left unfiltered to give it a stout, authentic taste. Lunch and dinner are served daily from February to December.

The Mysterious White Doe of Roanoke Island

For centuries, people have puzzled over the fate of the Lost Colonists of Roanoke Island, who shortly after landing in 1587 disappeared without a trace. Legends abound as to their fate. One of the most romantic concerns Virginia Dare, the first English child born in the New World.

According to the tale, little Virginia was adopted into the friendly Croatan tribe on the island and grew up to become a maiden of exquisite beauty. She was loved by one and all, yet she loved only one, a young chief named Oskisko. Chico, a witch doctor, was so infuriated that Virginia did not return his love that he determined to make her unable to marry anyone. Summoning all his powers, he bewitched her with a curse and turned her into a white doe.

Heartbroken, Oskisko resolved to get his love back. He learned from another local shaman that the only way to release Virginia from the body of the white doe was to pierce the doe's heart with an arrow made of an oyster shell.

Another spurned lover, Wanchese, a former friend to the colonists but now a sworn enemy, learned of Oskisko's plan. Like Chico, Wanchese decided that if he could not have Virginia, then nobody would. He set about finding a way to kill the doe and the maiden. Having received a silver arrow from Queen Elizabeth during an earlier voyage to England he'd made with the colonists, he set about stealthily following Oskisko on his mission to regain Virginia.

Creeping through the forest on Roanoke Island, Oskisko furtively searched for the white doe. She suddenly sprang from the trees and ran quickly to the white sands of the sound. Oskisko acted quickly and shot the arrow, lodging it in the doe's heart. But unbeknownst to him, Wanchese had acted just as quickly and shot his arrow into the doe's heart as well. Before either man could react, the restored Virginia fell to the sand, bleeding to death.

His mission accomplished, Wanchese slunk back into the forest, leaving Oskisko to say good-bye to his love. Carefully removing the arrows from Virginia's heart, Oskisko held her close as she lay dying. Stricken with grief, he then rushed to the sound and threw the arrows as far as he could into the deep blue water. When he turned back to his dying lover, she was gone.

Oskisko returned to where her body had lain and grieved all that day and into the night. Early the following morning, as the frost shimmered in the sunrise and the island started to come to life, he was awakened by the sound of pawing. Opening his eyes, he discovered a perfect white doe standing before him. They locked eyes for only a moment before the doe disappeared into the forest.

Some people say they have spotted a white doe wandering the forests of Roanoke Island. If you're lucky, you may spot her, too. Whether or not you believe it's Virginia Dare is up to you.

Bodie Island Lighthouse
COURTESY OF THE NORTH CAROLINA DIVISION OF TOURISM, FILM & SPORTS DEVELOPMENT

BODIE ISLAND
by Sunny Smith Nelson

odie Island provides a glimpse into what the Outer Banks looked like long before tourists arrived, when the only people inhabiting the area were the lighthouse keepers. It is a unique place, to say the least.

Bodie Island is really just the southern tip of the northern Banks and not an island at all. The pronunciation of the name is also a little quirky. I've heard many lifelong North Carolinians pronounce it "Bo-dee," although the correct way of saying the name is "Body." As with every place on the Outer Banks, there are several explanations of how the island came to be named. Some say the name honors the vast number of bodies that washed ashore from ships wrecked in the Graveyard of the

Atlantic. Others a little less melodramatic claim the name comes from the island's actually being a body of land. Still others say Bodie Island was named after a now-unknown person who helped build the lighthouse or was stationed there.

Established in 1953, Cape Hatteras National Seashore was the first national seashore in the country. It begins on Bodie Island and extends 75 miles through Hatteras and Ocracoke Islands, covering over 30,000 acres. Some of the country's best fishing and surfing are found in the national seashore.

JUST THE FACTS

Driving south from the northern Banks, you'll take either U.S. 158 (Virginia Dare Trail) or N.C. 12 (the Beach Road). From Roanoke Island, take U.S. 64/U.S. 264 East until you reach Whalebone Junction, then head south down N.C. 12.

Bodie Island has no airport of its own. Charters into the area will need to land at the Dare Country Regional Airport on Roanoke Island.

Your best bet for gathering information is the Outer Banks Visitors Bureau, 704 U.S. 64/U.S. 264, P.O. Box 399, Manteo, N.C. 27954 (800-446-6262 or 252-473-2138; www.outerbanks.org).

Things to Do

HISTORIC PLACES, GARDENS, AND TOURS

■ Encircled by its one-of-a-kind horizontal black and white bands, the **Bodie Island Lighthouse** has claimed its small section of the coast since 1847. History has not always been kind to the lighthouse, though. Only 12 years after its creation, it was torn down and rebuilt because of improper construction. Three years later, in 1862, Confederate troops blew up the lighthouse so the Union wouldn't be able to use it. The lighthouse was rebuilt for the second (and so far last) time in 1872 at the staggering cost to Reconstruction North Carolina of $140,000. Shortly after it was reactivated, the lighthouse proved it was still on a bad-luck streak when a flock of wild geese flew into the lantern and damaged the lens.

Now long repaired, the Bodie Island Lighthouse still flashes its 160,000-candlepower beacon 19 miles into the dark night over the Atlantic Ocean. It is not open for climbing, but the keeper's quarters have been restored and now serve as a museum and gift shop. A nature trail winds through the marsh surrounding the lighthouse.

No admission fee is charged here. Hours are seasonal, so be sure to phone ahead. Call 252-441-5711 for more information.

RECREATION

▪ Almost directly across N.C. 12 from the entrance to Bodie Island Lighthouse is one of the best beaches on the Outer Banks, **Coquina Beach**. Named for the tiny white shells you'll find scattered all over, Coquina offers good swimming and surf fishing. Do take note that there is no lifeguard on duty, so use common sense while visiting here.

Coquina Beach is rich in history. The **Laura A. Barnes**, built in 1918, was one of the last schooners constructed in the United States. It lies not far from where it grounded after a nor'easter blew it ashore in 1921. The crew survived, due to the heroic actions of the nearby lifesaving station. In 1973, the National Park Service moved the remains of the ship to their present location.

During World War II, this area came to be known as "Torpedo Junction" because the United States suffered such heavy losses to German submarines. America also made one of its greatest comebacks here, though, when it sunk a German U-boat for the first time. The remains of that submarine now lie 15 miles offshore.

▪ ***Oregon Inlet Fishing Center and Full-Service Marina***, located just down N.C. 12 and operated by the National Park Service, is home to the largest and most modern fishing fleet on the East Coast. Facilities include a general store, boat ramps and docks, and areas to clean your catch. If you're driving past here in the late afternoon, be sure to stop to see the boats come in with their daily catch—sea bass, mullet, bluefish, billfish, and even shark. No fees are charged to use the facility. For more information, call 800-272-5199 or 252-441-6301, or visit their website at www.oregon-inlet.com.

■ The National Park Service also operates the only place to stay on Bodie Island, the **Oregon Inlet Campground**. Here, you'll find 120 sites with only the basics—cold showers, toilets, picnic tables, and grills. No utility connections are offered, but the reasonable price makes up for the no-frills accommodations. The campground is open from April to late September. Availability is on a first-come, first-served basis; no reservations are accepted. The National Park Service recommends that campers bring longer-than-normal tent stakes, due to the shifting sands and winds of the area. Insect netting and bug spray are a good idea, too. Call 252-473-2111 for more information.

Offshore Fishing
COURTESY OF OUTER BANKS VISITORS BUREAU

Cape Hatteras Lighthouse
COURTESY OF NORTH CAROLINA DIVISION OF TOURISM, FILM & SPORTS DEVELOPMENT

Hatteras Island
by Sunny Smith Nelson

*T*he largest island of the Outer Banks, Hatteras Island has a heritage rich in maritime history and lore. Even the trip between Bodie Island and Hatteras Island is a history lesson. Going from one island to the next, you'll cross Oregon Inlet, a body of water that came into existence in 1846, after a large storm blew a channel open. The *Oregon*, the first ship to sail through this passageway, gave the inlet its name. Oregon Inlet is now the main entrance to Pamlico Sound. The meandering, three-mile Herbert C. Bonner Bridge connects the two islands. It requires constant dredging, as sand is perpetually deposited along the stone pillars of the bridge.

Once on Hatteras Island, you'll find several small towns connected by N.C. 12—Rodanthe, Waves, Salvo, Avon, Frisco, Buxton, and Hatteras. Each has a story and flavor all its own.

The most recognized symbol of the island is the Cape Hatteras Lighthouse. Threatened by the same winds and tides that created Oregon Inlet, the lighthouse underwent a monumental move in 1999 to preserve it from the forces of nature.

While hazardous to lighthouses, the waves are a boon to surfers. Hatteras Island is one of the best spots to catch a wave on the East Coast.

Just the Facts

Driving south from the northern Banks, you'll take either U.S. 158 (Virginia Dare Trail) or N.C. 12 (the Beach Road). From Roanoke Island, take U.S. 64/U.S. 264 East to Whalebone Junction, then go south on N.C. 12.

Hatteras Island has no airport of its own, so charters will need to land at the Dare Country Regional Airport on Roanoke Island.

The best place to turn for information is the Outer Banks Visitors Bureau, 704 U.S. 64/U.S. 264, P.O. Box 399, Manteo, N.C. 27954 (800-446-6262 or 252-473-2138). You can visit their website at www.outerbanks.org.

Things to Do

HISTORIC PLACES, GARDENS, AND TOURS

▪ In 1873, the United States Life Saving Service was established by Congress to assist poor souls caught in storms or grounded by sand bars and reefs. The treacherous "Graveyard of the Atlantic" was one of the areas most in need of such service. **Chicamacomico Life Saving Station**, located in Rodanthe, was one of the stations at seven-mile intervals along this portion of the North Carolina coast. Crews patrolled the beaches by foot or on horseback. They used Lyle guns to fire rescue lines to sinking ships or rowed out to rescue endangered crews. A bigger, improved Chicamacomico station was built in 1911.

The most famous rescue by the men at Chicamacomico occurred in 1918, when the English tanker *Mirlo* was torpedoed by a German U-boat. Captain John Allen Midgett, Jr., and his crew of five braved the surf and flames to save 47 of the 57 men aboard the ship. They were awarded medals by the British government in 1921 and were later recognized by the United States government.

Chicamacomico Life Saving Station now serves as a museum. Visitors enjoy the shipwreck exhibit with actual artifacts from, and pieces

Chicamacomico Life Saving Station
COURTESY OF OUTER BANKS VISITORS BUREAU

of, the ships themselves. Lifesaving equipment is also on display. The station is open limited hours from May to October. A reenactment of a shipwreck rescue is performed Thursdays at 2 P.M. from mid-June to Labor Day. The grounds are open year-round. Admission is free. For more information, call 252-987-1552.

▪ *Little Kinnakeet Life Saving Station*, located off N.C. 12 in Avon, was another of the lifesaving stations scattered along the North Carolina coast. The original building, commissioned in 1874, was condemned and modified twice before it was finally moved to its current position to rescue it from the encroaching tides. Like the Chicamacomico station, Little Kinnakeet was decommissioned in 1954 and turned over from the Coast Guard to the National Park Service. It is undergoing repairs and is closed to visitors, though the grounds are open for exploring. Admission is free. Call 252-473-2111 for more information.

▪ The tallest and most famous lighthouse in the United States is the 208-foot *Cape Hatteras Lighthouse*, located off N.C. 12 at Cape Point near Buxton. Over the years, it has come to be the unofficial emblem of the Outer Banks.

Like the other lighthouses along the Banks, the Cape Hatteras Lighthouse has a long and complicated history. Built in 1803 over a mile from the shoreline, the first version of the lighthouse was poorly constructed and gave out only a weak signal to passing ships. The lighthouse was damaged by Union naval shells in 1861. Shortly thereafter, the Confederate army removed the lamp from the lighthouse altogether.

The lighthouse was rebuilt in 1870 more than 1,000 yards from the sea. It rested on a floating foundation this time, meaning that it sat on yellow pine timbers in fresh water on compacted sand with a brick-and-granite foundation on top. As long as the sands held steady and no salt water seeped into the foundation, the lighthouse was safe. What the engineers did not account for, though, was that Hatteras Island itself was moving westward. The federal government abandoned the lighthouse in 1935 due to the constant erosion. The following year, it set up a temporary skeletal steel light tower. Once the 1870 lighthouse was abandoned, vandals damaged its lens.

It wasn't until 1950 that the light was moved back to the old lighthouse, after extensive repairs. But beach erosion continued. In 1980, a storm washed away the foundation of the original 1803 lighthouse, which until then had stood more than 600 feet from the shore. That storm reinforced the idea that something had to be done to save the existing lighthouse. In 1989, after much debate, the National Park Service decided to move the aged structure.

It wasn't until a decade later that the move was approved by Congress. The 1870 lighthouse closed its doors on November 22, 1998, as the National Park Service readied for the move. Engineers lifted the lighthouse from its foundation, sunk eight feet deep into the sand. They moved it 2,900 feet and reanchored it in a safer spot, leaving it about the same distance from the sea as back in 1870. After being closed for 550 days, the lighthouse reopened for visitors on May 26, 2000. The beam again lights up the night sky to a distance of 20 miles offshore.

Also on the grounds are the double keepers' quarters, which house a museum and visitor center, the principal keeper's quarters, and the Hatteras Island Visitor Center. Admission to the lighthouse was free prior to its $12 million move. The lighthouse is now scheduled to become part of the National Park Service Fee Demonstration Program; admission rates will be announced during the 2001 season. The grounds are traditionally open year-round except Christmas from 9 A.M. to 5 P.M.; hours are extended in the summer. The lighthouse is open for climbing from Easter weekend to Columbus Day weekend, weather permitting. For information, call 252-473-2111, or visit their website at www.nps.gov/caha.

■ Off Cape Hatteras is the **USS Monitor National Marine Sanctuary**. The *Monitor* and its Confederate counterpart, the CSS *Virginia* (or *Merrimack*) inaugurated a new age in naval warfare during their famous fight in 1862. Only nine months after battling the *Virginia*, the *Monitor* met a watery end in a ferocious storm while en route to Beaufort. It wasn't until 1974 that the *Monitor* was discovered. The site of the wreck became the first national marine sanctuary only a year later. Archaeologists and engineers believe the ship cannot be recovered without further damage, so the *Monitor* will continue to rest in the same spot where it met its end over 100 years ago.

The Coast Guard strictly enforces restrictions on activity in the sanctuary to preserve the wreck, so the closest history buffs can get is the reduced-scale reproduction at the North Carolina Aquarium at Roanoke Island.

MUSEUMS AND SCIENCE CENTERS

■ Museums and exhibits where you can learn about the life of the early colonists dot the Outer Banks. But there are few places to learn about the people who inhabited the area hundreds of years before the English arrived. The **Frisco Native American Museum and Natural History Center**, located off N.C. 12 in Frisco, sheds light on this often-overlooked group of people. Founded and operated by Carl and Joyce Bornfriend, this is a nonprofit educational foundation that displays collections of authentic Native American artifacts and explores the origins of different tribes, their tools, their religions, and their ways of surviving. Also on the grounds are nature trails, a pavilion, and a gift shop. The first annual Inter-Tribal PowWow, held in May 1999, featured dancers and drummers from all over the country. The museum is open year-round Tuesday through Sunday from 11 A.M. to 5 P.M. and Monday by appointment. Call 252-995-4440, or visit their website at www.nativeamericanmuseum.com.

RECREATION

The sportfishing and surfing are legendary here. But visitors should use common sense while exploring the waters of the island, as the weather can change at a moment's notice. Riptides and strong currents can surprise even the hardiest swimmer.

■ For fishermen, the places to go include **Hatteras Island Fishing Pier** (252-987-2323) in Rodanthe, **Avon Fishing Pier** (252-995-5480), and **Frisco Pier** (252-986-2533). All offer about the same features, including bait, tackle, ice, and snacks. For those interested in Gulf Stream fishing, the **Hatteras Fishing Center** (252-986-2365) offers charters. The island's largest marina, it has docks, boat slips, and a hotel.

- Surfers and windsurfers turn to **Hatteras Island Surf Shop** (252-987-2296) in Waves; **Kitty Hawk Sports** (252-441-9200) and **Avon Windsurf Company** (252-995-5441) in Avon; and **Fox Watersports** (252-995-4970) in Buxton. **Canadian Hole** in Pamlico Sound has been called the "Windsurfing Capital of the East Coast," thanks to its good waves and steady breezes.

- **Pea Island National Wildlife Refuge**, located at the northern tip of Hatteras Island, is a feeding and resting area for more than 265 species of migratory birds. Established in 1938 by an act of Congress, the refuge covers 5,195 acres of Hatteras Island and 25,700 acres of Pamlico Sound. No migratory waterfowl hunting is allowed here. The name comes from the acres of "dune peas" that cover the refuge. These beans, packed with protein, are a good source of energy for the birds on their long flights. Birds spotted here include piping plovers, peregrine falcons, Canada and snow geese, tundra swans, herons, egrets, ibises, bald eagles, and over 25 species of ducks. Observation decks and nature trials enable visitors

Windsurfing
COURTESY OF OUTER BANKS VISITORS BUREAU

Pea Island National Wildlife Refuge
COURTESY OF OUTER BANKS
VISITORS BUREAU

to view all the different winged visitors. Pea Island is also home to river otters, muskrats, rabbits, and raccoons. In addition, loggerhead turtles use the refuge as their northernmost nesting ground. The temperature at which the eggs incubate determines the sex of loggerheads; this northern nesting ground produces many members of the male loggerhead population.

The refuge's visitor center offers wildlife exhibits and a gift store; it is open daily from 9 A.M. to 4 P.M. from April to November and on most weekends during the winter months. The refuge is administered by Alligator River National Wildlife Refuge. Admission is free. For more information, call 252-473-1131.

▪ *Buxton Woods Reserve* is a 500-acre maritime forest on the southern end of Hatteras Island. It is the largest maritime forest in North Carolina.

▪ There are a dozen campgrounds to choose from on Hatteras Island, many offering over 100 sites. Most have the same kind of amenities— hot and cold water, electrical and sewer hookups, and access to water. Campers should contact *Cape Hatteras KOA* (800-562-5628 or 252-987-2307; www.koa.com/where/nc/33166), *North Beach Campground* (252-987-2378), or *St. Clair Landing* (252-987-2850 or 252-441-0599) in Rodanthe; *Camp Hatteras* (252-987-2777) or *Ocean Waves Campground* (252-987-2556) in Waves; *Sands of Time RV Park and Campground* (252-995-5596; www.members.aol.com/seau124593/index) in Avon; *Capewoods Campground* (252-995-5850) or *Island Hide-Away* (888-826-7098 or 252-995-6628) in Buxton; *Frisco Cove* (252-995-4242) or *Frisco*

Woods Campground (800-948-3942 or 252-995-5208) in Frisco; or *Hatteras Sands Camping Resort* (252-986-2422) or *Village Marina Campground* (252-986-2522) in Hatteras.

Places to Stay

The majority of hostelries on Hatteras Island are no-frills hotels and motels that cater to fishermen and those on a budget. For those wanting a little more luxury, there are a handful of bed-and-breakfasts. Everyone visiting Hatteras Island should be able to find a place to suit their needs and tastes.

RESORTS, HOTELS, AND MOTELS

Chain hotels on Hatteras Island include *Comfort Inn–Hatteras Island* (800-432-1441 or 252-995-6100) and *Holiday Inn Express Hotel and Suites* (800-361-1590 or 252-986-1110).

■ *Avon Motel*. Moderate. N.C. 12, Avon (800-243-5774 or 252-995-5774; www.avonmotel.com). This oceanside motel has been family owned and operated since 1954. Rooms include the basics, like air conditioning, phones, and televisions; some feature fully equipped kitchens. A guest laundry and a lighted fish-cleaning station are available. The motel is open from March to December.

■ *Cape Hatteras Motel*. Moderate. N.C. 12, Buxton (800-995-0711 or 252-995-5611; www.capehatterasmotel.com). Offering six rooms, seven efficiencies, 23 apartments, and one cottage, this motel has much to choose from. All rooms have a television, a microwave, a small refrigerator, and a coffee maker. Fully equipped kitchens and linens are provided in the efficiencies and apartments. All guests have access to a pool, a Jacuzzi, and a freezer for the day's catch. This motel is the closest place to stay to Canadian Hole and is only a 20-minute walk from the lighthouse.

■ *Hatteras Harbor Hotel*. Moderate. N.C. 12 at the Hatteras Harbor Marina in Hatteras (800-676-4939 or 252-986-2565; www.hatterasharbor.com/apts). This motel's 15 rooms and six efficiencies are located on the second floor of the marina building—the perfect place for sincere fishermen. Some rooms can accommodate up to six people and offer a full kitchen with a microwave and a coffee maker. Each room has a private balcony, from which guests can enjoy watching the boats come in and the sun setting over the sound.

■ *Lighthouse View Motel.* Moderate. N.C. 12, Buxton (800-225-7651 or 252-995-5680; www.lighthouseview.com). Guests staying here are located almost at the foot of the lighthouse. This large complex offers over 75 units ranging from single rooms to cottages and villas. The amenities include cable television, private porches and decks, washers and dryers, a pool, and a hot tub.

■ *Sea Gull Motel.* Moderate/Inexpensive. N.C. 12, Hatteras (252-986-2550; www.seagullhatteras.com). This motel, located within a mile of Hatteras Fishing Center, offers 45 oceanfront units, all of which have televisions and phones and a few of which have refrigerators and microwaves. A fish-cleaning area and outdoor showers are provided for fishermen. Kids love the outdoor pool and private beach. The motel is open from March to December.

INNS AND BED-AND-BREAKFASTS

■ *Cochran's Way.* Expensive. N.C. 12, Hatteras (800-278-1406 or 252-986-1406; www.cochransway.com). If you're looking for privacy, this is the place for you. Each of the three guest rooms offers its own distinctive style. The Sizer Room has a mahogany four-poster bed and Federal-style furniture; the Chinese Quilt Room has Mexican pine furniture; the Wicker Garden Room features white wicker. Each room has a private entrance and a Mexican-tile private bath. A swimming pool and tennis courts are around the corner at Club Hatteras. A gourmet breakfast is served each morning, and afternoon refreshments are provided. Rooms are available from April to November.

- **Castaways Oceanfront Inn**. Expensive/Moderate. N.C. 12, Avon (800-845-6070 or 252-995-4444). This is one of the largest places to stay on Hatteras Island. Castaways features 66 oceanfront rooms with private balconies; each room has a wet bar, a refrigerator, and cable television. A pool, a Jacuzzi, outdoor showers, and grills round out the amenities. The inn's restaurant is open for breakfast and dinner during the spring, summer, and fall. Two banquet rooms are available for large gatherings.

- **Seaside Inn at Hatteras**. Expensive/Moderate. N.C. 12, Hatteras (252-986-2700; www.seasidebb.com). Established in 1928, the Seaside Inn was the island's first hotel. It was built to accommodate the wealthy businessmen who came to Hatteras for the excellent hunting and fishing. The inn underwent a complete renovation in the 1990s. It now has 10 guest rooms, each individually decorated with antiques. Some of the rooms have separate sitting areas and Jacuzzis. A gourmet breakfast is served every morning.

- **Cape Hatteras Bed-and-Breakfast**. Moderate. Old Lighthouse Road, Buxton (800-252-3316 or 252-995-6004). The street address for this bed-and-breakfast lets you in on how close it is to the lighthouse. It is only 500 feet from the ocean as well. Its nine rooms and one suite include basic amenities like private baths and cable television. Guests can also take advantage of the sun deck, surfboard and sailboard storage, bicycles, beach chairs, coolers, and beach bags. A hearty breakfast is served each morning. The bed-and-breakfast is open from March to December.

Places to Eat

You'll find a surprising number of restaurants on Hatteras Island. Most are located on the sound side of the island near the lighthouse. Visitors can find everything here, from gourmet fare to a quick bite on the run. Most people will also be surprised and pleased at the lack of chain eateries.

■ **Bluewater Grill and Wine Bar**. Expensive. N.C. 12, Waves (252-987-1300). If you're looking to dine rather than to merely eat, Bluewater Grill is the place to go. Aged Angus beef and fresh seafood are grilled over a mesquite fire here, and the wine list, needless to say, is pretty impressive. Dinner is served Wednesday through Sunday from April through November.

■ **Austin Creek Grill**. Expensive/Moderate. N.C. 12, Hatteras Landing (252-986-1511). This casual waterfront bistro, a relative newcomer to the Outer Banks, has quickly gained a reputation among locals and visitors alike for some of the best steaks, seafood, and pasta on Hatteras Island. It is so popular, in fact, that reservations are highly recommended. Lunch and dinner are served year-round.

■ **The Breakwater Restaurant**. Expensive/Moderate. N.C. 12 at Oden's Dock, Hatteras (252-986-2733). The second-story dining room, deck, and bar of this restaurant overlook Pamlico Sound and afford great views of the sunset and of boats on their way to dock for the evening. The specialties include seafood, prime rib, veal, and pasta. Just try not to fill up on the freshly baked bread first! Live entertainment is offered on the deck on Sunday evenings in summer. Dinner is served nightly from February through November.

■ **The Channel Bass**. Expensive/Moderate. N.C. 12, Hatteras (252-986-2250). A Hatteras institution for over 30 years, this restaurant, owned and operated by the Harrison family, offers just about anything your heart and stomach could desire. Seafood and steaks are the specialties. The hush puppies are made from a secret family recipe, and the desserts are homemade. Be sure to compliment one of the restaurant staff on Mrs. Shelby's fishing trophies adorning the foyer. The Channel Bass is open for dinner nightly from mid-March to November.

■ **Harbor Seafood Deli**. Moderate. N.C. 12, Hatteras (252-986-2331). Located adjacent to the marina, this eatery offers a menu heavy on seafood. Try the scallop burger or the shrimp pasta salad. The porch is a nice place to go in the afternoon to enjoy hand-dipped ice cream and to watch the boats come in. Fishermen will appreciate the deli's special prepacked breakfasts and lunches for those all-day trips; call a day ahead to request what you want. Breakfast and lunch are served daily year-round.

- **Sonny's Restaurant**. Moderate/Inexpensive. N.C. 12, Hatteras (252-986-2922). If you're looking for down-home eats, Sonny's is your place. The regulars know all about the hot cakes, the omelets, the hash browns, and the stick-to-your-ribs sausage gravy that will get you through a long, hard day of fishing. Sonny's also offers an 18-item salad bar, a seafood buffet, prime rib, macaroni and cheese, and a variety of desserts. Alcohol is not served here, but you're more than welcome to brown-bag. Breakfast and dinner are served daily year-round.

A Well-Weathered Past

Excerpted from Jan DeBlieu's *Hatteras Journal*

Theodore Stockton Midgett was the son of a commercial fisherman. His wife, Ersie, a short, red-haired, and jovial woman, was the daughter of Effica and Jethro Anderson Midgett, who ran a business delivering food and dry goods that they brought to the island by sailboat. At the time Stockton and Ersie built the white house, Hatteras Island was still little more than a sparsely vegetated bar of sand. There were no paved roads, no running water, no electricity, no dunes. Construction on the Oregon Inlet bridge was forty years away. With no reliable weather forecasting system, the island's residents stayed continually prepared for major blows. . . .

. . . When the Civilian Conservation Corps set up a base camp in Rodanthe to headquarter their dune-building project,

Stockton realized the crews of men needed a source of food and supplies. In 1936 he built a general store just west of the white house. At first he intended to turn the store's operation over to his sons, Harold, Anderson, and Stockton, Jr. But the boys soon tired of staying inside to clerk and put up stock. Within two years the storekeeping had been delegated to Ersie, who was quick at figuring prices and balancing books. Stockton had other plans for his sons. In the fall of 1938 he went to Baltimore and came back with a franchise for the island's first transportation system, a bus line from Hatteras village to Manteo. . . .

. . . Harold and Anderson were determined to start running their new business as soon as they could. To help drive their first "bus"—a brand-new Ford station wagon—they recruited their young brother, Stocky. Once a day the station wagon made its way from Hatteras village to a ferry at Oregon Inlet, then on to Manteo and back. "We called the route one-O-one—a hundred and one different ways," Stocky recalled. "At low tide we drove the beach. At high tide we drove the bank—the top of the beach, where the dunes are now—or the inside road, which consisted of several different tracks. There were always more people than we had room for; most of the time we'd put 'em on the running boards and in each other's laps, and sometimes on the hood. If we got stuck, which we often did, everybody got out and pushed."

The modern world had begun to discover Hatteras Island. In addition to the debut of public transportation, 1938 brought electricity to Hatteras village with the formation of a municipal cooperative. Electricity meant running water, indoor toilets, refrigeration. Slowly residents began to enjoy more luxuries and to have more contact with the outside world. Occasionally a hurricane or a strong wind blow would disrupt the island's development, but storms were accepted as sporadic, shortlived dangers, like tornados in the Midwest. In 1944 a major hurricane pushed eight feet of water through Rodanthe. As Ersie, Joyce, and Anderson sat in the wood-frame house, a sudden blast of wind twisted the structure and sent it sliding twelve feet off its foundation. When the eye passed overhead, the family rushed to the home of a relative—only to have that house picked up beneath them by a surge and floated fifty yards, tossing and lurching in the waves. The receding tide left the relative's house perched on top of Anderson's brand-new Ford.

And still the pace of progress quickened. In 1948 the electric cooperative extended its service to the north section of Hatteras Island, and the state paved the first portion of Highway 12, a twenty-mile stretch between Hatteras village and Avon. In 1952 the surfaced road reached the length of the island. Although easier to drive than the beach, it was frequently overwashed or covered with sand, and the Midgett brothers' vehicles continued to get stuck. One evening as Stocky was driving back from Manteo in a school bus loaded with people, he suddenly found himself driving through water. "The sea had backed up right behind the dunes, and one of the dunes broke through," he says. "Water came rushing through like a funnel. I had on a pair of leather boots, so I climbed around on the fenders trying to get the hood up without getting my feet wet. By the time I dried off the engine, the front wheels of the bus had settled down through the highway. And before we could do anything else, the rear wheels fell through. The bus started settling down just like you'd put a casket in a grave."

Passengers piled out of the vehicle and climbed a dune while Stockton [Jr.] started north, walking and swimming toward the nearest Coast Guard station. An hour later when he returned with help, the bus had disappeared. "When the tide fell, the highest point of the bus was the left front corner. It was about eighteen inches above the surface of the road. I called my brother to tell him I'd lost the bus. He wanted to know if I'd been off drinking someplace."

OCRACOKE ISLAND
by Sunny Smith Nelson

*T*he last of the barrier islands that make up the thin, long, wind-swept Outer Banks, Ocracoke has always been known for its seclusion. Over the centuries, it has been the haunt of wild ponies, pirates, and German U-boats. Tourism didn't develop on the island until after World War II; it was only then that electricity, telephone lines, and paved roads were installed here. Even today, the island is accessible only by ferry and plane. This seclusion and slow pace of life attract people looking to get away from it all. Regulars have made Ocracoke their destination for vacations and retreats for generations. Ocracoke village, the only town on the island, wraps around the beautiful Silver Lake. The island has only one major road; walking and biking are the ways most people get around. You definitely don't want to miss a thing Ocracoke has to offer.

JUST THE FACTS

Ocracoke is accessible only by water or air. A free ferry crosses from Hatteras Island to Ocracoke about every half-hour in the summer. No reservations are accepted; passengers cross on a first-come, first-served basis. Two ferries operate between Ocracoke and mainland North Carolina, one from the west from Swan Quarter in Hyde County and one from the south from Cedar Island in Carteret County. Reservations are required for these ferries, and a fee is charged. For information on ferry schedules, fees, and crossing times, call 800-BY-FERRY. For information on the Hatteras ferry, call 800-368-8949; for information on the Cedar Island ferry, call 800-856-0343; for information on the Swan Quarter ferry, call 800-773-1094. The toll-free number for the Ocracoke terminal is 800-345-1665.

The Outer Banks Visitors Bureau is a great resource for information on every island along the Outer Banks; contact the bureau at 704 U.S. 64/U.S. 264, P.O. Box 399, Manteo, N.C. 27954 (800-446-6262 or 252-473-2138; www.outerbanks.org). You may also contact the Greater Hyde County Chamber of Commerce, P.O. Box 178, Swan Quarter, N.C. 27885 (888-HYDE-VAN or 252-925-5201).

Ocracoke Lighthouse
COURTESY OF NORTH CAROLINA DIVISION OF TOURISM, FILM & SPORTS DEVELOPMENT

Things to Do

HISTORIC PLACES, GARDENS, AND TOURS

■ When many people think of Ocracoke, the **Ocracoke Lighthouse** comes to mind. Built in 1823, this lighthouse is the oldest still in operation in North Carolina and the second oldest in the United States. It's the shortest on the North Carolina coast, too, standing only 75 feet in height. Its beam penetrates 14 miles out to sea. The lighthouse was built on the highest point of the island, which has saved it from flooding several times. When a hurricane in 1944 flooded many of the island's homes with as much as 30 inches of water, the waves merely lapped at the lighthouse's doorstep. The lighthouse is not open for climbing.

■ Some people strolling Ocracoke are surprised to find a British flag flying here. The **British Cemetery**, located not far from Silver Lake, is a memorial to the men of the HMS *Bedfordshire*, a British antisubmarine ship that was torpedoed and sunk off Cape Lookout by a German U-boat in May 1942. All aboard perished. Four bodies washed ashore on Ocracoke Island and were given a burial befitting men serving their country and helping to protect the United States. The graveyard, surrounded by a white picket fence and maintained by the Coast Guard, contains bronze plaques on concrete crosses. One features the words of Rupert Brooke: "If I should die, think only this of me; That there's some corner of a foreign field, That is forever England."

■ Another British legacy on the island may be the **wild ponies of Ocracoke**. Legend has it that on at least one of Sir Walter Raleigh's expeditions to explore the New World, he left ponies on Roanoke Island. The ponies spread throughout the Outer Banks, as the islands used to be connected by land bridges until various hurricanes and nor'easters shifted sands and created channels. A second theory postulates that the ponies may be descended from mustangs that swam ashore from Spanish galleons that met their watery end in the Atlantic. In either case, thousands of wild ponies roamed the Banks until the advent of development and tourism after World War II. The small number of ponies now left are protected by the National Park Service. In 1959, those on Ocracoke were corralled into a 160-acre pasture near the northern end of the island. They have been there ever since. While viewing them, you can conjecture for yourself whether they are descended from shipwreck survivors or Raleigh's brood.

MUSEUMS AND SCIENCE CENTERS

■ Though Ocracoke isn't large, it is steeped in history and legend. The island was originally called Wokokon by the Native Americans of the area. Legend has it that the infamous Edward Teach, better known as Blackbeard the Pirate, renamed the island on his final night. Anxious to do battle against the British who were trying to capture him, he cried out "O Crow Cock!" during the night, beckoning the morning to appear. You can find out the complete history of the island by visiting the **Ocracoke Visitor Center**, located in Ocracoke village by Silver Lake. The entire village was placed on the National Register of Historic Places in

Aerial view of Ocracoke
COURTESY OF NORTH CAROLINA DIVISION OF TOURISM, FILM & SPORTS DEVELOPMENT

July 1990. The visitor center offers exhibits detailing the important events in the island's history. The National Park Service administers the site. Rangers are on hand to answer questions or to guide you to a good book in the book shop. To contact the visitor center, or for information on docking at Ocracoke, call 252-928-4531.

SPECIAL SHOPPING

Ocracoke offers a handful of distinctive shops where visitors can find anything from the basic necessities to memorabilia and souvenirs to commemorate their trip.

▪ The *Ocracoke Variety Store*, located on N.C. 12, the main road in town, offers exactly what its name implies—a variety of everything. You'll find grocery items, T-shirts, tools, postcards, and just about everything in between.

▪ Offering much the same merchandise is the *Community Store*, an old country store with convenient benches outside where you can enjoy ice cream while you people-watch.

▪ Not to be missed is *Teach's Hole*, a self-proclaimed "Blackbeard Exhibit and Pyrate Specialty Shop." A 14-minute film tells shoppers about Blackbeard's connection to the island, his supposed haunts, what flags he flew and what they meant, and his death. Souvenirs include books, art, flags, and even pirate party supplies. For information, call 252-928-1718, or visit their website at www.teachshole.com.

RECREATION

▪ One of the best ways to get away from it all on Ocracoke is through the kayak ecotours offered by *Ocracoke Adventures*. Several different tours are available, including a sunrise tour, a Blackbeard tour, a sunset tour, a full-moon tour, and a clamming tour, during which you can rake your own clams. The Portsmouth Island tour takes you to the small is-

Ron Hubble

Nanzetta Way 260

Lewisville - NC

Zip: 27023

land just south of Ocracoke, where one of the largest towns on the Outer Banks was located until bad weather drove the 600 inhabitants off to other sections of the Banks; be sure to bring bug spray for this tour. Call 252-928-7873 for more information.

- Fishermen will want to make *Anchorage Marina* one of their first stops. Only 18 miles from the Gulf Stream, this marina is one of the closest jumping-off places for those in search of yellowfin tuna, wahoo, big amberjack, and bluefish. The marina offers dockage, gas and diesel, and water and power hookups. A café on the premises sells drinks, lunches, and fishing supplies. Call 252-928-6661 for more information.

- The National Park Service operates a campground on N.C. 12 north of Ocracoke village. Features include cold showers, restrooms, drinking water, tables, and fire grills. No utility hookups are available. The campground is open from early April to mid-September. Sites may be reserved from May to September; the campground operates on a first-come, first-served basis during April. A modest fee is charged. For information, call 800-365-2267.

Places to Stay

Many Ocracoke regulars have a certain hotel or bed-and-breakfast that they come back to time and again. You're sure to find your favorite spot, too. Be sure to book early, since lots of other new "regulars" visit Ocracoke each season.

RESORTS, HOTELS, AND MOTELS

■*Anchorage Inn.* Moderate. N.C. 12 (252-928-1101; www.theanchorageinn.com). The largest place to stay on Ocracoke Island, the Anchorage Inn has five floors and 35 rooms and offers double- to king-sized beds and kitchenettes. The inn overlooks the harbor and Pamlico Sound, providing a view of gorgeous sunsets and boats on their way home to dock. Complimentary continental breakfast, a café, a pool, and grills are among the popular features here.

- **Blackbeard's Lodge**. Moderate. N.C. 12 (800-892-5314 or 252-928-3421). A friend of mine's family has made Blackbeard's Lodge their regular place to stay. It could be the friendly staff, the second-story sun deck, or the front desk made of a ship's prow. You'll find the basic amenities here, like private baths and color cable television.

- **Boyette House**. Moderate/Inexpensive. N.C. 12 (800-928-4261 or 252-928-4261). The Boyette House offers two different experiences in lodging—the classic Boyette House I, which has 12 bedrooms with double beds, refrigerators, and televisions, and the newer and more upscale Boyette House II, which has 10 bedrooms with queen-sized beds, in-room breakfast bars, steam baths, and semiprivate porches. Some rooms even have Jacuzzis and living-room areas. All guests are invited to use the outdoor hot tub and the physical fitness center.

INNS AND BED-AND-BREAKFASTS

- **Berkley Manor**. Expensive. On the harbor (252-928-5911). Identifying itself as a secluded island estate, this former hunting and fishing lodge sits on three private acres of scenic woods and well-tended lawns. The 12 guest rooms are decorated with antiques and local art and feature private baths. Some rooms have private sitting areas and two-person Jacuzzis. A full breakfast is provided every morning. The manor is open year-round.

- **Pelican Lodge**. Expensive/Moderate. 27 Ammunition Road (888-7-PELICAN or 252-928-1661). This rustic-looking lodge prides itself on its attention to guests' special needs and desires. A registered dietitian supervises the lodge's breakfast, ensuring a healthy meal for all. A car rental service and even the lodge's own air service, Pelican Airways, provide transportation; aerial sightseeing tours are available through Pelican as well. The nine guest rooms have private baths and cable television. Complimentary bicycles are available if you'd like to explore the island.

- **Thurston House Inn.** Moderate. N.C. 12 (252-928-6037). Listed on the Registry of Historic Places in North Carolina, the Thurston House Inn was built in the 1920s by Captain Tony Thurston Gaskill and is now operated by his granddaughter. This charming inn offers nine guest rooms with private baths, televisions, and phones; some rooms have private decks and entrances. An expanded continental breakfast greets each guest before the day's activities, all of which can be easily reached from the inn's ivy-covered front door. The inn is open year-round.

- **Ocracoke Harbor Inn.** Moderate/Inexpensive. 135 Silver Lake Road (888-456-1998 or 252-928-5731; www.ocracokeharborinn.com). Overlooking Silver Lake, the Ocracoke Harbor Inn offers 16 rooms and seven suites, each with a private porch that provides a stunning view of the village and the harbor. All rooms and suites have televisions, telephones with modem ports, coffee makers, and refrigerators; the suites include kitchenettes and Jacuzzis. Guests enjoy the luxury of strolling to dinner or biking to nearby shops. The inn is open year-round.

Places to Eat

You really can't go wrong with any of the eateries on Ocracoke Island, so be adventurous and try a new one each opportunity you get. The variety is enough to satisfy any palate—fresh-off-the-boat seafood, good old meat and potatoes, Italian, gourmet, casual, or just about anything else you're in the mood for. As with every place on the Outer Banks, hours are seasonal, so it's best to call ahead to make sure your restaurant of choice is serving.

- **The Back Porch.** Moderate. 1324 Country Road (252-928-6401). This restaurant prides itself on being out of the way on the already out-of-the-way Ocracoke Island. Secluded from N.C. 12 by trees and cacti, the Back Porch does indeed feature a lovely back porch where you can enjoy your dinner. Or you can select the indoor dining room. You can taste from the first bite that all the sauces, condiments, and breads are made on-site. Freshly ground coffee and homemade desserts round out the evening. If you'd like to try your hand at any of the Back Porch's unique dishes, a cookbook is available at the hostesses' station. Dinner is offered seven nights a week during peak season.

■ **Creekside Café**. Moderate. N.C. 12 (252-928-3606). Creekside Café, overlooking Silver Lake, is a nice place to take a rest from your island explorations and get a cool drink and a bite to eat. Light fare like soups, salads, and sandwiches are offered. The truly hungry can choose from the seafood, pasta, and chicken selections. Try to get a seat on the porch to enjoy the breeze and the great view. Lunch and dinner are served daily during peak season.

■ **Howard's Pub and Raw Bar**. Moderate. N.C. 12 (252-928-4441; www.howardspub.com). Open 365 days a year, this place is a popular hangout for locals and visitors alike. The only raw bar on the island, Howard's features more than 200 imported, domestic, and microbrewed beers. So it follows that they're famous for things like the spicy "Ocracoke Oyster Shooter." The dishes most in demand include steaks, barbecued ribs, blackened tuna, and marinated mahi-mahi. The hand-shaped half-pound burgers, hand-cut fries, homemade salsa, chili, chowder, and desserts are popular, too. The screened-in porch invites you to sit back and relax—and to see if you can spot Portsmouth Island from your lounge chair.

■ **Island Inn Restaurant**. Moderate. At the Island Inn on Lighthouse Road (252-928-7821). You don't have to be a guest of the Island Inn to enjoy this appealing restaurant; you just have to be hungry and looking for a great meal. One of the oldest restaurants on Ocracoke, it serves meals on china like you'd find at Sunday dinner at Grandma's house. The cooking here, though, is definitely not Grandma's. You'll discover shrimp and oysters in your morning eggs, sometimes accompanied by a side of salsa. And you won't be disappointed by the grilled, fried, boiled, or broiled seafood or shellfish and the homemade bread and desserts. Breakfast and dinner are served daily during the busy season.

■ **¾ Time Ristorante**. Moderate. N.C. 12 (252-928-3434). This Italian restaurant serves some of the best pizza, subs, and pasta on the island.

To wash it all down, you'll find close to a dozen beers on tap and a good wine selection. Dinner is available outdoors during the warm months. The cozy indoor dining room serves dinner nightly year-round except during February.

Nearby

■ **Lake Mattamuskeet**, located on the Hyde County mainland, is accessible from Ocracoke by the Swan Quarter ferry. This is the largest natural lake in North Carolina, covering 40,000 acres and stretching for 18 miles at a width of about five to six miles. But the water is surprisingly shallow, averaging a depth of only two feet. This massive lake is a bird watcher's paradise; thousands of tundra swans winter here every year.

It comes as a surprise to some that Lake Mattamuskeet has not always been here. *Mattamuskeet* is, in fact, Algonquian for "Dry Dust." Some conjecture that the lake came into existence only when wildfires burned deep into the peat soil, transforming the flat, dry land into a lake bed.

A group of investors tried to drain the lake in 1914. They renamed the area New Holland, after similar drainage projects in Holland. A network of canals, a model community, and the largest pumping station in the world—capable of pumping up to 1.2 million gallons of water a minute—were built. When investors discovered that the project was too expensive, however, they abandoned New Holland.

The United States government bought the lake in 1934 and established Mattamuskeet National Wildlife Refuge. The pumping station was converted into a lodge, and the nearby smokestack was transformed into a 100-foot-tall observation tower. The lodge closed in 1974 and was added to the National Register of Historic Places in 1980.

Visitors to Lake Mattamuskeet and Mattamuskeet National Wildlife Refuge now enjoy crabbing, fishing, bird-watching, and hunting. The refuge is open during daylight hours. For more information, contact Refuge Manager, Mattamuskeet National Wildlife Refuge, Route 1, Box N-2, Swan Quarter, N.C. 27885 (252-926-4021).

Battle of Ocracoke Inlet
Excerpted from Robert E. Lee's
Blackbeard the Pirate: A Reappraisal of His Life and Times

Lieutenant Maynard, during the early gray light before sunrise on Friday, November 22, ordered the anchors weighed and headed for what in later years became known as "Teach's Hole." Off the tip of Ocracoke Island, and before passing into the sound waters, men in a rowboat were lowered with instructions to proceed ahead of the sloops and take soundings. Maynard did not care to run the risk of being grounded on a shoal, so the men in the rowboat signaled the course to be followed. Upon coming into firing range of the *Adventure*, the men in the rowboat were greeted with a round of shot and immediately "scurried back to the protection of the sloops" . . .

Blackbeard roared rudely across the water: "Damn you for villains, who are you? And from whence come you?"

"You may see by our colors we are no pirates," answered Maynard.

"Send your boat on board so that I might see who you are," demanded Blackbeard.

"I cannot spare my boat, but I will come aboard you as soon as I can with my sloop," replied Maynard.

Seeing that they intended to board by storm, Blackbeard took up a bowl of liquor; and calling out to the officers of the other sloops, drank to them with these words: "Damnation seize my soul if I give you quarter or take any from you."

In reply to this, Maynard yelled back, "I expect no quarter from you, nor shall I give any."

For the moment, the fortunes of war were in Blackbeard's favor. The two royal sloops had crunched the sands of the submerged bar and their crews set to working feverishly to dislodge them. The rising tide would shortly set them afloat again. Blackbeard acted with dispatch, ordering Philip Morton, his gunner, to train the eight cannons of the *Adventure* towards the attackers in a general broadside. . . .

This single broadside of eight cannons was devastating. . . . With a single broadside from his eight cannons, Blackbeard had reduced the attacking force to half its original size. . . .

At this juncture Maynard came up with a typical trick of sea warfare. He ordered all his men below deck, their pistols and swords ready for close fighting, to remain in the hold until he gave the signal. . . . Maynard's strategy was to ensnare the pirates into doing the fighting aboard his own ship. Maynard himself went into the cabin, ordering the midshipman at the helm and William Butler, the pilot, to inform him of anything that happened.

Blackbeard, seeing Maynard's sloop approaching, alerted his men to prepare to board, with grappling irons and weapons ready for instant use. In addition, he had a lethal surprise which he intended to introduce to His Majesty's Royal Navy—hand grenades: in this case, bottles filled with powder, small shot, and pieces of iron and lead and ignited by fuses worked into the center of the bottle. Captain Teach's own invention, it had served him well during numerous pirate attacks, the resulting explosion invariably creating pandemonium on deck.

Most of the light grenades landed on the deck of Maynard's sloop, exploding resoundingly and rendering the sloop almost invisible in the enveloping smoke. Since most of the men were below deck, the grenades this time failed to achieve their effect. The royal sloop continued to drift forward. Seeing through the smoke only a few or no hands aboard, Blackbeard jubilantly shouted to his crew: "They were all knocked on the head but three or four. Blast you—board her and cut them to pieces!"

Maynard's sloop bumped against the side of Blackbeard's sloop. . . . Teach was the first aboard. . . . According to Maynard's version, ten pirates followed their leader and scrambled aboard, howling and firing at anything that moved. Maynard's men in the hold burst out, shouting and shooting.

The effect of the men pouring out of the hold was as shocking as Maynard had calculated. Everything was in confusion. The pirates were taken aback. Blackbeard instantly saw what was happening. Like the leader he was, he paused to rally and inspire his men.

The blood of the twenty British seamen wounded or killed by the terrific broadside had slickened the deck. The bodies of the dead were still there. Additional blood was to flow from the butchery and the savage melée that was to follow—the bloodiest battle ever fought on the deck of a small craft. . . .

Blackbeard waded into the melée, swinging his great cutlass. It was a wild windmill attack that no one in front of him could repel with a blade. He had to be stopped by a pistol shot or by someone from the rear. Both methods were tried. Blackbeard from time to time supplemented his blade swinging with a pistol snatched from the bandolier of pistols across his chest. These were single-shot pistols, thrown aside after being used.

An heroic touch was given to the battle by the ferocious confrontation of Maynard and Blackbeard—the champion of law and order and the champion of piracy—face to face. In this epic struggle, one or the other had to be annihilated. . . .

In the heat of combat they engaged each other with swords. A powerful blow of Blackbeard's cutlass snapped off Maynard's sword blade near its hilt. A blow of such terrific force would ordinarily have knocked the sword flying, but apparently Maynard was holding it with a frenzied grasp. Hurling the hilt at his adversary, Maynard stepped back to cock his pistol, and at the same instant Blackbeard moved in for the finishing blow with his cutlass. But at the moment in which he swung his cutlass aloft, a British seaman approached Blackbeard from the rear and "gave him a terrific wound in the neck and throat." The cutlass, raised for the finishing blow, swerved as it came down, merely grazing the knuckles of Maynard, cutting them slightly.

The blood spurted from Blackbeard's gashed neck. He staggered, but fought on. Shouting defiance, he continued to swing the heavy cutlass about him. The bullet and sword wounds which he had sustained were, however, weakening him. Others saw that he was approaching his end. The British seamen, who had kept clear of him until now, closed in for the kill. They ducked in behind him to stab him with their swords. "At length, as he was cocking another pistol, having fired several before, he fell down dead." Edward Teach died a violent death, but was in the heat of battle, as he would have wished, still fighting as he fell with the insensate rage of a mortally wounded lion.

Lieutenant Maynard afterwards conducted an informal autopsy, to discover that his opponent had fallen with five pistol shots in him and no less than twenty severe cuts in various parts of his body. Maynard unquestionably recognized Blackbeard as a man superior to others in talent, in courage, and, moreover, in physical strength. . . .

Maynard ordered Blackbeard's head severed from his body and suspended from the bowsprit of Maynard's sloop. The rest of Blackbeard's corpse was thrown overboard. According to legend, when the headless body hit the cold water it defiantly swam around the sloop several times before it sank.

The Coastal Plain

Albemarle Region

Elizabeth City
Edenton
Bath

Neuse River Region

New Bern
Morehead City
Beaufort
Bogue Banks

Cape Fear Coast

Topsail Island
Wilmington
Wrightsville Beach
Pleasure Island
Southport and the Brunswick Islands

S preading across the eastern third of the state is North Carolina's vast coastal plain.

Inland are small river towns known for their manufacturing—and, more importantly, their barbecue—and countless farming communities that produce the majority of the state's agricultural products, as well as a politician or two. Much like the Mississippi Delta, the flat landscape can be monotonous, but a closer look reveals lush, fertile fields that yield such crops as tobacco, corn, and peanuts.

Along the coast, a series of seven sounds gives North Carolina one of the longest shorelines in the United States. Dotting it are what are quite possibly the state's most beautiful, historic, and fascinating destinations.

In the north, the region surrounding Albemarle Sound is home to the state's oldest towns, Edenton and Bath. One of the area's most vibrant communities, Elizabeth City, has been called the "South's prettiest city." Also here, stretching across 210,000 acres, is the Great Dismal Swamp, the continent's only live peat bog.

In the coastal plain's midsection, the Neuse River region encompasses some of the state's premier beaches, collectively called the Crystal Coast, as well as picturesque fishing and sailing villages such as Morehead City, Beaufort, and Oriental. Pirates were fond of the protective coves within the enormous Pamlico Sound, and legends of their antics abound. At the North Carolina Maritime Museum in Beaufort, artifacts from Blackbeard's ship, the *Queen Anne's Revenge*, are on display. Upriver, along the banks of the Neuse River, historic New Bern and its impeccably reconstructed colonial governor's mansion, Tryon Palace, should not be missed.

Farther south, the Cape Fear River region and its crown jewel, Wilmington, are among the state's fastest-growing areas. Among those drawn to this fair metropolis are filmmakers, who since the 1980s have given the city the distinction of being the "Hollywood of the East." A visit to the area would not be complete without a stop at one of the sparkling beaches at Topsail Island or Pleasure Island or the legendary Wrightsville Beach.

South of Wilmington, the hamlet of Southport and the pristine Brunswick County beaches round out the lower Cape Fear area. As the midway point along the bustling Intracoastal Waterway, Southport is a port of call for all manner of pleasure boats. If golf is your game, there are over 35 public courses in the vicinity to choose from. Or if your idea of a vacation is lounging on an uncrowded beach all day, then enjoying a sumptuous meal of fresh Calabash-style seafood, be sure to head for Oak Island, Holden Beach, or Sunset Beach.

by Sunny Smith Nelson
and Anne Holcomb Waters

Moth boats
COURTESY OF NORTH CAROLINA DIVISION OF TOURISM, FILM AND SPORTS DEVELOPMENT

ALBEMARLE REGION

By Sunny Smith Nelson

While attending the University of North Carolina at Chapel Hill, I met people from all over the state. I found that some of the students most proud of where they came from were those from the Albemarle region. From them, I learned that Albemarle Sound is the largest freshwater sound in the United States; that Washington, North Carolina, is the "original" Washington; and that the state's oldest communities, including North Carolina's very first town, are located here. In the Albemarle region, you'll find historic sites maintained by the Colonial Dames of America. Unlike other Southerners, when these ladies speak of "the War," they're referring to the Revolutionary War, not the Civil War. History and heritage are a large part of the culture of the Albemarle region, and the extraordinarily gracious people of the area are happy to share them with you.

Another thing I associate with the area is wild naturalness. When I was a child, my father would look forward to the crisp fall days when he and a group of his buddies would go to their patch of swampy woodland outside Windsor in Bertie County to hunt. He would come back and tell my brothers and me about the clear, cold nights sitting alone in his tree stand, where stars as big and bright as lamps were his only companions and the silence was so great he could almost hear them twinkling. Once I visited the area on my own, I saw what he was talking about. Passing along tar-patched, winding country roads by gum tree swamps, old to-bacco barns falling in on themselves, and fields of corn that went on forever showed me that there are still parts of the world that "progress" hasn't visited, and that leaving land as untamed as your great-grandfa-ther knew it is far better than putting a minimart at every crossroads. The people of the Albemarle know that the beauty of the woods and swamps is easily superior to anything we could replace it with.

If you visit the Albemarle region, remember to soak up the stories and family histories you're sure to hear from the proud residents. And be sure to enjoy the trip to your destination as much as you expect to love the final stop.

ELIZABETH CITY

A self-proclaimed "Main Street waterfront community," Elizabeth City sits on the banks of the Pasquotank River, whose Indian name means "Where the Currents Divide." Water played a major role in the develop-ment of Elizabeth City. The area was first explored and navigated in the late 1500s. Settlements started appearing along the river the following century. Elizabeth City was settled in the 1650s. The Dismal Swamp Canal, the oldest canal still in operation in the United States, brought the likes of George Washington and Patrick Henry to Pasquotank County in the 18th century to survey for rich farmland and good hunting and fish-ing. Planters used the port to trade with the East Indies. During the Civil War, the Union army captured Elizabeth City and used it as a port.

Though not the important trading center it used to be, Elizabeth City is now home to the largest Coast Guard command complex in the lower 48 states. The Pasquotank River serves as an alternate route to the Intra-coastal Waterway between Chesapeake Bay and Albemarle Sound. Elizabeth City takes great pride in this nautical heritage. Most of its cultural activities are centered around the river. Here, you'll find Southern hospitality in its highest form. For example, boats are given free dockage for two days at Mariners' Wharf; members of a volunteer group, the Rose Buddies, greet each disembarking newcomer with a rose and an invitation to a wine-and-cheese party. The town boasts museums, galleries, parks, and five historic districts listed on the National Register. It's no wonder that Elizabeth City was recently named in Norm Crampton's *The 100 Best Small Towns in America.*

JUST THE FACTS

Elizabeth City is accessible by land, water, and air.

U.S. 17 leads directly into town from the north and south. U.S. 158 leads into town from the west.

The Intracoastal Waterway and the Pasquotank River lead to the city's docks, which offer free docking for 48 hours.

The nearest large commercial airport is 50 miles to the north in Norfolk, Virginia. The Elizabeth City/Pasquotank County Regional Airport, located at 1028 Consolidated Road, shares runways with the Coast Guard. For information, call 252-335-5634, or visit their website at www.ecgairport.com.

The Trailways bus station is at 118 Hughes Boulevard. Call 252-335-5183 for information.

The Elizabeth City/Pasquotank County Tourism Board, located at 502 East Ehringhaus Street, is a great resource for learning about the area. Contact them at P.O. Box 426, Elizabeth City, N.C. 27907 (252-335-4365), or visit their website at www.elizcity.com.

PHOTOGRAPH USED IN THE BACKGROUND ON PAGE 73—

Nags Head
PHOTOGRAPHY BY WILLIAM RUSS
COURTESY OF NORTH CAROLINA DIVISION OF TOURISM, FILM AND SPORTS DEVELOPMENT

$\mathcal{T}hings\ to\ \mathcal{D}o$

HISTORIC PLACES, GARDENS, AND TOURS

The best way to begin your sightseeing is to stop by the Elizabeth City/Pasquotank County Tourism Board, located at 502 East Ehringhaus Street, to pick up a self-guided tour brochure.

- One of the most popular tours covers the **Elizabeth City commercial district** on Main Street. The commercial district sites let you see for yourself what eastern North Carolina downtowns looked liked before the Civil War. This area includes the largest number of brick antebellum commercial buildings in the state. An amalgamation of restaurants, antique shops, galleries, and boutiques perfect for browsing occupies the storefronts today.

- Also listed on the National Register of Historic Places are the **Episcopal Cemetery** and **Christ Episcopal Church**, located at 200 McMorrine Street. The graves in the Episcopal Cemetery date back to 1724. Many of eastern North Carolina's most prominent citizens have been laid to rest here, including John C. B. Ehringhaus, governor of North Carolina from 1933 to 1937. In the southeastern corner of the cemetery is a plot containing the remains of at least four unknown Confederate soldiers. The church was built in 1856, during the ministry of the Reverend Edward M. Forbes, a well-known local Civil War hero. The church's large stained-glass window depicts the life of Christ. The cemetery is open year-round during daylight hours. Admission is free, though donations are accepted.

MUSEUMS AND SCIENCE CENTERS

- The **Museum of the Albemarle**, located at 1116 U.S. 17 South, is a regional branch of the North Carolina Museum of History. The history of the Albemarle region is explored here. Exhibits chronicle the work, culture, and folklore of the area over the past 400 years. Included are Native American artifacts, antique duck decoys, lumber-camp supplies,

78   The Coast

Woodland Indian exhibit at
Museum of the Albemarle
COURTESY OF MUSEUM OF THE ALBEMARLE

and early-20th-century farm equipment. Guided tours are available, and kids will enjoy the hands-on history presentations. The gift shop sells items relating to the many exhibits. The museum is open Tuesday through Saturday from 9 A.M. to 5 P.M. and Sunday from 2 P.M. to 5 P.M.; it is closed Mondays and state holidays. Admission is free. For more information, call 252-335-1453, or visit their website at www.northeast–nc.com. The Museum of the Albemarle is scheduled to move to a new complex over four times its current size in early 2002.

▪ The **Elizabeth City State University Planetarium**, located at 1704 Weeksville Road, is open to groups of 10 or more who wish to learn about space exploration and astronomy. Admission is free, but reservations are required. Call 252-335-3759 for more information. One of the 16 campuses in the University of North Carolina system, Elizabeth City State was established in 1891 as a two-year institution serving African-American students. By 1937, the school had grown into a four-year teachers' college. It still concentrates on turning out some of the state's best teachers.

SPECIAL SHOPPING

▪ The **Pasquotank Arts Council Gallery**, located at 609 East Main Street, provides opportunities to view and purchase local artwork. The gallery is open Monday through Friday from 10 A.M. to 4 P.M. and Saturday from 10 A.M. to 5 P.M. Admission is free. For more information, call 252-338-6400.

RECREATION

Elizabeth City boasts an impressive list of activities and recreational opportunities. Any of the town's parks is a nice place to spend a lazy afternoon.

▪ **Fun Junktion**, located at 983 Simpson Ditch Road, is a 133-acre park built on land that was originally slated for landfill expansion. Once the county leaders decided to use the land for purposes other than garbage, they came up with plans for an area that would bring people together and provide them with opportunities for relaxation and—as the name says—fun. Visitors to the park will find a handicapped-accessible playground, basketball courts, picnic areas, hiking trails, and several lakes, including a catch-and-release fishing pond, a man-made swimming lake, and a 20-acre competition skiing lake. Canoe rentals are available. Admission is free. Call 252-337-6600 for more information.

▪ The waterfront parks of Elizabeth City, including **Charles Creek Park, Moth Boat Park, Waterfront Park**, and **Dog Corner Park**, provide visitors with great views of the Pasquotank River and chances to fish, boat, grill, play volleyball, or just fall asleep while reading a good book. Admission is free to all parks. For more information, call 252-338-3981.

SEASONAL EVENTS

Just as you'd expect, the festivals and celebrations in Elizabeth City center around the river.

▪ The annual **Elizabeth City Harbor Days**, held the third weekend in September on the waterfront, features an array of activities including a fine-arts festival, a pig pickin', live music, theater readings, book signings, and the biggest draw of all, the **Moth Boat Regatta**. The regatta honors the tiny moth boat, a one-person sailboat created in Pasquotank County in 1929. As the story goes, Captain Joel Van Sant stopped in Elizabeth City on his way from Atlantic City to Florida to have some work done on his yacht, the *Siesta*. He met with Ernest Sanders of Elizabeth City to

Moth boat
COURTESY OF NORTH CAROLINA
DIVISION OF TOURISM, FILM AND SPORTS
DEVELOPMENT

design a boat that could be raced on rivers and lakes. They came up with the moth boat, named because it looks like a quick-winged moth floating over the water. The moth boat quickly caught on because of its great speed and relative inexpensiveness. The regatta celebrates this heritage of boat racing and Elizabeth City's role in the creation of the boat. Call 252-335-4365 for information.

Places to Stay

RESORTS, HOTELS, AND MOTELS

▪ The majority of hotels and motels in Elizabeth City are of the chain variety. They include **Hampton Inn** (252-333-1800), **Holiday Inn** (252-338-3951), **Comfort Inn** (252-338-8900), and **Days Inn** (252-335-4316).

■ **Church Street Bed-and-Breakfast.** Moderate. 1108 West Church Street (252-335-1441). Church Street Bed-and-Breakfast is only six blocks from the water, making it a nice place to retreat to after exploring the waterfront. Intimacy is the word here, as only two guest rooms are offered. The rooms are decorated in mauve, gold, and green, reflecting a Victorian mood. A Jacuzzi, a game room, and a reading room are all available to guests. The bar is a nice place to spend a moment in the evening with a good friend and a drink. A full breakfast is served each morning. Evening refreshments are a nice extra to enjoy on the deck on a pretty evening.

■ **The Culpepper Inn.** Moderate. 609 West Main Street (252-335-1993). This lovely inn, located in the heart of one of the city's historic districts, offers 10 guest rooms individually decorated with antiques. The rooms have cable television and phones with modem ports. Some include king-sized beds and fireplaces. A full breakfast is offered every morning. The outdoor pool is a nice place to relax and catch a few rays. An evening social gives guests the opportunity to mix and mingle. A meeting room is available. Government and corporate rates are offered.

■ **Elizabeth City Bed-and-Breakfast.** Moderate/Inexpensive. 108 East Fearing Street (252-338-2177). This charming little bed-and-breakfast features four guest rooms, each with a private bathroom. The big attraction here is the peace and quiet. The Pasquotank River, only a few minutes' walk from the front door, might prove a nice destination after your candlelit dinner in the Secret Room, an English-style gourmet restaurant on the premises.

Places to Eat

You'll be surprised by the number of really good restaurants in this small town. The choices range from light fare to casual gourmet to down-home Southern cooking.

■ *Cypress Creek Grill*. Moderate. 218 North Poindexter Street (252-334-9915). Located in downtown Elizabeth City, this restaurant serves an all-inclusive menu—seafood, chicken, steaks, pasta, sandwiches, and vegetarian dishes. The atmosphere is relaxed yet upscale. Cypress Creek Grill affords the opportunity to have a special dining experience without emptying your wallet. Lunch and dinner are served Monday through Saturday year-round.

■ *Mulligan's Waterfront Grille*. Moderate. 400 South Water Street (252-331-2431). Located, as the name says, on the waterfront, Mulligan's offers off-the-boat seafood, steaks, chicken, and pasta in a casual atmosphere. Outside dining is especially lovely around sunset, when the boats are coming in. Live entertainment is offered on the weekends. Lunch and dinner are served daily year-round.

■ *Arena's Bakery and Deli*. Moderate/Inexpensive. 700 East Main Street (252-335-2114). The smell wafting from this shop alone is temptation enough to stop. Once inside, you'll find an array of baked goods ranging from fresh breads to still-warm sticky cinnamon buns. Besides the tempting breakfast and brunch items, visitors can order tasty sandwiches, crisp salads, and homemade soups. Arena's is open Monday through Saturday year-round for breakfast and lunch.

■ *Comstock's*. Moderate/Inexpensive. 115 South Water Street (252-335-5833). Known as "Stalk's" by the locals, Comstock's is an Elizabeth City institution. Ever since it opened in 1953, this old-fashioned lunch counter has served good old down-home, stick-to-your-ribs grub. You'll find big, juicy burgers, hot, salty fries, thick chocolate malts, cool, tangy lime-aids, and a variety of other time-tested foods. Stalk's "Museum of North Carolina Sports History," featuring local and state athletes and teams, decorates the premises. You can get breakfast, lunch, and dinner at Stalk's Monday through Saturday year-round.

Nearby

The Albemarle region was the cradle of colonial society in North Carolina. Today, it abounds with small towns that, like Elizabeth City, boast rich histories and interesting attractions. Any one of the following would make a wonderful day trip.

■ Historic **Halifax** is located near N.C. 125 and U.S. 301 about an hour and a half west of Elizabeth City. This is where North Carolina's Fourth Provincial Congress met to declare independence from England. A visitor center and a guided tour of several different historic structures are offered. For more information, call 252-583-7191, or visit their website at www.visithalifax.com.

■ Historic **Jackson** is about an hour west of Elizabeth City near N.C. 305 and U.S. 158. This town was home to some of the biggest aristocrats in the state. Several historic structures, including some antebellum homes, are open for viewing. Call 252-534-1383 for more information.

■ Historic **Murfreesboro**, about a 45-minute drive from Elizabeth City on U.S. 158 West, features a 12-block National Historic District containing homes from the 18th and 19th centuries. A guided tour is available from the Roberts-Vaughan Village Center. The Brady C. Jefcoat Museum of Americana, located in Murfreesboro, is home to the largest collection of washing machines, irons, and dairy items in the United States. For information, call 252-398-5922, or visit their website at www.murfreesboronc.com.

■ The **Great Dismal Swamp** begins just north of Elizabeth City and covers almost 600 square miles of North Carolina and Virginia. The only live peat bog on the continent, it contains some of the wildest and most untamed land on the East Coast. Colonel William Byrd II gave the area its name in 1728, when he stated that the place was so dismal that no one could or would want to inhabit it. But when George Washington came to the area in 1793, he saw the swamp as an economic opportunity. An investment group bought 40,000 acres in the Dismal Swamp and set about converting it to farmland by draining it. When the investors found this endeavor too expensive, they turned to lumbering the swamp for shingles and other wood products instead.

Canals were built in the swamp to make travel and trade easier. Among these were the 22-mile Dismal Swamp Canal, started in 1787, and the Jericho Canal, built in 1810. However, easier transportation brought greater deforestation during the 19th and early 20th centuries. Fortunately, the swamp recovered. Most of it is now second-growth vegetation. The Great Dismal is still nearly impenetrable because of its thick bogs, murky waters, and dense forests.

In 1973, the Union Camp Corporation donated 49,100 acres of the swamp to the Nature Conservancy, which in turn handed the land over to the federal government. That tract has since grown to over 109,000 acres. It is operated as the Great Dismal Swamp National Wildlife Refuge.

The Dismal Swamp Canal Welcome Center, located a few miles north of Elizabeth City on U.S. 17, offers film and slide programs, information on the history and wildlife of the swamp, hiking and biking trails, fishing, and boating. Among the wildlife you may be able to spot in the swamp are 209 species of birds, 21 varieties of reptiles, skinks, bear, bobcats, mink, otters, muskrats, foxes, and deer. From Memorial Day to the end of October, the center is open daily from 9 A.M. to 5 P.M.; from November to Memorial Day, it operates Tuesday to Saturday from 9 A.M. to 5 P.M. Call 252-771-8333 for more information.

■ *Merchants Millpond State Park*, located about 30 miles northwest of Elizabeth City off U.S. 158 near Gatesville, is one of North Carolina's ecological treasures. The 3,252-acre park is home to a mingling of coastal pond and swamp forest habitats, which has created one of the most diverse ecosystems on the East Coast. Over 190 species of birds have been spotted here, along with a wide variety of reptiles, amphibians, and mammals such as otters, beaver, mink, deer, and bear. The 760-acre millpond is home to bald cypresses and tupelo gums draped with Spanish moss and resurrection ferns. The tupelo gums' trunks have been twisted into wild shapes by the creeping mistletoe, giving rise to an "enchanted forest" that is a sight to behold. Pine and hardwood forests stand nearby.

Because there is so much to see and explore at Merchants Millpond

State Park, many people choose to camp here. The park offers both primitive campgrounds and family campsites for tents and trailers. No water or electrical hookups are available. Canoe rentals are offered. Fees are charged for camping and canoe rentals. The park is open daily year-round. For more information, contact Merchants Millpond State Park, 71 U.S. 158 East, Gatesville, N.C. 27938 (252-357-1191).

- Located south of Elizabeth City almost halfway to Edenton is the small town of *Hertford* in Perquimans County. Recently declared a state Heritage Tourism Community, Hertford was settled by Pennsylvania Quakers in the early 18th century and owes much of its heritage to that group.

- The *Newbold-White House*, located off U.S. 17 Bypass in Hertford, was built in 1730 by the Quaker Abraham Sanders. It is the oldest brick home in the state. Period pieces on display in the house show what life was like during North Carolina's pioneer days. An admission fee is charged. The Newbold-White House is open Monday through Saturday from 10 A.M. to 4 P.M. from March to Thanksgiving. Call 252-426-7567 for more information.

ALL GOOD THINGS

Excerpted from David Cecelski's *A Historian's Coast: Adventures into the Tidewater Past*

Even our wildest swamps have a natural history—sometimes gradual, other times cataclysmic—that has been influenced by settlement, exploitation, and other human practices. Most of this past has never been written down and is often not apparent, but you can find traces of it in the land itself if you spend the time and look closely. . . .

. . . A tar pit or rosin mound indicates a site where naval stores were produced, hence where a longleaf pine forest once stood. A tangle of narrow-gauge railroad track reveals that the swamp forest was timbered, most likely between 1880 and 1920, when Northern lumber companies moved into the old-growth forests of the South. Coils of copper wire and rusted barrels are of course evidence of the moonshine liquor industry that thrived on the Carolina coast during Prohibition. The East Lake and "CCC" (Craven County Corn) brands of homemade whiskey were famous in speakeasies from Norfolk to Boston. And when we stumble upon a sunken shad boat on a creek off the Alligator River or a hand-hewn bow net hidden along the White Oak River, we know that we have discovered traces of the springtime fishery that was the largest in the state in the late nineteenth century.

Other times, when we run up against cypress pilings on the waterfronts of tiny river communities like Rockyhock and Colerain, we are reminded of the great herring fisheries that flourished in the Albemarle Sound vicinity before the Civil War. Using seines that were often a mile and a half in length, thousands of slaves and free black fishermen caught the herring as they migrated out of the Atlantic to spawn in tidewater rivers. The pilings mark the old sheds where the laborers headed and salted the herring by the millions.

The canals that pass through coastal swamps also reveal a great deal about the past. Sometimes, all you notice is a narrow, all-too-straight line of visibility through a cypress swamp, but you can bet that it is an old canal once used to float white oak timbers, cypress shingles, and cedar staves to a mill. Along intertidal marshes, I have inadvertently paddled into a labyrinth of intersecting, narrow canals, a sign of rice cultivation in the slavery era, when large gangs of men and women in bondage cultivated the "golden grain" along the Lower Cape Fear. In places like Lake Phelps and Lake Mattamuskeet, I have followed other, larger canals that date to the late eighteenth and early nineteenth centuries, when slaves dug canals to drain swampland for agriculture and to raft crops and lumber to market.

In my travels, I have floated down even larger passages, known as "ships' canals," that bring to life the golden age of canal building between the American Revolution and the Civil War. During that period, many political leaders believed that

ships' canals held the greatest promise for overcoming the navigational hazards of North Carolina's shallow sounds and dangerous, shifting inlets. Between 1794 and 1805, for example, slaves dug the twenty-two-mile-long Dismal Swamp Canal to serve as a shipping route between Albemarle Sound and Chesapeake Bay and to skirt the dangerous swash and bar at Ocracoke Inlet.

Though it was antiquated by the opening of the Albemarle and Chesapeake Canal in 1859, the Dismal Swamp Canal had lasting consequences that had nothing to do with shipping. The canal blocked the Great Dismal Swamp's natural water flow from west to east, which eventually dried up the vast wetlands east of the canal and opened them for agriculture. The canal also lowered water levels throughout the moister parts of the Great Dismal, drying out the highly combustible upper layers of peat during summer droughts. Even as early as 1860, unprecedentedly hot peat fires burned much of the old-growth forests of cypress, juniper, and gum in the Great Dismal.

Millponds also have a story to tell. Quite often, [my brother] Richard and I stumble upon old millponds along remote blackwater creeks. We frequently discover relics of the mills' dams and foundations. When on a millpond, I find it easy to imagine what much of our coastal landscape looked like from the Revolutionary War well into the twentieth century, when millponds could be found in practically every tidewater community. Local people dammed creeks and harnessed the water's flow to power sawmills and gristmills. . . .

Millponds, like all wetlands, are an example of what ecologists refer to as an ecotone, a transitional zone between two diverse ecological communities. Ecotones support life native to each of the two communities (woods and river, for instance), as well as plants and animals endemic to only the ecotone. The heightened diversity and density of life in these transitional zones—a phenomenon known as the "edge effect"—is what makes millponds so remarkably rich in life. . . .

Sometimes when I am staying overnight in a coastal swamp, I get a glimpse of an even more distant past. It is often not easy to find a dry campsite in a swamp forest. A few times, I have had to paddle well into the night before finding a place to rest my head. More than once on waking the next morning, I have discovered clusters of arrowheads and shards of pottery around my camp, letting me know that I was hardly the first person who found shelter on that knoll or hammock. The coastal Algonquians—or their ancestors—used these same places for fishing camps long before European contact in the sixteenth century. . . .

Above all, I am haunted by the fragility of these freshwater wetlands—our most endangered and underappreciated coastal habitats. Everybody admires the beauty of ocean beaches and salt marshes, and I think most people understand their importance for tourism and the seafood industry. But far fewer people have had the chance to fall in love with the natural beauty and ecological uniqueness of these coastal wetlands—the cypress swamps, blackwater creeks, river bottom lands, pine savannas, pocosins, and Carolina bays.

EDENTON

One of the oldest communities in the state, Edenton proclaims itself "the South's prettiest small town." Some say it's the profusion of well-maintained colonial and antebellum homes that justifies that claim. The long, tree-lined streets boast 18th- and 19th-century homes that once belonged to governors, aristocrats, and shipping magnates. South King Street is dotted with homes that predate the Civil War, with the exception of two "newcomers" built shortly thereafter. Others attribute Edenton's charm to the perfectly manicured lawns and the abundance of flowers and trees—roses, tulips, lilies, magnolias, crepe myrtles—along the blue water of Edenton Bay and Albemarle Sound. Still others say Edenton is so beautiful because of the warm people living and working here. Edenton's fiercely proud residents will stop whatever they're doing to give you a history lesson and welcome you to their small piece of paradise.

When it was incorporated in 1715 as "the Towne on Queen Anne's Creek," this area became the first permanent settlement in North Carolina. A few years and a few name changes later, it came to be called Edenton in honor of the Royal governor who made his home here, Charles Eden. The town was designated the first capital of the colony.

But good feelings toward Britain did not last forever. By August 1774, the citizens of Edenton decided that they had suffered enough of Britain's infamous taxation without representation. Daniel Earle, rector of St. Paul's Church, rallied citizens by the courthouse and publicly denounced the Boston Port Act, signifying support of the revolutionaries in Massachusetts. That October, the ladies of Edenton decided to do their part to support the cause. Vowing not to purchase or drink any more tea or to wear clothes or fabrics from England until the unfair taxation was stopped, the ladies disrupted trade with Britain and proved themselves a force in the battle for independence. A colonial teapot now standing atop one of the Revolutionary War cannons on the courthouse green celebrates the ladies' contribution.

Among Edenton's notable citizens were a pair of signers of the two most important documents in the establishment of our country. Joseph Hewes, a ship owner and merchant, signed the Declaration of Independence, while Hugh Williamson, surgeon general of the state's colonial troops, signed the Constitution in 1787. Both assisted the cause by donating and outfitting ships for the burgeoning United States Navy. Samuel Johnston, another patriot from Edenton, was the first United States senator from North Carolina. Johnston's brother-in-law, James Iredell, was appointed to the United States Supreme Court by President George Washington.

Thanks to its many influential and powerful residents and its favorable location as an inland port, Edenton developed into an important commercial center around the time of the Revolution. But following the construction of various canals in the area at the beginning of the 19th century, Edenton fell out of favor as a trading post. Ever since then, the citizens have worked to maintain their heritage as the home of the revolutionary spirit of North Carolina.

JUST THE FACTS

Edenton is located on Albemarle Sound at the mouth of the Chowan River. You can reach the town from the east or west by U.S. 17 and from the north or south by N.C. 32.

Edenton Marina, located at 607 West Queen Street, offers full-service dockage for boaters passing by on Albemarle Sound. Call 252-482-7421 for information.

The nearest large commercial airport is in Norfolk, Virginia. Northeastern Regional Airport, located at 113 Airport Drive in Edenton, accepts small charter flights; call 252-482-4664 for more information.

Edenton's bus station is located at 810 Broad Street. Call 252-482-2424 for information.

Historic Edenton State Historic Site, located at 108 North Broad Street, offers written information, guided walking tours, and trolley tours. Call 252-482-2637, or visit their website at www.ah.dcr.state.nc.us/sections/hs/iredell/iredell.htm. The Chowan County Tourism Development Authority, located at 116 East King Street, offers a great deal of written information on the area. Call 800-775-0111 or 252-482-3400, or visit their website at www.edenton.com.

Things to Do

HISTORIC PLACES, GARDENS, AND TOURS

The draw for most people coming to Edenton is the state's largest collection of 18th-century homes. Most are listed on the National Register of Historic Places, and a few are on the National Historic Landmarks list. You can wander the streets on your own, soaking up the Georgian, Federal, Jacobean, Greek Revival, and Victorian architecture, or you can take a guided tour on foot or by trolley.

▪ Regardless of which way you choose to see the town, your first stop should be **Historic Edenton State Historic Site**, at 108 North Broad Street. Here, you can pick up maps and pamphlets detailing the architecture and history of each building for exploration on your own, or you can sign up for a guided tour. Tours are given daily from April through October. A fee is charged; students and school groups receive discounted rates. Trolley tours are offered Tuesday through Saturday in the morning and afternoon. A fee is charged; children under five are free. The historic site is open daily year-round except for major winter holidays; extended hours are in effect during the summer. Call 252-482-2637 for more information.

▪ One must-see stop in Edenton is **St. Paul's Episcopal Church**, located at Church and Broad across the street from Historic Edenton State Historic Site. St. Paul's Parish was formed in 1701 on Hayes Plantation. Construction on St. Paul's Church—sometimes called "the Westminster Abbey of North Carolina"—started in 1736. It was here, at the second-oldest church in North Carolina, that Edenton's Revolutionary War effort had its beginnings. The membership log at St. Paul's is a who's who of the state's most important colonial leaders. An active congregation still worships here.

▪ South down Broad Street from St. Paul's is the **Cupola House**, the home of the **Edenton Museum**. This Jacobean-style home, built in 1758 by Francis Corbin, a land agent of Lord Granville, is the oldest house still standing in Edenton.

Cupola House
COURTESY OF NORTH CAROLINA
DIVISION OF TOURISM, FILM AND
SPORTS DEVELOPMENT

Barker House

■ The **Barker House**, located near Edenton Bay farther down Broad Street, was the home of Penelope Barker, who initiated the Edenton Tea Party in 1774. Her husband, Thomas, was the London agent for the colony. The Barker House dates to 1782.

■ At the water's edge is the 1767 **Chowan County Courthouse**, where you'll see cannons and the famous teapot commemorating the bold actions of the town's ladies during the Edenton Tea Party. This is the oldest courthouse in North Carolina and one of the best examples of Georgian architecture in the state. Upstairs is the lodge room of the local Masons, which features a chair used by George Washington in the lodge in Alexandria, Virginia.

■ The **Chowan County Jail**, the oldest working jail in the nation, is located next to the courthouse.

■ Also of interest is the **Iredell House** on East Church Street. Built in 1773, this was the home of James Iredell, United States Supreme Court appointee of President George Washington.

Iredell House
COURTESY OF NORTH CAROLINA DIVISION OF TOURISM, FILM AND SPORTS
DEVELOPMENT

MUSEUMS AND SCIENCE CENTERS

■ *Edenton National Fish Hatchery*, located at 1104 West Queen Street, is one of over 80 federal fish hatcheries spread throughout the United States. Established in 1899, this is one of the oldest hatcheries in the country. In its time, it has bred a wide assortment of warm-water fish, including largemouth bass, striped bass, channel catfish, bluegill, redear sunfish, shad, and herring. The hatchery currently produces only striped bass. The 2 million to 4 million striped bass hatched here every year are used to stock the sounds, lakes, and coastal rivers of the state. Edenton National Fish Hatchery also distributes warm-water fish from other hatcheries to the state's farm ponds and reservoirs. Admission to the hatchery is free. It is open weekdays from 7 A.M. to 3:30 P.M. and weekends from 8 A.M. to 4 P.M. year-round. For more information, call 252-482-4118.

CULTURAL OFFERINGS

■ *Chowan Arts Council Gallery and Gallery Shop*, located at 200 East Church Street, features the work of local and national artists. The eclectic mix here ranges from commissioned portraits to folk art.

A permanent exhibit entitled "A Century of Chowan through Photographs" traces life in the county from 1850 to 1954; it includes portraits of many of the area's most important figures and chronicles events significant in the county's history. You might consider this look at post–Revolutionary War Chowan County a natural extension of your colonial tour of Edenton homes. The Gallery Shop sells original art and reproductions of some of the works displayed throughout the facility. Admission is free. The gallery and shop are open Monday through Saturday from 10 A.M. to 4 P.M. and Sunday from 1 P.M. to 4 P.M. year-round. Call 252-482-8005 for more information.

RECREATION

▪ If walking around Edenton and viewing all the lush lawns gets you in the mood for some golf, try **Chowan Golf and Country Club**, located at 1101 West Sound Shore Drive. Driving and putting greens are available in addition to the 18-hole course. Call 252-482-3606 for additional information.

SEASONAL EVENTS

▪ The *Biennial Pilgrimage Tour of Homes and Countryside in Edenton and Chowan County* takes place on a Friday and Saturday in mid-April every two years. Buildings of historic merit, including private homes usually not open to the public, are made available to visitors wanting to satisfy their curiosity as to exactly what lies behind those doors. Fifteen in-town homes, three country homes, three public homes, the courthouse, and local churches are included in the tour. A single ticket is good for the entire weekend; breakfast, lunch, dinner, and transportation are included in the price. All proceeds go to the preservation and promotion of historic sites in the area. For more information or to buy advance tickets, contact the Edenton Women's Club, P.O. Box 12, Edenton, NC 27932 (800-775-0111 or 252-482-3400).

▪ Edenton's Christmas festivities include the *Iredell House Groaning*

Board, held the second weekend in December. A dessert groaning board, harpsichord music, and 18th-century-style Christmas decorations fill the 1773 home of former United States Supreme Court justice James Iredell.

Places to Stay

INNS AND BED-AND-BREAKFASTS

A couple of motels are located outside Edenton's historic district, but since you're here to see the beautiful buildings downtown, the best places to stay are the historic inns and bed-and-breakfasts. The rates are so reasonable at many of these establishments that they're comparable to what a room at a hotel would cost, and they offer much more personal attention, a better location, and prettier surroundings.

■ **The Lords Proprietors' Inn**. Deluxe. 300 North Broad Street (800-348-8933 or 252-482-3641; www.lordspropedenton.com). A member of the Historic Hotels of America and the Independent Innkeepers' Association, this inn is comprised of three historic homes covering two acres. It offers 16 rooms and four luxury suites. All rooms have private baths, televisions, and VCRs and are sumptuously decorated with antiques and reproductions crafted by a local cabinetmaker and woodworker. A full gourmet breakfast is included. A four-course gourmet dinner prepared by the inn's chef can be reserved for an additional fee Tuesday through Saturday.

■ **Granville Queen Inn**. Expensive/Moderate. 108 South Granville Street (252-482-5296; www.Edenton.com/granvillequeen). Guests will have a hard time choosing which of the nine themed bedrooms they'd like to try in this 1907 mansion. The Egyptian Queen Room features bronze sphinxes and cobra-handled faucets. Hand-crafted furniture from an Italian estate graces the Peaches and Queen Room. All rooms have a fireplace, a private balcony, cable television, and a phone. Other bonuses include a five-course gourmet breakfast and, if you're a weekend guest, an evening wine tasting.

- **Albemarle House Bed-and-Breakfast**. Moderate. 204 West Queen Street (252-482-8204). The guest rooms of this circa-1900 home are decorated with antiques and period reproductions and have queen-sized beds, air-conditioning, cable television, and private baths. The two-room suite features a connecting bath good for families and groups traveling together. A full country breakfast is served each morning. Privileges at the Chowan Golf and Country Club are extended to guests who want to burn off those extra calories from the eggnog French toast and the pecan waffles. Innkeeper Reuel Schappel will even take you on a three-hour afternoon or evening cruise on his 28-foot sloop, *Wanderer*, for a small fee.

- **Captain's Quarters Inn**. Moderate. 202 West Queen Street (800-482-8945 or 252-482-8945; www.captainsquartersinn.com). Located in a 1907 Colonial Revival home, the Captain's Quarters offers eight individually decorated and nautically themed guest rooms, each with a private bath, a sitting room, a telephone, and cable television. The 65-foot wraparound porch puts you within walking distance of Edenton's major attractions and the waterfront. A three-course gourmet breakfast and afternoon refreshments are included in the price of your stay, and you can request a gourmet dinner for parties of four or more in advance. Sailing, golfing, and mystery-weekend packages are available.

- **Governor Eden Inn Bed-and-Breakfast**. Moderate. 304 North Broad Street (252-482-2072). This Neoclassical home, dominated by large Ionic columns and oval beveled-glass windows, features four individually decorated guest rooms tastefully appointed with antiques. Guests enjoy catching the bay breeze on the upstairs front balcony and the downstairs wraparound porch. Continental breakfast is offered.

- **Trestle House Inn at Willow Tree Farm**. Moderate. 632 Soundside Road (800-645-8466 or 252-482-2282; www.edenton.com/trestlehouse). This bed-and-breakfast, nestled on a private six-acre lot five miles outside town, is named after the Southern Railway trestles used as exposed support beams in the ceiling and roof. Its five guest rooms have private baths, ceiling fans, and central air. Guests can canoe from the pond behind the inn to Albemarle Sound and into Edenton. Both canoes and bikes are available for rent. A homemade breakfast is served daily.

Places to Eat

You'll find the usual trusty chains in Edenton, but the independent, locally owned restaurants are, as usual, superior in atmosphere and quality of food.

■ **Creekside Restaurant and Bar**. Expensive/Moderate. 406 West Queen Street (252-482-0118). This restaurant is conveniently located near the heart of the historic district. You can't go wrong with Creekside's famous prime rib or any of their other dishes, from pasta to chicken to salads. Lunch is served Monday through Friday and dinner seven days a week.

■ **Waterman's Grille**. Expensive/Moderate. 427 South Broad Street (252-482-7733). Located one block from Edenton Bay and within walking distance of all the town's major historic sites, this restaurant specializes in good, fresh seafood. Daily lunch and dinner specials are offered. Lunch is served Monday through Saturday and dinner Tuesday through Saturday.

■ **Nixon Family Restaurant**. Moderate. 327 River Road (252-221-2244). Don't let the casual atmosphere at this restaurant fool you into thinking that food is taken lightly around here. The big draws are the oyster bar and the large variety of other just-off-the-boat seafood. Breakfast, lunch, and dinner are served Tuesday through Sunday.

■ **Lane's Family Barbecue**. Moderate/Inexpensive. 421 East Church Street Extension (252-482-4008). This family-style restaurant specializes in barbecue, but those looking for something else won't be disappointed either, as seafood, chicken, and vegetables also grace the menu. At Lane's, you'll get well fed without breaking the bank. Lunch and dinner are served daily.

**Somerset Place
State Historic Site**

Nearby

- About 45 minutes south of Edenton is the small town of Creswell, home of **Somerset Place State Historic Site**. Located down the oak- and cypress-lined Lake Shore Drive near Phelps Lake, Somerset Place was formerly one of the four largest plantations in North Carolina. Home to several generations of the Josiah Collins family beginning in 1785, the plantation encompassed up to 100,000 acres. Upwards of 300 slaves worked the plantation at any given time, digging irrigation and transport canals, building sawmills, gristmills, and other structures, and cultivating rice, wheat, and corn. When the Civil War ended, the Collinses were unable to maintain Somerset Place without their source of unpaid labor, and the plantation ceased operation.

Archaeological research has been under way since the early 1950s to uncover facts about Somerset Place's many residents. Today, visitors can see what life was like for both the Collinses and their slaves through educational programs and tours of the mansion, the detached kitchen, the smokehouse, the dairy, and the Colony House, which was the Collinses' home before the completion of the current plantation house. Somerset Place State Historic Site is open Monday through Saturday from 9 A.M. to 5 P.M. and Sunday from 1 P.M. to 5 P.M. from April through October. From November through March, it is open Tuesday through Saturday from 10 A.M. to 4 P.M. and Sunday from 1 P.M. to 4 P.M. Admission is free. For more information, call 252-797-4560, or visit their website at www.ah.dcr.state.nc.us/hs/somerset/somerset.htm.

■ Approximately 20 miles west of Edenton and four miles outside the town of Windsor on N.C. 308 is **Hope Plantation**, the former home of North Carolina governor David Stone. The 1803 buff-colored, two-story Georgian- and Federal-style plantation house is authentically furnished with period antiques. Also on the grounds is the 1763 **King-Bazemore House**, built of handmade brick. Originally situated five miles away, the King-Bazemore House was constructed by William King, a successful area planter and cooper. In 1840, the home was purchased by Stephen Bazemore. In 1974, the Bazemore family donated the house to the Historic Hope Foundation. Also relocated to Hope Plantation was the **Samuel Cox House**, built in 1800 in the western part of Bertie County. This structure is significant because it is considered a typical North Carolina farmhouse of the period. The house was donated to the foundation in 1970 and serves as a caretaker's residence today.

Hope Plantation is open Monday through Saturday from 10 A.M. to 5 P.M. and Sunday from 2 P.M. to 5 P.M. from January 3 to December 20. It is closed Thanksgiving. An admission fee is charged. Call 252-794-3140 for more information.

■ Historic **Windsor**, located near N.C. 308 and U.S. 17 about 20 minutes west of Edenton, was established in 1768 when William Gray offered 100 acres for a town. That original land is now recognized as a National Historic District. Call 252-794-4277 for more information.

■ Historic **Williamston** is 45 minutes west of Edenton near U.S. 64 and U.S. 17. Its two National Historic Districts feature homes and buildings from the 19th and early 20th centuries. Railroad and tobacco money helped build the town, including the outstanding former county courthouse, constructed in the Italianate style in 1885. Call 800-766-8566, 252-792-6605, or 252-792-0409 for more information.

■ Historic **Plymouth**, located south of Edenton near N.C. 32 and U.S. 64, is one of the top Civil War destinations in the state. Union and Confederate soldiers fought it out here for three days in 1864. Today, visitors can relive the action at the **Port O' Plymouth Civil War Museum**. Call 252-793-1377 for more information.

BATH

Established in 1705, Bath is North Carolina's oldest town. As such, it is home to many of the state's "firsts," including the first church, the first public library, the first port of entry, and the first shipyard, among others. Thanks to its advantageous location near Pamlico Sound, Bath became a major port for naval stores, tobacco, and furs only a few years after French Protestants from Virginia founded the town. The area became home to such notable personages as John Lawson, the surveyor general of the colony and the author of the first history of Carolina, published in 1709, and Edward Teach, better known as Blackbeard the Pirate, who is rumored to have taken a wife here for a short time in 1716. Stories still float around that some of Blackbeard's treasure is buried around Bath, though none has ever been found.

Problems started to beleaguer the town early on. Despite Bath's status as the first town in the state, it failed to grow. In 1711, Cary's Rebellion, a struggle over religion and politics in the area, turned violent. That same year, the town was ravaged by a drought and an outbreak of yellow fever. The Tuscarora War further debilitated Bath. When neighboring towns like Edenton and Washington were founded, many people moved from Bath to pursue other economic and political opportunities.

Today, Bath is a small community measuring only a few blocks. The original town limits survive as the boundaries for a National Historic District; the district includes four buildings that connect Bath to its once-prosperous past. Visitors can enjoy an afternoon exploring the town on foot and learning about the old homes and church.

JUST THE FACTS

Bath is in Beaufort County on the Pamlico River about 15 minutes east of Washington. It can be reached by N.C. 92 or by a free ferry that crosses the Pamlico from N.C. 306 north of Aurora.

Historic Bath State Historic Site, located on Carteret

Things to Do

HISTORIC PLACES, GARDENS, AND TOURS

■ Four historic buildings that date to colonial and antebellum times are open for visitors. In order to learn about these landmarks, stop by the visitor center at **Historic Bath State Historic Site**. Here, you can view a short film entitled *Bath—The First Town* and pick up maps and pamphlets on the history of the town. The visitor center is open Monday through Saturday from 9 A.M. to 5 P.M. and Sunday from 1 P.M. to 5 P.M. from April through October. From November to March, it operates Tuesday through Saturday from 10 A.M. to 4 P.M. and Sunday from 1 P.M. to 4 P.M. Call 252-923-3971 for more information.

■ The visitor center offers guided tours of the three 18th- and 19th-century homes in the National Historic District. Participants should plan on spending about an hour and a half going through these houses. The **Bonner House**, a two-story white frame house built in 1830, was home to Joseph Bonner, a local businessman who operated a steam sawmill and a turpentine distillery. Visitors can learn what daily life was like for an eastern North Carolina family between the Revolutionary and Civil Wars. The 1751 **Palmer-Marsh House** is the oldest home in Bath. It features an imposing double chimney that no doubt kept the premises warm on cool Carolina nights. The house is decorated in 18th-century antiques and reproductions. The **Van der Veer House** was built in 1790 by Jacob Van der Veer, a rope manufacturer and a partner with Bonner in his sawmill. The house now operates as a museum. A modest admission fee is charged for the Bonner House and the Palmer-Marsh House but not for the Van der Veer House. All three operate the same hours as the visitor center.

Palmer-Marsh House
COURTESY OF NORTH CAROLINA
DIVISION OF TOURISM, FILM
AND SPORTS DEVELOPMENT

Van Der Veer House
COURTESY OF NORTH CAROLINA
DIVISION OF TOURISM, FILM
AND SPORTS DEVELOPMENT

■ *St. Thomas Episcopal Church*, located on Craven Street near the visitor center, rounds out Bath's roster of historic structures open for visitation. This is the oldest church in North Carolina. It houses the state's first public library, which was donated to St. Thomas Parish in 1701, four years before Bath was incorporated. No admission fee is charged, though donations are accepted. Tours here are self-guided; the simple one-story brick church never closes its doors.

Nearby
_____

■ *Belhaven Memorial Museum*, located in city hall in Belhaven, is within easy driving distance of Bath on N.C. 99. Started as a collection of buttons by Mary Eva Blount Way, the holdings quickly grew to include all kinds of antiques and artifacts of life in Beaufort County, eastern North Carolina, and the South in general. "Miss Eva" decided to open her home to visitors in 1940 in order to share her collection—which by then included over 10,000 items—in an effort to aid the American Red Cross. After her death in 1962, a group of citizens purchased the collection in order to keep Miss Eva's memory and work alive. They reopened the museum in city hall three years later. Today, visitors will find all kinds of interesting testimonials to the culture and people of the area dating all the way back to the beginning of the 19th century—war memorabilia, toys, household utensils, clothing, tools, and much more. The museum is open Thursday through Tuesday from 1 P.M. to 5 P.M. Admission is free, but donations are accepted. For more information, contact the museum at P.O. Box 220, Belhaven, N.C. 27810 (252-943-6817).

▪ Visitors to Belhaven have the opportunity to stay in a couple of noteworthy inns. *River Forest Manor*, built in 1899 by John Aaron Wilkinson, has hosted the likes of James Cagney, Tallulah Bankhead, Twiggy, and Walter Cronkite over the years. For information, contact the inn at 738 East Main Street, Belhaven, N.C. 27810 (252-943-2151; www.riverforestmanor.com). The charming *Thistle Dew Inn Bed-and-Breakfast* offers three guest rooms in a Queen Anne home overlooking the Pungo River. Contact the inn at 443 Water Street, Belhaven, N.C. 27810 (252-943-6900).

▪ *Aurora Fossil Museum*, located at 400 Main Street in Aurora, is a free ferry ride over the Pamlico River from Bath. The museum, which grew out of discoveries made by the PCS Phosphate Company during mining operations in the 1950s and 1960s, uses fossil research and an 18-minute video presentation to explain the formation of the coastal plain. The area around Aurora and much of the rest of eastern North Carolina once lay under the ocean. As time passed, calcium phosphate collected on the seabed and preserved the remains of many of the creatures that had lived in the water. After millions of years, the sea finally receded, leaving a thick layer of phosphate buried underneath layers of sand and clay. It was in this fashion that coastal animals from eons ago were preserved. Visitors to the museum learn about the history of these sea creatures through exhibits that show what ocean life was like millions of years ago and through displays of fossilized bones, teeth, shells, and coral. Kids especially love the small phosphate yard near the museum, where they can search for their own fossils. The museum is open Tuesday through Friday from 9 A.M. to 4:30 P.M. and Saturday from 9 A.M. to 2 P.M. in June, July, and August. From September to May, it is open Monday through Friday from 9 A.M. to 4:30 P.M. Admission is free. For more information, call 252-322-4238.

■ *Bennett Vineyards*, located half an hour south of Bath and three miles from the Aurora ferry at 6832 Bonnerton Road in the community of Edward, is the largest muscadine and scuppernong vineyard in the Carolinas. It is situated between the Pamlico and Neuse Rivers on a 138-acre parcel of colonial land-grant soil. The grapes this winery uses are indigenous only to the Southeast and are what the colonists used for their wines. Tours are given daily by appointment. Call 877-762-9463 or 252-322-7154 for more information.

■ Historic *Washington*, located about 15 minutes from Bath near U.S. 17 and U.S. 264, was founded in 1775 and named in honor of George Washington. The town quickly became a major port on the Pamlico River. When the Beaufort County seat was moved from Bath to Washington in 1785, Washington started to eclipse Bath in importance.

Though the War for Independence was a major factor in the development of Washington, the War Between the States was devastating to the town. Union troops captured the city in 1864 and pillaged and burned it before their departure. The town was rebuilt, but fire destroyed much of the downtown area again in 1900, when a faulty stove flue caught one of the buildings on fire. But Washington was rebuilt a second time. Today, the town's National Historic District includes about 11 blocks of 19th- and early-20th-century buildings, including many Gothic churches.

■ The *North Carolina Estuarium*, located at 223 Water Street in Washington, is the only estuarium in the state. It is dedicated to educating visitors about the Albemarle-Pamlico estuarine system, the second-largest in the nation. Estuaries, which are aquatic areas made up of both fresh and salt water, line the state's shoreline and are a vital part of the area's ecology. Visitors to the estuarium will find an aquarium, artifacts from local estuaries including boats and fishing equipment, and an audiovisual presentation concerning humans' effects on the estuarine system and the system's effects on man. A gift shop is on the premises. The estuarium is open Tuesday through Saturday from 10 A.M. to 4 P.M.; extended hours are offered in the summer. A modest admission fee is charged. For more information, call 252-948-0000, or visit their website at www.estuarium.com.

■ Overnight visitors to Washington might consider staying at *Pamlico House Bed-and-Breakfast*. This 1906 Colonial Revival house, listed on the National Register of Historic Places, was recently awarded a Three-Diamond rating by AAA. For information, contact the inn at 400 East Main Street, Washington, N.C. 27889 (800-948-8507 or 252-946-7184). Another excellent choice is *Carolina House Bed-and-Breakfast*, an 1880 home located only two blocks from the Pamlico River. Carolina House is also listed on the National Register. Contact the inn at 227 East Second Street, Washington, N.C. 27889 (252-975-1382).

New Bern at dusk
PHOTOGRAPH © STEVE UZZELL

NEUSE RIVER REGION

by Anne Holcomb Waters

he Neuse River region encompasses some of North Carolina's most fascinating historical and natural sites. The towns and villages that populate the Neuse River region—named for the Neusiok Indians, who once inhabited the river's shores—date primarily to the 18th century.

Among these is New Bern, the state's colonial capital. Overlooking the point where the Neuse and Trent Rivers converge, New Bern is home to the magnificent Tryon Palace, which has secured the town a premier spot on the state's heritage trail. This year-round destination is not only for those interested in Revolutionary War history, however. Over the course of several years, New Bern's downtown has undergone a renaissance, as more and more interesting shops and excellent restaurants have opened to serve the tourist trade. The town's most recent addition is a brand-new convention center on the banks of the Neuse.

Forty-five minutes east of New Bern is Morehead City, where world-class fishing tournaments attract fishermen from far and wide. Be sure to plan a meal here, as Morehead City's bustling waterfront restaurants serve up some of the area's best seafood. Morehead City is also the jumping-off point for the stunning sands of Bogue Banks.

Historic Beaufort is nothing less than idyllic. Overlooking Taylor Creek, this former pirates' hideout now quietly greets sailors of a different ilk. Across the creek from Beaufort's serene waterfront, wild ponies graze amid thousands of seafowl on Shackleford Banks. Kayaking has become a fashionable way to sightsee here.

Situated on the Intracoastal Waterway is another quaint fishing hamlet, Oriental. Regarded by many as the East Coast's premier yachting destination, Oriental offers a sailing school that serves both beginners and experienced sailors wishing to hone their skills.

For outdoor enthusiasts, Croatan National Forest is an oasis for birdwatching, hiking, camping, and boating. Hunting and fishing are also permitted for visitors holding the proper permits. Indigenous insect-eating plants thrive here, including the pitcher plant, sundew, and Venus flytrap. This vast 159,000-acre park is surrounded by water and has several lakes within its borders.

And of course, there are the beaches. Atlantic Beach, Pine Knoll Shores, and Emerald Isle—all on Bogue Banks—are among the state's most popular seaside resorts. Fort Macon State Park at Atlantic Beach offers a history lesson and a day at the beach all in one. Or if you'd rather escape the masses, you can ferry over to Cape Lookout National Seashore, where a diamond-painted lighthouse continues in service 150 years after it was built. Another ferry ride away is pristine Hammocks Beach State Park, perhaps the land of buried treasure.

Whether you intend to tour the historic sites, to fish or boat, or just to hang out on the beaches, the Neuse River region is sure to please.

NEW BERN

New Bern is located 35 miles from the Atlantic Ocean at the confluence of the Neuse and Trent Rivers. North Carolina's second-oldest town, it was named by its Swiss founder, Christophe von Graffenried, in honor of his home capital. Throughout the city, you will see New Bern's symbol, the black bear, which it shares with its European mother city.

In 1710—the same year that North and South Carolina were divided—von Graffenried and two partners purchased an 18,750-acre parcel for a colony for German and Swiss emigrants. The purchase was inspired by colonial surveyor general John Lawson, who had returned to London extolling the virtues of the New World in his book, *A New Voyage to Carolina*. Subsequently dispatched by von Graffenried to select a site for the colony, Lawson laid out the town plan in the form of a crucifix, which served the dual purpose of religious expression and defense against Indians.

The latter goal proved unsuccessful, however. Although King Taylor of the Tuscaroras had been paid for the land where New Bern was settled, the influx of immigrants proved too much for him to stand. In September 1711, Lawson and von Graffenried embarked on a canoe trip up the Neuse River. A few days into the journey, they were captured by the Tuscaroras. Von Graffenried managed to save himself by persuading the Tuscaroras that his connections to the English Crown would serve them well should he live. Lawson wasn't so fortunate. The Tuscaroras supposedly pierced him with splinters of wood, then lit him afire and burned him to death.

The three years of fighting that followed drove von Graffenried back to Europe, which left New Bern in the hands of Colonel Thomas Pollock. With the help of some of the Tuscaroras' traditional enemies, the colonists eventually vanquished the tribe. The Indians who survived migrated north, where they gave their new land the name of their Carolina home—Chattawka, now Chautauqua, New York.

Once the Indian threat was removed, white settlers flocked to New Bern, which prospered as a port for shipping tar, pitch, and turpentine. In 1723, New Bern was incorporated and made the seat of Craven County, which it remains today. By the time the colonial assembly convened here in 1737, New Bern was well established as the most vital city between Virginia and Charleston, South Carolina.

In 1776, North Carolina's first governor, Richard Caswell, was heralded into office in New Bern, the state's first capital. When the capital was moved to Raleigh in 1794, New Bern's political role diminished, but the city continued to thrive as a shipping center. It was during this period that many of its lovely homes and buildings were constructed.

In 1862, New Bern was captured by Union forces under General Ambrose Burnside. The city remained a Union outpost for the rest of the Civil War.

During Reconstruction, lumber mills and the seafood industry kept the city going. After World War II, manufacturing and the military were at the heart of New Bern's development.

Since the reconstruction of Tryon Palace in the 1950s, New Bern has seen a steady increase in tourism. Today, the city boasts a collection of National Register buildings second in number only to Charleston. In and around the historic district, dozens of antique and specialty shops, art galleries, and restaurants have sprouted up, making a trip to New Bern a delight.

JUST THE FACTS

New Bern is accessible by land, water, or air.

Car travelers can take either U.S. 70, U.S. 17, or N.C. 55 to reach town. Those planning to take the bus should contact the Trailways station, located at 504 Guion Street; the number is 252-633-3100.

New Bern is located on the Neuse River, portions of which double as the Intracoastal Waterway. Those arriving by water can stay at any of the private marinas along the river.

For those flying into New Bern, US Airways and Midway Airlines offer commuter flights into Craven County Regional Airport. Fuel and maintenance are available here. Call 252-638-8591 for more information.

The Craven County Convention and Visitors Bureau, located at 314 South Front Street, offers an abundance of information on the area. For information, call 800-437-5767 or 252-637-9400, or visit their website at www.visitnewbern.com.

The *New Bern Journal* is the local daily newspaper.

Tryon Palace
COURTESY OF TRYON PALACE HISTORIC SITES AND GARDENS

Things to Do

HISTORIC PLACES, GARDENS, AND TOURS

■ ***Tryon Palace Historic Sites and Gardens*** is the cornerstone of historic New Bern. It is located at 610 Pollock Street, one block south of U.S. 17 and U.S. 70 Business. The complex consists of Tryon Palace, its surrounding 14 acres of gardens and grounds, and four other historic landmarks—the John Wright Stanly House, the Dixon-Stevenson House, the Robert Hay House, and the New Bern Academy Museum.

    Tryon Palace is a reconstruction of the state's first Capitol, built before the population shifted west and before Raleigh became the capital city in 1794.

In 1765, Royal Governor William Tryon commissioned English architect John Hawkes to design and supervise the construction of Tryon Palace, an elegant Georgian mansion containing public rooms for government functions on the ground floor and family living quarters upstairs. Cooking and laundry facilities were in a wing on the left, while livery stables were in a wing to the right.

In 1770, just 13 months after moving his family into the home, Tryon was appointed governor of New York. His successor, Josiah Martin, subsequently moved into Tryon Palace with much fanfare. Martin commissioned Hawkes to add a poultry house, a smokehouse, and a pigeon house. Martin spent four years lavishly furnishing his abode, impervious to the growing resentment around him. In 1775, patriots forced Martin to flee the house. He left all his possessions behind.

In 1777, the first North Carolina General Assembly convened at Tryon Palace, the newly designated Capitol of North Carolina. By 1798, however, when fire destroyed the main building, Raleigh had been made the state capital, and the role of New Bern and Tryon Palace was greatly diminished.

Through the years, portions of the grounds were sold. Tryon Palace languished, only the west wing remaining intact. Recovery began in 1939, when the original architectural plans were discovered in New York. A restoration trust fund was established by Mrs. Maude Moore Latham, a New Bern native whose dedication to the project and philanthropy were largely responsible for its success.

Noted architect William G. Perry of the Boston firm that restored Colonial Williamsburg began his work in New Bern in 1951. Mrs. Latham died that same year but passed along her legacy to her daughter, Mrs. John A. Kellenberger, who headed the state commission in charge of the project. On April 8, 1959, Tryon Palace opened its doors to the public.

Tours of Tryon Place begin in the visitor center, located across Pollock Street from the northern side of the building. Following a 20-minute orientation film, visitors make their way along a lovely oak-canopied drive leading to the main entrance; don't be surprised if you are cheerfully greeted along the way by one of the many historical interpreters, busy with his or her chores. A costumed guide will greet you at the door and lead you into the marble entrance hall, through the public rooms downstairs, and up the pegged mahogany staircase to the private rooms. Thanks to an inventory of William Tryon's original furnishings, the palace contains some 7,000 pieces of art and 18th- and 19th-century American and English antiques that reflect the opulent world of Governor Tryon. Among his personal possessions that remain at Tryon Palace is a library of 400 books.

- After your tour of Tryon Palace, take time to stroll the formal *Colonial Revival Gardens*, designed by Morley Jeffers Williams, an expert in 18th-century landscaping. The Latham Garden is designed in the style of cutwork parterre. Hedges define the beds, creating ornate patterns. Nearby is the private Green Garden, designed to be viewed from the palace. The Kellenberger Garden illustrates how ornamentals were grown for their decorative qualities. The wonderful Kitchen Garden produces heirloom varieties of herbs and vegetables.

- The *John Wright Stanly House*, an elegant 1779 Georgian home located at 307 George Street, is one of the properties that is part of Tryon Palace Historic Sites and Gardens. On his Southern tour in 1891, President George Washington dined and danced at Tryon Palace, but he laid his head to rest at the John Wright Stanly House, which he described as "exceedingly good lodgings." The house is named for a powerful New Bern citizen who aided the American cause by raiding British vessels. Ironically, John Wright Stanly traced his lineage to King Edward I of England. The home served as General Ambrose Burnside's headquarters while Union forces occupied the city. The house's interior is noted for its intricate woodwork, especially its Chippendale staircase.

- Built between 1826 and 1833, the *Dixon-Stevenson House*, located at 609 Pollock Street, is a fine example of Neoclassical architecture. Constructed on a lot that was originally part of Tryon Palace's gardens, it was the home of George W. Dixon, a merchant, tailor, and one-time mayor of New Bern. During the Union occupation, the house was used as a regimental hospital. Inside, you'll find hand-carved woodwork and antiques of the Federal and Empire periods.

- The **Robert Hay House**, located on Eden Street next to the Tryon Palace Museum Shop, was home to a Scottish wagon maker and a founding member of First Presbyterian Church in New Bern.

- The **New Bern Academy Museum** is located four blocks from Tryon Palace at the corner of New and Hancock Streets. Completed in 1809, it was a leading school in the area for 162 years. The museum contains four rooms, each focusing on an aspect of local history: the founding and early history of New Bern, the architecture of the city, the Civil War and Reconstruction, and education in New Bern. This is a great place to get a broad overview of the city. The museum is open daily from 1 P.M. to 5 P.M. Admission is included with your ticket to the Tryon Palace complex or can be purchased separately.

  Tryon Palace Historic Sites and Gardens is open Monday through Saturday from 9 A.M. to 4 P.M. and Sunday from 1 P.M. to 4 P.M. It is closed Thanksgiving, December 24, 25, and 26, and New Year's. An admission fee is charged. Special events include garden tours in April and October and Christmas tours in December. Its two gift shops—the Tryon Palace Museum Shop and the Crafts and Garden Shop—are open daily. For more information, call 800-767-1560 or 252-514-4900, or try their website at www.tryonpalace.org.

- The **Attmore-Oliver House**, located at 513 Broad Street, is another museum house well worth visiting. Now home to the New Bern Historical Society, the house was constructed in 1790 and enlarged in 1834. It is furnished with 18th- and 19th-century antiques and features Civil War

Attmore-Oliver House
PHOTOGRAPH © STEVE UZZELL

artifacts and a doll collection. The home is open Tuesday through Saturday from 1 P.M. to 4:30 P.M. from April to early December, or by appointment. No admission fee is charged, but donations are accepted. For information, call 252-638-8558.

- **Christ Episcopal Church**, located at 320 Pollock Street, is a splendid Gothic Revival structure built around 1875 over an existing shell constructed in 1824. It traces its roots to a parish established here in 1741. The church possesses a silver communion service, a Bible, and a *Book of Common Prayer* that were gifts from King George II. It is open to the public on weekdays.

- **First Presbyterian Church**, located at 412 New Street, is a magnificent structure built from plans drawn by Sir Christopher Wren.

MUSEUMS AND SCIENCE CENTERS

- **Firemen's Museum**, located at 408 Hancock Street, honors New Bern's firefighting outfits through the years. It houses an array of 19th-century man- and horse-drawn fire engines, 20th-century steam and motorized fire engines, sundry firefighting equipment, and Civil War relics. Children will enjoy learning about Fred the fire horse, whose mounted head hangs near equipment he once pulled. Fred joined the Atlantic Company in 1908 and valiantly served until his death in 1925, long after motorized engines came into use. The museum is open Monday through Saturday from 10 A.M. to 4:30 P.M. and Sunday from 1 P.M. to 5 P.M. It is closed Thanksgiving, Christmas, and New Year's. An admission fee is charged. Call 252-636-4087 for more information.

CULTURAL OFFERINGS

- **Bank of the Arts**, home of the Craven County Arts Council and Gallery, is located at 317 Middle Street in a 1913 granite Neoclassical Revival building that was once the Peoples Bank. This gallery displays an array of pottery, sculpture, paintings, and photography. Exhibits change every six

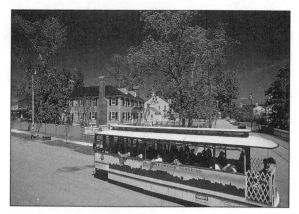

Trolley tour in New Bern
PHOTOGRAPH © STEVE UZZELL

weeks. The gallery is open Monday through Friday from 10 A.M. to 4 P.M. Admission is free. During the summer months, the arts council offers concerts in the park. For information, call 252-638-2577.

▪ **The New Bern Civic Theatre** stages performances at the Saax Bradbury Playhouse, located at 414 Pollock Street. Professional and local actors perform a variety of dramas, comedies, musicals, and even sign-language productions. Call 252-633-0567 for information.

SPECIAL SHOPPING

▪ Visitors to New Bern can cool off with an ice-cold glass of "Brad's Drink" at the **Birthplace of Pepsi-Cola** (252-636-5898), a souvenir shop located at Middle and Pollock Streets. It was here that pharmacist Caleb "Doc" Bradham formulated his famous soft drink behind his soda fountain in the 1890s. The concoction was instantly popular with his customers. In his search for a catchier name, Bradham spent $100 to acquire a registered brand name, Pep Kola, from a New Jersey company. Still not satisfied, he modified the name to Pepsi-Cola. Unfortunately, Bradham was forced into bankruptcy by the collapse of the sugar market following World War I, and the rights to the drink were purchased by a New York company. Bradham died in 1934, never realizing any of the profits his drink produced.

- **Carolina Creations** (252-633-4369), located at 321 Pollock Street, offers wonderful hand-crafted pottery, sculpture, jewelry, cards, and prints by local and nationally known artists.

- **Mitchell Hardware** (252-638-4261), located at 215 Craven Street, is a turn-of-the-century hardware store complete with enamelware, crockery, pottery, and more.

- **Weavers Web** (252-514-2681), located at 602 Pollock Street, sells hand-woven sweaters, skeins and skeins of beautiful yarn, and all manner of patterns for cross-stitch, weaving, and needlepoint.

RECREATION

- One of four national forests in North Carolina, **Croatan National Forest** is the only true coastal forest east of the Mississippi. Spreading over 159,000 acres south from New Bern to Bogue Sound, the forest encompasses ecosystems ranging from upland hardwoods to pocosins. It provides habitat for a variety of flora and fauna, including such endangered species as Venus flytraps, alligators, and red-cockaded woodpeckers. The forest offers numerous boating access areas and hiking trails, including the 21-mile Neusiok Trail, which stretches from the Neuse River to the Newport River. Primitive camping is permitted except in developed day-use areas and actively managed sites. Other outdoor recreational opportunities include bird-watching, camping, and picnicking. Fishing, hunting, and trapping are regulated by the North Carolina Wildlife Resources Commission; information is available where licenses are sold. The ranger's office, located in New Bern, is open Monday through Friday from 8 A.M. to 4:30 P.M.; a map machine is located outside. For information, contact the Ranger's Office, Croatan National Forest, 141 East Fisher Avenue, New Bern, NC 28560 (252-638-5628).

SEASONAL EVENTS

- **Spring Historic Homes and Gardens Tour** is held every April, when the azaleas and dogwoods are in full bloom. Cosponsored by the New Bern Historical Society and the New Bern Preservation Foundation, the tour includes many private houses usually closed to the public, as well as churches and other historically significant buildings. A fee is charged. For information, contact Spring Historic Homes and Gardens Tour, P.O. Box 207, New Bern, NC 28563 (252-633-6448 or 252-638-8558).

■ *Rotary Cup Sailing Regatta* is a sailboat race held every Labor Day weekend at Fairfield Harbor. Festivities include a concert and a five-kilometer race. The event is sponsored by the Rotary Club of New Bern.

■ The annual *Chrysanthemum Festival* is held downtown in mid-October. Food, entertainment, and an antique-and-crafts show are offered. Call 252-638-5781 for information.

Places to Stay

Not surprisingly, a number of bed-and-breakfasts operate in New Bern's elegant historic houses. At the other end of the spectrum are newly constructed, well-known chains situated on the waterfront; some of these offer marinas.

RESORTS, HOTELS, AND MOTELS

■ *Sheraton Grand New Bern*. Expensive/Moderate. 1 Bicentennial Park (800-326-3745 or 252-638-3585). At least half the rooms here offer a view of the Trent and Neuse Rivers. The hotel has 156 boat slips for mariners. Its restaurant overlooks the marina and pool. Senior-citizen discounts are offered.

■ *BridgePointe Hotel and Marina*. Moderate. 101 Howell Road, at the junction of U.S. 70 and U.S. 70E Bypass (877-283-7713 or 252-636-3637). The newly renovated rooms here all have river views. Amenities include in-room coffee makers, cable television, a swimming pool, a marina, and the BridgePointe Landing Restaurant. Senior-citizen, military, and business rates are offered.

- **Comfort Suites Riverfront Park**. Moderate. 218 East Front Street (800-228-5150 or 252-636-0022). Comfort Suites is situated next to Union Park along the banks of the Neuse. All the suites are equipped with microwaves, coffee makers, and refrigerators. Some have waterfront balconies and whirlpool baths. A fitness room and an outdoor swimming pool are available for guests. Complimentary continental breakfast is offered.

INNS AND BED-AND-BREAKFASTS

- **Harmony House Inn**. Expensive/Moderate. 215 Pollock Street (800-636-3113 or 252-636-3810). Housed in a handsome 1850s Greek Revival structure, this friendly inn offers eight spacious guest rooms and two suites, all with private baths. A full breakfast is served.

- **The Aerie**. Moderate. 509 Pollock Street (800-849-5553 or 252-636-5553). This charming 1880s inn with a lovely garden is located one block from Tryon Palace. Each of its seven guest rooms has a private bath, color cable television, and a telephone. A full breakfast with a choice of three entrées is served in the dining room.

- **Howard House**. Moderate. 207 Pollock Street (800-705-5261 or 252-514-6709). This lovely Victorian inn features period antiques in its guest rooms, private baths, and gourmet breakfasts. Homemade desserts and refreshments are also provided.

- **The Meadows Inn**. Moderate. 212 Pollock Street (800-872-9306 or 252-634-1776). The Meadows Inn is a Colonial-style structure built in 1847. It offers one suite and eight guest rooms with fireplaces and private baths. Breakfast and a morning newspaper are brought to guests' rooms.

- **The New Berne House.** Moderate. 709 Broad Street (800-842-7688 or 252-636-2250). This stately Colonial-style home has seven rooms containing charming antiques and traditional furnishings. Each has a private bath. Breakfast and refreshments are included in the price of your stay.

Places to Eat

- **Henderson House.** Expensive. 216 Pollock Street (252-637-4784). Housed in a lovely Federal-style brick home listed on the National Register of Historic Places, Henderson House offers gourmet fare served in an Old World atmosphere. The specialties include steak and seafood entrées. Dinner is served Tuesday through Saturday. Henderson House is available for private parties.

- **Corina's Restaurant.** Expensive/Moderate. 415 Broad Street (252-633-9898). Chef Bryan Fisher, a graduate of the Culinary Institute of America, has twice been head chef for the U.S. Open tennis tournament. The menu at Corina's features soups, crepes, salads, and quiches for lunch and fresh seafood, lamb, duck, and veal for dinner. Dinner is served Monday through Saturday.

- **The Harvey Mansion Historic Inn Restaurant and Lounge.** Expensive/Moderate. 221 South Front Street (252-638-3205). The Harvey Mansion has six formal dining rooms, where it serves up award-winning duck, veal, and seafood. The cellar pub offers an equally delicious but more casual menu. The mansion overlooks the Trent River and is listed on the National Register. It is open for dinner Tuesday through Sunday.

- **The Chelsea.** Moderate. 335 Middle Street (252-637-5469; www.thechelsea.com). This restaurant offers "Fusion Cuisine." French, German, Italian, Cajun, and American regional entrées are either on the menu or featured as specials. The Chelsea is housed in the second drugstore operated by Caleb Bradham, the inventor of Pepsi-Cola. Lunch and dinner are served Monday through Saturday.

- **Fred and Claire's Restaurant**. Moderate. 247 Craven Street (252-638-5426). This brightly decorated place features omelets, quiches, sandwiches, and salads. Credit cards are not accepted. Lunch and dinner are served Monday through Saturday.

- New Bern has a couple of gourmet coffee shops. They are the **New Bern Roasting Company** (252-634-1952), located at 215 Middle Street, and **Trent River Coffee Company** (252-514-2030), located at 208 Craven Street. Trent River Coffee Company hosts monthly musical events sponsored by the Downeast Folk Arts Society.

- The **Cow Café** (252-638-1131), located at 305 Avenue C, is an ice cream parlor operated by Maola Milk and Ice Cream Company.

Nearby

- Located at the gateway to Pamlico Sound, **Oriental** is considered by some to be the sailing capital of the East Coast. This quaint fishing village and growing retirement center beckons sailors of all skills, including yachtsmen from the nearby Intracoastal Waterway and novices who come to hone their skills at the Oriental Sailing School. To reach Oriental, take U.S. 17 North from New Bern, then follow N.C. 55; it's about a 25-mile drive.

- If you decide to stay in Oriental, you're sure to find a welcome at **The Cartwright House** (252-249-1337), **The Inn at Oriental** (252-249-1078), or **Oriental Marina Motel** (252-249-1818), all of which are within easy walking distance of the harbor.

- **CSS Neuse State Historic Site** and the **Richard Caswell Memorial** are located north of New Bern on U.S. 70 just within the city limits of Kinston. An audiovisual program and a statue at the Richard Caswell Memorial honor North Carolina's first governor. Under a shelter outside lie the remains of the last ironclad built by the Confederacy, the CSS *Neuse*. In 1865, its crew sank the vessel to keep it from enemy hands.

It remained embedded in mud for nearly 100 years before it was extracted and put on display. The sites are open Monday through Saturday from 9 A.M. to 5 P.M. and Sunday from 1 P.M. to 5 P.M. from April to October. From November to March, they are open Tuesday through Saturday from 10 A.M. to 4 P.M. and Sunday from 1 P.M. to 4 P.M. Admission is free. For information, call 252-522-2091.

■ *Minnesott Beach* is located a free 20-minute ferry ride across the Neuse. Take the Cherry Branch ferry to U.S. 306; check the ferry schedule for times.

■ *Neuse River Recreation Area* is located approximately 11 miles southeast of New Bern on U.S. 70. Camping, hiking, fishing, and swimming are the main activities here. Call 252-638-5628 for information.

Oriental
PHOTOGRAPH BY BILL RUSS
COURTESY OF NORTH CAROLINA DIVISION OF TOURISM, FILM AND SPORTS DEVELOPMENT

The Barbecue Trail

One of the first books I publicized when I came to Blair was Bob Garner's *North Carolina Barbecue*, a history of the tradition and guide to some of the state's outstanding restaurants. I quickly discovered that North Carolinians are boastful about their barbecue. This is ironic because there's not even a consensus within the state about the proper way to fix it. Hailing from Razorback country, where we cook up some good barbecue ourselves, both pork (nod to Memphis) and beef (nod to Texas), I was skeptical of North Carolina's grandiose claims. Especially the first time I *saw* it. Don't let looks deceive you, though. It is pretty good stuff.

If you're traveling to the Albemarle beaches via U.S. 70 from Raleigh, you'll pass through prime "eastern-style" barbecue country. You see, there is a longstanding rivalry between barbecue buffs at opposite ends of the state. In the eastern half, you've got eastern-style barbecue, which uses the whole hog. In the western half, you've got "Lexington-style," which uses the shoulders only.

"No one quite knows why two distinct barbecue styles developed in North Carolina . . . ," Bob Garner writes. "But that distinction, together with differences between eastern and western sauces and the regional variations in what's considered an appropriate barbecue side dish, has provided grist for an endlessly revolving mill of barbecue debate. It has also given North Carolina something of an undeserved national reputation for barbecue schizophrenia that, to outsiders, sullies the state's claim to have the best barbecue on the planet. *The New Yorker's* Calvin Trillin wrote in his book *Alice, Let's Eat* of being 'subjected to stern geographical probings' when he mentioned to former North Carolina residents that he had sampled barbecue in their state. And in *Southern Food*, John Egerton sniffs, 'There are two basic styles of North Carolina barbecue, and proponents of each are so disdainful of the other that doubt is cast on both.'"

That said, here are some of Bob Garner's recommendations.

"The White Swan is one of those tiny, unprepossessing places off the beaten track that you're always really smug about discovering. Of course, it's only off the beaten track for those who don't live around the Smithfield area, and not far off the track at that: just a mile-and-a-half from Interstate 95. For area residents, though, it's not only a place with consistently delicious eastern-style barbecue, superb fried chicken, and championship-caliber hush puppies—it's a place with a colorful past. . . .

"Ava Gardner, the movie star, grew up and is buried in Smithfield, and you can easily combine an excursion to the White Swan with a visit to the Ava Gardner museum downtown. . . .

"To get [to the White Swan], take I-95 south to Exit 90, then go a mile-and-a-half toward Smithfield on U.S. 301/N.C. 96 North."

"Ken's Grill is an unobtrusive little place,

the kind of spot you might blow right past without noticing as you travel on U.S. 70 to Morehead City or Beaufort. Before I had a chance to visit, I had received several phone calls about the barbecue at Ken's over a period of several months. I finally found myself passing through the area on a Wednesday—one of only two days of the week Ken's Grill prepares barbecue, the other being Saturday—so I decided to pick up a sandwich for the road. . . .

"Besides barbecue, Ken's offers thick, hand-patted hamburgers, which are typically served country-style—topped with cheese, coleslaw, and homemade chili. There's also a different special every day, including Fridays, when Ken's serves its own version of the thick fish stew that's probably the number one local delicacy in the area—surpassing even barbecue.

"Ken's Grill occupies a small, square building on the south side of U.S. 70 outside LaGrange, roughly halfway between Goldsboro and Kinston."

". . . Today, many of those who live outside Goldsboro are familiar with the family name through the visibility of Scott's Famous Barbecue Sauce, a quintessential eastern North Carolina style, vinegar-based sauce that's sold commercially in several grocery chains in North Carolina, South Carolina, and Virginia. The yellow label features the red silhouette of a pig and the legend: 'It's the best ye ever tasted' . . .

"Scott's is a cheerful, sunlight-filled place, with chrome-and-formica tables and comfortable booths upholstered in light green vinyl. . . .

"The restaurant isn't highly visible to non-Goldsboro residents, although it's easy to find. From U.S. 70, which skirts the northern edge of Goldsboro, take the Williams Street exit and travel south toward town; you'll see the restaurant on the right."

"Wilber's is one of the biggest names in barbecue in eastern North Carolina, and unlike a few other famous places in the coastal plain, this is a restaurant where the name above the door still means *exactly* what it did thirty-four years ago when Wilber Shirley opened the place.

"As far as I can determine, Wilber's is one of only four remaining restaurants anywhere in the eastern part of the state where barbecue is cooked entirely over hardwood coals. . . .

"Wilber's has a homey, laid-back feel to it: red brick and white trim on the outside, knotty pine paneling and red-checked tablecloths inside. . . .

"Wilber's serves combination plates, featuring barbecue and either fried or pit-barbecued chicken, along with the potato salad, Brunswick stew, coleslaw, and hush puppies. There are even some seafood selections available, as well. These side offerings all get high marks for quality and consistency, but the main thing you'll remember after a visit to Wilber's is the barbecue itself, which is absolutely superb.

"Wilber's is located four miles east of Goldsboro on U.S. 70."

This Morning, we set out early, being four *English*-men, besides four *Indians*. We went ten miles, and were then stopp'd by the Freshes of the *Enoe* River, which had rais'd it so high, that we could not pass over, till it was fallen. I enquir'd of my Guide, Where this river disgor'd it self? He said, It was *Enoe*-River, and run into a place call'd *Enoe*-Bay, near his Country, which he left when he was a Boy; by which I perceiv'd, he was one of the *Cores* by birth: This being a branch of the *Neus*-River. . . . This River is near as large as *Reatkin*; the South-side having curious Tracts of good Land, the Banks high, and Stone-Quarries. The *Tuskeruros* being come to us, we ventur'd over the River, which we found to be a strong Current, and the Water about Breast-high. However, we all got safe to the North-Shore, which is but poor, white, sandy Land, and bears no Timber, but small shrubby Oaks. We went about 10 Miles, and sat down at the Falls of a large Creek, where lay mighty Rocks, the Water making a strange Noise, as if a great many Water-Mills were going at once. I take this to be the Falls of *Neuse*-Creek, called by the *Indians*, *Wee quo Whom*.

MOREHEAD CITY

Morehead City is for fishermen what Oriental is for sailors: a mecca. Morehead City is also the gateway to two alluring destinations—charming Beaufort to the east and lively Atlantic Beach to the south. But don't make the mistake of visiting the area without taking a look around Morehead City. At the very least, make the trip to its picturesque waterfront to gaze at its fleet of charter boats, to eat at its famous boat-to-shore seafood restaurants, and to shop at its fish markets and gift and antique shops.

Morehead City is the product of the ambitions of John Motley Morehead, governor of North Carolina from 1841 to 1845. Together with an associate, Silas Webb, Morehead purchased a 600-acre tract in 1853, which he dreamed of developing into a deepwater port that would eventually be linked by rail to the Piedmont and to cities on the Ohio and

Morehead City waterfront
COURTESY OF CARTERET COUNTY TOURISM DEVELOPMENT BUREAU

Mississippi Rivers. That town, Carolina City, met an early demise when Morehead decided to subdivide his holdings. He subsequently planned a new town just to the east of the original, sketching out 50-by-100-foot lots that he put up for sale in November 1857. Two months later, excursion trains were bringing regular crowds from Goldsboro. By May 1858, every new lot in town had sold, earning Morehead $1 million. A post office was established here on February 28, 1859.

Morehead City was occupied during the Civil War. It rebounded at the turn of the 20th century to become a fashionable summer resort. Meanwhile, the fishing industry continued to grow. In 1952, a deepwater port was established at Morehead City, fulfilling John Motley Morehead's dream. The town has since become known as a port for shipping bulk cargo, particularly coal and phosphate.

Today, Morehead City is world-renowned for its fishing waters, fed by the Gulf Stream. Fishermen come to test their skills against marlin, amberjack, mackerel, tarpon, and bluefish. The town is also becoming known as an excellent diving destination among those in search of shipwrecks and buried treasure.

Morehead City
COURTESY OF NORTH CAROLINA DIVISION OF TOURISM, FILM AND SPORTS DEVELOPMENT

JUST THE FACTS

Morehead City is located on U.S. 70. It is accessible from the north by N.C. 101, from the west by N.C. 24, and from the south by N.C. 58.

Three airports serve the area. Craven County Regional Airport in New Bern offers US Airways and Midway Airlines express and charter flights; call 252-638-8591 for information. To the west in Jacksonville, Albert J. Ellis Airport offers US Airways commuter flights; call 910-324-3001. Michael J. Smith Airport, located in Beaufort, offers private and charter services; call 252-728-1777 or 252-728-2323.

The bus station is located at 206 North 15th Street; call 252-726-3029.

For information on the area, contact the Carteret County Tourism Bureau, 3409 Arendell Street, Morehead City, N.C. 28557 (800-786-6962 or 252-726-8148; www.sunnync.com).

The *Carteret County News Times* is the local weekly newspaper.

Diver at Morehead City shipwreck
COURTESY OF CARTERET COUNTY TOURISM DEVELOPMENT BUREAU

Things to Do

MUSEUMS AND SCIENCE CENTERS

▪ The **Carteret County Historical and Geological Society**, located at 100 Wallace Drive near the Crystal Coast Civic Center, houses an interesting collection of artifacts and memorabilia reflecting the county's Native American, military, and maritime past. It also contains an excellent research library, a small art gallery, and a gift shop. It is open Tuesday through Saturday from 1 P.M. to 4 P.M. The museum is run by volunteer docents. Admission is free. For more information, call 252-247-7533, or visit their website at www.rootsweb.com/~ncchs.

RECREATION

Fishing is the reason most people visit Morehead City. Opportunities to test your skills abound. Onshore and offshore fishing trips are available, as are charter rigs. Or you can bring your own boat or rent one at the waterfront. A list of charters and head boats is available from the Carteret County Tourism Bureau.

▪ Scuba-diving adventures can be booked through a number of outfits. You might try **Olympus Dive Center**, located on the waterfront at 713 Shepard Street. Call 252-726-9432, or try their website at www.olympusdiving.com.

SEASONAL EVENTS

- The **Big Rock Marlin Tournament**, held the second week in June, is part of the World Billfish Series. Blue marlin fishermen come from near and far to compete for cash prizes totaling over $1 million; the winner takes home nearly $500,000. For information, call 252-247-3575. For a listing of all fishing tournaments and for information on obtaining tournament licenses, call the North Carolina Division of Marine Fisheries at 252-726-7021, or visit www.ncdmf.net.

- The **North Carolina Seafood Festival** is held the first weekend in October on the Morehead City waterfront. Thousands flock to the festival to enjoy the music, to admire the arts and crafts, and, of course, to sample the delicious seafood. For information, call 252-726-6273.

- The **Bald Is Beautiful Convention and Contest** originally sought to gather at Bald Head Island, off the Cape Fear coast. But Morehead City, which proved to have a sense of humor about its name, is glad the convention opted to meet here instead. Every summer, the bald and the proud compete for such titles as "Most Kissable" and "Shiniest Head." For information, call 252-726-1855, or visit their website at www.members.aol.com/baldusa.

Places to Stay

RESORTS, HOTELS, AND MOTELS

Accommodations in Morehead City tend to be a little less expensive than in Beaufort and Atlantic Beach, especially in the high season. Chain hotels and motels have secured the market here.

- **Hampton Inn on Bogue Sound**. Expensive/Moderate. 4035 Arendell Street (800-538-6338 or 252-240-2300). This hotel overlooks Bogue Sound. It offers complimentary continental breakfast, free in-room movies, an exercise room, and an outdoor pool. Its suites have separate living rooms, microwaves, refrigerators, and wet bars.

- **Best Western Buccaneer Motor Inn**. Moderate. 2806 Arendell Street (800-682-4982 or 252-726-3115). The Best Western offers complimentary breakfast and newspaper, cable television, a pool, and golf and fishing packages. Rooms with king-sized beds and Jacuzzis are available.

- **Comfort Inn**. Moderate. 3100 Arendell Street (800-422-5404 or 252-247-3434). This motel offers comfortable rooms, free cable television, complimentary continental breakfast, a newspaper delivered to your door, a pool, a fitness room, and golf packages.

- **Econo Lodge**. Moderate. 3410 Bridges Street (800-533-7556 or 252-247-2940). A motor inn with a colonial theme, the Econo Lodge offers free continental breakfast, cable television, a pool, and golf and fishing packages.

Places to Eat

- **Nikola's**. Expensive. Fourth and Bridges Streets (252-726-6060). This local favorite offers classic Italian entrées like shrimp scampi and veal Marsala, served with an appetizer, soup or pasta, a salad, vegetables, homemade bread, dessert, and a beverage. It offers both a fixed-price menu and an à la carte menu. Dinner is served Tuesday through Saturday.

- **Amos Mosquito's Swampside Café**. Expensive/Moderate. 509 Evans Street (252-247-6222). Located on the waterfront, this café offers an array of fresh salads, sandwiches, pastas, and seafood entrées, some bearing Asian and Southwestern influences. Dockside dining is available. Guests love the tableside hibachis, where they can make their own s'mores. Lunch and dinner are served daily.

- **Bistro by the Sea**. Expensive/Moderate. 4301 Arendell Street (252-247-2777; www.bistrobythesea.com). Bistro by the Sea has a diverse menu that includes soups, salads, beef and chicken entrées, and fresh seafood specials. Its piano-and-cigar bar offers specialty martinis. Dinner is served Tuesday through Saturday; the restaurant is closed during January.

- **Windandsea**. Expensive/Moderate. 708 Evans Street (252-247-3000). This bright new restaurant on the Morehead City waterfront offers fine dining and wood-oven pizzas. Dinner is served Tuesday through Sunday.

- **Calypso Café**. Moderate. 506 Arendell Street (252-240-3380). The Calypso specializes in Caribbean-style cuisine with an emphasis on seafood. Dinner is served Tuesday through Saturday.

- **Mrs. Willis' Restaurant**. Moderate. 3114 Bridges Street, behind Morehead Plaza (252-726-3741). Mrs. Willis began cooking barbecue, chicken, and pies in 1949. Her family carries on the tradition today. Lunch and dinner are served daily.

- **Rockefellers**. Moderate. 405 Arendell Street (252-808-3280). Rockefellers has two outdoor decks overlooking the Intracoastal Waterway. One of its two indoor dining areas is casual, while the other is more formal. The formal dining room includes an oyster bar.

- **The Sanitary Fish Market**. Moderate. 501 Evans Street (252-247-3111). A Tar Heel institution, the Sanitary Fish Market has been serving up fresh seafood on the Morehead City waterfront since 1938. This vast, 600-seat restaurant offers broiled and fried seafood, steaks, lobster, and homemade soup, chowder, and hush puppies. It is open daily for lunch and dinner from February through November.

- **Raps Grill and Bar**. Moderate/Inexpensive. 715 Arendell Street (252-240-1213). Housed in a 1912 building with a 35-foot oak bar, Raps offers seafood, pasta, chicken, burritos, burgers, and Maryland-style crabs. Lunch is served Monday through Saturday; dinner is offered daily.

Beaufort town docks
COURTESY OF CARTERET COUNTY TOURISM DEVELOPMENT BUREAU

BEAUFORT

Beaufort is a lovely old fishing village that has the distinction of being North Carolina's third-oldest town. At the time of the American Revolution, Beaufort was the third-largest port in the state. Today, it boasts a 12-block National Historic District on the original "Plan of Beaufort Towne," platted by Henry Somerset in 1713.

When French Huguenots and immigrants from Germany, Sweden, England, Scotland, and Ireland arrived here around 1708, the place was known to the Indians as Wareiock, or "Fish Town." It was renamed Beaufort for the duke of Beaufort, one of the Lords Proprietors.

Beaufort was an important military port during the War of 1812, when much privateering occurred here. Privateering was a sort of licensed piracy, in which ship captains and financial backers were entitled to the spoils of war. One of the most famous and successful privateers was Otway Burns, captain of the *Snap Dragon*, who captured cargoes worth millions of dollars between 1812 and 1814. After the war, he stayed in Beaufort and became a successful shipbuilder, merchant, and politician.

In the 19th century, Beaufort continued to prosper as a port and as an agricultural, commercial, and governmental center. Wealthy planters and their families sought its pleasant and healthful environment.

Early in the Civil War, Beaufort was again called to military duty, this time aiding blockade runners bringing supplies to the Confederacy. On March 25, 1862, the town was occupied by Union forces. It was from Beaufort that the Federals launched the formidable fleet that helped conquer the South.

After the war, Beaufort remained a seasonal resort town, though its economic importance was diminished. Fishing became its major industry. The harvesting and processing of menhaden—used for fish meal and industrial oils—were particularly important.

By the 1970s, Beaufort's waterfront was in serious decline. Residents embarked upon a mission to save their old village. The result of their efforts is one of the most attractive and appealing destinations in the entire state.

JUST THE FACTS

From the north or south, drivers can take U.S. 17 to U.S. 70 to reach Beaufort.

Craven County Regional Airport in New Bern offers express and charter flights via US Airways and Midway Airlines; call 252-638-8591 for information. Michael J. Smith Airport, named in honor of the Beaufort son who perished in the *Challenger* space shuttle accident, offers private and charter services; call 252-728-1777 or 252-728-2323.

The nearest bus station is located at 206 North 15th Street in Morehead City; call 252-726-3029.

Boaters can stop at the Beaufort Municipal Docks (252-728-2503) or Town Creek Marina (252-728-6111).

For information on the area, contact the Carteret County Tourism Bureau, 3409 Arendell Street, Morehead City, N.C. 28557 (800-786-6962 or 252-726-8148; www.sunnync.com).

Things to Do

HISTORIC PLACES, GARDENS, AND TOURS

■ **Beaufort Historic Site** includes three restored homes built between 1767 and 1825; the Carteret County Courthouse, constructed in 1796; the Carteret County Jail, built in 1829; and the Apothecary Shop and Doctor's Office, erected in 1859. It offers guided tours and living-history demonstrations. The **Old Burying Ground**, a Civil War–era cemetery located on Ann Street, is administered by the historic site. Like all ancient cemeteries, it has many tales to tell. Among those interred here are Otway Burns, privateer hero of the War of 1812; a 13-year-old girl buried in a whiskey keg; and Nancy Manney French, who died shortly after reuniting with her long-lost love. Tours are conducted Tuesday, Wednesday, and Thursday at 2:30 P.M. A fee is charged. The historic site also offers **English Double-Decker Bus Tours**, operated by the Beaufort Historical Association. These entertaining tours run about 45 minutes and are offered Monday, Wednesday, and Friday at 11 A.M. and 1:30 P.M. and Saturday at 11 A.M. A fee is charged. You may contact Beaufort Historic Site at 130 Turner Street, P.O. Box 1709, Beaufort, N.C. 28516-0363 (800-575-7483 or 252-728-5225; www.blackbeardthepirate.com or www.nccoastonline.com/BHA.html).

MUSEUMS AND SCIENCE CENTERS

■ A visit to the **North Carolina Maritime Museum**, located at 315 Front Street, is a wonderful way to learn about coastal and maritime history. The museum offers exhibits on the United States Life Saving Service, coastal marine life, North Carolina watercraft, and commercial fishing. An exhibit in the lobby features Blackbeard the Pirate and the search for his ship, the *Queen Anne's Revenge*. The museum's library is available for reading and research.

■ Across the street from, and administered by, the museum is the

North Carolina
Maritime Museum
Courtesy of Carteret
County Tourism
Development Bureau
© Henderson Photography

Harvey W. Smith Watercraft Center, a boat shop where visitors can watch the restoration of wooden boats and models. The museum's educational arm, it provides field trips to tidal flats and barrier-island beaches and runs the Junior Sailing School for children age eight and over.

The museum's gift shop stocks books on maritime and natural history. The North Carolina Maritime Museum is open Monday through Friday from 9 A.M. to 5 P.M., Saturday from 10 A.M. to 5 P.M., and Sunday from 1 P.M. to 5 P.M. Admission is free. Call 252-728-7317.

RECREATION

- **Lookout Cruises** sails to Cape Lookout twice daily. Interested visitors can also try a morning dolphin watch or a sunset cruise aboard the company's 42-passenger catamaran. Call 252-504-SAIL for information.

- If you want to try a guided snorkel or dive in search of shipwrecks, you might try **Discovery Diving Company**. If you are an experienced diver and would like to join up with others, Discovery can help out, too. Call 252-728-2265 for information.

- If kayaking interests you, you might try **AB Kayaks** (252-728-6330), **Barrier Island Kayaks** (252-393-6457; www.barrierislandkayaks.com), or **Island Rigs** (252-247-7787; www.islandrigs.com).

■ The *Old Homes and Antique Show* is held the last week in June. Sponsored by the Beaufort Historical Society, it features tours of historic homes, churches, gardens, and the Old Burying Ground. Antiques are shown at the Morehead City Civic Center. Double-decker bus tours are conducted throughout the weekend, and entertainment is provided. For more information, call the Beaufort Historical Association at 800-575-7483 or 252-728-5225.

■ Beaufort Historic Site sponsors the *Traditional Thanksgiving Feast* each year during the week of Thanksgiving. Call 252-728-5225 for information.

Places to Stay

INNS AND BED-AND-BREAKFASTS

■ *Beaufort Inn*. Expensive. 101 Ann Street (800-726-0321 or 252-728-2600). Beaufort Inn's 44 waterfront rooms overlook the harbor. All have private baths. The inn provides a full breakfast, boat slips, and a hot-tub spa.

■ *The Cedars*. Expensive. 305 Front Street (252-728-7036). The Cedars is located across from Taylor Creek. All 11 of its guest rooms have private baths. The inn offers a full breakfast, a wine bar, a deck, and bicycles.

■ *Inlet Inn*. Expensive. 601 Front Street (800-554-5466 or 252-728-3600). The harbor-front rooms here all have a seating area, a refrigerator, a bar, and cable television. Many have private porches with rocking chairs, while others have fireplaces or window seats with a view of Cape Lookout. Continental breakfast is provided. Boat slips are available.

■ *Captain's Quarters*. Expensive/Moderate. 315 Ann Street (800-659-7111 or 252-728-7711). Captain's Quarters is a charming Victorian inn with a wraparound porch. Its three guest rooms have private baths. Continental breakfast is provided. Children under 12 are not allowed.

- **Delamar Inn**. Expensive/Moderate. 217 Turner Street (800-349-5823 or 252-728-4300). This 1866 inn offers three guest rooms furnished with antiques. Each room has a private bath. The gracious hosts will provide beach chairs and bicycles if asked. Refreshments are served in the afternoon. The inn is closed from December to February.

- **Langdon House**. Expensive/Moderate. 135 Craven Street (252-728-5499). This hospitable inn has three guest rooms, each with a private bath. The rooms are decorated in a simple 18th-century style. A full breakfast is included.

- **Pecan Tree Inn**. Expensive/Moderate. 116 Queen Street (252-728-6733). This inn has seven guest rooms and three suites, all with private baths. Two of the suites have king-sized canopy beds and Jacuzzis, while the third consists of two adjoining rooms. Pecan Tree Inn also has a lovely flower and herb garden. Continental breakfast is provided.

Places to Eat

- **Beaufort Grocery Co**. Expensive/Moderate. 117 Queen Street (252-728-3899). This restaurant offers a creative menu of local seafood, beef, lamb, veal, freshly made breads, and desserts. It is open daily for lunch and dinner. Sunday brunch is also served. Dinner reservations are recommended.

- **The Spouter Inn**. Expensive/Moderate. 218 Front Street (252-728-5190). The Spouter Inn offers fine dining in a relaxed setting overlooking Taylor Creek. Sandwiches and homemade chowders are featured at lunch and fresh seafood dishes and delicious desserts at dinner. Lunch and dinner are served Thursday through Tuesday.

- **Clawson's 1905 Restaurant.** Moderate/Inexpensive. 425 Front Street (252-728-2133). Clawson's offers casual dining in a former grocery store filled with memorabilia from Beaufort's past. The specialties include ribs, steaks, seafood, and salads. Lunch is served Monday through Saturday and dinner daily.

- **Loughry's Landing.** Moderate/Inexpensive. 510 Front Street (252-728-7541). Guests here have two dockside dining options with views of the boats and the wild ponies. On the upper deck, you can enjoy pizza and ice cream. On the lower deck, you can get entrées like grilled game fish, steamed shellfish, steaks, ribs, and pasta. Lunch and dinner are offered daily.

- **The Net House.** Moderate/Inexpensive. 133 Turner Street (252-728-2002). The steamed and lightly battered seafood served here has earned the Net House bragging rights for years. The nightly specials and the creamy seafood bisque are favorites, too. Dinner is served nightly.

- **The Royal James Café.** Inexpensive. 117 Turner Street (252-728-4573). This local landmark is the oldest continuously operated business in Beaufort. Visitors enjoy the signature burgers and secret sauce before a game of pool on the nearly 50-year-old tables. Lunch and dinner are served daily.

Nearby

- **Cape Lookout National Seashore** is the famous Atlantic headland located off Beaufort Inlet. Extending over 55 miles of barrier islands, it is a protected loggerhead turtle breeding ground, as well as a great spot for shelling and fishing. The rangers here give programs daily during the summer.

  The black-and-white diamond-painted **Cape Lookout Lighthouse**, built in 1859 and located within Cape Lookout National Seashore, is still signaling sailors today. Though it is not open for tours, its renovated keeper's quarters and summer kitchen are.

For ferry information, see the ferry schedule or call the National Park Service office on Harkers Island at 252-728-2250.

■ Across Taylor Creek from the Beaufort waterfront is **Rachel Carson National Marine Estuarine Sanctuary**, the home to a herd of wild Banks horses. The sanctuary is comprised of a series of islands called Shackleford Banks. Accessible only by boat, it is available for hiking, shelling, swimming, camping, research, and education. Brochures for a self-guided trail are available from the North Carolina Maritime Museum and from the sanctuary office, located at 135 Pivers Island Road. For information, call 252-728-2170, or visit their website at www.ncnerr.org.

■ The inner islands around the marsh and sound are dominated by **Cedar Island**, the port for a ferry that travels to Ocracoke Island. Home to about 350 permanent residents, Cedar Island offers miles and miles of deserted beaches without the undertow and drop-offs of the Atlantic. **Cedar Island National Wildlife Refuge** provides feeding grounds for migratory waterfowl. This area is ideal for kayaking.

■ **Harkers Island**, located approximately 15 miles northeast of Beaufort at the southern end of Core Sound, is famous for boat building, in particular the Core Sound sharpie, a shallow-draft boat with sails on either side. Many of the current residents are descended from the original 18th-century settlers, as their "hoi toide" (high tide) accents attest.

■ The **Core Sound Waterfowl Museum** (252-728-1500), located on Harkers Island, is dedicated to the preservation of traditional decoy carving and the history of waterfowl hunting "Down East," as this entire area is called.

Fort Macon State Park
COURTESY OF CARTERET COUNTY TOURISM
DEVELOPMENT BUREAU
© COPYRIGHT HENDERSON PHOTOGRAPHY

BOGUE BANKS

Bogue Banks is a 29-mile-long barrier island that stretches from Beaufort Inlet on the east to Bogue Inlet to the west. Until the 1950s, Bogue Banks was virtually undeveloped. But once people came to recognize it as one of the state's longest, most accessible barrier islands, its beautiful, expansive white beach became one of the most popular vacation destinations on the coast. After several decades of development, much of the native landscape has been supplanted by condominiums, beach houses, hotels, and resorts. However, Bogue Banks still boasts one of the prettiest beaches in the state.

The eastern end of the island is dominated by Atlantic Beach, the oldest town on Bogue Banks. Its bustling commercial area includes shops, restaurants, and entertainment parks; children and teenagers love it. Adjacent to Atlantic Beach is Fort Macon State Park, the most-visited state park in North Carolina, attracting 1.24 million guests a year.

Midway down the island, at Salter Path and Pine Knoll Shores, beach cottages are the norm. Pine Knoll Shores was developed by Theodore

Roosevelt's children, who were heirs of his distant cousin Alice Hoffman, the owner of most of the island from 1918 until 1953. The Roosevelt family donated 322 acres of local land, including 2,700 feet of beachfront, to the state. In 1973, Pine Knoll Shores was incorporated. It is now home to Theodore Roosevelt State Natural Area.

Past Indian Beach at the island's western end is the town of Emerald Isle. Things are slower and quieter here. Few of the local buildings reach over two stories.

JUST THE FACTS

Bogue Banks is a barrier island sandwiched between Bogue Sound and the Atlantic Ocean. N.C. 58 runs almost the entire length of the island. Visitors coming from the north can connect to N.C. 58 from U.S. 70. Those coming from the south can take U.S. 17 to N.C. 24 in Jacksonville or connect directly to N.C. 58 from U.S. 17 near Croatan National Forest.

Air access is via Craven County Regional Airport (252-638-8591) in New Bern, Albert J. Ellis Airport (910-324-1100) in Jacksonville, or Michael J. Smith Airport (252-728-1777 or 252-728-2323) in Beaufort.

For information on the area, contact the Carteret County Tourism Bureau, 3409 Arendell Street, Morehead City, N.C. 28557 (800-786-6962 or 252-726-8148; www.sunnync.com).

Things to Do

HISTORIC PLACES, GARDENS, AND TOURS

- The top historical draw on Bogue Banks is without a doubt **Fort Macon State Park**, located east of Atlantic Beach at the tip of the island. For over 150 years, Fort Macon has stood guard over Beaufort Inlet. The pentagon-shaped fortress, completed in 1834, was named to honor Nathaniel

Macon, a former speaker of the House of Representatives and United States senator. Not long after it was garrisoned, Fort Macon began to give way to erosion and storms, so the United States Army sent one of its young West Point engineers, Robert E. Lee, to rectify the problem. The stone jetties designed by Captain Lee are still in use today. During the Civil War, the 500 Confederate troops at Fort Macon were forced to surrender to Union general Ambrose Burnside following an 11-hour bombardment. The fort was garrisoned again during the Spanish-American War and World War II.

A self-guided tour with audiovisual displays provides historical background on the fort for visitors of all ages. The museum on the premises exhibits tools, weapons, and artifacts and offers a slide presentation. The bookstore has a variety of historical material.

The 385-acre park is a favorite spot for bird-watching, sportfishing, and shelling. In the summer, the lifeguard-protected swimming area, the bathhouses, and the picnic areas are popular with visitors.

Fort Macon State Park is open from 9 A.M. to 5 P.M. daily except for Christmas. Admission is free. For information, call 252-726-3775.

MUSEUMS AND SCIENCE CENTERS

- The **North Carolina Aquarium at Pine Knoll Shores** is one of the island's most popular attractions. Its 16-tank viewing gallery, exhibits, touch tank, and two nature trails are designed to educate visitors about North Carolina's fragile and fascinating marine life. Included are the 200-gallon Precious Waters exhibit, a salt-marsh tank, and a riverbank display featuring live alligators. The Loggerhead Odyssey exhibit includes a nursery for injured turtles. The aquarium is located five miles west of Atlantic Beach at Milepost 7. It is open from 9 A.M. to 7 P.M. from Memorial Day through Labor Day and from 9 A.M. to 5 P.M. the rest of the year. An admission fee is charged. Call 252-247-4003 for information.

RECREATION

- **Theodore Roosevelt State Natural Area**, a 250-acre nature preserve at Pine Knoll Shores, is the perfect place to observe the local wildlife and get a glimpse of the island in its native state. Few facilities are offered here. Call 252-247-4003 for information.

■ Water enthusiasts should check out the opportunities offered at **Britannia Watersports and Windsurfing School**, located at 1245 N.C. 58 in Salter Path. Call 252-247-5245 for information.

■ Those interested in fishing might try **Oceana Resort Fishing Pier**, located on Fort Macon Drive in Atlantic Beach. During the off-season, the fishing is free for guests at the resort; otherwise, a fee is charged. For information, call 252-726-0863. **Sportsman's Pier** is on Money Island Drive in Atlantic Beach. A fee is charged. For information, call 252-726-3176.

SEASONAL EVENTS

■ **Worthy Is the Lamb** is an inspirational musical drama of the last days of Christ. It is performed in the Crystal Coast Amphitheatre, located three miles north of the bridge to Emerald Isle. The nation's only fully orchestrated passion play, it is performed Thursday through Saturday at 8:30 P.M. from mid-June through the end of August. During the first half of September, it is offered on Friday and Saturday at 8 P.M. An admission fee is charged. For information, call the amphitheater at 800-662-5960 or 252-393-8373.

■ The **Emerald Isle Beach Music Festival**, held in May at Holiday Trav-L-Park on Coast Guard Road in Emerald Isle, features live bands playing beach music. This is a great chance to hone your shagging skills. Call 252-354-2872 for information.

■ The **Atlantic Beach King Mackerel Tournament**, the largest all-cash king mackerel contest in the country, is held each September. Call 252-247-2334 for information.

Places to Stay

RESORTS, HOTELS, AND MOTELS

■ **Sheraton Atlantic Beach**. Expensive. West Fort Macon Road, Atlantic Beach (800-624-8875 or 252-240-1155). The Sheraton offers ocean-view suites with king-sized beds, Jacuzzis, and in-room movies. Among its amenities are indoor and outdoor pools, an exercise room, a restaurant, and a nightclub.

■ **Vacation Properties/A Place at the Beach**. Expensive. Fort Macon Road, Atlantic Beach (800-334-2667 or 252-247-2636). Situated on the ocean, this resort offers one-, two-, and three-bedroom units, along with surf fishing, golf packages, two pools, lighted tennis courts, and children's programs in the summer.

■ **Best Western Crystal Coast Resort**. Expensive/Moderate. Salter Path Road, Atlantic Beach (800-733-7888 or 252-726-2544). Children sleep free in their parents' rooms here. A pool and a wading pool are available.

■ **Ramada Inn**. Expensive/Moderate. Salter Path Road, Atlantic Beach (800-338-1533 or 252-247-4155). All the rooms here have private balconies overlooking the beach. A pool and cable television are among the amenities.

■ **Oceana**. Moderate. Fort Macon Road, Atlantic Beach (252-726-4111). Located near Fort Macon, Oceana is an old-fashioned beach place for the whole family. It offers a pool, a playground, a pier, and a lifeguard on the beach during the summer.

■ **Royal Pavilion**. Moderate. 125 Salter Path Road, Pine Knoll Shores (800-533-3700 or 252-726-5188). Royal Pavilion enjoys a solid reputation. It offers an 1,100-foot private beach, two outdoor swimming pools, a restaurant, and a lounge. Suites are available.

Places to Eat

- **Konstantin's Steakhouse.** Expensive. Atlantic Station, West Fort Macon Road, Atlantic Beach (252-240-2224). Catch-of-the-day specials, steaks, and chicken entrées are the main attractions at Konstantin's. Dinner is served Wednesday through Monday. A nightclub is on the premises.

- **Channel Marker.** Expensive/Moderate. Morehead City–Atlantic Beach Causeway, Atlantic Beach (252-247-2344). Channel Marker offers outdoor dining overlooking Bogue Sound. Dinner specialties include fresh seafood, served steamed or grilled, and Black Angus beef. Ample boat dockage is available. Call for serving hours.

- **Pizzuti's.** Moderate. 201 West Fort Macon Road, Atlantic Beach (252-222-0166). This restaurant offers northern Italian specialties and continental cuisine. It is open daily for dinner.

- **Rucker John's.** Moderate. Emerald Isle Plantation Shopping Center, Emerald Isle (252-354-2413). Rucker John's offers freshly prepared sandwiches, salads, pasta, grilled seafood, shrimp, steaks, and chicken. Outdoor dining is available. Lunch and dinner are served daily.

- **New York Deli.** Inexpensive. Morehead City–Atlantic Beach Causeway, Atlantic Beach (252-726-0111). This deli is noted for its authentic Philly cheesesteaks and its subs and salads. It also offers meat-and-cheese party trays and homemade desserts to go. It is open daily.

Nearby

- **Swansboro** is a pretty, historic fishing village located on the White Oak River. This "Friendly City by the Sea," as locals like to refer to it, has been greeting visitors for over 250 years. Among its historic structures are the William Pugh Ferrand Store, erected in 1839, and the Jonathan Green Jr. House, built in the mid-18th century and thought to be the

town's oldest home. Swansboro offers a picture-perfect look at coastal North Carolina life in days gone by. It is a great place to have lunch and browse antique and craft shops. Swansboro is located just over the Emerald Isle bridge on N.C. 24.

- *Hammocks Beach State Park* is considered one of the most beautiful and most unspoiled beaches on the Atlantic coast. Ironically, our nation's ugly segregationist past is largely the reason. In 1914, Dr. William Sharpe, a pioneer in brain surgery, bought the island. Shortly thereafter, he named a black couple, John and Gertrude Hurst, as caretakers. When Sharpe began to receive unsigned letters stating that a black man was unfit to manage the property, he bought an ad in the local paper offering $5,000 for information leading to the arrest and conviction of anyone damaging the island or its occupants. The threats ended.

In the 1940s, when he was an old man, Sharpe decided to leave the island to the Hursts. Mrs. Hurst persuaded him to instead leave it to the North Carolina Teachers Association, a black teachers' alliance. His beloved Hammocks Beach thus fulfilled Sharpe's dream of a "refuge and a place for enjoyment for some of the people whom America treated so badly."

On May 3, 1961, at the dawn of the civil-rights movement, the property was presented to the state. Visitors to Hammocks Beach today enjoy swimming, primitive camping, picnicking, shelling, surf fishing, and nature programs. For information, call 910-326-4881. To reach the park, take the ferry from Hammocks Beach Road (S.R. 1511), located off N.C. 24. Consult the ferry schedule for times.

Wilmington
COURTESY OF NORTH CAROLINA DIVISION OF TOURISM, FILM AND SPORTS DEVELOPMENT

CAPE FEAR COAST

by Anne Holcomb Waters

*T*he name will probably draw you in, just as it did Hollywood. Since the 1980s, the Cape Fear coast has been the location of such feature films as *Billy Bathgate, The Hudsucker Proxy,* and *Blue Velvet.* Currently, it is the film location of the popular television series *Dawson's Creek.* Wilmington, the area's thriving city, has come to be known as the "Hollywood of the East." It is third only to Los Angeles and New York in cinematic productivity.

But this is much more than a pretty, inexpensive place to make movies. The southern promontory of North Carolina's coast gets its name from the deadly shoals at the mouth of its like-named river, the Cape Fear. At the northern edge of the region is Topsail Island, whose name honors its legacy of crafty pirates. Next comes the exclusive Figure Eight Island, where Vice President Gore and family vacationed shortly before this writing. Wilmington, the largest deepwater port in the Southeast, is situated on the banks of the Cape Fear River, as is the quaint port town of Southport, a popular stopover for boaters cruising the Intracoastal Waterway. Along the Atlantic coast east and south of Wilmington are some of the state's premier beaches, including Kure Beach, Carolina Beach, and the fabled Wrightsville Beach. Off Southport is the exclusive Bald Head Island, accessible only by boat. Stretching from Southport to the South Carolina line are the lovely, uncrowded beaches of Brunswick County.

While summer is certainly the most popular time to visit the Cape Fear coast, the area's mild climate makes it an inviting destination any time of year. In the spring, Wilmington is at its showiest during its annual Azalea Festival. In the fall, when the king mackerel are running, fishing tournaments abound. And in winter, Wilmington's vibrant cultural scene heats up the chilly nights. Whenever you choose to visit, the area's abundant recreational opportunities and cultural diversions will make it an ideal destination.

TOPSAIL ISLAND

Midway between Cape Lookout and Cape Fear is the 26-mile barrier island known as Topsail. Although the name sounds like the product of 21st-century resort marketing, legend has it that it dates back to the golden age of piracy, when marauding pirates would moor their vessels in the sound behind the island, waiting to spring on unsuspecting cargo ships. It wasn't long before word spread among ship pilots to keep an eye out for the pirate ships' topsails over the dunes—hence the name. Chances are the infamous pirates Blackbeard and Stede Bonnet roamed these shores. Treasure hunters still flock here with their metal detectors and scuba gear to search for loot.

Written records describing Topsail date from the 1500s, when early European explorers ventured into its protected inland waterways. Artifacts from the Tuscaroras and other Native Americans reveal that the island was a favorite hunting and fishing spot long before white settlers came along.

Interestingly, Topsail Island played an important role in both the Civil

War and World War II. During the Civil War, it was the site of a Confederate saltworks. In World War II, Camp Davis, an enormous antiaircraft training center, was constructed on Topsail. Following the war, Camp Davis was deactivated. The island was subsequently selected as a testing ground for missiles, and Operation Bumblebee was thus born. Some 200 missiles were launched here, resulting in the development of the ramjet engine, which enabled aircraft to break the sound barrier. Concrete observation towers from this era still dot the landscape.

When the military left in 1948, civilians moved in. The island has steadily grown as a resort destination since then. The town of Surf City was incorporated in 1949, followed by Topsail Beach in 1963 and North Topsail Beach in 1990. In 1954, Hurricane Hazel leveled nearly all the buildings on the island. Two more hurricanes, Donna and Diane, later wreaked more havoc. The most recent catastrophic weather came in 1998, but the tenacious islanders rebuilt and are once again ready to welcome visitors to their lovely stretch of sand and surf.

JUST THE FACTS

The island can be reached from U.S. 17 via the bridges at North Topsail Beach and Surf City.

The nearest airports are at Wilmington, to the southwest, and Jacksonville, to the north. There is also a public airstrip in nearby Holly Ridge.

The Greater Topsail Island Chamber of Commerce is located at Treasure Coast Landing on N.C. 50 in Surf City. For information, call 800-626-2780 or 910-329-4446, or visit their website at www.topsailcoc.com.

Things to Do

MUSEUMS AND SCIENCE CENTERS

■ *Topsail Island Museum: Missiles and More*, located at 720 Channel

Boulevard in Topsail Beach, offers Indian artifacts and displays on pirate activity and World War II operations. From April to October, it is open from 2 P.M. to 4 P.M. on Monday, Tuesday, Thursday, Friday, and Saturday. Admission is free, though donations are accepted. Call 800-626-2780 for information.

- The **Surf City Town Hall** has a loggerhead turtle exhibit that uses photographs and a nest facsimile to teach visitors about this area's favorite endangered species. The hall is open daily from 8 A.M. to 5 P.M.

- The **Karen Beasley Sea Turtle Rescue and Rehabilitation Center**, located behind the Topsail Beach Town Hall, offers special tours for groups by appointment. For information, call 910-328-3377, or visit their website at www.seaturtlehospital.org.

RECREATION

- **Surf City Pier**, located in the heart of Surf City, is a favorite local fishing spot. It is open 24 hours a day, seven days a week. No alcoholic beverages are allowed. A fee is charged. Call 910-328-3521.

- Five public golf courses are located within 15 miles of Topsail Island. Call the chamber of commerce at 800-626-2780 or 910-329-4446 for a list.

Places To Stay

RESORTS, HOTELS, AND MOTELS

Though cottage and condominium rentals dominate Topsail Island's accommodations, there are a few other options as well.

- **Breezeway Motel.** Moderate. At the corner of Channel and Davis Streets in Topsail Island (800-548-4694 or 910-328-7751). Located on Topsail Island Sound, the Breezeway offers spacious rooms, a pool, balconies, boat docks, a fishing pier, and a waterfront restaurant.

- **Jolly Roger Motel.** Moderate. 803 Ocean Front Boulevard, Topsail Beach (800-633-3196 or 910-328-4616). Jolly Roger offers 65 oceanfront rooms, efficiencies, and suites, as well as a pier.

- **Tiffany's Motel.** Moderate. N.C. 210 North, Surf City (800-758-3818 or 910-328-1397). This intimate motel has 14 charmingly appointed rooms. On weekends in season, a complimentary breakfast is served in a gathering room that has a dartboard and a fireplace.

- **Sea Vista Motel.** Moderate/Inexpensive. 1521 Ocean Boulevard, Topsail Beach (800-SEA-VISTA or 910-328-2171). Located on the ocean at the south end of N.C. 50, Sea Vista is a five-minute walk from Topsail Sound Pier, where you'll find a general store.

Places to Eat

- **The Breezeway Restaurant.** Moderate. 636 Channel Boulevard, Topsail Beach (910-328-4302). The Breezeway enjoys a solid reputation for its fresh seafood and steaks. It offers waterfront dining. Dinner is served Thursday through Monday.

- **Mollie's Restaurant.** Moderate. 107 North Shore Drive, Surf City (910-328-0505). This friendly restaurant serves breakfast, lunch, and dinner every day but Tuesday. Its specialties include seafood, steaks, pasta, salads, and sandwiches.

- **Soundside Restaurant.** Moderate. 209 North New River Drive, Surf City (910-328-0803). Chef and owner Stephen Sellers takes pride in using fresh local seafood and produce to create his Southern coastal cuisine with a Portuguese flair. From March to November, Soundside serves dinner nightly and brunch on Sunday.

- **Sneads Ferry** is a busy fishing community located on the New River near the northern tip of Topsail Island on N.C. 172. Every August since 1971, the annual **Sneads Ferry Shrimp Festival** has attracted seafood lovers from all over. Proceeds from the festival have enabled the town to build the Shrimp Festival Community Building and acquire a 14-acre park. For information, call 910-327-4911.

- If you're looking for a bite to eat in Sneads Ferry, try the **Riverview Café** (910-327-2011), located at Fulcher's Landing. The Riverview has been offering fresh local seafood since 1946.

Wilmington waterfront
PHOTOGRAPH BY MICHAEL WOLF
COURTESY OF SPROCKET BOX FILM WORKS

WILMINGTON

Until the turn of the 20th century, Wilmington was North Carolina's largest city. Today, it remains one of its most vibrant and interesting.

Thanks to the city's preservation efforts, a large section of downtown spreading out from the banks of the Cape Fear River is recorded on the National Register of Historic Places. Down along the river's edge are Riverfront Park and Riverwalk, a lovely pedestrian path that runs alongside Water Street, a mostly brick-and-cobblestone lane lined with antique lamps. Also along the water are cozy specialty shops and restaurants at Chandler's Wharf and the Cotton Exchange. Many of the city's tour operators are based at the foot of Water Street.

Wilmington's historic and cultural attractions include an array of stunning colonial- and antebellum-era homes, such as the Burgwin-Wright House and Bellamy Mansion, as well as splendid museums like St. John's Museum of Art and the Cape Fear Museum. Boasting more than 200 houses of worship, Wilmington is a showcase of church architecture.

Wilmington's charm has not been lost to popular culture. Over the past two decades, the city has evolved into the third-busiest movie mill in the country. What began in 1983 when Dino DeLaurentiis built a $1.5 million studio has evolved into a multimillion dollar industry. Star spotting is a favorite pastime here. Some Wilmingtonians have caught the acting bug, appearing as extras in the 400-plus films and television shows that have been shot in and around the city.

Much of Wilmington's appeal lies in its long and illustrious history. White settlement in the area came in 1725 at Brunswick Town, located south of the city. Wilmington, founded in 1732, was originally called New Liverpool and subsequently New Carthage and Newton before it was finally named for Spencer Compton, earl of Wilmington. Wilmington proved to be more strategically located than Brunswick Town, which was ultimately abandoned.

From 1720 to 1870, North Carolina led the world in the production of naval stores—tar, pitch, and turpentine—and Wilmington was the primary export center. Its protected position upriver from the turbulent storms and marauding pirates of the Atlantic Ocean would prove the city's salvation again and again.

During the Revolutionary War, the area was spared major bloodshed save for the battle at Moores Creek Bridge, 20 miles north. There, 1,060 clever Patriots outwitted 1,600 Loyalists by tricking them into attacking their evacuated camps by leaving the fires burning. When the Tories attempted to cross the bridge in pursuit, they discovered that only two logs remained—two logs slathered with grease. On April 12, 1781, Lord Cornwallis and company occupied the city following their costly victory at Guilford Courthouse near Greensboro. The troops reconnoitered here for two weeks before their fateful march to Yorktown.

Wilmington grew slowly for the next 50 years, until the Wilmington and Weldon Railroad arrived in 1840. By 1850, Wilmington was the largest city in the state. Over the decade that followed, many of its most impressive buildings—including Thalian Hall, the Zebulon Latimer House, and Bellamy Mansion—were constructed.

In the latter stages of the Civil War, the city became the lifeline of the Confederacy before the fall of Fort Fisher, which overlooked the mouth of the Cape Fear River to the south. Under the fort's protection, stealthy and daring blockade runners played cat and mouse with the formidable Union navy to provide much-needed supplies to the Rebels and to maintain the city's economy. It took the largest war fleet ever assembled to bring down the fort on January 15, 1865. Six months later, Lee surrendered at Appomattox.

After the war, Wilmington endured a brief period of depression until the export of cotton helped the economy rebound. Expansion continued into the 20th century. During the two World Wars, Wilmington flourished as a shipbuilder. In 1952, the North Carolina Ports Authority opened here. Economic decline followed in 1960 when the railroad, the area's chief employer, moved its corporate headquarters. About the same time, recognition of the city's treasure trove of historic architecture spurred a preservation movement. In 1974, much of Wilmington's downtown was recorded on the National Register.

Today, the population of Wilmington is 75,000 and growing. Also growing more numerous are the golf and other resort communities that lure thousands of retirees to the area to bask in its temperate climate and enjoy the dynamic cultural scene. Both those who come to stay and visitors here for the historic sites can testify that another heyday has arrived in Wilmington.

JUST THE FACTS

Wilmington can be reached by Interstate 40 and U.S. 421 from the northwest, U.S. 74/U.S. 76 from the west, and U.S. 17 from the south.

Wilmington International Airport is served by US Airways,

United Express, Midway Corporate Airlines, and A.S.A. Atlantic Southeast, the Delta connection. Call 910-341-4333 for information.

The Trailways bus station is at 201 Harnett Street; call 910-762-6625. The Wilmington Transit Authority provides local bus service; call 910-343-0106.

The Cape Fear Coast Convention and Visitors Bureau is located in the 19th-century courthouse. For information, contact the bureau at 24 North Third Street, Wilmington, N.C. 28401 (800-222-4757 or 910-341-4030; www.cape-fear.nc.us). The Riverfront Information Booth at the foot of Market and Water Streets also provides information. It operates from 9 A.M. to 4:30 P.M. on a seasonal basis.

The local newspaper is the *Wilmington Morning Star*, the state's oldest daily. The free weekly newspapers *Encore* and *Scene* provide up-to-date event listings.

Things to Do

HISTORIC PLACES, GARDENS, AND TOURS

Sightseeing in Wilmington is a treat, especially in the spring and autumn. Although its historic district is one of the largest in the country—over 200 blocks—many of the most interesting sites are concentrated near the Cape Fear River and can easily be seen on foot. However, if you would prefer a nostalgic ride aboard a horse-drawn carriage, a trolley, or a riverboat, opportunities abound.

▪ Information on the **Self-Guided Walking Tour of Attractions and Historic Buildings** and the **River Circle Tour** is available from the Cape Fear Coast Convention and Visitors Bureau. The self-guided River Circle Tour offers a terrific overview of the entire lower Cape Fear area. The driving portion of the tour takes about two hours, including the 40-minute ferry ride from Southport to Fort Fisher. You determine how long to stay

at the sites along the way. Those sites include the Battleship *North Carolina*, Orton Plantation, Brunswick Town, Southport, Fort Fisher, and the North Carolina Aquarium at Fort Fisher. Call 910-341-4030.

■ Engaging guides with straw hats and canes lead **Wilmington Adventure Walking Tours** from the corner of Market and Water Streets. Tours are offered Monday through Saturday from 10 A.M. to 2 P.M. from April to November. A fee is charged. Call 910-763-1785.

■ **Horse-Drawn Carriage and Trolley Tours**, based at Market and Water Streets, offers narrated tours between 10 A.M. and 10 P.M. Tuesday through Sunday from April to October; off-season times vary. A fee is charged. Call 910-251-8889.

■ **Wilmington Trolley Company**, based at Dock and Water Streets, offers an eight-mile, 45-minute narrated tour Tuesday through Sunday from April to October. A fee is charged. Call 910-763-4483 to learn the schedule.

■ **Henrietta III** *Riverboat Cruises* board at the foot of Dock Street for narrated sightseeing, dinner dance, and moonlight cruises. The sightseeing cruise lasts 90 minutes and is offered Tuesday through Sunday at 11:30 A.M. and 2:30 P.M. during the summer. A fee is charged. Call 910-343-1611.

■ Narrated sightseeing tours and a water taxi over to the Battleship *North*

Carolina are offered by **Captain J. N. Maffitt Harbor Tours**. Tours leave from the junction of Dock and Water Streets. A fee is charged. Call 910-343-1611.

- **Screen Gems Studios** offers tours most Saturdays and Sundays. The studios are at 1223 North 23rd Street, near the airport. A fee is charged. Call 910-343-3433.

- **Thalian Hall**, located at 310 Chestnut Street, is an impressive Neoclassical structure built in 1858 and renovated most recently in 1990. Housing both city hall and the Thalian Hall Center for the Performing Arts, the building was designed by John M. Trimble, whose credits include the New York Opera House.

In 1788, the Thalian Association, the oldest amateur theatrical group in the United States, was formed in Wilmington. At the beginning of the 19th century, the group used an auditorium where Thalian Hall now stands. By the time the city acquired that land and announced plans for a new city hall, the Thalians were so entrenched in the cultural scene that citizens demanded the new building also house a theater for the players.

The tradition of excellence has continued through the years. Among the luminaries who have performed or lectured here are Oscar Wilde, Marian Anderson, Charles Dickens, and William Jennings Bryan.

Thalian Hall is open for tours. Prices and hours vary according to group size. For tour information, call 910-343-3660. For box office information, call 800-528-2820 (outside North Carolina) or 910-343-3664. The hall's website may be reached at www.thalianhall.com.

- The **Burgwin-Wright House**, located at 224 Market Street, was built in 1770 upon a foundation of stone from an old jail. This lovely Georgian-style home features 18th- and early-19th-century furnishings and is surrounded by three gardens and an orchard. It was the home of colonial treasurer John Burgwin. When Burgwin fled at the outbreak of the Revolutionary War, Lord Cornwallis and his staff occupied the home. Legend has it that one of Cornwallis's staff members fell in love with a young woman from South Carolina and etched her name in a windowpane. Years later, their son was a guest in the room and spotted his mother's name.

Colonial cooking demonstration at the Burgwin-Wright House
COURTESY OF CAPE FEAR COAST CONVENTION AND VISITORS BUREAU

Now the headquarters of the North Carolina Society of Colonial Dames, the house is open for tours Wednesday through Saturday from 10 A.M. to 5 P.M. Open-hearth cooking demonstrations are offered on the second Saturday of each month in the detached three-story kitchen. An admission fee is charged. For information, call 910-762-0570.

■ The *Zebulon Latimer House*, located at 126 South Third Street, was built in 1852 for a prosperous merchant who had migrated to Wilmington from Connecticut in the 1830s. An elegant, four-story Italianate house, it is a wonderful example of the ornate style so popular in the city at that time. It serves as the headquarters of the Lower Cape Fear Historical Society, which purchased the house and its furnishings from the Latimer family in 1963. Family portraits still adorn the walls. The fourth floor, which is unrestored, is open so visitors can get an idea of what the home looked like prior to restoration. The house is open Monday through Friday from 10 A.M. to 3:30 P.M. and Saturday and Sunday from noon to 5 P.M. Admission is charged. For more information, call 910-762-0492, or visit their website at www.latimer.wilmington.org.

■ *Bellamy Mansion*, at 503 Market Street, is a magnificent antebellum home constructed in 1859 by free black and slave artisans. Designed by James F. Post, it was the residence of Dr. John D. Bellamy and family, who lived here only briefly before fear of the Union army and a yellow-fever epidemic caused them to flee. They returned after the war. The house remained in the family until 1946, when the last surviving daughter, Ellen Bellamy, died. Since then, it has been under the stewardship of

Preservation North Carolina. The restored mansion and Victorian gardens are open for tours. Plans are under way for restoration of the slave quarters and carriage house. The home is open Wednesday through Saturday from 10 A.M. to 5 P.M. and Sunday from 1 P.M. to 5 P.M. Admission is charged. For more information, call 910-251-3700, or visit their website at www.bellamymansionmuseum.org.

■ The *Battleship* **North Carolina**, moored across the Cape Fear River at Eagles Island, was the mightiest sea fighter in World War II. In 1941, as the ship was undergoing sea trials, it passed in and out of New York Harbor so frequently that journalist Walter Winchell dubbed it the "Show Boat" for the Edna Ferber novel and subsequent musical. During the war, it earned 15 battle stars and participated in every major offensive in the Pacific. Decommissioned in 1960, the battleship was relegated to the mothball fleet until North Carolina's citizens—most notably its school-children—raised the necessary $236,000 to bring it to the state.

Tours of the ship take visitors to the engine room, the cobbler's shop, the ship's store, the laundry, the print shop, the crew's mess and quarters, the officers' quarters, the sick bay, the combat information center, and the pilothouse. Audio stations along the way provide insight. The Battleship Memorial Museum, located aboard the ship, displays photographs and artifacts. On permanent display is the "Roll of Honor," a roster of all North Carolinians who died in service during World War II. The visitor center includes bathrooms, a snack bar, and a picnic area. The site is open daily from 8 A.M. to 5 P.M. between September 16 and May 15 and from 8 A.M. to 8 P.M. the rest of the year. Admission is charged. To reach the ship, drive over the Cape Fear Memorial Bridge from Wilmington

Battleship North Carolina
PHOTOGRAPH BY BILL RUSS
COURTESY OF NORTH CAROLINA DIVISION OF TOURISM,
FILM AND SPORTS DEVELOPMENT

or take a water taxi from the bottom of Market Street. Call 910-251-5797.

■ **Oakdale Cemetery** is a very special place often overlooked by visitors. Canopied by tremendous live oak trees, the cemetery is a garden oasis whose stone monuments chronicle the lives of Wilmington's citizenry. It is located on 15th Street off Market Street.

MUSEUMS AND SCIENCE CENTERS

■ **Cape Fear Museum**, located at 814 Market Street, features exhibits and photographs tracing Wilmington's history. It includes a scale model of the city as it looked in 1863. Founded in 1898 by the Daughters of the Confederacy, the museum originally focused on the Civil War. Now, the collection includes material on contemporary Wilmingtonians such as basketball superstar Michael Jordan, football great Rosie Greer, and musician Charlie Daniels. The museum is open Tuesday through Saturday from 9 A.M. to 5 P.M. and Sunday from 2 P.M. to 5 P.M. Admission is charged. Call 910-341-4350.

■ *St. John's Museum of Art*, located at 114 Orange Street, houses note-worthy art by North Carolinians and some outstanding works of well-known 18th- and 19th-century artists from beyond the state's borders, among them Henry Bacon and Daniel Chester Finch, creators of the Lincoln Memorial, and Mary Cassatt. The North Carolina artists represented here include African-Americans Minnie Evans and Romare Bearden. The works are housed in a complex consisting of three historic buildings, one of them the former St. Nicholas Greek Orthodox Church. The museum is open Tuesday through Saturday from 10 A.M. to 5 P.M. and Sunday from 1 P.M. to 4 P.M. Admission is charged except on the first Sunday of each month. For more information, call 910-763-0281, or visit their website at www.stjohnsart.wilmington.org.

■ The *Wilmington Railroad Museum*, at Red Cross and Water Streets, celebrates the glory days of the old iron horse, which once contributed greatly to Wilmington's prosperity. This small museum, staffed by volunteers, is open Monday, Tuesday, Thursday, Friday, and Saturday from 10 A.M. to 5 P.M. and Sunday from 1 P.M. to 5 P.M. Admission is charged. Call 910-763-2634.

CULTURAL OFFERINGS

■ *Opera House Theatre Company*, at 2011 Carolina Beach Road, is a nonprofit organization that presents professional productions featuring guest artists. Call 910-762-4234.

SPECIAL SHOPPING

■ The **Cotton Exchange**, located in the 300 block of Front Street, houses a variety of specialty shops and restaurants in several turn-of-the-century buildings, many of which were cotton warehouses. Most of the shops are open Monday through Saturday from 10 A.M. to 5:30 P.M.

■ **Chandler's Wharf** is located on the waterfront at the corner of Water and Ann Streets. Its boutiques and restaurants offer a range of choices.

RECREATION

■ **Greenfield Gardens**, located on Carolina Beach Road (U.S. 421 South) features a 180-acre cypress-studded lake, paddleboats, and a playground. A path for walking or biking winds around the well-tended flower beds. In summer, the amphitheater is filled with music. Call 910-341-7855.

■ Some 39 golf clubs dot the Cape Fear coast, and that number is growing annually. Contact the Cape Fear Convention and Visitors Bureau to ask for a free **Area Golf Guide**. Some notable course designers who have worked in the area include George Cobb, Willard Byrd, Tom Fazio, and Dan Maples.

SEASONAL EVENTS

■ The **North Carolina Azalea Festival** lures thousands of visitors to Wilmington each April, just when the city is looking its best. Guests enjoy the annual coronation of Queen Azalea, a variety show, a parade, a street fair, a circus, and a concert. The main attraction, of course, is the gardens bursting with dogwood trees and the South's signature azaleas.

- **Riverfest** is held each October in Riverfront Park. Boat races, a raft regatta, music, dancing, and booths offering arts, crafts, and deep-fried food attract visitors and locals alike to the banks of the Cape Fear River. Call 910-452-6862.

Places to Stay

RESORTS, HOTELS, AND MOTELS

- **Best Western Coastline Inn**. Expensive/Moderate. 503 Nutt Street (800-617-7732 or 910-763-2800; www.coastline.com). All the rooms here overlook the river. In-room coffee service, phones with data ports, and fax and copier service are offered. A complimentary continental breakfast is served at your door.

- **Hilton Wilmington Riverside**. Expensive/Moderate. 301 North Water Street (910-763-5900; www.wilmingtonhilton.com). The Hilton has a commanding view of the river. It offers an outdoor pool, an outdoor whirlpool, exercise facilities, two ballrooms, a gift shop, a restaurant and lounge, and a boat dock for those arriving by water. Children stay free with their parents.

- **Greentree Inn**. Moderate. 5025 Market Street (800-225-7666 or 910-799-6001; www.cape-fear.nc.us/greentree). Greentree is centrally located four miles from downtown Wilmington and six miles from Wrightsville Beach. It offers 121 clean, fresh rooms, a pool, cable television, and continental breakfast. Some rooms have mini-bar refrigerators.

INNS AND BED-AND-BREAKFASTS

- **The Graystone Inn**. Deluxe. 100 South Third Street (888-763-4773 or 910-763-2000; www.graystone.com). Originally called Bridgers Mansion, this place was built for Elizabeth Haywood Bridgers in 1905. Innkeepers Paul and Yolanda Bolda have taken care to return it to its turn-of-the-

20th-century grandeur. The Graystone Inn features a spacious parlor, a baby grand piano ready for playing, and an elegantly set dining room.

- **The Inn at St. Thomas Court.** Deluxe/Expensive. 101 South Second Street (910-343-1800; www.innatstthomascourt.com). Located two blocks from the river next door to the 1841 deRossett House, this inn offers Old World charm with modern comforts.

- **The Taylor House Inn.** Expensive. 14 North Seventh Street (800-382-9982 or 910-763-7581). This beautiful Neoclassical home, built in 1908, features large guest rooms with private baths, antique furnishings, ceiling fans, and fireplaces. A full breakfast is served in the dining room.

- **The Wine House.** Expensive. 311 Cottage Lane (910-763-0511). The Wine House features a brick-walled courtyard and two private guest houses. Each suite has a queen-sized bed, a fireplace, a ceiling fan, a refrigerator, a wet bar, and a private bath.

- **Blue Heaven Bed-and-Breakfast.** Expensive/Moderate. 517 Orange Street (910-772-9929; www.bbonline.com/nc/blueheaven). This lovely 1897 Victorian home is a peaceful place to unwind and get a good night's rest. All the rooms have private baths, fireplaces, phones, cable television, VCRs, and air conditioning.

- **Catherine's Inn.** Expensive/Moderate. 410 South Front Street (800-476-0723 or 910-251-0863; www.catherinesinn.com). This Victorian inn, built in 1883, has a wraparound front porch. Its screened-in two-story back porch overlooks a sunken garden and affords a breathtaking view of the Cape Fear River.

- **The Worth House.** Expensive/Moderate. 412 South Third Street (800-340-8559 or 910-762-8562; www.worthhouse.com). This 1893 Queen Anne–style home is located a short stroll from the river. Antiques and period art grace the seven guest rooms, some of which have fireplaces.

- **The Front Street Inn.** Moderate. 215 South Front Street (910-762-6442; www.frontstreetinn.com). This place offers peace and privacy in the midst of the historic district. The Front Street Inn is alive with American art gathered from galleries, fairs, auctions, and attics. The combination bar and breakfast room serves an extensive continental breakfast, along with beer, champagne, and wine.

Places to Eat

The restaurant scene in Wilmington is vibrant and eclectic. Many of the current hot spots are located downtown within easy walking distance of the river.

■ *Deluxe Café*. Expensive. 114 Market Street (910-251-0333). This café offers "Nouveau American" fare with a local flavor. It is open nightly for dinner.

■ *The Under Currant*. Expensive. 10 Market Street (910-815-0810). This excellent restaurant is located in a two-story Federal-style building. Chef Tripp Engel serves up progressive American fare from a menu that changes daily. An extensive wine list has garnered the restaurant accolades. Its signature china and crystal lend a sophisticated air. Upstairs is a sofa bar. Dinner is served daily; reservations are recommended.

■ *Elijah's Restaurant*. Expensive/Moderate. 1 Ann Street in Chandler's Wharf (910-343-1448). Located on the bank of the Cape Fear River, this grill serves delicious local seafood. Guests enjoy dining al fresco here and at Elijah's parent restaurant, the Pilot House. Lunch and dinner are served daily.

■ *Pilot House Restaurant*. Expensive/Moderate. Water Street in Chandler's Wharf (910-343-0200). The venerable Pilot House has been serving fresh seafood for many years. The restaurant overlooks the river and offers outdoor dining. Lunch and dinner are served daily.

■ *Caffé Phoenix*. Moderate. 9 South Front Street (910-343-1395). Caffé

Phoenix is an American bistro offering Mediterranean-influenced food. Lunch and dinner are served daily.

■ **Cedars Authentic Lebanese Taste**. Moderate. 128 Front Street (910-763-5552). This restaurant offers traditional Lebanese food, such as falafel, couscous, and baba ghanouj. It serves dinner Thursday through Sunday; lunch fare is available in the adjoining deli Tuesday through Saturday.

■ **Courtyard Seguin Café**. Moderate. 414 Village Road in nearby Leland (910-383-3222). Louisiana transplants Billy and Rose Seguin have brought their extended family and Cajun cuisine to coastal North Carolina. The café offers seafood gumbo, jambalaya, and other favorites. Lunch is served Monday through Friday and dinner Tuesday through Saturday.

■ **Genki**. Moderate. 419 College Road (910-796-8687). This Japanese restaurant and sushi bar features Maki sushi, sashimi, beef curry, vegetarian entrées, and homemade sauces. It is open nightly for dinner.

■ **German Café**. Moderate/Inexpensive. 316 Nutt Street in the Cotton Exchange (910-763-5523). This café offers delicious and authentic German cuisine. Lunch is served daily and dinner Tuesday through Sunday.

■ **Front Street Brewery**. Inexpensive. 9 North Front Street (910-251-1935). This brewpub offers ribs, steaks, pasta, and sandwiches to go along with its great beer. It is open daily for lunch and dinner.

■ **Front Street Diner**. Inexpensive. 118 South Front Street (910-772-1311). Front Street Diner offers everything from eggs Benedict to fried chicken, muffins, and homemade desserts. Breakfast and lunch are served Wednesday through Monday.

■ **Wilmington Hollywood Connection**. Inexpensive. 1223 North 23rd Street at Screen Gems Studios' commissary building (910-343-1818). Visitors here can get deli sandwiches on freshly baked bread, along with soups and salads. Lunch is served Monday through Saturday.

Basketweaver at Poplar Grove
COURTESY OF CAPE FEAR COAST
CONVENTION AND VISITORS BUREAU

Nearby

■ **Poplar Grove Historic Plantation** is located nine miles north of Wilmington on U.S. 17 at Scotts Hill. The estate was purchased from Joseph Mumford by James Foy, Jr., in 1795. Its 628-acre farm produced peas, corn, and beans and held some 64 slaves. In 1849, the manor house was destroyed by fire. It was rebuilt on its present site in 1850. Relying on peanuts as its staple crop, Poplar Grove remained a focal point of the community under the ownership of the Foy family until its sale in 1971.

Renovated and opened to the public in 1980, the estate now serves as a museum complex consisting of the house, its outbuildings, and 16 acres of grounds. A host of craftspeople demonstrate traditional skills, such as weaving, spinning, basket making, and blacksmithing. The plantation is open Monday through Saturday from 9 A.M. to 5 P.M. and Sunday from noon to 5 P.M. A fee is charged. For more information, call 910-686-9518, or visit their website at www.poplargrove.com.

■ **Orton Plantation Gardens** is located on the Cape Fear River 18 miles south of Wilmington on U.S. 133. The beautiful gardens were the inspiration of Luola Murchison Sprunt and her husband, James, who began constructing terraces overlooking the river and planting avenues of live oak trees in 1910. Five years later, they erected the quaint Luola's Chapel. The gardens were greatly expanded by the Sprunts' son and daughter-in-law under the supervision of landscape architect Robert Swann Sturtevant. The impressive house is not open for tours. Built around 1725 by "King" Roger Moore, the founder of Brunswick Town, it was expanded twice, once in 1840 and again in 1910.

A tour of the gardens takes about an hour, but many choose to stretch a visit into a full morning or afternoon. The gardens open daily at 8 A.M. from March to August and at 10 A.M. from September to November. Admission is charged. Call 910-371-6851.

▪ *Duplin Winery* is located in Rose Hill, 40 miles north of Wilmington on U.S. 117. It follows traditional recipes and methods passed down from the Swiss and German immigrants who settled this part of North Carolina in the 1700s. For groups of 10 or fewer, free tours and tastings of its award-winning scuppernong and muscadine wines are offered Monday through Saturday from 9 A.M. to 5 P.M. The winery is closed on major holidays. On select dates, it offers dinner and a stage show. Call 800-774-9634 or 910-289-3888 for a schedule, or visit their website at www.duplinwinery.com.

Orton Plantation Gardens
COURTESY OF CAPE FEAR COAST CONVENTION AND VISITORS BUREAU

Wrightsville Beach
PHOTOGRAPH BY BILL RUSS
COURTESY OF NORTH CAROLINA DIVISION OF TOURISM, FILM AND SPORTS DEVELOPMENT

WRIGHTSVILLE BEACH

Wrightsville Beach consists of two islands: the inland Harbor Island, connected to the mainland by a drawbridge, and outlying Wrightsville Beach, a four-mile barrier island across Banks Channel. In the past several years, resort and golf communities here have become permanent homes for retirees and others drawn to Wrightsville Beach's beauty and climate. Year-round residents number around 3,200, but when summer rolls around, that number explodes to about 25,000. Although Wrightsville Beach is heavily developed, it is still an exquisite destination. If you don't mind the crowds, head here in the summer. If you do, wait until the off-season, when you can share this bit of coastal paradise with the few who call it home.

Wrightsville Beach is one of the oldest resorts in North Carolina. "The Banks," as it was originally known, was developed in 1853 by a group of enterprising businessmen who erected a clubhouse they called the Carolina Yacht Club. The club remains one of the oldest of its kind in the country. In 1888, the Wilmington Sea Coast Railway accessed Harbor

Island. Shortly thereafter, two bathhouses and a restaurant were built, establishing the island as a resort. After the place was advertised as Ocean View for a time, Wrightsville Beach became the official name in 1900.

In 1905, electric trolleys brought their first passengers to Wrightsville Beach, ushering in its most romantic period. Hoping to entice Wilmingtonians and others to ride the trolleys out to the island, the Tidewater Power Company built several attractions, the foremost of which was the now-legendary Lumina Pavilion, so called for the thousands of incandescent lights that made it sparkle. In the daytime, the Lumina provided bathers with amusements that included bowling alleys, snack bars, and slot machines. In the evening, it shone so brightly that it served as an aid to mariners. Wilmingtonians and visitors from all over the South danced the nights away to the music of Tommy Dorsey, Guy Lombardo, Cab Calloway, and Louis Armstrong in the Lumina's grand ballroom. Outside, silent pictures projected on a large movie screen entertained people on the beach. Sadly, the Lumina fell to the wrecking ball in 1973. But its legend lives on in memory and lore.

Like Pleasure Island and the Brunswick County beaches, Wrightsville Beach was practically demolished by the furious Hurricane Hazel in 1954. Few buildings that stood before Hazel remain today. Luckily, one of them is the 1907 Myers Cottage, which houses Wrightsville Beach's small but alluring museum. Other attractions here include world-class fishing, great shopping, fine dining, and, of course, the seashore and all its pleasures.

JUST THE FACTS

Wrightsville Beach is located about 10 miles east of Wilmington on U.S. 74/U.S. 76. A small drawbridge separates the island from the mainland.

Air service is available through Wilmington International Airport; call 910-341-4333.

For information about the area, contact the Cape Fear Coast Convention and Visitors Bureau, 24 North Third Street, Wilmington, N.C. 28401 (800-222-4757 or 910-341-4030; www.cape-fear.nc.us). The number for the Wrightsville Beach Chamber of Commerce is 800-232-2469.

The local newspaper is the *Wilmington Morning Star*. The free weekly newspapers *Encore* and *Scene* provide event listings.

Wrightsville Beach Museum
COURTESY OF CAPE FEAR COAST
CONVENTION AND VISITORS BUREAU

Things to Do

MUSEUMS AND SCIENCE CENTERS

- The **Wrightsville Beach Museum of History** is housed in the island's fourth-oldest cottage, Myers Cottage. In addition to a collection of artifacts and archival photographs, the museum has a scale model of Wrightsville Beach as it looked around 1910. The museum also hosts traveling exhibits. It is located at 303 West Salisbury Street. The museum is open from noon to 6 P.M. Tuesday through Sunday. A modest admission fee is charged. For information, call 910-256-2569, or visit their website at www.wilmington.org/wbmuseum.

SPECIAL SHOPPING

- **Roberts Market**, located at 32 North Lumina Avenue, has been providing beach residents and visitors with the necessities since 1919. Call 910-256-2641.

- **Boombatti's Homemade Ice Cream** is sure to cool off even the most sunburned vacationer. It is located at 1924-E Eastwood Road. Call 910-256-8330.

RECREATION

This area has one of the largest recreational fishing fleets north of Florida. Numerous charter boats and head boats are available for hire. Contact the Wrightsville Beach Chamber of Commerce at 800-232-2469.

■ The landmark *Johnny Mercer Pier* is currently undergoing reconstruction but should again be open for business about the time this edition hits the stores. Call 910-256-2743.

■ *Wrightsville Beach Park* has a fitness trail, basketball and tennis courts, a children's play area, and sports fields. It is located in the middle of Harbor Island.

■ *The Loop* is a popular 2.5-mile path that runs from downtown to Wrightsville Beach Park. If you're tired of running on the sand, this provides an ideal morning outing, as long as you don't mind sharing it with others walking, jogging, biking, and skating.

SEASONAL EVENTS

■ King mackerel is indeed king around here. The *Wrightsville Beach King Mackerel Tournament* is held in September. For information, call the North Carolina Marine Fisheries Department at 910-395-3900.

Places to Stay

RESORTS, HOTELS, AND MOTELS

■ *Blockade Runner Resort Hotel.* Expensive. 275 Waynick Boulevard (800-541-1161 or 910-256-2251). Although a tad pricey, the Blockade Runner offers an excellent stay at the beach. Celebrating 30 years in business, this well-managed establishment has one of the prettiest, best-maintained stretches of sand on the whole island. Amenities include an outdoor pool, a fitness center, and breakfast. Children under 12 stay free with their parents.

- **Carolina Temple Apartments**. Expensive. 550 Womack Boulevard (910-256-2773). This is the place to go when you've had all the plastic, chrome, and imitation-ivy hanging baskets you can stand. Carolina Temple offers 16 beachfront apartments with kitchenettes. It has a boat dock.

- **Silver Gull Oceanfront Resort Motel**. Expensive/Moderate. U.S. 74 at the ocean end of Salisbury Street (800-842-8894 or 910-256-3728). Like the name says, this motel offers oceanfront rooms. Guests enjoy the private balconies and kitchenettes. Silver Gull was completely refurbished in 1994.

Places to Eat

- **Oceanic Restaurant**. Expensive/Moderate. 703 South Lumina Avenue (910-256-5551). Oceanic's local awards include "Best Water View," "Best Grilled Seafood," and "Best Restaurant." In addition to seafood, it offers superb steaks and fresh pasta dishes. Lunch and dinner are served daily.

- **Brown Dog Grill**. Moderate. 7105 Wrightsville Avenue (910-256-2688). Brown Dog serves a delicious array of seafood and other meats cooked on a wood-burning grill. It offers daily chef's specials, an excellent wine list, and beer from Wilmington's Front Street Brewery. Dinner is served Monday through Saturday.

- **The Olympia Restaurant**. Moderate. 212 Causeway Drive (910-256-5514). The Olympia offers fresh seafood, Mediterranean specialties, steaks, Greek salads, a full bar, and an eclectic wine list. Dinner is served daily; brunch is offered on Sunday.

- **Southbeach Grill**. Moderate. 100 South Lumina Avenue (910-256-4646). This grill offers outdoor dining overlooking Banks Channel. Its creative beach cuisine centers around fresh seafood and innovative seasonal entrées. Lunch and dinner are served daily.

Pleasure Island
PHOTOGRAPH BY S. CROWDER
COURTESY OF THE CAPE FEAR CONVENTION
AND VISITORS BUREAU

PLEASURE ISLAND

Carolina Beach, Kure Beach, and Fort Fisher make up Pleasure Island. This area prides itself on its clean, uncrowded beaches, reasonably priced accommodations, and friendly atmosphere. Don't be discouraged by the commercial nature of the drive in on U.S. 421—the beaches on the other side of all the buildings are well worth the visit.

Carolina Beach occupies the northern end of the island, while Kure is located at its southern end, next to Fort Fisher. Both beaches are characterized by cottages, family-owned motels and restaurants, and a small-town air. Carolina Beach is the livelier and more developed of the two.

Despite its lack of old buildings, Carolina Beach dates from the late 19th century, when Joseph L. Winner, a Wilmington merchant, purchased 108 acres to develop into a resort town. Although his town, which he called St. Joseph, never took off, other developers followed his lead. By 1915, Carolina Beach had both electricity and a paved road leading to Wilmington.

In 1954, Hurricane Hazel devastated the town, leveling some 362 cottages and other buildings and damaging that many again.

Today, Carolina Beach takes pride in its post-Hazel renaissance. With its boardwalk, pier, Ferris wheel, merry-go-round, gazebo, and arcade, it is a slice of coastal Americana. And of course, it wouldn't be the beach without the requisite water slides and miniature golf courses. Fishing is also a major activity here; anglers can test their skills on piers, in the surf, and on deep-sea charters. Carolina Beach State Park invites hikers, picnickers, and campers to explore the area's vast array of vegetation.

As you drive across the island to Kure Beach, you'll no doubt notice the devices along the road that look like solar panels. For decades, the federal government has been conducting an experiment here to determine the corrosive effects of salty sea air on various types of metals.

Kure Beach is a small, family-oriented community dominated by vacation cottages and mom-and-pop motels and restaurants. It is named for its founder, Hans Kure, who acquired land here in 1891. In the 1930s, Kure Beach was the site of the world's first installation for the extraction of bromine from seawater. (Years ago, ethylene dibromide was the ingredient that made leaded gasoline safe—or so they thought.) Among other riches discovered while testing the seawater were gold, silver, copper, and aluminum. During World War II, a German U-boat fired—actually, misfired—upon the plant, despite heavy security. Shortly after the war, the laboratory closed.

Popular pastimes here today include fishing and strolling on the 711-foot-long Kure Beach Fishing Pier, picnicking at nearby Fort Fisher, and enjoying the sand and surf.

JUST THE FACTS

Pleasure Island is located about 12 miles south of Wilmington on U.S. 421.

It can also be reached via the Southport/Fort Fisher toll ferry.

Air travelers will need to make arrangements through Wilmington International Airport; call 910-341-4333.

For information on the area, contact the Pleasure Island Chamber of Commerce at 1140-B North Lake Park Boulevard, Carolina Beach, N.C. 28428 (910-458-8434; www.caro-kure.wilmington.net).

The weekly newspapers of Pleasure Island are the *Island Gazette* and the *Weekly News*.

Cannon at Fort Fisher
COURTESY OF CAPE FEAR COAST
CONVENTION AND VISITORS BUREAU

Things to Do

HISTORIC PLACES, GARDENS, AND TOURS

■ *Fort Fisher State Historic Site* is located on U.S. 421 south of Kure Beach. Named for Colonel Charles Fisher, a North Carolina hero who died at First Manassas, Fort Fisher was the Civil War's largest earthen fortress, built to protect the port of Wilmington. In January 1865, some 10,000 Federal troops and history's heaviest naval bombardment to that date finally brought down the fort, signaling the end of the Civil War. What remains of the fort today is slowly being eroded by the effects of time and the sea, despite efforts to protect it. The state has seeded the mounds that remain; a trail leads around them and offers views of the Cape Fear River.

A trip to the visitor center will give you an idea of the fort's former stature and its role in protecting Wilmington and the daring blockade runners that ran supplies to the Confederacy. Visitors can enjoy a slide show, dioramas, artifacts, and a complete model of Fort Fisher, which was studied in classrooms at West Point following the Civil War. The grounds include a picnic area. From April to October, the site is open Monday through Saturday from 9 A.M to 5 P.M. and Sunday from 1 P.M. to 5 P.M. From November to March, it is open Tuesday to Saturday from 10 A.M. to 4 P.M. and Sunday from 1 P.M. to 4 P.M. It is closed Christmas and New Year's. Admission is free. Call 910-458-5538.

MUSEUMS AND SCIENCE CENTERS

■ The *North Carolina Aquarium at Fort Fisher* is located across the road from Fort Fisher State Historic Site. The southernmost of the three marine resource centers along the coast, it features aquariums and exhibits and houses conference rooms and laboratories. The aquarium is currently closed due to a major renovation and expansion; it is expected to reopen in the spring of 2002. For more information, call 910-458-8257.

RECREATION

■ *Carolina Beach State Park* is 10 miles south of Wilmington on U.S. 421. Located inland on the Intracoastal Waterway, it encompasses 712 acres of varying ecosystems, including dune ridges of longleaf pine and turkey oak, longleaf and evergreen savannas, pocosins, and brackish tidal marshes. It is home to the indigenous carnivorous Venus flytrap, red sundew, and pitcher plant. Five hiking trails are offered, as are a marina and facilities for camping, fishing, and picnicking. During the summer, nature programs are held in the park's amphitheater. Call 910-458-8206.

■ At *Fort Fisher State Recreation Area*, located near Fort Fisher State Historic Site, visitors can picnic in the shade of lovely live oak trees after enjoying a morning on the four-mile stretch of undeveloped beach. Restrooms, showers, and a snack bar are provided. Call 910-458-8206.

- **Kayak Carolina** offers a two-hour introduction to the sport, as well as an interpretive nature tour. For information, call 910-458-9111, or visit their website at www.kayakcarolina.com.

The convergence of the Cape Fear River, the Intracoastal Waterway, and the Atlantic Ocean make Pleasure Island one of the premier bottom-, pier-, and surf-fishing destinations on the East Coast. The Carolina Beach yacht basin is a center for boating activities. A number of charter boats (limited to six passengers) and head boats (up to 150 passengers) are based there.

Seasonal Events

- Pleasure Island hosts two fishing tournaments a year: the **East Coast Classic King Mackerel Tournament** in July and the **Carolina Beach Surf-Fishing Tournament** in October. Call the chamber of commerce at 910-458-8434 for information.

- The second weekend of October ushers in the annual **Pleasure Island Seafood, Blues, and Jazz Festival**. The event takes place overlooking the Cape Fear River at the Fort Fisher Air Force Base Recreation Area. Call 910-458-8434 for information.

- All of Pleasure Island is illuminated with Christmas displays during the annual **Island of Lights** celebration from mid-November through New Year's Eve. The festivities include a parade, a flotilla, and a tour of homes. Call 910-458-7116 for information.

Places to Stay

Pleasure Island is thick with accommodations, so the following list is by no means inclusive. Be mindful that rates vary greatly according to the season. Many places have a two-day minimum, particularly on weekends. In summer, some even have a week's minimum. The chamber of commerce can provide you with a list of rental cottages and condominiums; call 910-458-8434.

RESORTS, HOTELS, AND MOTELS

■ **Sand Dunes Motel**. Expensive/Moderate. 133 Fort Fisher Boulevard, Kure Beach (800-535-4984 or 910-458-5470; www.thesanddunes.com). Sand Dunes has 39 rooms and efficiencies, 29 of which are oceanfront. A lifeguard is on duty during the summer. The motel offers beach-side Adirondack chairs for relaxing.

■ **Savannah Inn**. Expensive/Moderate. 316 Carolina Beach Avenue North, Carolina Beach (910-458-6555). This inn offers clean oceanfront rooms and efficiencies individually decorated with beach decor. A three-night minimum is required during the summer.

■ **Golden Sands**. Moderate. 1211 South Lake Park Boulevard, Carolina Beach (888-458-8334 or 910-458-8334; www.coastalcarolinas.com/goldensands). This place has 88 rooms and efficiencies and offers a pool.

■ **Surfside Motor Lodge**. Moderate. 234 Carolina Beach Avenue North, Carolina Beach (910-458-8338). Located half a block from the boardwalk, Surfside offers oceanfront rooms and efficiencies, two pools, and color cable television.

■ **Admiral's Quarters Motel**. Moderate/Inexpensive. U.S. 421, Kure Beach (910-458-5050; www.admiralsquartersmotel.com). Admiral's Quarters has 37 rooms, all but three of which are oceanside. All have private porches or balconies with rocking chairs. The motel offers two pools, a gazebo, and a sandy playground for the kids.

■ **Docksider Inn**. Moderate/Inexpensive. U.S. 421, Kure Beach (910-458-4200; www.docksiderinn.com). Located on the ocean, Docksider offers rooms with a nautical theme. Its suites have whirlpool baths.

■ **Sandstep Motel**. Moderate/Inexpensive. 619 Carolina Beach Avenue North, Carolina Beach (800-934-4076 or 910-458-8387; www.sandstep.com). Located at the north end of the beach, this 40-room family-run motel complex is housed in five buildings, two of them oceanfront. It has rooms with two double beds and a bath, a coffee maker, and a refrigerator. It offers two pools. Pets are allowed, but call ahead to let them know.

- **Sea Ranch Motel.** Moderate/Inexpensive. 1123 Lake Park Boulevard, Carolina Beach (800-849-8977 or 910-458-8681). For 24 years, the Vernon family has run Sea Ranch, located at the southern end of Carolina Beach.

INNS AND BED-AND-BREAKFASTS

- **Darlings by the Sea.** Deluxe/Expensive. 329 Atlantic Avenue, Kure Beach (800-383-8111 or 910-458-4200; www.darlingsbythesea.com). This inn offers five oceanfront rooms complete with whirlpool baths. Fitness rooms, a courtyard, and a sun deck are on the premises. Darlings by the Sea markets itself primarily to couples.

- **Dolphin Watch Inn Bed-and-Breakfast.** Expensive. 910 Carolina Beach Avenue North, Carolina Beach (800-846-8191 or 910-458-5355; www.dolphinwatchbandb.com). This 1950s beach cottage, renovated in 1990, features a wraparound porch and private dune walkover. Complimentary beach chairs and boogie boards are provided for guests. Children under 16 are not allowed.

Places to Eat

- **The Cottage Restaurant.** Expensive/Moderate. 1 North Lake Park Boulevard, Carolina Beach (910-458-4383). Indoor and outdoor dining are offered at this restaurant, located in a 1916 beach cottage. The Cottage has a contemporary menu featuring fresh seafood, pasta, chicken, veal, lamb, and steak. Lunch and dinner are served Monday through Saturday.

- **Big Daddy's Restaurant.** Moderate. 206 Kure Avenue, Kure Beach (910-458-8622). Big Daddy's has been serving "seafood at its best" since 1968. It offers steak, prime rib, and chicken, too, as well as a full bar and special menus for seniors and children. Dinner is served nightly; lunch is served on Sunday.

- **Kiva Grill.** Moderate. 8211 Market Street, Kure Beach (910-686-8211). The fare at Kiva Grill has Southwestern and Pacific Rim influences. Lunch and dinner are served daily.

- **Marina's Edge.** Moderate. 300 North Lake Park Boulevard, Carolina Beach (910-458-6001). For seafood lovers, Marina's Edge offers fresh fish, lobster, and a raw bar. For the rest, it has plenty of chicken and steak entrées. Dinner is served nightly; lunch is served Saturday and Sunday.

The Blockade Takes the Life of a Rebel Spy

Excerpted from Dawson Carr's *Gray Phantoms of the Cape Fear*

Rose O'Neal Greenhow's brief career as a Southern spy had already exposed her to danger. Her husband, Dr. Robert Greenhow, had been a native Virginian whose position in the State Department had brought him to Washington. There, Rose quickly endeared herself to members of government and the city's elite. After her husband's death, she continued to reside in Washington, although her heart was in the South.

When the war broke out, she resolved to do all in her power to help the Rebels. Upon learning details of the North's plan to attack at Manassas in July 1861, she passed the word to Confederate general P. G. T. Beauregard. Some say this information allowed the Rebels to make advance preparations that led to a major triumph.

Greenhow was later held under arrest in Washington and nearly thrown in prison for passing information to Southern military leaders. At her trial, she was given the option of swearing allegiance to the United States, but she haughtily declined. Uncertain what to do with such a woman, the Union eventually agreed to pardon her if she would at least swear to leave the North and never return. To this, she agreed.

But that did not mean she would abandon the cause. Greenhow understood the importance of good relations between England and the South. She decided to try her hand at being a Confederate agent in Europe. . . .

Her trip to Europe proved more successful than even she had hoped. Honored by high officials in both England and France, Greenhow also won popularity among the residents of those two nations, especially the British. While in England, she published her memoirs, entitled *My Imprisonment and the First Year of Abolition Rule at Washington*. The book was well received all over England, helping further her goal of influencing public opinion in favor of the Confederacy. Copies were snatched up eagerly by people anxious to read a firsthand account of the war across the Atlantic—and especially to hear the story of such an attractive and popular spy.

Now, as she prepared to travel back to Wilmington, Greenhow carried several thousand dollars in gold coins, her share of the profits from the book's sales. Of all the Southern patriots who came across the sea to win over the English, it's unlikely that any was as well liked as she, and it was with some regret that she was leaving. Yet she missed her friends back across the Atlantic and wanted to see them again in spite of the dangers of the forthcoming voyage. Also, it was rumored that she carried secret dispatches for President Jefferson Davis.

She stepped aboard the new blockade runner *Condor*—a magnificent gray behemoth with three stacks and remarkable speed—as the vessel prepared to leave Scotland in September 1864. The captain was a furloughed British naval officer using the alias Samuel Ridge. . . .

It was the first week of October when the *Condor* reached the vicinity of New Inlet. Guiding her was Thomas Brinkman, one of the small cadre of Smithville pilots who helped blockade runners reach the Cape Fear River through the maze of sand bars and shoals. Brinkman directed the shadowy vessel along the shoreline, taking advantage of her seven-foot draft to cruise at the very edge of the surf. The skies were stormy that night, and although waves rocked the ship, the crewmen were thankful for the additional cover. . . .

In the darkest part of the night, just before dawn, the *Condor* increased speed as she approached the mound battery at Fort Fisher, now faintly visible a couple of miles ahead. Unfortunately, the omnipresent *Niphon* was waiting. . . .

Rose O'Neal Greenhow was desperate, believing that the enemy would board the *Condor* momentarily and that she would be arrested. She pleaded with Captain Ridge to take her to shore, but he tried to reassure her that once daylight arrived, they could make it to the beach safely. He explained that the stormy weather made the sea too dangerous for an attempt in the dark. Still, she begged him until he finally relented.

The captain asked three of his most experienced crewmen to launch a lifeboat and deliver her to shore. As soon as they were aboard the small craft, a monstrous wave overturned it, and all aboard were tossed into the swirling waters. The men all surfaced and made their way to land. But Greenhow was never seen alive again, as the heavy gold coins she carried in her garments pulled her to the bottom. . . .

Greenhow [is] . . . buried in Oakdale Cemetery in the heart of [Wilmington].

Waterfront Park in Southport
COURTESY OF PHILLIP MORGAN AND SOUTHPORT-OAK ISLAND CHAMBER OF COMMERCE

SOUTHPORT AND THE BRUNSWICK COUNTY BEACHES

Just walking underneath the huge, sprawling oak trees that line Southport's avenues takes you back to a gentler time. Although a laid-back attitude is pervasive, Southport is a bustling town. Originally named Smithville for Benjamin Smith, a Continental Army general who later became governor, Southport was renamed in 1887 to reflect its geography.

Located midway between New York and Miami along the Intracoastal Waterway, Southport is a vibrant port of call for boaters. It has also become well known for its concentration of antique shops, its historic sites, and its wonderful restaurants, art galleries, and parks. The most popular park in Southport is Waterfront Park. From there, you can watch ocean ships pass on their way up the Cape Fear River to Wilmington, a remarkable photographic opportunity. Southport itself is so photogenic that a number of motion pictures and television films have been made here.

A good place to begin is Southport 2000, the town's visitor center, located on West Moore Street. Here, you can pick up maps, brochures, and information for self-guided walking tours. Just around the corner is the North Carolina Maritime Museum at Southport. Take time out to enjoy Southport's historic business district, especially the many antique shops along Howe and Moore Streets. Also, be sure to stroll the Southport Riverwalk and visit the shops around the yacht basin and near the marina. Finally, take time to enjoy some local seafood.

Wind-swept live oaks and yaupon trees grace Oak Island, a 10-mile stretch of beach with quiet surf and moderate tides. This family-oriented community offers water activities for all ages. Its three piers, its marina, and its public launch facilities make it popular with fishermen, especially those looking for king mackerel.

Oak Island grew from a few prewar cottages to a community of over 300 homes after World War II. In 1954, Hurricane Hazel destroyed all but five houses here. Incorporated in July 1999, the town of Oak Island consists of the communities once known as Long Beach and Yaupon Beach.

Named after the historic Fort Caswell, located at the top of the island, Caswell Beach is home to the brightest lighthouse in the United States. It also boasts a Coast Guard Station reminiscent of the old lifesaving stations. Deep dunes and sprawling beach cottages line the ocean. On the marsh side, cottages on pilings overlook the Cape Fear River's shipping channel. The only souvenirs available at Caswell Beach are the shells collected on quiet, low-tide walks along the beautiful shore.

Caswell Beach
Courtesy of North Carolina's Brunswick Islands

Holden Beach is an 11-mile south-facing island. It, too, was devastated by Hurricane Hazel in 1954, but developers lost no time in making certain that there was ample rental space for its numerous visitors. The western end of Holden overlooks Shallotte Inlet, a shrimp-boat harbor said to possess waters with curative powers. At Windy Point, the story goes, people have been mysteriously cured of infections. The most plausible reason is a type of reed that grows here but nowhere else. Although the water's curative power is unsubstantiated by scientists, people have come here from as far away as Canada to put it to the test.

Ocean Isle Beach and Sunset Beach round out the Brunswick County beaches. Ocean Isle boasts the terrific Museum of Coastal Carolina. Sunset Beach is considered by many to be the most beautiful of North Carolina's southern islands.

JUST THE FACTS

Southport, located about 25 miles south of Wilmington, can be reached via N.C. 133 or N.C. 87. Beware that numerous logging trucks use these roads and that some of their drivers are aggressive. For a more scenic approach, take the Fort Fisher ferry from Pleasure Island. Oak Island can be reached by N.C. 133. The three southern Brunswick islands are connected to U.S. 17 by small state roads.

Several agencies supply information about the area. You may contact the Southport–Oak Island Chamber of Commerce at 4841 Long Beach Road SE, Southport, N.C. 28461 (800-457-6964). You may contact Southport 2000 at 113 West Moore Street, Southport, N.C. 28461 (910-457-7927; www.oak-island.com). For information on Holden Beach, Ocean Isle Beach, and Sunset Beach, contact the South Brunswick Islands Chamber of Commerce, P.O. Box 1380, Shallotte, N.C. 28459 (800-426-6644 or 910-754-6644).

The *State Port Pilot* and the *Brunswick Beacon* are the local weekly papers.

Things to Do

HISTORIC PLACES, GARDENS, AND TOURS

■ **Southport Trail** is a self-guided tour map available from the visitor center and the Southport Historical Society (800-388-9635). This one-mile walk through town visits many interesting sites. A few are described below.

■ The **Adkins-Ruark House**, located at 119 North Lord Street at the corner of Nash Street (and now privately owned), is where author and journalist Robert Ruark spent his childhood summers. His book *The Old Man and the Boy* is an account of his time in Southport.

■ **Keziah Memorial Park**, located on Moore Street, features the Indian Trail Tree, which is several hundred years old. This live oak was deliberately bent by Native Americans to create a landmark to guide them.

■ Gentleman pirate Stede Bonnet was making repairs to his ship, *The Revenge*, when Colonel William Rhett caught up with him at what is now called **Bonnet's Creek**. A one-time wealthy planter, Bonnet is said to have taken to piracy to get away from his shrewish wife.

MUSEUMS AND SCIENCE CENTERS

■ The **North Carolina Maritime Museum at Southport**, located at 116 North Howe Street, houses materials pertaining to the nautical history of the lower Cape Fear. A self-guided tour leads among 12 exhibits linked to each other through a story line. Shipwrecks, navigational aids, and fishing are covered, as is the history of Southport. The museum is open Tuesday through Saturday from 9 A.M. to 5 P.M. An admission fee is charged for visitors over age 16. Call 910-457-0003.

■ The **Museum of Coastal Carolina**, located at 21 East Second Street in Ocean Isle Beach, is a handsome, 7,500-square-foot building constructed in 1991. A hands-on interactive museum, it explores the natural history and heritage of the area. From Memorial Day to Labor Day, it is open Tuesday, Wednesday, Friday, and Saturday from 9 A.M. to 5 P.M., Monday and Thursday from 9 A.M. to 9 P.M., and Sunday from 1 P.M. to 5 P.M. The rest of the year, it is open Friday and Saturday from 9 A.M. to 5 P.M. and Sunday from 1 P.M. to 5 P.M. Call 910-579-1016 for more information.

CULTURAL OFFERINGS

■ Housed in a 1904 schoolhouse that subsequently became city hall, then the library, the **Franklin Square Art Gallery** features the work of local artists working in a variety of media. Legend has it that if you drink from the hand pump in Franklin Square Park, you're sure to return to the town. The gallery is closed from Christmas to Valentine's Day. Call 910-457-5450.

Franklin Square Art Gallery
COURTESY OF PHILLIP MORGAN AND
SOUTHPORT-OAK ISLAND CHAMBER OF COMMERCE

SPECIAL SHOPPING

Southport has a reputation for its antique shops. More than 15 shops and 75 dealers trade here. Head for Howe and Moore Streets to visit a concentration of them.

Oyster Bay Golf Links at Sunset Beach
COURTESY OF NORTH CAROLINA'S BRUNSWICK ISLANDS

RECREATION

■ *Scuba South Diving Company* is located at 222 South River Drive in Southport. Owner and skipper Wayne Strickland leads shipwreck scuba tours amid Frying Pan Shoals. A boat leaves at 7 A.M. daily to explore the ruins of such crafts as the *City of Houston* (a steamship) and the *Sherman* (a blockade runner). Call 910-457-5201.

SEASONAL EVENTS

■ Two annual fishing tournaments—the *U.S. Open King Mackerel Tournament* (based at Southport Marina) and the *South Brunswick Islands King Mackerel Classic* (based at Holden Beach Marina)—offer $100,000 in prizes each. Call 800-426-6644 for details.

■ The *North Carolina Oyster Festival* is held in Shallotte in mid-October. What began as a tiny oyster roast in 1979 has now grown into the official North Carolina oyster celebration. The highlight is an oyster-shucking championship. Call 910-754-6644 for information.

■ Every December, Southport's *Christmas by the Sea* celebration offers home tours and a parade of decorated seafaring vessels. Call 800-457-6964 for information.

- The **North Carolina Festival by the Sea** is held the last full weekend of October in Holden Beach. More than 150 arts-and-crafts vendors congregate here to show their wares. Call 910-842-3828 for details.

Places to Stay

RESORTS, HOTELS, AND MOTELS

- **The Winds Inn and Suites**. Expensive/Moderate. 310 East First Street, Ocean Isle Beach (800-334-3581 or 910-579-6275; www.TheWinds.com). The Winds offers a complimentary breakfast buffet, three pools, a garden bar and restaurant, and golf packages.

- **Blue Water Point Motel and Marina**. Moderate. 5710 West Beach Place, Oak Island (888-634-9005 or 910-278-1230; www.bwpresort.com). This motel offers rooms with a view of the water, cable television, mini-refrigerators, coffee pots, a restaurant, and free sunset cruises for guests during the summer season.

- **Cape Fear Inn**. Moderate. 308 East Bay Street, Southport (910-457-5989). This inn offers 12 rooms furnished with antiques; each has a private bath. Guests enjoy cable television, telephones, a complimentary breakfast, and afternoon refreshments.

- **The Driftwood Motel**. Moderate. 604 Ocean Drive, Oak Island (910-278-6114). Family-owned and operated for 25 years, this motel has a pool, a central guest kitchen, laundry facilities, outdoor grills, and picnic tables. Every room has a refrigerator.

- **Lois Jane's Riverview Inn**. Moderate. 106 West Bay Street, Southport (800-457-1152 or 910-457-6701). This 1890s home was built by Lois Jane's grandfather and restored by her children in 1995. The inn is furnished with period antiques, many of them family heirlooms. It offers two rooms with private baths and two with a shared bath. Breakfast is included in the room rate.

Places to Eat

- **Betty's Waterfront Restaurant.** Moderate. Off Old Ferry Road in Holden Beach (910-842-3381). Betty's offers fresh seafood any way you want it: grilled, fried, blackened, or broiled. Chicken and steak are also on the menu. Dinner is served Monday through Saturday.

- **Bogeys Restaurant.** Moderate. 5908 East Oak Island Drive, Oak Island (910-278-4400). Bogeys features jazz on Friday and Saturday evenings. Lunch and dinner are served Tuesday through Saturday.

- **Crabby-Oddwaters Restaurant.** Moderate/Inexpensive. 310 Sunset Boulevard, Sunset Beach (910-579-6372). This place is located upstairs from Bill's Seafood Market, the source of its fare. To get fresher seafood, you'd have to catch it yourself. Dinner is served Thursday through Saturday.

- **Jones' Seafood House.** Moderate/Inexpensive. 6404 East Oak Island Drive, Oak Island (910-278-5231). This family-owned restaurant specializing in Calabash-style seafood has been a local favorite since it opened its doors in 1964. Dinner is served daily.

- **Ship's Chandler Restaurant.** Moderate/Inexpensive. 101 West Bay Street, Southport (910-457-6595). The Ship's Chandler serves seafood, sandwiches, and salads for lunch and steaks, specialty dishes, and more seafood for dinner. It is open daily except Monday.

- **Buck's Pizza.** Inexpensive. On the causeway at Holden Beach (910-842-2858). Buck's uses only fresh ingredients in its hand-tossed pizzas, stromboli, and hoagies. Lunch and dinner are offered daily.

Nearby

- For nearly 50 years, seafood lovers have flocked to the small town of **Calabash,** located off U.S. 17 just north of the South Carolina line, for some original "Calabash-style" seafood, lightly battered and fried. It has been estimated that there is one restaurant for every 75 of Calabash's 1,300 citizens. Try **Barracuda Bar & Grille** at 1224 Riverview Drive (910-579-5066), **Dockside Seafood House** on the Calabash River (910-579-6775), or any of the restaurants along U.S. 179. Be prepared for a wait in summer.

▪ Once a haven for pirates, **Bald Head Island** is a pristine triangle of land south of Wilmington. It is accessible only by water. You can ferry over to the island from Southport or cruise in your own boat to the harbor. On my first Blair staff retreat, we stayed in Wilmington and took a day trip to Bald Head. While we didn't get a glimpse of any of Bald Head's famous loggerhead turtles, we did enjoy a pleasant tour that included a hike into the island's remaining patch of maritime forest and a climb up Old Baldy, the oldest lighthouse in the state. Old Baldy is privately owned, so access is restricted.

Aside from a handful of utility vehicles, automobiles are not allowed on the island, so the speediest way to get around is by golf cart. Since 1986, the state's portion of the island—10,000 acres—has been designated a "day-use state park." The remaining land is privately owned and under careful development. The upscale resort here consists of the **Marsh Harbour Inn and Conference Center**, a championship golf course, a variety of rental cottages and condominiums, and **Theodosia's**, a deluxe inn featuring 10 individually decorated rooms; for information, call 800-656-1812 or 910-457-6563, or visit their website at www.southport.net/theodosia. Some vacation packages include round-trip ferry passage and use of the club. Contact the information center at 5079 Southport-Supply Road, Southport, N.C. 28461 (800-432–RENT; www.southport.net).

▪ Museum artifacts, crumbling foundations, and the walls of St. Philips Church are all that is left of historic **Brunswick Town**, located 18 miles south of Wilmington on N.C. 133. Founded in 1726 by Maurice Moore, one of the enterprising sons of a former South Carolina governor, Brunswick was the site of the first colonial rebellion against British rule. In 1766, eight years before the Boston Tea Party, some 150 armed citizens known as the "Sons of Liberty" encircled customs officials and forced them to take an oath that they would issue no more stamped paper.

"Old Baldy"
COURTESY OF NORTH CAROLINA'S BRUNSWICK ISLANDS

Brunswick Town initially flourished as a port for shipping tar, pitch, and turpentine. But despite its early promise, it was abandoned soon after New Bern took over as the state capital and Wilmington assumed prominence.

After decades of calm, the site again took on a historic role in 1861, when an earthen fortress, **Fort Anderson**, was constructed to protect Confederate blockade runners against the Union navy. In 1865, following the fall of Fort Fisher at the mouth of the Cape Fear River, Union forces attacked Fort Anderson by land and water. After three days of fighting, the Confederates evacuated the fort in the dark of night.

Now a State Historic Site, Brunswick Town is open Monday through Saturday from 9 A.M. to 5 P.M. and Sunday from 1 P.M. to 5 P.M. from April to October. From November to March, it is open Tuesday to Saturday from 10 A.M. to 4 P.M. and Sunday from 1 P.M. to 4 P.M. It is closed major holidays. Admission is free. For information, call 910-371-6613, or visit their website at www.ah.dcr.state.nc.us/hs/brunswic/brunswic.htm.

THE PIEDMONT

The Triangle

Raleigh

Durham

Chapel Hill and Carrboro

Research Triangle Park

Triangle Nearby

*W*hat history we have of pre-European North Carolina tells us that trade and settlement along the Eno and Haw Rivers, on up to the Tar and the Dan, drew so much traffic that the area eventually became part of the Great Indian Trading Path, a corridor of roads and trails between the Chesapeake Bay region and the Indian towns in the Carolinas and Georgia. The path served Indian commerce prior to European colonization and was the principal avenue for joining cultures in the southeastern Piedmont of what became the United States. It ran directly through what is now the Triangle.

The number of tribes that converged at the path in this area was significant: the Eno, the Occoneechi, the Algonquin, the Tuscarora. Diversity and the spirit of cultural exchange have characterized this vibrant area since at least those times.

This triangular spot now sits on the great American trading path that runs from New York to Atlanta and Miami. More importantly, it sits at the convergence of three major universities and nearly a dozen colleges. These educational riches prompted the placement of Research Triangle Park, and the rest is history.

The three-city area of Raleigh, Durham, and Chapel Hill is now one of the fastest-growing technical communities in the world. The effects, of course, are at least two-sided. The rapid development is slowly but surely eliminating the area's famed greenery, despite concerted efforts to develop an ecological consciousness. But what has also grown, geometrically, is the area's cultural diversity. The tribes of the North come down to mix and mingle with those of the South. They share life, culture, and information with representatives from all over the world who come to join the educational and technological growth. The result is a Southern anomaly: In this 60-mile spread, you can find almost anything you can imagine. There is world music, and there is world food. There are art films, and there are Southern barbecue houses. There are world-class museums, and there are rivers to raft. You can buy arugula, or you can buy okra. There is hi-tech conversation in magnolia-scented air. There is modern dance next to a Gothic cathedral. There is gospel, and there is opera. And there are celebrations of every group that can be celebrated.

You can't possibly do everything there is to do here in a couple of days, so spend a week. Walk around each one of these towns if you can, because each has a very specific flavor. Take the time to find the streets where people like to walk, and look around. This is our very own melting pot in the South.

by Deb Baldwin

North Carolina State Capitol
COURTESY OF NORTH CAROLINA DIVISION OF TOURISM, FILM AND SPORTS DEVELOPMENT

RALEIGH

by Deb Baldwin

*R*aleigh's capital status boiled down to the power of the punch. In 1771, when Wake County was formed from parts of Cumberland, Johnston, and Orange Counties, a courthouse and jail were erected on the hillside in front of the residence of Joel Lane, who, with his brothers Joseph and Jesse, had moved there in 1741. Their house proved so popular with travelers that they officially made it a tavern.

In 1788, over the objections of North Carolina's principal towns, a state convention seeking a central location for an "unalterable seat of government" resolved that the site should fall within "ten miles of Isaac Hunter's plantation." Hunter's land was indeed among the 17 tracts considered, but the legislators instead purchased 1,000 acres of Joel Lane's land. It has been suggested that the strong punch Lane used to ply the legislators played a role in the decision. The placement of the capital was an especially hard blow to Fayetteville, which had constructed a prospective statehouse of its own and even an inviting tavern—the Cool Spring—to compete with Lane's. Though the new nation's residents had left the Old World, they still carried some of its traditions: the spirited exchanges of the public house were essential for the establishment of the rules of government. In the years since, more than one person has chuckled over the public-house origins of North Carolina's capital city, which has become known as the home of some of the most conservative politics in the nation.

In 1792, a city was established on Lane's land and named in honor of navigator and historian Sir Walter Raleigh. Raleigh has the distinction of being the only state capital established on land specifically purchased by a state for its government seat. The city's founding fathers called Raleigh the "City of Oaks," and that remains its moniker. It retains the original grid layout bequeathed by its first surveyor. The legislative buildings lie within the central square, so they are all easily accessible by foot.

The city has had its moments in history. The 17th president of the United States, Andrew Johnson, was born in Raleigh in 1808. In 1865, some 60,000 Union troops were quartered in Raleigh when word came of President Lincoln's assassination. Upon hearing the news, the angry troops, carrying torches and bent on revenge, headed downtown. General John Alexander Logan stopped them at gunpoint, thus saving Raleigh.

Still, Raleigh remained a rather sleepy state capital until 1959, when an initiative by the state carved out the now-famed Research Triangle Park just west of the city. This nucleus of research has transformed Raleigh into one of America's fastest-growing and most desirable places to live, being predominantly a city of comfortable, beautiful, unpretentious homes with broad lawns and lush gardens underneath the signature oaks. The people here pride themselves on their historic districts and their architecture, especially the famed Executive Mansion. The atmosphere reflects the city's varied functions as a governmental, educational, social, and shopping center.

Raleigh's colleges have played a significant role in the development of the city. Meredith College is the largest four-year women's college in the Southeast. North Carolina State University, founded in 1887 as a land-grant university, now boasts a fine reputation in design and technology. Its 27,000-plus students exert a major impact on the city, as do its Wolfpack teams. Peace College, a liberal arts and sciences college for women, is affiliated with the Presbyterian Church. Founded in 1857 by William Peace, it saw use as a Confederate hospital and later as a Freedman's Bureau office. Its main building is listed on the National Register of Historic Places. St. Augustine's College was founded in 1867 to serve freedmen by educating teachers of black students. Its curriculum has since shifted from teacher training to liberal arts. Shaw University began educating students in 1865, making it the oldest historically black university in the South. Founded by Baptist missionary Henry Martin Tupper in what is now the heart of the city, it was renamed in 1870 to honor its Massachusetts benefactor, Elijah Shaw.

Today's Raleigh is a mixture of the political, the traditional (personified by the Southerners whose families have been in the city for generations), and the upscale (the young urban professionals who have moved to the city in droves). The conservative tide is turning because of the influx of highly educated professionals. This trend has changed the economics, the demographics, and the face of the city, where development in recent years has included multimillion-dollar museum complexes and increased attention to the arts.

JUST THE FACTS

Getting to Raleigh is easy. You can come by plane, train, or automobile.

The area is home to Raleigh-Durham International Airport, which is just a 15-minute drive from downtown Raleigh. The airport offers more than 300 daily departures—including international flights to London, Toronto, Ottawa, and the Bahamas—on 14 major and 10 regional airlines.

Interstate 40, which connects the East and West Coasts of the United States, serves as one of Raleigh's main thoroughfares. The area's first-rate system of state highways and the I-440 Beltline provide easy access to the city, surrounding communities, and Research Triangle Park. Interstate 95 and Interstate 85 run within 25 miles of the city.

The Greyhound bus terminal is located at 314 West Jones Street; call 919-834-8410 for information. Within greater Raleigh, the Capital Area Transit (CAT) bus system and CAT

Connectors provide riders with an extensive network of routes. The Raleigh Trolley serves the downtown area from 11:30 A.M. to 2 P.M. Monday through Friday and provides rides for monthly historic tours on Saturday.

Greater Raleigh is accessible by Amtrak train. The station is located at 320 Cabarrus Street; call 919-833-7594 for information.

One of the best sources for information on Raleigh is the Capital Area Visitor Center, located at 301 North Blount Street; call 919-733-3456. The Greater Raleigh Convention and Visitors Bureau is located at 9421 Fayetteville Street Mall; call 800-849-8499 or 919-834-5900, or contact their website at www.raleighcvb.org/index.html.

Raleigh's morning newspaper is the *News and Observer*, one of the largest in the state. The weekly papers the *Independent* and the *Spectator* are good resources for finding local activities and entertainment, as well as dining and shopping information.

Things to Do

HISTORIC PLACES, GARDENS, AND TOURS

▪ The **North Carolina State Capitol** is located at 1 East Edenton Street on Capitol Square; the front entrance to the grounds is on Wilmington Street. Built between 1833 and 1840, this National Historic Landmark is one of the finest and best-preserved civic buildings in the Greek Revival style of architecture. A reconstruction of the original statehouse, which burned in a fire in 1831, it originally housed the governor's office, cabinet offices, legislative chambers, and the state library. The biggest tragedy of the fire, some say, was the destruction of the marble statue of George Washington by Italian sculptor Antonio Canova, reputed to have been the most precious work of art in the United States. Now, a replica of that statue has been placed in the Capitol. The copper dome, over 97 feet tall, has been restored, along with the rest of the building.

Confederate president Jefferson Davis lay in state here in 1893.

The monuments on the grounds of the Capitol include the Vietnam Memorial and the Confederate Memorial.

Tours are offered regularly. You can see the old Senate and House Chambers, complete with fireplaces, desks, and original furniture. (The legislature got its own building in 1963.) The Capitol is open to the public from 9 A.M. to 5 P.M. Monday through Saturday and from 1 P.M. until 5 P.M. on Sunday. Admission is free. Call 919-733-4994 for more information.

▪ The **North Carolina State Legislative Building** is at 16 West Jones Street at the corner of Salisbury Street. Completed in 1963, this was the first building in the United States constructed for the sole purpose of housing a state general assembly. It includes the facilities of the North Carolina General Assembly, including the Senate and House Chambers, committee rooms, offices for members, and space for clerical personnel. The building has been described as "classic modern architecture with an oriental atmosphere." It is open Monday through Friday from 8 A.M. until 5:30 P.M.; tours are also offered on weekends. When the legislature is in session, visitors get a firsthand look at the governmental process. Call 919-733-7928 for information and the legislative schedule.

▪ The **Executive Mansion**, at 210 North Blount Street, stands on Burke Square, which in 1792 was suggested as a "proper situation for the Governor's house." After a great deal of bickering, $25,000

Executive Mansion
COURTESY OF NORTH CAROLINA
DIVISION OF TOURISM, FILM AND
SPORTS DEVELOPMENT

was begrudgingly approved for the project in 1885. Despite the use of convict labor and convict-created brick instead of sandstone, the price tag swelled; one historian puts the total at $58,000 by the time the home was finished in 1891.

Legislative reluctance notwithstanding, the house has long been a source of North Carolina pride. Crowds regularly wait in line for tours. The mansion was described by Franklin Delano Roosevelt as having "the most beautiful governor's residence interior in America." The home was built completely of materials from within the state, and each brick bears the moniker of the inmate who made it.

Admission is free. Call 919-733-3456 for tour hours.

■ *Mordecai Historic Park*, at 1 Mimosa Street, is a museum and garden surrounding a two-story frame plantation house built as a country estate. Named for its second owner, Moses Mordecai, it was purchased in 1968 by the city of Raleigh. The house holds the family's fine Victorian furniture and original library. The park includes the Ellen Mordecai Garden, which features a plot of flowers designed from early 1800s diaries.

Also located at the park—and its real claim to fame—is the structure where Andrew Johnson was born. The building was a kitchen for the tavern where the parents of the future president worked. Johnson was born in the loft above the kitchen. There's a story behind the birth. On December 29, 1808, as young Peggy Casso danced at her wedding ball in the statehouse, a little girl came to summon her, saying that Jacob Johnson needed her. His wife, Polly, had just given birth to a son. Would the young bride come name him? She would indeed. Dropping to the floor beside the new baby, Peggy said, "I name thee, on this my wedding night, Andrew." On his return to Raleigh in 1867, President Johnson called first on Mrs. Peggy Stewart, his godmother.

Tours are offered from 10 A.M. to 3 P.M. on Monday, Wednesday, Thursday, Friday, and Saturday and from 1 P.M. until 3 P.M. on Sunday. Admission is charged. Call 919-834-4844 for more information.

■ The *Joel Lane House* is located at 728 West Hargett Street at the corner of St. Mary's. Built in the 1760s, this is Raleigh's oldest dwelling. During the 18th century, it was the home (and tavern) of Colonel Joel

Lane (1760–95) and the site of numerous historic events. Lane is considered the "Father of Raleigh," since he sold 1,000 acres of his plantation to the state of North Carolina in 1792 for the site of the new state capital. Informative guided tours of the fully restored and authentically furnished house and kitchen and the re-created 18th-century herb and formal gardens are provided by costumed docents. Tours are offered Tuesday through Friday from 10 A.M. to 2 P.M. and Saturday from 1 P.M. to 4 P.M. from March 1 through mid-December. A small admission fee is charged. Annual events include a Christmas open house and a Fourth of July celebration. Call 919-833-3431 for more information.

While many of the cities in North Carolina have wonderful gardens, Raleigh is particularly blessed.

▪ The *J. C. Raulston Arboretum* at North Carolina State University, located on Beryl Road off the I-440 Beltline near the fairgrounds, is a nationally acclaimed garden containing one of the most diverse collections

Joel Lane House
PHOTOGRAPH BY DEB BALDWIN

of landscape plants in North America. As part of the Department of Horticultural Science at the university, the arboretum is primarily a research and teaching garden that focuses on the evaluation, selection, and display of plant material from around the world. Named in honor of its late founder and director, this eight-acre masterpiece includes such wonders as the Klein-Pringle White Garden, a Japanese garden meditation space, the Paradise Garden (designed to delight all five senses in the fashion of the ancient Persian gardens), and, famously, the 450-foot Perennial Border, created by nationally known designer Edith Eddleman. The gardens are open from 8 A.M. until 8 P.M. every day of the year. For more information, call 919-515-3132, or contact their website at www.arb.ncsu.edu.

- The **Martha Frank Fragrance Garden** at the Governor Morehead School for the Blind, on Ashe Street between Hillsborough Street and Western Boulevard, is a new and emerging garden that provides a sensory experience through scent, sound, and touch for the blind, the visually impaired, and the sighted. It is open from 8 A.M. to 4:30 P.M. daily. Admission is free. Call 919-834-0686 for more information.

- The **Martin Luther King, Jr., Memorial Gardens**, at 1500 Martin Luther King Boulevard, are dedicated to the memory of Dr. King. The facility features an award-winning, life-sized bronze statue of King and a 12-ton granite monument honoring heroes of the civil-rights movement; both rest amid a colorful variety of trees and flowering plants. This is the only public park in the United States devoted to the civil-rights movement. Call 919-834-6264 for more information.

- The **Raleigh Municipal Rose Garden**, at 301 Pogue Street off Hillsborough Street, is host to over 60 varieties of roses, including English roses, miniatures, floribundas, grandifloras, tree roses, and climbers. Call 919-821-4579 for information (and maybe even growing tips).

MUSEUMS AND SCIENCE CENTERS

- The **African-American Cultural Complex**, at 119 Sunnybrook Road, is home to a unique collection of items created by African-Americans who have contributed to the development of North Carolina and America. Innovations in science, business, politics, medicine, sports, and the arts are included in the exhibit. A replica of the slave ship *Amistad* and an outdoor pageant of its events are featured. The complex is open by appointment only. For more information, call 919-212-3598, or visit their website at www.aaccmuseum.org.

▪ *Exploris*, at 201 East Hargett Street, is another of the bright and shiny new attractions in downtown Raleigh. This $40.2 million interactive museum (for kids of all ages, of course) uses its 84,000 square feet to celebrate diversity and teach technology. It is open every day but Monday. An admission fee is charged. For more information, call 888-287-5411, or visit their website at www.exploris.org.

▪ The **North Carolina Museum of Art**, at 2110 Blue Ridge Road, houses the art collections of the state of North Carolina. The paintings and sculpture held here represent more than 5,000 years of artistic heritage from ancient Egypt to the present. The collection of Renaissance and Baroque paintings—including works by Van Dyck, Jan Breughel, and Raphael—is internationally recognized. Significant American paintings include works by John Singleton Copley, Winslow Homer, and Georgia O'Keeffe. Also represented are collections of African, Oceanic, Egyptian, Greek, Roman, 20th-century, and Jewish ceremonial art.

In the summer of 2000, the museum was in the international spotlight after its innovative presentation of a 130-piece Auguste Rodin installation. This exhibition marked a turning point in the museum's life and inspired a citywide celebration of all things French, entitled Festival Rodin.

An admission fee is charged. The museum is open every day except Monday. For more information, call 919-839-6262, or visit their website at www.ncartmuseum.org.

▪ The **North Carolina Museum of Natural Sciences**, at 11 West Jones Street, opened in the spring of 2000 on Bicentennial Plaza with round-the-clock festivities showcasing four floors of exhibits and more than 3,000 live animals. The largest natural-history museum in the Southeast, it is nothing short of spectacular. Highlights include four enormous whale

North Carolina Museum of Natural Sciences
PHOTOGRAPH BY WILLIAM RUSS
COURTESY OF NORTH CAROLINA DIVISION OF TOURISM, FILM AND SPORTS DEVELOPMENT

skeletons from coastal North Carolina, a 20-foot waterfall, and an ar-thropod zoo crawling with critters from butterflies to tarantulas.

After finishing runner-up when Sue, the most complete *T. rex* ever found, was sold at auction, the museum successfully acquired an equally rare find—the world's only Acrocanthosaurus, a 112-millon-year-old crea-ture that lived 45 million years before *T. rex*. Scientists at the museum and North Carolina State University recently discovered a 66-million-year-old Thescelosaurus, the world's first dinosaur specimen with a fossilized heart.

The museum offers free hands-on programs every day. It is open Monday through Saturday from 9 A.M. to 5 P.M. and Sunday from noon to 5 P.M. Admission is free. For more information, call 877-4NATSCI or 919-733-7450, or visit their website at www.naturalsciences.org.

▪ The **North Carolina Museum of History**, at 5 East Edenton Street, is a 170,000-square-foot-facility completed in 1994. It houses both short- and long-term exhibits describing how North Carolinians have lived from the state's beginnings to the present day. Joined recently on Bicentennial Plaza by the North Carolina Museum of Natural Sciences, it has put on a new face with exhibits focusing on the state's folklife, its struggles during the Civil War, and the role of African-Americans in the state. The North

Carolina Sports Hall of Fame is also housed here.

Special programs include dramatic presentations, demonstrations, and family nights. Guided tours are available. The museum is open Tuesday through Saturday from 9 A.M. until 5 P.M. and Sunday from noon to 5 P.M. Admission is free. For more information, call 919-715-0200, or visit their website at www.nchistory.dcr.state.nc.us.

CULTURAL OFFERINGS

▪ *Artspace*, at the corner of Blount and David Streets in downtown Raleigh, is a nonprofit center for the visual and performing arts. It offers the public the opportunity to visit and interact with over 40 artists working in open studios. Three exhibition galleries feature regional, national, and international artists. The arts-education programs offered here include lectures, demonstrations, gallery talks, and art classes for adults and children. Admission is free. Artspace is open from Tuesday to Saturday from 10 A.M. to 6 P.M. Special opening receptions are sponsored on the first Friday of each month. For more information, call 919-821-2787, or visit their website at www.artspace.citysearch.com.

▪ *Carolina Ballet* has its office at 336 Fayetteville Street Mall. The company performs a classically based repertoire and features the work of George Balanchine, artistic director Robert Weiss, and other well-known contemporary choreographers. Performances are held at Raleigh Memorial Auditorium, R. J. Reynolds Theatre in Durham, and the Stevens Center for the Performing Arts in Winston-Salem. For more information, call 919-303-6303, or visit www.carolinaballet.com.

▪ The *North Carolina Symphony* was founded in 1933 by a group of orchestra lovers meeting in Chapel Hill. Despite the scarcity of money for such luxuries, the symphony struggled to a reorganization in 1940, when it gained some support from the state. It now has 15 chapters that help raise funds for travel expenses for the symphony's public and school concerts throughout the state.

The symphony offers a classical and pops series, an outdoor summer series in June and July, and children's concerts year-round. Most area performances are in Memorial Auditorium, located at South Wilmington and South Streets, but the new Meymandi Concert Hall is scheduled to open in February 2001 next to the old facility. Call 919-733-2750 for more information.

- Founded in 1936, **Raleigh Little Theatre** (RLT) is one of the oldest continuously operating community theaters in the country. It offers entertainment, educational, and community programs year-round. Named the "Best Theatre Organization in the Triangle" by *Spectator* magazine, RLT stages three different series, 12 productions, and more than 150 performances each year. The Main Stage series includes five Broadway musicals, comedies, and dramas; the City Stage series includes four contemporary works; and the Youth Series features five shows aimed at a young audience. Performances are held in RLT's theater at 301 Pogue Street, except for the popular holiday production of *Cinderella*, which is presented at North Carolina State University's Stewart Theatre. Call 919-821-4579 for information or 919-821-3111 for tickets.

- **Theatre in the Park** is located at 107 Pullen Road off Hillsborough Street near the Bell Tower at North Carolina State University. Under the direction of Ira David Wood, it presents contemporary and classical productions, original world premieres, experimental drama, musicals, and the internationally known original musical production of *A Christmas Carol*. The company offers open auditions, classes, and workshops. It also invites community volunteers to participate. For more information, call 919-831-6058, or visit their website at www.tip.dreamhost.com.

- **North Carolina Theatre** bills itself as the "theatre of live musicals in North Carolina." Every year since 1983, it has brought popular Broadway fare—including classics like *A Chorus Line* and *My Fair Lady*, as well as newer sensations like *5 Guys Named Moe* and *The Secret Garden*—to the stage of Raleigh Memorial Auditorium. All the shows are produced in Raleigh using professional talent from the Triangle, New York, and across the country, under the musical direction of McRae Hardy. Call 919-831-6950 for information or 919-831-6941 for tickets.

- Raleigh has through the years become a real theater town. Such independent groups as the **Raleigh Ensemble Players**, under the direction of Deb Royals, and the **Burning Coal Theatre Company** offer serious theater ranging from experimental presentations to known works to premiere pieces. Meredith and Peace Colleges have theaters. North Carolina State's **University Theatre** presents five major student productions per year, as well as TheatreFest, a summer season featuring local, professional, and student artists. For information on these companies, call the Raleigh Arts Commission at 919-857-4372.

SPECIAL SHOPPING

■ Numerous restaurants and galleries keep visitors occupied at the **City Market**, located at the intersection of Blount and Martin Streets. The market is so colorful that it has recently been showcased in the *New York Times*. It serves as a good meeting place for jaunts to the museums. Call 919-828-4555 for more information.

■ The **North Carolina State Farmer's Market** is 75 acres of the finest products that Triangle farmers have to offer. Visitors enjoy the special areas for flowers, plants, and gardening supplies, as well as the Farmer's Market Restaurant and the N.C. Seafood Restaurant. To get there, take the Lake Wheeler Road/Dorothea Dix/Farmer's Market exit off Interstate 40 and follow the signs. The market is open seven days a week until 6 P.M. It opens at noon on Sunday. Call 919-733-7417 for more information.

RECREATION

■ **Pullen Park**, founded in 1887, was named in honor of Richard Stanhope Pullen, who donated the land to the city of Raleigh. Pullen began the development of the park by planting trees, shrubbery, and crops to feed the city's horses.

The park offers a variety of recreational opportunities for all ages, including amusement rides, swimming, a playground, picnic shelters, lighted tennis courts, classes, fitness programs, workshops, and art classes. The park's magnificent carousel draws children from far and wide. The

train and the paddleboats are fun, too.

Pullen Park is located in the downtown area at 520 Ashe Avenue. It is open year-round. Its hours of operation vary with the season. Call 919-831-6468 for more information.

- **Lake Wheeler Metropolitan Park**, at 6404 Lake Wheeler Road, includes a 700-acre lake and 150 acres of land. Managed by the Raleigh Parks and Recreation Department, this popular location offers a variety of kayak, canoe, johnboat, and sailboat rentals and is open to all types of private boating. Superb fishing and picnicking opportunities are also offered. Although swimming is not allowed, visitors may indulge in various water-related activities, such as windsurfing, water-skiing, and kayaking. The award-winning Waterfront Program Center overlooks the lake; it boasts a popular lakeside conference room, restrooms, and a huge, open deck area with rocking chairs and picnic tables.

Recently cited as a favorite getaway by the *News and Observer*, Lake Wheeler is open seven days a week from sunrise to sunset year-round. It hosts a variety of special events, including the annual Tar Heel Powerboat Regatta, the Atlantic Coast University Team Rowing Regatta, boat shows, canoe and kayak festivals, seasonal bass tournaments, Great Outdoor Provision Company fly-fishing schools, *Carolina Adventure Magazine*'s freshwater fishing school, and the Kid's Fishing Derby. Windsurfing, water-skiing, and boating classes are also offered. For more information, call 919-662-5704.

• The success of the North Carolina State Wolfpack teams has long given Raleigh a taste for athletic competition, but the new *Entertainment and Sports Arena*, located on Edwards Mill Road, has ratcheted the excitement level up. The *Carolina Hurricanes* of the National Hockey League, the *Cobras* of the Arena Football League, and the *North Carolina State men's basketball team* play at the $152 million state-of-the-art facility. This venue reaches a height of 120 feet, a width of 495 feet, and a length of 635 feet. Its four seating levels can accommodate 19,000 fans for hockey games, 20,000 for basketball games, and about 21,000 for concerts. To contact the box office, call 919-861-2323; for other information, call 919-861-2300.

■ The *North Carolina State women's basketball team* plays at Reynolds Coliseum, located at 103 Dunn Avenue on the university campus. Call 919-515-2106 for ticket information.

■ The *Carolina MudCats*, the Triangle's class AA baseball team, play at Five County Stadium in Zebulon. Call 919-269-2287 for information.

■ Golf has long been a southern Piedmont tradition. Raleigh has over 20 quality courses. The city hosts a couple of tournaments every year, the *Buy.com Classic* and the famous *Jimmy V. Classic*. Of course, Pinehurst is close by, so many golf aficionados head south.

SEASONAL EVENTS

■ *Artsplosure Spring Art Festival* is held downtown the third weekend in May. The two-day, city-sponsored free outdoor festival features regional, national, and local jazz, blues, country, and pop musicians in continuous shows. Included are 150 booths for artists and lots of interactive and educational activities for children. For information, call 919-832-8699.

■ *Divine Destiny* is held at the Raleigh Convention Center. Pastor Shirley Caesar's annual conference features performances by such gospel greats as Patti LaBelle, Gladys Knight, Kirk Franklin, Vickie Winans, the Williams Brothers, Lou Rawls, and, of course, Pastor Shirley herself. Those attending the conference must pay a fee, but the concerts each night are free to the public. For more information, call 919-683-1161.

- **First Night Raleigh** is an alcohol-free New Year's Eve celebration of the arts held at various locations downtown. Throughout the afternoon and evening, participants enjoy art exhibits, music, dance, comedy, theater, and children's activities. The event culminates in a countdown to midnight; the traditional "Acorn Drop" is followed by fireworks. For information, call 919-832-8699.

- The **North Carolina Renaissance Faire** has become a regular event on Raleigh's spring calendar. It includes jousting, knightings, singing, dancing, puppetry, fencing, sword fighting, and the inevitable quest for the Holy Grail. The event takes place at the fairgrounds, in the Village of Yesteryear/Heritage Village area. Camping and RV hookups are offered. The fair runs from 10 A.M. until 6:30 P.M. An admission fee is charged except for children five and under. Call 919-878-8537 for more information.

- The **North Carolina State Fair**, a rich tradition in the state, takes place in mid-October. North Carolina State's homecoming weekend always falls within its stay, guaranteeing some excitement on the Raleigh highways. Approximately 700,000 people attend the fair every year to enjoy the livestock, the agriculture displays, and the Midway, as well as such top-name performers as Ray Charles and Merle Haggard. This is the largest annual event in the state. An admission fee is charged. The fairgrounds are at 1025 Blue Ridge Road. Call 919-733-2145 for more information.

Places to Stay

RESORTS, HOTELS, AND MOTELS

- **The Sheraton Capitol Center Hotel.** Deluxe/Expensive. 421 South Salisbury Street (800-325-3535 or 919-834-9900). This elegant, fun hotel sits across from the new Memorial Auditorium theater complex, so the entertainment includes some first-rate people-watching in the two-story atrium and the lobby. The service here is polished. Amenities include an indoor pool and Jacuzzi, a workout facility, room service, and more. The business-class accommodations include a data port on all telephones, coffee makers, hair dryers, and irons. Express check-in and checkout are available. For an added level of service, guests can stay in one of the concierge-level rooms. As with most hotels, making reservations in advance will significantly lower your rates.

▪ *Crabtree Summit Hotel.* Expensive/Moderate. 3908 Arrow Drive (800-521-7521 or 919-782-6868). This European-style hotel is a jewel. Located near Crabtree Valley Mall, it has 84 rooms, including deluxe rooms and several suites. Each room and suite has a refrigerator, a hair dryer, luxurious bathrobes, special bath amenities, a coffee maker, an iron, and an ironing board. A breakfast buffet is offered every day. A lounge, an outdoor pool, and an exercise room are on the premises. A car wash is also available. Pets are welcome with some restrictions.

▪ *The Velvet Cloak Inn.* Expensive/Moderate. 1505 Hillsborough Street (800-334-4372 or 919-823-0333). This hotel is located 12 blocks from North Carolina State University. Its wrought-iron balconies with flower boxes and its brick driveways give it an appearance reminiscent of New Orleans. It has 172 guest rooms, including eight suites.

▪ *Hampton Inn–Crabtree.* Moderate. 6209 Glenwood Avenue (919-782-1112). This inn is less than eight miles from the airport, the State Capitol, the fairgrounds, and North Carolina State University. Research Triangle Park is located within 11 miles, Duke University within 21 miles, and Crabtree Valley Mall within just one mile. The inn offers a free deluxe continental breakfast, local calls, a fitness center, a pool, in-room coffee makers, and a guarantee of satisfaction. Airport shuttle service is available.

- **The Oakwood Inn**. Expensive. 411 Bloodworth (919-832-9712). This elegant inn was built in 1871. Though it is only blocks from the Executive Mansion, you'll feel you've gone back in time in this peaceful setting so quiet you can hear the clock ticking in the front room. Restored in 1984 as a bed-and-breakfast, the inn occupies a lavender gabled house with a wraparound porch and lush gardens. Its six guest rooms have period antiques and accessories, footed tubs, and fireplaces. Modern amenities like computer ports, cable television, and private telephone lines are offered for those who can't sever their ties to the world. A full breakfast is served daily; continental breakfast is available for those on a varied schedule. Afternoon tea is served daily; beverages and snacks are available around the clock. The gracious hosts are more than willing to point you in the right direction for a walking or driving tour.

- **The William Thomas House**. Expensive. 530 North Blount Street (800-653-3466 or 919-755-9400). Sometimes called the Gray Fish Richardson House, after the attorney for whom it was built in 1881, this is a good example of middle-class Victorian construction. The inn offers four famously decorated rooms with air conditioning, ceiling fans, and modern amenities like color televisions and private telephone lines. Breakfast is served under a 12-foot ceiling in the dining room. Wine and cheese are offered in the afternoon.

Places to Eat

- **Angus Barn**. Expensive. U.S. 70 West at Aviation Parkway (919-787-3505). Don't let the rustic interior, the homey staff, and the checkered tablecloths fool you: this revered house of meat is a place where deals are made. The steaks, the prime rib, and the châteaubriand are famous. They are joined by oysters, lobster, baked potatoes, traditional French onion soup, and delicious, old-fashioned desserts. The famous Angus Barn cheese spread, breads, pickles, and crackers will put you in danger of premeal overconsumption. Make no mistake, this restaurant is upscale;

the Angus Barn has been the recipient of the Institution Design Award, the Ivy Award of Distinction, the Business Executives Dining Award, the Distinguished Restaurant of North America Award, and the coveted *Wine Spectator* Grand Award (the wine cellar holds over 50,000 bottles). You can buy gifts at the country shop or listen to jazz (yes, jazz!) in the upstairs lounge. And don't miss the realistic bovines on the restroom doors! Reservations are not accepted on weekends, and vegetarians need not apply. Weekend lines begin to queue up at 5 o'clock. Dinner is served daily.

■ *Bistro 607*. Expensive. 607 Glenwood Ave. (919-828-0840). Once my bed-and-breakfast hostess let it slip that Bistro 607 was, in her opinion, the best restaurant in town, I had to include it. The presentations here are dramatic and the dishes unusual—like "Duck Breast with Charred Peaches and Red Wine Sauce" and "Lobster with Roasted Pineapple." The chefs and owners, Jean-Paul Fontaine and Lofton Heath Holloman, are truly creative, and the staff is gracious. The restaurant bakes all its own breads and desserts. Outdoor dining is available. Lunch is served Monday through Friday and dinner Monday through Saturday.

■ *42nd Street Oyster Bar*. Moderate. 508 West Jones Street (919-831-2811). It wouldn't be possible to discuss Raleigh dining without mentioning this place, open since 1931. Oysters, oysters, oysters, plus drinks, drinks, drinks, lights, color, and action—that's what you'll find here. This is another of the political watering holes for which Raleigh has always been famous. Lunch is served Monday through Friday and dinner seven days a week.

■ *Irregardless Café*. Moderate. 901 West Morgan Street (919-833-8898). These days, it seems increasingly difficult to find a creative menu that caters to the vegetarian as vigorously as it does to the carnivore. So it is with great pleasure that I revisit Irregardless (which turned 25 in the year 2000) to enjoy the exquisite wild mushroom and artichoke crepes, the vegan house salad, and the home-baked bread. Okay, okay, many of their dishes now include something with a face, but you'll also find an actual vegan entrée, and the menu carefully specifies all ingredients. The staff is guaranteed gracious. And these days, there is dancing on Saturday nights.

Irregardless has both a food hot line (919-833-9920) and a music hot line (919-790-4340). It has been voted Best Restaurant in the Triangle and Best Vegetarian Restaurant by the *Spectator*, so I'm not the only one who loves it. Lunch and dinner are served Monday through Saturday. Brunch is offered on Sunday.

▪ ***Tír na nÓg*** (pronounced "Tear na noag"). Moderate. 218 South Blount Street (919-833-7795). This Irish pub is known by the locals to be a worthy place for either dining or raising a pint. The fare includes the standard (like fish and chips and shepherd's pie) and the unusual (like fried oyster salad, boxty, and wild mushroom strudel). The hosts have graciously included a number of vegetarian-friendly dishes. The traditional Irish bread pudding should top off your night, if you have any room after a few frothy stouts. Lunch is served Monday through Saturday and dinner Tuesday through Sunday. Brunch is offered on Sunday.

▪ ***Fox and Hound***. Moderate/Inexpensive. Suite 119, MacGregor Village Shopping Center (919-380-0080). A friend of mine, a displaced Brit now living in Chapel Hill, swears by Fox and Hound as necessary for his sanity and survival. He and his wife regularly make the drive over for the specialties of the isle, including shepherd's pie, fish and chips, bangers and mash, Yorkshire pudding, and especially the British ales and the 15 different single-malt Scotches. Lunch is served Monday through Saturday and dinner seven nights a week.

▪ ***Char-Grill***. Inexpensive. 618 Hillsborough Street (919-821-7636). Okay, I don't eat meat, but if I did, I'd be all over Char-Grill, which serves old-fashioned grilled cheeseburgers, great, great French fries, and extra thick and creamy milk shakes at an old-fashioned drive-in. Make that three drive-ins—there are also Raleigh locations on Atlantic Avenue and Edwards Mill Road. A camaraderie comes from hanging around outside the drive-in window, waiting for great American food. This is where fast food started, and where it should have remained. Lunch and dinner are served seven days a week.

An Uncivil Argument

Excerpted from the *News and Observer's Raleigh: A Living History of North Carolina's Capital*, edited by David Perkins

Letter from an English gentleman, on his travels through the United States, to his friend in London:

March 12, 1798

. . . Raleigh is situated more than an hundred miles from any seaport, and nearly thirty from any boatable waters, has no stream of water capable of making it a manufacturing town; has therefore no prospect of becoming anything more than the solitary residence of a few public officers, containing a few ordinary taverns, gaming houses and dram shops, and this is in fact what the metropolis now is. It might probably have been expected by the founders, that being in a hilly country, it would become the summer residence of many people in the eastern sickly parts of the state, but it has been found on experience not to have the degree of healthiness which its elevated situation would seem to promise. . . .

The plan of Raleigh (which by the bye is dignified with the name of city) would have been tolerably good, had it been situated in a place in which it could have been completed; but neither power nor superstition, as in the east, have any effect here to help its completion; for it contains neither the castle of the Lord's anointed, nor the coffin of a departed saint. The necessities of the government, and the groveling dissipation of a few, are its whole support.

The ground is divided into four quarters by as many spacious streets, which terminate in the public square, in the center of which stands the state house, a clumsy brick building, built without any regular design of architecture, and totally devoid of taste or elegance.

Disgraceful as the appearance of the state house is at best, they have contrived to place it yet in a more disadvantageous point of view, by erecting the court house, the palace of the governor, and most of the other buildings, on one of the streets which has only an end view of the statehouse, which makes but a forty appearance. . . .

At the four corners of the public square are groves which might have been made agreeable walks; I thought this was their design, and seeing a small house in two of them, I took them for summer houses, and began in my mind, to applaud the state for constructing such charming places for the recreation of the people in a warm climate, and going to visit one of them, was arrested in my progress by a terrible stench issuing from four doors, which informed me it was a temple of Cloacina.

The streets of this city are honored with the names of some of the great men who have distinguished themselves in the service of the state . . . and to do them justice the state ought, in imitation of the ancients, to place statues of them in their favorite temples.

Raleigh citizens reply

June 4, 1798

Mr. Hodge,

Your No. 295 contains much entertaining matter, particularly the curious piece pretended to have been written by the English gentleman on the tour through the United States. . . . We contend he has offered a high affront and gross indignity to the state; and if he is in fact an Englishman, in return for his civility we can but advise him through you to return to the Nabobs of his own country, where the appearance of public and private buildings is more pleasing to an English eye, and the fare of their tables better suited to an English stomach.

We are not disposed to enter into a reasoning detail with this man of the world . . . but you will indulge us a minute while we briefly refute a few of his statements. . . .

He approves the plan of the our city, but it wants water, power and superstition to complete it, and of course it cannot be done without a cottage of the Lord's anointed, and a coffin of a departed saint. . . . The Lord's annointed [sic], and the corpse of a departed saint, we consign to the gentleman for his ingenuity and labour in writing our history—we know not his meaning by the necessities of the government, for we believe it is as well supplied here as if the metropolis had been planted on the water side, except with crabs and frogs.—It is to be lamented that there are too many dissipated people among us, but they are running away fast, and our hope is, a better race will take their place.

Were we to venture an opinion of this traveling gentleman, we should pronounce him a disappointed partisan, who had formerly struggled in the interest of that grave-yard called Fayetteville—rankling at the heart, he has assumed the character of an Englishman to vent his spleen.—That he is a natural born son, begotten by Vulcan on the body of Cloacina, at her devotion, and raised in and upon the offerings of her temples in his favourite village, where we presume the stench is not so offensive to him, as there is a material difference in the qualities of aliments that sustain human life—in one place it is mostly of the skin and bones of swine and sand-hill turkeys, in another it is very different—sound and wholesome.

Excuse scurrility—It is diamond cut diamond—and we must meet the gentleman on his own ground—we are, &c.

The Citizens of Raleigh.

Durham Skyline
COURTESY OF DURHAM CONVENTION & VISITORS BUREAU

DURHAM
by Deb Baldwin

*I*n 1701, explorer John Lawson called Durham "the flower of the Carolinas." During the mid-1700s, Scots-Irish and British newcomers to America settled on land granted to John Carteret, the earl of Granville, by King Charles I. Those early settlers worked the land and built gristmills such as West Point.

But the official birth date of the city did not come until the 1850s, when landowner William Pratt refused to give land for a train station and Dr. Bartlett Durham stepped in to offer four acres of his own property. The railroad detoured around the Pratt tract, and Bartlett Durham's name went down in history. Durham was incorporated in 1867. When Durham County was created from Orange and Wake Counties in 1881, the town of Durham was made the seat.

In the spring of 1865, General Joseph E. Johnston surrendered to General William T. Sherman at the Bennett House in Durham. That same year, a young man named Washington Duke, mustered out of the Confederate army, walked 137 miles to his old farm near Durham to restart his life after the war. He began to grind tobacco, which he packed, labeled *"Pro Bono Publico,"* and sold to soldiers and others, who soon spread the reputation of his "brightleaf" far and wide. The venture proved so successful that he was joined by his three sons—Brodie, Benjamin N., and James B. "Buck"—in the tobacco business. In 1880, Buck Duke decided to escape the competitive market for plug tobacco by making cigarettes. By 1890, he formed the American Tobacco Company, which eventually pushed the family's wealth into league with the likes of the Rockefellers and the Carnegies.

Durham's history, though shaped by tobacco, is also marked by another trait. The area has been a center of ethnic diversity since it was home to at least four Native American tribes, some of which had relocated by the time the first English and Scots-Irish settlers secured land grants in 1750. These communities drew traffic and trade along the Great Indian Trading Path and the Eno River. It is likely that the brightleaf tobacco that the town was famous for was itself introduced to settlers by the Indian tribes. Diversity still characterizes Durham, which was once known as the "Capital of the Black Middle Class." Indeed, North Carolina Central University in Durham holds the honor of being the nation's first four-year public liberal-arts institution founded for African-Americans. The city celebrates different cultures through such events as the Bimbé Cultural Festival, the North Carolina Gay and Lesbian Film Festival, the North Carolina Jewish Film Festival, the Black Diaspora Film Festival, the International Jazz Festival, the American Dance Festival, and, of course, the wonderful Bull Durham Blues Festival.

Today, Durham is known as the "City of Medicine," thanks to its medical, diet, and fitness centers. It is home to 13 historic sites, 15 arts centers or performance halls, 12 science and nature centers, great baseball and basketball, 20 major annual events, and dozens of nightclubs.

JUST THE FACTS

Durham sits at the northern point of the Triangle; Raleigh lies southeast and Chapel Hill southwest. Durham can be reached by Interstate 85, Interstate 40, U.S. 15/U.S. 501, and U.S. 70.

Raleigh-Durham International Airport is less than 20 minutes away; it can be reached by the Durham Expressway leading to Interstate 40 East.

The Amtrak station is at 400 West Chapel Hill Street; for reservations, call 800-872-7245.

The Triangle Transit Authority runs buses from Duke University Medical Center to the airport and to Chapel Hill; call 919-549-9999 for information. Duke University Transit sends buses between the school's East and West Campuses; call 919-684-8111. The Greyhound bus station is located at 820 West Morgan Street; call 919-687-4800.

The daily newspaper is the *Herald-Sun,* which offers a special-events insert on Friday called "The Preview." The *News and Observer* of Raleigh has a special Durham section every day. Some of the most comprehensive listings of local events can be found in the *Independent* and the *Spectator,* free papers published on Wednesday.

The Durham Convention and Visitors Bureau is located at 101 East Morgan Street. Call 800-446-8604 or 919-687-0288 for information.

Things to Do

HISTORIC PLACES, GARDENS, AND TOURS

■ Tobacco may have put Durham on the map, but **Duke University** has kept it in the public eye. The university was created in 1924 by James B. "Buck" Duke as a memorial to his father, Washington Duke. The Dukes long felt an interest in Trinity College, which had its origin in 1838 in nearby Randolph County when the Methodist and Quaker communities joined forces to form a school. After a brief period as Normal College (1851–59), the school changed its name to Trinity College and affiliated with the Methodist Church. It moved to Durham in 1892 with financial assistance from Washington Duke and the donation of land by Julian S. Carr. In December 1924, the trustees gratefully accepted the provisions of James B. Duke's indenture, creating the family's philanthropic foundation, the Duke Endowment, which provided in part for the expansion of Trinity College into Duke University.

As a result of the Duke gift, the college underwent massive expansion. The original Durham campus became known as "East Campus" when it was rebuilt in its current Georgian style. West Campus, which has a Gothic style fashioned after the Ivy League, opened in 1930. East Campus served as the home of the Woman's College of Duke University until 1972, when the men's and women's undergraduate colleges merged. In 1995, East Campus became the home for all first-year students.

Duke has achieved an outstanding record of academic excellence, and its schools of engineering, medicine, law, and business—among others—are renowned. The campus is home to the Fuqua School of Business, Duke Medical Center, the Terry Sanford Center, the Duke Museum of Art, performing-arts spaces, labs, and countless other facilities. The players on the Duke Blue Devils men's basketball teams are known by name around the state and beyond.

■ **Duke Chapel,** on Chapel Drive on the West Campus, is the university's most recognizable landmark. Its 210-foot tower is visible for miles. Based architecturally on the Canterbury Cathedral, this awe-inspiring Gothic-style structure is built from North Carolina stone, as is the rest of the impressive West Campus. The chapel holds a 5,200-pipe organ and a 50-bell carillon resting in an impressive structure of intricately detailed stone, wood, and stained glass. Visitors are welcome to tour the chapel and to participate in the interdenominational services held on Sundays at 11 A.M. They can even take the ride all the way up to watch the carillonneur. In the summer, dancers and the dance audience gather on the chapel's lawn before entering neighboring Page Auditorium for performances of the American Dance Festival. The chapel is host to frequent world-class musical presentations. Call 919-684-2572 for more information.

■ **Sarah P. Duke Gardens**, located on the West Campus, encompasses 55 acres of spectacular landscape right in the midst of the university. All told, it offers five miles of walks and pathways that visit the Blomquist Garden of native North Carolina plants, the Asiatic Arboretum, a fishpond, and beds featuring floral displays that change throughout the year. These magnificent gardens also serve as a backdrop to live per-

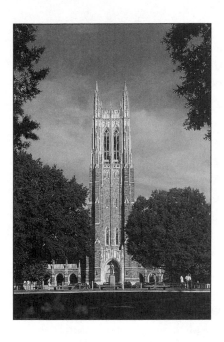

Duke Chapel
PHOTOGRAPH BY WILLIAM RUSS
COURTESY OF NORTH CAROLINA DIVISION OF
TRAVEL AND TOURISM

formances of dance and music. They are open daily until sunset. Guided tours are available. Call 800-367-3853 or 919-684-3698 for more information.

▪ **West Point on the Eno**, at 5101 North Roxboro Road in northern Durham, is a 371-acre natural and historic city park that features a reconstructed 1778 gristmill and part of the community that surrounded it, including a re-created blacksmith shop. The park also offers the Hugh Manghum Museum of Photography, hiking trails, and an amphitheater. It is open daily from 8 A.M. until dark. Admission is free. Call 919-471-1623 for information, or visit their website at www.geo.duke.edu.enowelco.html.

▪ **Bennett Place**, a small farmhouse at 4409 Bennett Memorial Road, once rested between Confederate general Johnston's headquarters in Hillsborough and Union general Sherman's headquarters in Raleigh. This is where those two soldiers met in 1865 to sign surrender papers for Southern armies in the Carolinas, Georgia, and Florida.

Today, James Bennett's reconstructed farmhouse, kitchen, and smokehouse give visitors a glimpse into the lifestyle of an ordinary Southern farmer during the Civil War years. The original buildings were destroyed by fire in 1921. The present structures were carefully reconstructed in the 1960s using sketches and early photographs as a guide.

A visitor center with exhibits and an audiovisual program help tell the Bennett Place story. Special events include a surrender reenactment in April, the Fall Living History Program in October, and a Christmas open house in early December. From April through October, Bennett Place is open from 9 A.M. to 5 P.M. Monday to Saturday and from 1 P.M. to 5 P.M. on Sunday. From November through March, it is open Tuesday through Saturday from 10 A.M. to 4 P.M. and Sunday from 1 P.M. to 4 P.M. Admission is free. Call 919-383-4345 for more information.

■ At *Duke Homestead*, located at 2828 Duke Homestead Road, you can see the humble beginnings of the Duke tobacco dynasty. It showcases the early home of Washington Duke and the farm and factories where he first grew and processed tobacco. Duke's sons later founded the American Tobacco Company, the largest tobacco company in the world. Museum exhibits trace the history of tobacco from Native American times to the present. From April through October, Duke Homestead is open 9 A.M. to 5 P.M. Monday to Saturday and 1 P.M. to 5 P.M. on Sunday. From November to March, it is open Tuesday to Saturday from 10 A.M. to 4 P.M. and Sunday from 1 P.M. to 4 P.M. Admission is free. Groups are asked to schedule their visits in advance. Call 919-477-5498 for more information.

■ *Historic Stagville* is a State Historic Site featuring 18th- and 19th-century buildings dedicated to African-American cultural and historic studies. This 71-acre site occupies the remnants of one of the largest plantations of the pre–Civil War South. The plantation belonged to the Bennehan and Cameron families, whose combined holdings totaled approximately 900 slaves and almost 30,000 acres by 1860. Historic Stagville is located at 5825 Old Oxford Highway. It is open Monday through Friday from 9 A.M. to 4 P.M. Admission is free. Call 919-620-0120 for more information.

■ *North Carolina Mutual Life Insurance Company*, at 114–116 West

Parrish Street, was once the home of the Mechanics and Farmers Bank, known as the "World's Largest Negro Business." It won Durham the reputation as the "Capital of the Black Middle Class." The white-brick building, erected in 1921 on the site of the company's first office building, is on the National Register of Historic Places and is a National Historic Landmark.

Magic Wings
Butterfly House
COURTESY OF DURHAM
CONVENTION & VISITORS BUREAU

MUSEUMS AND SCIENCE CENTERS

■ The *Duke University Primate Center* is the world's leading facility dedicated to prosimian primates. Over 420 animals representing 28 species and subspecies are housed here, including lemurs from Madagascar, loris from Asia, galagos from Africa, and tarsiers from islands of eastern Asia. Only about a quarter-mile from Duke's campus, this facility provides an extraordinary opportunity to see and appreciate these increasingly endangered creatures. The center is open for tours six days a week. Tours are by appointment only; due to an increase in tour requests, you should call at least two weeks in advance of the date you wish to come. In accordance with USDA regulations, all visitors must be accompanied by a trained docent or staff member while on the premises. Call 919-489-3364 for more information.

■ The *North Carolina Museum of Life and Science*, located at 433 Murray Avenue, is more fun than a kid (of any age) ought to have. Featuring a real 15-foot tornado, a percussion hut, dozens of interactive exhibits, over 75 live animal species from owls to wolves, the Magic Wings Butterfly House, the new Insectarium, an outdoor nature park, and the Ellerbee Creek Railway, this is guaranteed entertainment for hours. The museum is one of only 35 institutions in the world accorded "full member" status by the Association of Science-Technology Centers. It operates every day except Thanksgiving, Christmas, and New Year's. It is open Monday through Saturday from 10 A.M. to 5 P.M. and Sunday from noon to 5 P.M. An admission fee is charged. For more information, call 919-220-5429, or visit their website at www.ncmls.citysearch.com.

CULTURAL OFFERINGS

▪ The *Carolina Theatre*, located at 309 West Morgan Street, is part of the Durham Civic Center complex. This theater is nothing short of gorgeous, and the events that take place here are a thrill. You can sit back in the renovated glory of the historic 1926 Beaux-Arts auditorium and see first-run art shows, live music by such artists as Emmylou Harris, Richard Thompson, Joan Armatrading, and the Durham Symphony, or live theater and opera companies performing classic and modern pieces. The parking is easy, and the courtyard is lovely. All in all, this is a splendid night's entertainment. For more information, call 919-560-3040, or visit their website at www.carolinatheatre.org.

▪ *Broadway at Duke* features up to six major touring Broadway productions per year in the 1,636-seat Page Auditorium on the Duke campus. The theater is located on Towerview Road. For more information, call 919-684-4444, or visit their website at www.auxweb.duke.edu/boxoffice.

▪ *Duke Drama* makes its home in the 600-seat Reynolds Industries Theatre. It presents both student productions and specially produced Broadway previews featuring some of the biggest names from New York. It's worth your while to check their schedule. Call 919-684-4444 for more information.

▪ *Manbites Dog Theater*, now at 703 Foster Street, is one of the reasons you'll want to stay in Durham. This courageous theater takes on the community and the world with controversial issues that leave audiences talking about the performances for days. One of the most popular events is the annual performance of Ludlam's *Mystery of Irma Vep*. Call 919-682-3343 for more information.

■ *Hayti Heritage Center*, at 804 Old Fayetteville, is located in Durham's historic Hayti community. The St. Joseph's Historic Foundation/Hayti Heritage Center is an integral part of the Triangle's cultural landscape. The 1890s church that houses the St. Joseph's complex is a National Historic Landmark. The center offers innovative programming and exhibitions featuring local, regional, and national artists in its effort to educate and enrich the entire community about African-American life, history, and culture, as viewed through many artistic perspectives. Among the programs the Hayti Heritage Center coordinates are the Black Film Diaspora, the Bull Durham Blues Festival, and the Martin Luther King Festival. It is also host to the Lyda Moore Merrick Gallery. For more information, call 919-683-1709, or visit their website at www.hayti.org.

SPECIAL SHOPPING

■ When you're in Durham, make sure you visit *Ninth Street*, where a row of boutiques, galleries, cafés, a record store, and two good bookstores makes for a very pleasant afternoon walk. You'll also want to visit *Brightleaf Square*, located on Gregson Street toward the center of town.

■ *Patterson's Mill Country Store*, at 5109 Farrington Road between N.C. 54 and Old Chapel Hill Road, is an authentic country store and pharmacy with hundreds of pieces of historical memorabilia. A collector or amateur pharmaceutical historian could spend a day in this little store with nary a boring moment. The store includes a furnished early-20th-century doctor's office. Antiques, collectibles, and North Carolina crafts and gifts are for sale. The store is open Tuesday through Sunday. For more information, call 919-493-8149.

Durham Bulls Baseball
PHOTOGRAPH BY CHIP HENDERSON
COURTESY OF DURHAM CONVENTION
& VISITORS BUREAU

RECREATION

■ **Durham Bulls Athletic Park**, at 409 Blackwell Street, is the nationally acclaimed, 10,000-seat downtown home of the Durham Bulls class AAA baseball club. It replaced the historic Durham Athletic Park. The park includes skyboxes and the year-round Ball Park Corner, which sells Bulls memorabilia. Call 919-956-2855 for more information. **Durham Athletic Park**, at 426 Morris Street, is the old site where generations of fans gathered to watch the Bulls play. So charming is it that it was used as the location for the movie *Bull Durham*, starring Kevin Costner, Susan Sarandon, and Tim Robbins.

SEASONAL EVENTS

■ The **American Dance Festival** takes place on the Duke campus, primarily in Page Auditorium and the Reynolds Industries Theatre. One of the best modern-dance festivals in the world, it features premieres by well-known mavericks like the Paul Taylor Company and Pilobolus, as well as the work of avant-garde and unknown performers. The festival runs from early June to late July and attracts an exotic audience of art and dance aficionados from around the world. Call 919-684-6402 for information or 919-684-4444 for tickets.

■ The **Bimbé Cultural Festival**, sponsored by the Hayti Heritage Center, takes place at Durham Athletic Park in late May. This African-American music-and-arts festival is one of the oldest cultural festivals in the country and one of the region's most comprehensive celebrations of music, art, and dance from Africa and the Caribbean. Call 919-560-4355 for information.

- The **DoubleTake Film Festival** takes place in April, primarily in the Carolina Theatre's Royal Center for the Arts. It is presented in association with the Center for Documentary Studies at Duke University and has alliances with national and international institutions such as the Museum of Modern Art in New York, Exploris and the North Carolina Museum of Art in Raleigh, and the Hague Appeal for Peace in the Netherlands. The organization continues its presentation of documentaries throughout the year by offering film series, educational outreach, and the DoubleTake Documentary Traveling Festival. For information, call 919-660-3663, or visit their website at www.cds.aas.duke.edu/filmfestival.

- The **Festival for the Eno**, at West Point on the Eno city park, takes place on the Fourth of July weekend and has, after over two decades, become a rich Triangle tradition. It is a three-day, five-stage festival that raises money for the purchase and protection of land in central North Carolina's Eno River Basin. The festival offers diverse entertainment for

American Dance Festival
PHOTOGRAPH BY WILLIAM RUSS
COURTESY OF NORTH CAROLINA DIVISION OF TRAVEL AND TOURISM

Eno River near Durham
PHOTOGRAPH BY WILLIAM RUSS
COURTESY OF NORTH CAROLINA DIVISION OF
TRAVEL AND TOURISM

all ages; past performers have included Ralph Stanley, Chuck Davis and the African-American Dance Ensemble, and Dar Williams. The ambiance and the view of the beautiful Eno River are worth the trip and the admission fee by themselves. Camping is permitted at Eno River State Park but not in the city park. Call 919-477-4549 for information.

■ The ***Bull Durham Blues Festival*** takes place at Durham Athletic Park every year in early September. The groove is deep and wide at this wonderful festival that features national, regional, and local blues, along with booths offering everything from barbecue to Jamaican Jerk chicken. Tickets are available for one or both nights; you may bring a blanket or chair for the ball field seating. The cast of performers includes such names as the Neville Brothers, Buddy Guy, and Wilson Pickett. Sit back and have fun. For more information, call 800-845-9835 or 919-683-1709, or visit their website at www.hayti.org/Special-Events/Bluesfest/bull-durham-blues.html.

Places to Stay

RESORTS, HOTELS, AND MOTELS

■ ***The Regal University Hotel***. Deluxe. 2800 Campus Walk Avenue at U.S. 15/U.S. 501 Bypass off Interstate 85 (919-383-8575). Located a mile from Duke's West Campus and Duke University Medical Center, the Regal features 313 spacious guest rooms, including six suites. This inviting hotel draws some of the dancers, performers, and artists who visit the university, which makes for a lively happy hour. A swimming pool, a spa with a masseuse, and a full breakfast buffet (offered until a very civilized late hour in the morning) make this altogether a very hospitable place.

- **The Washington Duke Inn and Golf Club.** Deluxe. 3001 Cameron Boulevard (919-490-0999). One of only two Mobil Four-Star hotels in North Carolina, the Washington Duke Inn has 171 rooms, all with Internet access. The guest rooms overlook either the 18-hole championship golf course designed by Robert Trent Jones or the beautifully landscaped front grounds. The inn is within walking distance of most of Duke's West Campus and is a quick cab ride from downtown. Guests can dine at the on-site Four-Diamond Fairview Restaurant, which serves an international medley of specialties.

- **Durham Marriott at the Civic Center.** Deluxe/Expensive. 201 Foster Street (919-768-6000). If you want to stay at a major hotel in downtown Durham, this is your primary option. Located atop the Durham Civic Center four miles from Research Triangle Park, two miles from Duke University, and within walking distance of the Brightleaf district and Durham Bulls Athletic Park, the 187-room hotel offers guest rooms with executive work areas, two-line speaker telephones with voice mail and data ports, cable television with in-room movies, coffee makers, irons and ironing boards, and hair dryers. A restaurant/lounge/bar, an airline reservations desk, a rental-car desk, a gift shop, and meeting and banquet facilities are on the premises. Valet parking, room service, secretarial services, and laundry services are available. Guests have access to a gym one block from the hotel.

- **The Brownestone Inn.** Moderate. 2424 Erwin Road (919-286-7761). This inn is convenient to Duke University and the hospitals. Its 140 rooms are comfortable, and the staff is friendly. A pool, a sauna, and a whirlpool are on the premises. Complimentary continental breakfast is served. Again, you may have the fun of spotting some performers from the nearby theaters, which sit only a block away.

INNS AND BED-AND-BREAKFASTS

- **Arrowhead Inn.** Deluxe/Expensive. 106 Mason Road (800-528-2207 or 919-477-8430). Resting on six acres of gardens and lawns just minutes from Eno River State Park, Arrowhead Inn is luxury in a historical setting. The inn, built around 1775, has been carefully renovated; it has been featured in *Southern Living* and *Food and Wine*. The rooms range from an upscale rustic cabin to a carriage house; all offer private baths and phones with modem ports. A full gourmet breakfast and late-afternoon refreshments are served.

■ *Morehead Manor Bed-and-Breakfast.* Deluxe/Expensive. 914 Vickers Avenue (919-687-4366). This bed-and-breakfast is located in the historic Morehead Hill neighborhood just south of downtown, near Durham Bulls Athletic Park and Brightleaf Square. Built in 1910 for the man who ran Liggett and Myers Tobacco Company, the colorfully redecorated 8,000-square-foot Colonial Revival home features four distinct guest rooms.

Places to Eat

■ *Magnolia Grill.* Expensive. 1002 Ninth Street (919-286-3609). Magnolia Grill is the crème de la crème of Triangle dining. Ask anybody in Durham. While maintaining their modest location for over a decade, owners Ben and Karen Barker and chef Glenn Lozuke have made quite a splash, earning awards like Best Chef Southeast 2000, *Bon Appétit*'s "Best Pastry Chef in America" for 1999 (won by Karen), and an award from the James Beard Foundation. The *"Nouvelle* Southern" menu, which changes daily, includes nearly a dozen exciting appetizers (how's "House-Cured Majestic Salmon with Wild Rice Scallion Pancake" sound?), entrées like "Grilled Pork Confit" and "Pan-Roasted Cervena Venison," a gallery of gourmet desserts ("The Magnolia Grill is known for its desserts," says Ben Barker), and a very fine wine and liquor collection. Vegetarian offerings are limited, but the restaurant is willing to accommodate dietary preferences and restrictions. Reservations are essential at this busy restaurant. Dinner is served Tuesday through Saturday.

■ *Nana's Restaurant.* Expensive. 2514 University Drive (919-493-8545). Nana's, reopened after a lengthy renovation, enjoys a reputation for extraordinary food and service. Former Magnolia Grill chef Scott Howell, who studied at the Culinary Institute of America in New York City, created Nana's, he says, "to start makin' food happen." The combination of world-class cuisine, great service, and well-chosen wines has won the restaurant the coveted Award of Excellence from *Wine Spectator* magazine each year since 1994. Of course, you'll need to call for reservations. Dinner is served Monday through Saturday.

▪ *Café Parizade*. Expensive/Moderate. 2200 West Main Street at Erwin Square (919-286-9712). Café Parizade is the festive creation of Durham restaurant magnate Giorgios Bakatsias. Diners enjoy cool and elegant Mediterranean cuisine (with touches of France, Greece, Italy, and even Africa) under a brightly adorned ceiling (try to count the cherries). A vegetarian can have fun here while enjoying an uptown ambiance. While not great for intimate conversation, this place has good food, is entertaining, and is a great date restaurant. Lunch is served Monday through Friday and dinner every day.

▪ *Anotherthyme*. Moderate. 109 North Gregson Street (919-682-5225). Located just a block from Brightleaf Square, Anotherthyme is, after over a quarter-century in Durham, a dining staple. Under the continued guidance of chef and owner Mary Bacon, the restaurant offers Mediterranean and Southwestern creations alongside a 150-item wine list in a casually elegant setting. This restaurant is extremely vegetarian-friendly. It's also a great place to stop in for a nightcap. Dinner is served daily.

▪ *Fishmongers Restaurant and Oyster Bar*. Moderate. 801 West Main Street (919-682-0128; www.fishmongers.net). Fishmongers gives diners a real taste of the coast. You'll feel perfectly at ease pounding your crabs here or slurping down your fresh oysters. Open for over 15 years, Fishmongers offers frosty bottled and draft beers and friendly, intelligent service. Lunch is served Tuesday through Sunday and dinner every day.

▪ *Pops*. Moderate. 810 West Peabody in Brightleaf Square (919-956-7677). This restaurant offers consistently good food and a clientele as bright and colorful as the artwork on the walls. The cuisine is stylish, fresh Italian. The desserts and breads are baked in-house. The open-kitchen setting is perhaps a little loud for intimate conversation. Lunch is served Monday through Friday and dinner seven days a week.

- **Taverna Nikos**. Moderate. 905 West Main Street (919-682-0043). Located in historic Brightleaf Square, Taverna Nikos offers a beautiful Mediterranean atmosphere and hospitality to match. The staff is delightful, and the decor is very Greek market. Lunch and dinner are served Monday through Saturday.

- **George's Garage**. Moderate/Inexpensive. 737 Ninth Street (919-286-4131). George's is an upbeat smorgasbord of ethnic foods and activities in the hub of Ninth Street life. In addition to the excitement of finding sushi at 11 P.M., there's the added bonus of pull-back-the-table dancing on weekends. The lunch menu includes an array of food that may leave you stunned. Lunch and dinner are served every day.

- **Blue Corn Café**. Inexpensive. 716-B Ninth Street, adjoining Books on Ninth (919-286-9600). The fine used bookstore is reason enough to try Blue Corn Café. There are bigger and better reasons, however—the Latin American cuisine is colorful, interesting, very good, and very reasonably priced. Check out the Puerto Rican cornsticks, and watch for surprises like cactus in your quesadilla. Vegetarians recipes are available. Lunch and dinner are served Monday through Saturday.

- **Bullock's Barbecue**. Inexpensive. 3330 Quebec Drive (919-383-3211). Crowds come from miles around for Bullock's signature sliced barbecue, a rarity in the land of chopped. Don't worry about the long line; the crowd is chatty, and you can admire the wall of fame that showcases celebrities who have sampled the sauce through the years. Vegetarians can forget it, though the slaw and hush puppies are delicious.

- **Satisfaction Restaurant and Bar**. Inexpensive. 905 West Main Street in Brightleaf Square (919-682-7397). This is, strictly speaking, a sports bar. And you'll know it if the Blue Devils happen to be playing. But it's also a great pizza place. Freshly made dough, over 20 toppings to choose from, delicious sauce—what's not to like? Try the homemade potato chips to go with that microbrew or import beer you're sipping. Vegetarians are welcome. Lunch and dinner are served Monday through Saturday.

Franklin Street in Chapel Hill
COURTESY OF CHAPEL HILL / ORANGE COUNTY
CONVENTION AND VISITORS BUREAU

CHAPEL HILL AND CARRBORO

by Deb Baldwin

*I*t was the winter of 1795 when the first student at the University of North Carolina made his way to class—by walking the 170 miles from Wilmington to Chapel Hill. He was for weeks the sole student there, but his arrival had been heralded for nearly 20 years. The college was planned for in the first state constitution, drawn up in 1776. It asked for the establishment of "one or more universities" in which "all useful learning shall be duly encouraged and promoted." State support, the document stated, should be provided so that instruction might be available "at low prices."

Revolution slowed the process. It wasn't until 1789—the year George Washington became president of the new nation—that the university was chartered by the North Carolina General Assembly. Despite constitutional instructions to the contrary, no state appropriations were made, and the trustees were left to secure land and money themselves.

Three years later, on a warm November day in 1792, some 12 men on horseback finally rode up the dome that is now called Chapel Hill, having been commissioned by the legislature to search out a suitable site for the university. They sat down in an open glade beneath the leaves of a tulip poplar (allegedly the tree now known as the Davie Poplar) on a site said to be "inaccessible to vice." There was plenty of water, and the air was temperate. The site was beautiful, offering a 360-degree vista of the lower lands all around. Some say the men selected the spot and moved on, while others say they lolled about and consumed a fair amount of whiskey—a story most students find more plausible.

On October 12, 1793, in a Masonic ceremony led by legislator and trustee William R. Davie, the cornerstone was laid for the brick building now called Old East. The scene is depicted in a mural on a wall of the post office on Franklin Street; the school still celebrates University Day each year.

It was a little more than a year, then, before that lonely student made his famous trek. Others soon followed. The seclusion offered by the remote site seemed to free the students, rather than to tame them, however. For example, students chopped off the tail of a horse belonging to one university president, upended his privy, and assured him in writing that he would soon be "as secure as Pharaoh in a hieroglyphic of feathers and a balmage, sir, of delicious tar." The students' actions brought forth his resignation.

Since those early days, the university has cultivated a fine reputation for educational excellence in both the sciences and the arts. It boasts a fine medical school, the state's only dental school, a good liberal-arts school, and reputable law and business schools. The programs in public health and environmental health are some of the best in the country. Chapel Hill and neighboring Carrboro are now home to over 100,000 residents. More than 20,000 students attend the university. The notable beauty of the campus and the wild and rebellious nature of the students continue to be hallmarks of Chapel Hill. Both the town and the university draw bonds of affection that keep people coming back. Though the students come these days in convertibles, sports cars, and Jeeps, many claim they would still walk to the school if they had to. So liberal is this place that it often invokes the wrath of the state's conservatives; Jesse Helms called the town a "zoo." Chapel Hill is a haven of alternative lifestyles, education, and entertainment in a lush and hospitable Southern environment.

Meanwhile, nearby Carrboro, once simply the quiet and rustic neighbor of Chapel Hill, has developed its own identity, artists' galleries, and festivals.

JUST THE FACTS

Chapel Hill, in Orange County, is accessible by N.C. 54, U.S. 15/U.S. 501, and Interstate 40, which connects Chapel Hill, Durham, Research Triangle Park, and Raleigh. Hillsborough, the county seat, is just to the north; it can be reached from Interstate 40 or by heading north on N.C. 86.

The nearest major airport is Raleigh-Durham International Airport, about a half-hour away. Small planes can land just north of town at Horace Williams Airport, which has a 4,500-foot lighted landing strip; call 919-962-1337 for information.

The Greyhound/Trailways bus station is at 311 West Franklin Street; call 919-942-3356. Intercity bus service is offered among Chapel Hill, Durham, and Raleigh by the Triangle Transit Association; call 919-549-9999.

The Chapel Hill/Orange County Visitors Bureau is at 501 West Franklin Street, Suite 104 (888-968-2060 or 919-968-2060; www.chocvb.org).

The local newspapers are the *Chapel Hill Newspaper*, the *Chapel Hill Herald*, the *Daily Tar Heel*, and the *News and Observer* of Raleigh. The free weekly *Independent* offers good in-depth reporting and listings of activities; the *Spectator* offers listings of activities and restaurants.

Things to Do

HISTORIC PLACES, GARDENS, AND TOURS

■ Although the **University of North Carolina at Chapel Hill** is primarily flanked by Franklin Street, Hillsborough Street, Raleigh Road, and

Columbia Street, it continues to spread. The main historic campus lies between Franklin Street and Cameron Avenue. Visitors can enjoy a fine campus walking tour between those two streets.

The first building on the campus—indeed, the only building for two years—was the two-story brick structure that came to be called *Old East*, located on what is now Cameron Avenue. A National Historic Landmark, it is the oldest state-university building in America. The college opened to students on January 15, 1795, but its first and only professor had to wait as student Hinton James of New Hanover County walked from home, arriving on February 12. By March, two professors and 41 students were present. Old East still serves as a men's dorm.

■ At the heart of the campus on Cameron Avenue stands the visual symbol of the university, the *Old Well*. For many years, the Old Well served as the sole water supply for Old East and Old West dormitories. In 1897, it was given its present decorative form at the direction of President Edwin A. Alderman, who based his beautification on the Temple of Love in the Garden of Versailles. Though local custom has it that a sip from the well brings wisdom and good luck, frequent nocturnal visits by students from nearby North Carolina State University generally render a drink from this well unwise.

The Old Well
COURTESY OF CHAPEL HILL / ORANGE COUNTY
CONVENTION AND VISITORS BUREAU

■ The **Davie Poplar** marks the spot where, as legend has it, William R. Davie selected the site for the university in 1792. It sits in McCorkle Place, the large green that separates Franklin Street from the campus.

■ **Playmakers Theatre**, on Cameron Avenue, is considered by some to be the most beautiful building on campus. This Greek Revival temple is one of the masterworks of New York architect Alexander Jackson Davis, who designed it as an unlikely combination library and ballroom. In later years, it became the theater for the Carolina Playmakers, who, under the leadership of "Proff" Fred Koch and playwright Paul Green, were largely responsible for developing folk and outdoor drama in the United States.

■ **Forest Theatre**, on Country Club Road, sits on what was once Battle Park. The site was first utilized for theatrical presentation in 1916, on the tricentennial of Shakespeare's death. W. C. Coker, the faculty botanist who had developed the nearby arboretum, chose the location. Several years later, when Frederick Koch came to the university, the location was developed into a permanent theater. The outdoor amphitheater, dedicated to Koch, still serves as a performance space for local theater groups, including the relatively new Open Door Theatre company.

Forest Theatre
Courtesy of Chapel Hill / Orange County Convention and Visitors Bureau

North Carolina Botanical Garden
COURTESY OF CHAPEL HILL / ORANGE COUNTY
CONVENTION AND VISITORS BUREAU

- The *North Carolina Botanical Garden*, on Old Mason Farm Road near N.C. 54, encompasses nearly 600 acres. Its display of the state's native plants is separated into areas depicting coastal plain, Piedmont, and mountain habitat gardens. Also cultivated here are a shade garden, a fern collection, native perennial borders with rare plants, and an aquatic collection. Pieces of sculpture are featured among the collections. Call 919-962-0522 for more information.

- Visitors to the university campus can also enjoy the gardens and the heavenly, wisteria-covered arbor at the *Coker Arboretum*, on Hillsborough Road.

Coker Aboretum
PHOTOGRAPH BY DEB BALDWIN

Morehead Planetarium
COURTESY OF CHAPEL HILL / ORANGE COUNTY CONVENTION AND VISITORS BUREAU

MUSEUMS AND SCIENCE CENTERS

▪ *Morehead Planetarium*, on East Franklin Street, is, after 50 years, one of the landmarks of North Carolina. It was a gift of John Motley Morehead III (1870–1965), a former student at the university whose mission was to educate the community. Its purpose far exceeded that modest scope when, as the American space program took wing, it was used to train astronauts from the Mercury program to the Apollo-Soyuz program.

The planetarium was the first to be owned by a university. It still serves as an educational and instructional training ground, as well as a program- and education-oriented facility. It is home to one of the most spectacular pieces of equipment in the East—the magnificent Zeiss Model VI projector, which is capable of showing nearly 9,000 stars in a 68-foot dome. The complex also houses exhibits, an art gallery, a rose garden with a sundial, a gift shop, and banquet facilities. Public planetarium shows (offered Wednesday through Saturday evenings) and live sky shows narrated by planetarium staff members (offered on Fridays) teach the public about the night sky, lunar landings, the travels of the *Voyager* spacecraft, black holes, weather tracking, the Big Bang, and more. On occasion, music laser shows are offered, though the projector is seen to its best advantage in the star shows. An admission fee is charged. Call 919-549-6863 or 919-962-1247 for operating hours and show times, or visit their website at www.morehead.unc.edu.

▪ The *Ackland Art Museum*, on Columbia Street on the university campus, was founded through the bequest of William Hayes Ackland (1855–1940). The museum exhibits from a permanent collection of more than 14,000 works of art from around the world. The Ackland is rich in paintings and sculptures by artists such as Degas, Rubens, and Pissarro; Indian miniatures; Japanese paintings; North Carolina folk art; and prints, drawings, and photographs. It also exhibits four to six temporary loan exhibitions annually, including such innovative installations as "Contemporary Film and Video Art." The museum is open from Wednesday through Sunday from 10 A.M. to 5 P.M. and Sunday from 1 P.M. to 5 P.M. Admission is free. Call 919-966-5736 or 919-406-9837 for more information.

Cultural Offerings

▪ *Playmakers Repertory Company*, an offshoot of the original Carolina Playmakers, is a professional regional theater troupe offering up to six productions per year, including original works, in the Paul Green Theatre on the university campus. Call 919-962-PLAY for more information.

The Carolina Playmakers, founded by Koch, launched many of the school's alumni and associates into the arts. Among these were Thomas Wolfe, who performed the title role in his student-written play, *The Return of Buck Gavin*; Pulitzer Prize–winning playwright Paul Green; comedian Andy Griffith; band leader Kay Kyser; and author Richard Adler.

▪ The *ArtsCenter*, at 300-G East Main Street in Carrboro, has for 25 years been a dynamic artistic center for the community. It features a non-stop calendar of art classes, theater, jazz, family programming, and art exhibits. The facilities include a theater, classrooms, a dance studio, an informal performance space, and an art gallery. Activities include a wide array of classes and workshops taught by professional artists in a noncompetitive, hands-on environment. On weekends, musicians from locations ranging from the Appalachians to the Andes perform in the Earl Wynn Theater. The "World-Music" concert series highlights emerging and established artists, and the nationally recognized jazz series presents regional and national jazz artists. The family entertainment at the center includes a series featuring artists dedicated to sharing drama, musical theater, puppetry, storytelling, and music of all kinds with children and their families. Theater programs include the ArtsCenter Community Theater, which provides a venue for actors of all levels to explore and develop their craft. The West End Project series provides an informal theater space for artists to perform new material or learn new skills. The ArtsCenter also hosts productions by some of the Triangle's many professional theater companies. Call 919-929-2787 for more information.

SPECIAL SHOPPING

▪ You can't come to Chapel Hill and miss the scene on **East Franklin Street**, the drag that runs right beside the college. You'll see saxophone players, accordion players, bagpipe players, rappers, snake handlers, college students, flower ladies, college professors, homeless folks, lawyers, record stores, bars, galleries, cafés, old churches, trees, shops, and the Morehead Planetarium—all within the space of about a quarter-mile. Go down to **West Franklin Street** and you've got bakeries, art shops, antiquarian bookstores, vintage clothiers, designer boutiques, a wine bar, a teahouse, outfitters . . . you get the picture. These days, the action extends all the way to Main Street in Carrboro (just keep following Franklin Street West), where you'll find more galleries, the ArtsCenter, an army surplus store, on and on.

▪ Of special note is **A Southern Season**, at 1800 East Franklin Street in Eastgate Shopping Center. One of the first true gourmet stores in the area, it has been offering Southern and European specialties for over 25 years. It has expanded to include a café, a coffee bar, and a wine room. It also sells specialty baskets and fine gifts through telephone orders, a catalog, and a website (www.southernseason.com). Call 919-929-7133 for more information.

■ **Foster's Market**, at 750 Airport Road in Chapel Hill, offers a fine selection of gourmet and vegetarian dishes, baked goods, and groceries. This is a good place for afternoon coffee and conversation or for a pickup for a potluck party. Call 919-967-4383 for information.

■ **Weaver Street Market and Café**, in Carr Mill Mall at 101 East Weaver Street in Carrboro, is more than just a great co-op and organic-foods grocery. It's also a restaurant that offers baked goods and a unique salad bar, as well as a community center that offers musical presentations and art shows on the lawn. This is the place to get a feel for the Carrboro ambience. Just have a seat on the lawn on Thursday evening or Sunday morning (when they have live music), enjoy some gourmet coffee, and relax. Call 919-929-0010 for more information.

RECREATION

■ If you enjoy cycling, you'll be pleased to learn that Chapel Hill and Carrboro are extraordinarily bicycle friendly. The two towns have a well-developed system of bike trails and bike lanes and a commitment (through the Chapel Hill Greenway Commission) to eventually developing over 40 miles of trails. At least four good official trails are currently available. Maps are accessible at www.ils.unc.edu/hiking/chindex.html. Or you can contact the town clerk at 919-968-2743 to get more information about the system.

■ I'd be sorely remiss if I didn't mention the **Cat's Cradle**, at 300 East Main Street—that monster of a nightclub, that giant bus stop on the rock-'n'-roll route from Atlanta to New York City, that incubator of musical movers. This is a great music club known far and wide. Though it's moved around a bit in its 20 or 30 (who's counting?) years of life, it still brings in wonderful acts who actually *ask* to play here. And we're talking big, like the Smashing Pumpkins, T-Bone Burnett, Howling Wolf, the Squirrel Nut Zippers, Ben Folds Five, Arlo Guthrie, and Richard Thompson. And we all remember the days when REM used to play here, as did the Riders in the Sky, Brave Combo, and even Nirvana. What a club! Go on in and watch these greats (did I mention the Dirty Dozen Brass Band?) among a crowd of only about 300, and be sure to tell Billy the manager hello. Yes, it costs to get in, but you can listen to one of the world's greatest college stations (WXYC, 89.3 FM) for ticket giveaways or at least some information. Call 919-967-9053 to get the lowdown, or check the *Independent* for listings.

▪ The **North Carolina Tar Heels basketball team** is a subject that is sure to get a strong reaction from almost anyone you see on the street in Chapel Hill. Calling the 22,000-seat Dean E. Smith Center (the "Dean Dome") home has put the team a little farther away from many of its fans but has done nothing to hinder its success. ACC basketball is one of the most exciting spectator sports around, and you're right in the heart of it. You can reach the Dean Dome at 919-962-6000 or by visiting www.tarheelblue.fansonly.com.

▪ Golfing opportunities include **Twin Lakes Golf Course** (919-933-1024), at 648 William Way, six miles south of Chapel Hill, and the university's **Finley Golf Course** (919-962-2349), located two miles from Interstate 40 West on N.C. 54. In 1999, Finley Golf Course underwent an $8 million renovation by architect Tom Fazio. It has since been called a "masterpiece." The 18-hole, par-72 course offers reduced rates to students and faculty of the university.

SEASONAL EVENTS

▪ **Apple Chill** and **FestiFall**, Chapel Hill's street fairs, take place on Franklin Street in April and October, respectively. Sponsored by the Chapel Hill Parks and Recreation Department, they offer live music and other entertainment, a variety of foods, and lots of vendor stalls for a Sunday of fun. Call 919-968-2784 for information.

▪ Chapel Hill and Carrboro pride themselves on their diversity. **Fiesta del Pueblo**, which takes place in September at Chapel Hill High School, is where local citizens gather to celebrate Latin American art, music, food, and tradition. This weekend event boasts an attendance estimated around 35,000 to 40,000. A modest admission fee is charged.

La Fiesta del Pueblo
COURTESY OF CHAPEL HILL / ORANGE
COUNTY CONVENTION AND VISITORS
BUREAU

▪ *Fête de la Musique*, takes place, of course, in the Paris of the Piedmont, Carrboro. The town partakes of a tradition begun in Paris in 1982 to celebrate music, friendship, and freedom on the summer solstice. In 1998, Carrboro joined two other American cities—New York and San Francisco—to honor the occasion; overall, 100 nations participate. A rare event indeed, it brings every available musician to the mic and every able Carrboro citizen to the rank of celebrant. The festival continues to grow worldwide, so get the word out and go!

Places to Stay

RESORTS, HOTELS, AND MOTELS

▪ **The Governor's Club**. Deluxe. 11000 Governors Drive (800-891-3284 or 919-933-7500). At the Governor's Club, you'll find a group of cottages situated on a Jack Nicklaus golf course in a mountain setting. Each cottage offers four to seven comfortable suites, a large living area, and a fully equipped kitchen. Suites can be individually contained for single travelers, or they can access the adjoining living area for groups and families, allowing for mixing and mingling in ways not possible in standard hotel settings. The Governor's Club is popular for conferences, parties, and retreats. Tennis courts are available for those who don't enjoy golf.

▪ **The Carolina Inn**. Deluxe/Expensive. 211 Pittsboro Road (919-918-2795 or 919-933-2001; www.triangle.citysearch.com/E/V/RDUNC/0003/

03/95/1.html). This historic Four-Diamond hotel is the grand old lady of Chapel Hill. It offers elegant, magnolia-clad Southern hospitality in a location that is not beatable by Tar Heel standards. From its site right on the corner of the university campus, you can easily walk to the arboretum, the planetarium, the Playmakers Theatre, the Forest Theatre, or the Wilson Library. The inn is recognized as a National Trust Hotel of America and is listed on the National Register of Historic Places. It is indeed rich in history, as the walls and the staff will be glad to tell you. You'll have to book ahead here, since this gracious hotel is such a favorite for wedding parties and alumni gatherings. All 184 rooms are nicely decorated. Guests enjoy complimentary coffee and fresh-baked chocolate chip cookies on arrival. And yes, there is a ghost, but you'll have to wheedle the staff into telling you about it.

▪ *The Siena Hotel.* Deluxe/Expensive. 1505 East Franklin Street (800-223-7379 or 919-929-4000). Inspired by the ambiance of Italy, the Siena is an elegant hotel that has been a Four-Diamond recipient since 1989. It prides itself on having a distinctive European character based on a Tuscan villa. The 80 spacious guest rooms are individually appointed with antiques; the French doors open onto European balconies. The amenities include a complimentary buffet breakfast, a daily newspaper, bathrobes, and turndown service.

▪ *Hampton Inn.* Moderate. 1740 U.S. 15/U.S. 501 (919-968-3000). This 122-room hotel just outside the city limits offers a deluxe continental breakfast, in-room coffee, laundry service, health-club passes, an outdoor swimming pool, and discounted airport and local transportation service, among other things.

INNS AND BED-AND-BREAKFASTS

▪ *The Inn at Bingham School.* Expensive/Moderate. N.C. 54 at Mebane Oaks Road (800-566-5583 or 919-563-5583). Originally a prep school that opened in 1845, this quiet inn seems far from the ever-increasing madding crowd of the Triangle. Innkeepers François and Christina Deprez offer hospitality, history, gourmet breakfasts, and wine and cheese under

the tall pecan trees of central North Carolina. Though it has been renovated, the inn retains its historical authenticity in its original wood and
masonry and its period antiques in every room. The five rooms include a
1790s log cabin; depending on your choice, you may enjoy a fireplace, a
whirlpool, or a canopy bed. This historical house serves as a meeting
place for at least one secret society from the Triangle area. Try to get
François to tell you more.

Places to Eat

Okay, I *know* I'm including a lot of restaurants here, but dining out is
part of the lifestyle of the Chapel Hillian. These restaurants—all of them—
are among the best around.

■ ***Carolina Crossroads in the Carolina Inn.*** Expensive. 211 Pittsboro
Street (919-933-2001; www.crossroads.citysearch.com). At Carolina Cross-
roads, you can enjoy the elegant cuisine of world-class executive chef
Brian Stapleton while seated in the lap of hospitality at the Carolina Inn.
The California-born Stapleton has been voted chef of the year in the
Triangle; he came to the Crossroads after 10 years with the Ritz Carlton.
Recipes like "Seared Halibut with Spring Peas, Leeks, Jerusalem Artichokes,
White Grapes, and Cornmeal Dumplings" give a nod to both California
and the South. Breakfast and dinner are served every day; lunch is served
Monday through Saturday; brunch is offered on Sunday.

■ ***Il Palio Ristorante at the Siena Hotel.*** Expensive. 1505 East Franklin
Street (919-929-4000). This is the only Four-Diamond Italian restaurant
in the state of North Carolina. Internationally renowned executive chef
Gennaro Villella, late of Il Circo (a close relative of Le Cirque), offers
dishes such as house-smoked salmon, pasta filled with fresh Maine lobster, and seared sea bass. "Simplicity is the foundation of my cuisine,"
says Villella. "My philosophy is to treat ingredients with respect, to give
unique, healthy, flavorful dishes. Through this experience of food and
wine, I offer guests a moment of genuine Italian lifestyle." The award-
winning wine list and the seamless service rise to the occasion. Break-

fast, lunch, and dinner are served daily. Brunch is offered on Sunday.

- **La Résidence**. Expensive. 202 West Rosemary Street (919-967-2506). La Résidence offers regional and seasonal foods prepared with classical French techniques and served in a lovely garden setting. Now in operation for over a quarter-century, the restaurant, under the guidance of chef Joseph Walter, offers such creations as "Grilled Breast of Quail with Garlic-Herb Couscous and Pomegranate Demi-Glaze." It has an extensive wine and liquor list. Live jazz is offered some nights. Reservations are necessary at this popular Triangle tradition. Dinner is served Monday through Saturday.

- **Akai Hana**. Expensive/Moderate. 206 West Main Street in Carrboro (919-942-6775). Here is a great find if you're a sushi eater. This elegant and airy restaurant offers deliciously fresh and properly prepared sushi, sashimi, and Japanese dishes. If you're a sake fan, ask for a sake sampler; Akai Hana has a variety of high-quality sakes, served hot or cold. Live jazz is offered some nights, as is live Japanese flute and keyboard music. Lunch is served Monday through Friday and dinner Monday through Saturday.

- **Crook's Corner**. Moderate. 610 West Franklin Street (919-929-7643). Crook's Corner is Southern dining at its best. You'll find barbecue on the menu here, and grits served in one of their finer settings—alongside shrimp. This is a great place to check out the work of local artists, whose pieces you'll find hanging on the walls, in the restrooms, and even on the roof. You'll be able to check out the works of local artist Clyde Jones anytime you stop by—they're here permanently, hanging from the eaves and rafters all around. And of course, Bob Gaston's signature pink pig proudly hoofs the roof. Garden dining is available in season. If you're lucky, you'll catch sight of everybody's favorite Bill Smith, head chef *extraordinaire* and modest but unforgettable town historian. Dinner is served daily; brunch is offered on Sunday.

- **Pyewacket Restaurant**. Moderate. 431 West Franklin Street (919-929-0297; www.pyewacketrestaurant.com). This was one of the area's original vegetarian restaurants. Now, over two decades later, some of their old recipes are still on the menu. These days, seafood and meat are more prominently featured than vegetarian dishes. Drinks and wine are available, as is a late-night menu Thursdays through Saturdays. Patio dining is offered in season. Lunch is served Monday through Friday and dinner seven days a week.

■ *Acme Food and Beverage Co*. Moderate/Inexpensive. 110 East Main Street in Carrboro (919-929-2263). This stylish restaurant is worth a special trip to the Paris of the Piedmont. The "Uptown America" menu changes every six weeks, but tall cheeseburgers and crispy fries are always served. Don't forget to take a walk down Carrboro's Main Street after your meal. Lunch and dinner are served daily.

■ *Vespa Cibobuono*. Moderate/Inexpensive. 306 West Franklin Street (919-969-6600). After visiting numerous Italian restaurants one night, a friend and I stopped, discouraged, into Vespa around 10 P.M. Our evening had been one of enforced "plate-splitting" fees, store-bought bread, and overcooked, packaged pasta. "Are you closing soon?" we asked the waiter. "Please!" he boomed. "Not until you have finished. What may we serve you?" We proceeded to sample fresh and delicate pasta, freshly baked crusty bread, tasty sauces, good wine, and hearty espresso, all served with effusive hospitality. The menu includes seafood, sweet sausage, and veal alongside risotto, polenta, and scottata (homemade mozzarella), as well as some dishes for the vegetarian and some fine desserts. Other waiters came to greet us as well, and we were told that nearly all the staff are natives of Sicily. We had a great meal and a delightful time. Incidentally, I've been told that the Vespa in Cary is an equally delightful experience. Lunch and dinner are served Tuesday through Sunday.

■ *Allen and Son Pit-Cooked Bar-B-Q*. Inexpensive. N.C. 86 North at Mill House Road (919-942-7576). This is a bastion of hickory-cooked chopped barbecue. Order up a platter with some fries, slaw, hush puppies, and Brunswick stew and you're ready for a tailgating party Chapel Hill–style. Honey, don't forget the sweetened iced tea. If it's a football weekend, you'd better call ahead, because they're going to be busy. There's another location on U.S. 15/U.S. 501 near Pittsboro, if you've just gotta have it and you're headed south. My friends in New York demand that I bring Allen and Son's barbecue on every trip. Lunch and dinner are served Monday through Saturday.

■ *Mama Dip's Kitchen*. Inexpensive. 408 West Rosemary Street (919-942-5837). This Southern-style restaurant is owned by—you guessed it—Mama Dip. Though the famed owner has been acclaimed by such notables as Craig Claiborne of the *New York Times* and has had her own book published, she will likely be working in the kitchen when you eat here. She is deservedly famous for, among other things, her barbecue sauce, her sweet potato pie, her chicken and dumplings, and, yes, her chitlins. Southern-cooked vegetables are also a specialty. Lunch and dinner are served seven days a week.

■ *The Mediterranean Deli*. Inexpensive. 410 West Franklin Street (919-967-2666). This little place has been called "the best restaurant in Chapel Hill" by one reputable source. It offers a wide selection of authentic Middle Eastern food at reasonable prices. The offerings include dolmades, hummus, falafel, and spinach pie. The desserts include baklava, lady fingers, burma, and mammoul. After your meal, you can shop for olives, oils, and couscous from their shelves. Lunch and dinner are served seven days a week.

■ *Pepper's Pizza*. Inexpensive. 127 East Franklin Street (919-967-7766). Peppy Pepper's serves pizza with artichokes, broccoli, and whatever you can imagine. You can watch through the front window as they spin the pizzas, but I'm just as fond of counting the incidents of body piercing while I wait. This is great pizza, folks, and the be-studded staff is always friendly. Pepper's also whips up great calzones, stromboli, and salads. Did I mention that you can buy pizza by the slice? Lunch is served Monday through Saturday and dinner every day.

■ *Sutton's Drugstore*. Inexpensive. 159 East Franklin Street (919-942-5161). This is a comforting sight for returning Tar Heels who have seen lots of spots come and go. Go in and sit down at the counter and order a good, old-fashioned cheeseburger, crispy crinkle-cut fries, and a chocolate milk shake or an orangeade. You'll be served under a broad-bladed ceiling fan within walls full of pictures of students, athletes, cheerleaders, local kids, and townspeople. Have a chat with the cook (or the pharmacist, who'll take over if the cook steps out) and get a taste of the village. Breakfast and lunch are served daily.

There is a remarkable trend in Chapel Hill and Carrboro these days—lots and lots of Mexican restaurants, most of them really good, and all of them really inexpensive. I'd be disloyal not to mention that the Flying Burrito is one of my favorites and the leader of the pack.

▪ *Carrburritos Taqueria*. Inexpensive. 711 Rosemary Street (919-933-8226). Very inexpensive, very informal, and a very cool place to be, Carrburritos has perhaps three great patio tables (just try to get one), fresh food, and a salsa bar that can't be beat. Lunch and dinner are served Monday through Saturday.

▪ *The Cosmic Cantina*. Inexpensive. 128 East Franklin Street (919-960-3955). Based on the once-fabulous Cosmic Cantina in Durham, this one is equally inexpensive. It stays open late and is perfect for the post-bar or -performance bite. Lunch and dinner are served daily.

▪ *El Chilango*. Inexpensive. 506 Jones Ferry Road in Carrboro (919-960-0171). El Chilango is more than a dining experience; it's a cultural experience. This little Mexican bar and buffet is a place for people to mix and mingle in Spanish *or* English. In addition to a great buffet (which includes homemade tortillas and cactus salad!), it offers such activities as Conversation Night and live Latino music and dancing. Fun! Lunch and dinner are served every day.

▪ *The Flying Burrito*. Inexpensive. 746 Airport Road (919-967-7744). The Flying Burrito sits in the little mall on the right next to Fosters. These folks serve up the biggest, greatest burritos and the most delicious Margaritas (they have a great nonalcoholic Margarita, too!). Fresh fish, great salsa, a colorful atmosphere, and a lively crowd are what you'll find here. Lunch is served Monday through Friday and dinner seven days a week.

▪ *Margaret's Cantina*. Inexpensive. 1129 Weaver Dairy Road in Timberlyne Shopping Center (919-942-4745). A drive down the hill to

Margaret's will get you a subtler ambiance (if you can get in to enjoy it), good vegetarian selections, and a delicious, signature fresh-squeezed citrus Margarita. Margaret's has a die-hard following. Lunch is served Monday through Friday and dinner seven days a week.

This Fairy Godmother of Modern Times

Edward Kidder Graham, president of the University of North Carolina, spoke these welcoming remarks to an incoming freshman class in the early years of the 20th century: "There is nothing mysterious about the part the college will play in giving you the qualities that will equip you for this great adventure on which you are setting out. She cannot, by allowing you to room within sight of the well, nor by any system of examinations or lectures, give you a single virtue, nor has she a wishing cap by which she can 'wish on you' any capacity or quality that you do not have. Before she can answer your inquiry as to what she means to say to you as your foster mother, she asks you a very simple question. It is: 'What do you want; and what are you willing to pay?' You may remember in your mythology, and in your Grimm's fairy tales, that when the hero's fortune was so great that the kind fairies put themselves at his service, they always asked him what he wanted. He had at least to choose. It was the way with the wonderful youth Solomon. It is the way with you, O wonderful youth, whoever you are, that have come to this fairy godmother of modern times: She will mean to you what you will, and what you will she will give it to you. I should like to make this splendidly clear, and take the full responsibility for the promise: The college will give to you this year whatever gift you seriously ask of her. I challenge you, therefore, to answer with a choice, and I call upon you to consider with all intentness and manly intelligence what your momentous choice is, and that you put behind that choice, once made, every ounce of power you possess!"

The Earliest Days

Historian Kemp L. Battle described the Masonic ceremony that gave birth to the University of North Carolina this way: "The Chapel Hill of 1793 was covered with a primeval growth of forest trees, with only one or two settlements and a few acres of clearing. Even the trees on the East and West Avenue were still erect. The sweetgums and dogwood and maples were relieving with their russet and golden hues the general green of the forest. A long procession of people for the first time is marching along the narrow road, afterwards to be widened into a noble avenue. Many of them are clad in the striking, typical insignia of the Masonic Fraternity, their Grand Master [William R. Davie] arrayed in the full decorations of his rank. They march with military tread, because most of them have seen service, many scarred with wounds of horrid war. Their faces are serious, for they feel that they are engaged in a great work. They are proceeding to lay the cornerstone of the first building to be erected on the campus of the first American State University to open its doors."

Battle described the university's first official day this way: "The morning of the 15th of January [1795] opened with a cold, drizzling rain. As the sighing of the watery wind whistled through the leafless branches of tall oaks and hickories and the Davie poplar then in vigorous youth, all that met the eyes of the distinguished visitors were a two-storied brick building, the unpainted wooden house of the Presiding Professor, the avenue between them filled with stumps of recently felled trees, a pile of yellowish red clay, dug out for the foundation of the Chapel, or Person Hall, a pile of lumber, collected for building Steward's Hall, a Scotch-Irish preacher-professor, and not one student. . . . It was not until the 12th of February, 1795, that the first student arrived, with no companion, all the way from the banks of the lower Cape Fear, the precursor of a long line of seekers after knowledge. His residence was Wilmington, his name was Hinton James. For two weeks, he constituted the entire student body of the University. Two weeks later the next arrivals came, Maurice and Alfred Moore of Brunswick."

RESEARCH TRIANGLE PARK

by Deb Baldwin

*T*his 7,000-acre park in the middle of the Triangle is the result of a concept born in the 1950s to University of North Carolina sociology professor Howard Odum. He was joined by Romeo Guest, who coined the name of the unusual park, and investor Karl Robbins, who agreed to fund the purchase of large plots of land for the project. Now, the eight-mile-by-two-mile area is home to 140 organizations that employ an estimated 44,000 people (over 50,000, including contract employees). More than 99 percent of them work in research and development in fields that include biotechnology, biopharmaceuticals, microelectronics, telecommunications, public health, and environmental science. The average salary of a Research Triangle Park (RTP) employee is $54,145, so, needless to say, the park has had a major economic impact on the area.

You'll probably find RTP to be devoid of personality. It presents a rather featureless face of granite, brick, and high security, the only visitor-friendly venues being its small malls and large hotels. The dollars are high here, so the hotels are very competitive; most of them offer good service and excellent decor. And if you find the place inhospitable during the day, you'll find it deathly quiet at night. It shuts down; most of its restaurants do, too. Your best bet is to drive into Durham or Raleigh.

JUST THE FACTS

Research Triangle Park is northwest of Raleigh and southeast of Durham on Interstate 40 near the intersection of N.C. 54 and N.C. 55.

Raleigh-Durham International Airport is conveniently located several miles to the east.

The major papers in the area are the *News and Observer* of Raleigh and the *Durham Herald-Sun*. Dining and events information is available in the *Independent* and the *Spectator*, both free weeklies.

Places to Stay

RESORTS, HOTELS, AND MOTELS

■ **Radisson Governor's Inn**. Deluxe/Expensive. 919 N.C. 54 East (919-549-8631). This 193-room inn is the only hotel actually within RTP. Its business rate includes breakfast, a complimentary drink, and an in-room movie. Each room has a coffee pot and a desk with a data port and voice mail. A swimming pool and a fitness center are on the premises. Off-site laundry service is available.

■ **Sheraton Imperial Hotel and Convention Center**. Deluxe/Expensive. 4700 Emperor Boulevard, Durham (800-325-3535 or 919-941-5050). The Sheraton Imperial is widely acclaimed as one of the most luxurious of the Triangle's hotels. It offers 331 elegantly appointed guest rooms, a polished staff, and a list of amenities that includes a business center, a jogging trail, and two lighted tennis courts. Room service is available throughout the day. Complimentary shuttle service to nearby Raleigh-Durham International Airport may be arranged through the concierge.

Places to Eat

■ **Fortune Garden**. Moderate/Inexpensive. 5410-Y N.C. 55 (919-544-6009). Those mourning the sudden dearth of Chinese food in Chapel Hill will be somewhat mollified by a trip to RTP. Fortune Garden represents a marriage of Chinese and Thai both on the menu and in the kitchen; the owners, one from China and the other from Thailand, offer dishes from each tradition. Lunch is served Monday through Friday and dinner Monday through Saturday.

■ **The Deli Box**. Inexpensive. 10800 Chapel Hill Road in Morrisville (919-467-4163). A must-visit, the Deli Box is as close as RTP comes to having a tradition. It offers great sandwiches, a strange interior, interesting music, and local crooning legend and sandwich server Leroy Savage, if you're lucky. Vegetarians are lucky all the time at the Deli Box, thanks to the specialty sandwiches offered for the meat-free. Lunch is served Monday through Friday.

■ **Sarah's Empanadas**. Inexpensive. 5410 N.C. 55 in Greenwood Commons (919-544-2441). Sarah's offers the traditional Spanish pie with a variety of fillings—meats, cheese, or vegetables. For over a decade now, this little restaurant has been serving the park inexpensive and delicious lunches that can be eaten in or taken away. If only they'd change that font over the front door. Oh, well . . . Lunch is served Monday through Friday.

TRIANGLE NEARBY

*T*f you thought there was a lot to do in the Triangle, you were right. But wait, there's more! Here are a few places to visit in the red-clay land surrounding the Triangle proper.

■ **Historic Hillsborough** actually seems like two towns, one of which lies on the busy interstate and one of which is the peaceful village beyond. In town, you'll find more than 100 sites listed on the National Register of Historic Places, some dating back to pre–Revolutionary War times. You can take a self-guided walking tour that visits the majority of these sites, or you can arrange for a tour with guides in costume. Flyers and information on all the sites open to the public are available at the Orange County Visitor Center at 150 East King Street; call 919-732-7741. The center is in the late-18th-century Alexander Dickson House; the home's gardens include traditional 18th- and 19th-century plants used for cooking, medicine, and dyeing. The visitor center is also the place for information about the Christmas Candlelight Tour and the biennial Spring Historic Home and Garden Tour.

Occaneechi Indian Village
COURTESY OF CHAPEL HILL / ORANGE COUNTY CONVENTION AND VISITORS BUREAU

- *Occaneechi Indian Village* is located along the Eno River on South Cameron Avenue in downtown Hillsborough. The village—reconstructed to look as it did in the late 17th century—includes a palisade, huts, a cooking area, and a sweat lodge. This spot is often used for Native American powwows. Call 919-304-3723 for more information.

- One of the best places to stay in Hillsborough is the *Inn at Teardrop*, at 175 West King Street (919-732-1120). The old building, which dates to 1768, is beautifully decorated with wildly exotic antiques and world memorabilia. There are no televisions or telephones in the six rooms here, so guests are immersed in historic quiet. Another excellent choice is the *Hillsborough House Inn*, at 209 East Tryon Street (800-616-1660 or 919-644-1600; www.hillsboroughinn.citysearch.com). This large home, built in 1790, overlooks St. Mary's Road, an ancient Native American trading path. Its 80-foot-long veranda allows an excellent view of the landscaped gardens, the sweeping front lawn, the pond, and the in-ground pool.

- If you're hungry, it's worth noting that the *Colonial Inn* (919-732-2461), at 153 West King Street, has long been the object of pilgrimages

Inn at Teardrop
COURTESY OF CHAPEL HILL / ORANGE COUNTY CONVENTION AND VISITORS BUREAU

by students who make the drive over from Chapel Hill to taste the affordable country cooking. You can get your greens and cornbread here in a setting you won't soon forget. A tavern stood here as early as 1759. Cornwallis is said to have had his soldiers pave the muddy intersection of King and Churton Streets with flagstones like those in front of the inn. ***Hobgood's Family Barbecue***, at 636 North Churton Street (919-732-7447), is another local institution. Open for nearly three decades, Hobgood's is famous for its deluxe barbecue sauce.

▪ ***Pittsboro*** and ***Chatham County***, once dismissed as country cousins, are now reveling in their rural spaciousness and their growing community of artists. Simple ***Siler City*** has come into the news in the past few years with its rapidly growing Latino population. It is now the site of interesting celebrations like the annual Stations of the Cross procession, conducted in Spanish and English. Keep your eye on this small farm town.

▪ Of special interest is ***Fearrington Village***, on U.S. 15/U.S. 501 between Pittsboro and Chapel Hill. Some years ago, a portion of this 200-year-old farm was converted into a fine restaurant that came to be known for its prix fixe menu and its charming country setting. It has now grown to include an entire community of specialty shops, a market, a medical center, a bookstore, a flower and plant shop, and, perhaps most notably, a dairy barn and silo. The excellent bookstore—called ***McIntyre's***—is noted

Fearrington House
COURTESY OF FEARRINGTON HOUSE COUNTRY INN AND RESTAURANT

for bringing in names like Jimmy Carter for autographing events. Recently, arts events like sculpture tours and performances by such conservatories as the North Carolina School of the Arts have added to the allure of the famed country community. The renowned restaurant still stands, along with a bed-and-breakfast inn (919-542-2121). The inn is the only Five-Diamond winner in North Carolina and one of only a handful of country inns to earn AAA's highest accolade. Distinctive touches include ecclesiastical doors used as headboards and pine flooring from a workhouse along the Thames.

▪ The **General Store Café** (919-542-2432), at 39 West Street in Pittsboro, is a great place to catch up on Chatham news, to visit, and to pick up herbal elixirs, teas, a few groceries, and breakfast or lunch. Vegetarians will be pleased with the "Tofu Eggless Salad Sandwich" and other such offerings, and everybody will be happy with the yummy desserts and homemade scones. This is also a good place to pick up a map to the 50-plus studios and galleries in Pittsboro and the surrounding area. All the local artists—who include potters, sculptors, painters, jewelers, glass workers and blowers, designers, ironworkers, and more—can be accessed through the Chatham County Arts Council (919-542-0394). A grand studio tour is held in December. This is a great way to do some fine holiday shopping!

- **Beggars and Choosers** (919-542-5884), at 38 Hillsboro Street in Pittsboro, is a vintage store and collectible shop to die for. But don't go in if you don't have time to do it right! You could get lost in this place, which offers everything from feathers to beds.

- Anybody in Pittsboro will be glad to tell you about the **Piedmont Farm Tour**, which takes place in April. Twenty-five farms for $25 is the offer; you can get advance tickets for $20. You'll get a close look at the work done at dairies, apiaries, nurseries, vegetable farms, and horse farms. Call 919-542-2402 for more information.

- Speaking of dairies, weary travelers shouldn't miss the **Inn at Celebrity Dairy** (877-742-5176; www.theinn@celebritydairy.com) in Siler City. The famous goats here provide cheese to many of the finest stores and restaurants in the Triangle. Needless to say, guests get a fine breakfast— fresh goat cheese, homemade preserves, fresh eggs, and seasonal fruits and vegetables. The inn offers six rooms and a suite. Spinning and wool gathering are among the unusual activities available to guests, who can also enjoy a therapeutic massage from the nearby massage institute. And I've saved the best for last. Baby goats are available to climb all over you at any time. A friendly lot, they're just a bunch of kids.

- Lovers of fine crafts might like to make a short trip north of the Triangle to Granville County, where they'll find the **Cedar Creek Gallery** at 1150 Fleming Road in Creedmoor. This gallery, owned and operated by craftspeople, boasts the largest selection of fine crafts on the East Coast. A winner of the North Carolina Governor's Award for Excellence in the Arts and Humanities, Cedar Creek pulls in pilgrims from all over, who come to see the work of over 250 artists and artisans, many of whom have work displayed in permanent national collections. People come for the stoneware, quilts, baskets, jewelry, furniture, candles, wind chimes, musical instruments, and other items. The gallery is open seven days a week. For more information, call 919-528-1041, or visit their electronic gallery at www.cedarcreekgallery.com.

- The headquarters for *Falls Lake State Recreation Area* is at 13304 Creedmoor Road in the community of Wake Forest, 10 miles north of Raleigh. Falls Lake offers outdoor recreation at seven facilities on its 38,000 acres of woodlands and lake in Wake and Durham Counties. RV and tent sites, primitive sites, and sites for group camping are available year-round. Visitors also come for the swimming, the picnic facilities, the hiking trails, and the interpretative programs. A privately managed concessionaire, Rollingview Marina, offers boat launching, slips, mooring, rentals, and supplies. The recreation area is open from 8 A.M. to 6 P.M. November through February; from 8 A.M. to 7 P.M. during March and October; from 8 A.M. to 8 P.M. in April, May, and September; and from 8 A.M. to 9 P.M. June through August. For more information, call 919-676-1027.

The Sandhills

Fayetteville

Pinehurst and Southern Pines

$\mathcal{T}$ogether, Fort Bragg and Pope Air Force Base constitute one of the world's largest military complexes. It's easy to see, then, why many of the people who come to the Sandhills region of North Carolina are members of the armed services. But the Sandhills are also a magnet for anyone who loves to play golf or train horses.

The temperate climate and the beauty of the region's longleaf pine forests provide great conditions for the 40 championship courses located in this region. The climate and the sand footing have made the area one of the leading training and competition locations for horse lovers. Here, you can see hunters, jumpers, and dressage horses in training, especially during the mild winter months. You can also see Standardbreds working during the winter on the harness tracks. You can enjoy everything from steeplechases to polo matches.

Although the city of Fayetteville is primarily associated with Fort Bragg and Pope Air Force Base, it has a long history as a trading and cultural center. Today, in addition to visiting the museums that honor our nation's fighting men and women, you can visit some of the state's earliest historical sites.

Statue of Lafayette
COURTESY OF NORTH CAROLINA DIVISION OF
TOURISM, FILM AND SPORTS DEVELOPMENT

FAYETTEVILLE

by Deb Baldwin

*I*f you can get past Fayetteville's military trappings, you will discover a town that predates much of the rest of North Carolina. If you find yourself in Fayetteville, lost amid strips of pawn shops and signs proclaiming "Girls, Girls, Girls!" my advice is to relax and enjoy the otherworldly scenery. Where else can you find business names like Seven Dwarfs' Lounge, Cloud Nine, Pandora's Night Fantasy, and I Thee Wed? The names alone are enough for a few hours' amusement.

Fayetteville is one among dozens of cities named after the Marquis de Lafayette, but it is said to be the first one—actually, the only one—he really visited. The French hero of the American Revolution arrived in Fayetteville by horse-drawn carriage in 1825 and was welcomed by the residents.

Fayetteville has long tried to find its niche in North Carolina. The city sought to become the state capital, even building a statehouse as an enticement to legislators. More importantly, it then sought to add to its allure by building the all-important public house nearby, the Cool Spring

Tavern. After the disappointing outcome of the "War of the Taverns"—the Cool Spring versus Joel Lane's tavern in Raleigh—insult was added to injury when, in 1831, a kitchen fire at the home of a citizen named Kyle swept the downtown area, destroying over 600 buildings, including the would-be statehouse. Nonetheless, Fayetteville is still home to some of the oldest structures in the state. Some of the most beautiful examples of local architecture are the town's spectacular churches—St. Joseph's Episcopal, St. John's Episcopal, and Evans Metropolitan AME Zion, among others.

It was in 1918 that the city saw its most pivotal change. That year, Congress established Camp Bragg, an army field-artillery site. Pope Field, named for Harley H. Pope, an airman whose JN-4 "Jenny" crashed in the Cape Fear River, was added a year later. After five years, Camp Bragg became a permanent army post renamed Fort Bragg. Today, Fort Bragg and Pope Air Force Base comprise one of the world's largest military installations.

The military has brought diversity to this part of North Carolina. A 1997 study by the University of Michigan named Fayetteville the fourth most integrated city in the United States.

JUST THE FACTS

Fayetteville is located just east of Interstate 95 roughly 26 miles south of Interstate 40. It can be reached via U.S. 401, N.C. 24, or N.C. 87.

Fayetteville Regional Airport is just south of the city off Interstate 95 Business. For information, call 910-433-1160.

The Greyhound/Trailways bus station is located at 324 Person Street; call 910-483-2580.

Over 300,000 residents live in Cumberland County, nearly 120,000 of them in Fayetteville, the county seat. Fayetteville is among the fastest-growing cities in the state; since 1990, its population has climbed by 49 percent due to annexation.

The daily newspaper is the *Fayetteville Observer-Times*.

Paraglide is the official newspaper of Fort Bragg and Pope Air Force Base. You can find information and show times in the free publication *Up and Coming.*

The Fayetteville Area Convention and Visitors Bureau is located at 245 Person Street. For information, call 800-255-8217 or 910-483-5311, or visit their website at www.fayettevillenc.com/chamber.

Things to Do

HISTORIC PLACES, GARDENS, AND TOURS

■ **Fayetteville State University**, at 1200 Murchison Road, was established in 1877 as the Howard School, the first state-supported teacher-training institution for black North Carolinians. In 1939, it was renamed Fayetteville Teachers College. Since 1972, it has been a campus of the University of North Carolina system. One of the famed administrators of the school was Charles W. Chesnutt, who was appointed principal in 1880. Chesnutt was the author of *The Conjure Woman* and *The Wife of His Youth*, among other works; he was awarded the Springarn Medal by the NAACP in 1928. For more information about the university, call 910-486-1111.

■ **Cross Creek Cemetery #1**, on Cool Spring Street, is one of the few cemeteries in the country listed on the National Register. It contains a collection of the remarkable masonry of famed Scottish artist George Lauder and the graves of many Confederate and Union soldiers, as well as that of Lauder himself.

■ **Cool Spring Tavern**, at 119 North Cool Spring Street, is thought to have been built in 1788. Having survived the great fire of 1831, it is believed to be the oldest structure in the city. The tavern was built in a failed attempt to entice the men deliberating the location of the new state capital. The decision fell to Raleigh, of course. Since 1860, the structure has been privately owned by the MacKethan family. For more information, call 910-433-1990.

Market House
COURTESY OF FAYETTEVILLE CONVENTION
AND VISITORS BUREAU

■ The *Market House*, at the intersection of Green, Gillespie, Person, and Hay Streets, was built in 1832 on the foundation of the old statehouse, which burned in the fire of 1831. It was within those walls that North Carolina ratified the United States Constitution in 1789 and chartered the University of North Carolina. It was also there that North Carolina ceded its western lands to form the state of Tennessee.

The Market House is listed on the National Register of Historic Places. Its ground floor was used as a market for many years, and its upper level housed the town hall. The clock still chimes at 7:30 A.M. for breakfast, at 1 P.M. for dinner, at sundown, and at 9 P.M., which was once the local curfew. Call 910-483-2073 for more information.

■ *Liberty Point*, located at Bow and Person Streets, is the site where, on June 20, 1775, some 55 patriots signed what is generally known as the Liberty Point Resolves, a petition declaring independence from Great Britain. A granite stone notes the names of the patriots and their pledge to their country at that historic meeting: "We stand ready to sacrifice our lives to secure her freedom." The building at this site, constructed between 1791 and 1800, is the oldest known commercial structure in Fayetteville. Call 910-433-1612 for more information.

■ **St. Joseph's Episcopal Church**, located at Ramsey and Moore Streets, was established in 1873 by the black members of St. John's Episcopal Church with the assistance of that church's rector, the Reverend Joseph Caldwell Huske. Built in the Shingle style with Gothic and Spanish influences, it is notable for the five exquisite "Resurrection Windows" by Tiffany of New York and for its pipe organ, built in 1857 by Henry Erben of New York. The organ, purchased from St. John's for $100, has been powered by hand, water, gas, and now electricity. It is one of the oldest still in use in the country. For information, call 910-323-0161.

■ **St. John's Episcopal Church**, at 1817 Green Street, was rebuilt after the 1831 fire in basically the same design as the original structure, with a big exception: 10 pyramidal spires replaced the single spire that had topped the church. The extraordinary stained-glass windows, imported from Munich, Germany, and said to have been carried by oxcart from New York, were installed around the turn of the 20th century. Call 910-483-7405 for information.

■ **Evans Metropolitan AME Zion Church**, at 301 North Cool Spring Street, was established around 1800 by the remarkable Reverend Henry Evans, a free black shoemaker and preacher who passed through Fayetteville on his way to Charleston and decided to stay. His ministry served both black and white members until the founding of the predominantly white Hay Street Methodist Episcopal Church in the early 1830s. The current Gothic-style building, which dates to 1893–94, is a monument to the craftsmanship of African-American artisans James Williams and Joseph Steward. For more information, call 910-483-2862.

■ **Cape Fear Botanical Garden**, at 536 Northeastern Boulevard, (U.S. 301/Interstate 95 Business), sits at the confluence of the Cape Fear and the Cross Creek Rivers. The 85-acre garden contains old-growth forest and over 2,000 specimens of ornamental plants that keep it beautiful year-round. Included are the signature Camellia Garden, which boasts over 200 named varieties of camellias, and other formal gardens offering signs that provide both historical and horticultural information. Also on the grounds are a restored 100-year-old farmhouse, outbuildings, and garden, which help illustrate the local lifestyle of long ago. An admission fee is

Cape Fear Botanical Garden
COURTESY OF NORTH CAROLINA DIVISION OF
TOURISM, FILM AND SPORTS DEVELOPMENT

charged; reduced rates are offered for military personnel, retired persons, and children under 12. The garden is open from 10 A.M. to 5 P.M. Monday through Saturday and from noon to 5 P.M. on Sunday. Call 910-486-0221 for more information.

MUSEUMS AND SCIENCE CENTERS

■ The *Fayetteville Museum of Art*, located at 839 Stamper, was founded in 1971. It was originally housed in downtown Fayetteville's historic Market House. In 1978, it moved to its present facility, which has the distinction of being the first building in North Carolina designed and built as an art museum. The museum includes two galleries, classrooms, studio space, a library that lends art reference materials and slides, and a museum store. The 5.8-acre grounds and pond give visitors a place to relax. This parklike setting, an oasis in the midst of a heavily trafficked area, is the site of large-scale sculpture displays, art festivals, and public concerts. Admission is free, though donations are appreciated. The museum is open from 10 A.M. to 5 P.M. on weekdays and from 1 P.M. to 5 P.M. on Saturday and Sunday. Call 910-485-5121 for more information.

■ The *Museum of the Cape Fear Historical Complex*, at 801 Arsenal, combines a modern museum building, the 1897 Poe House (yes, that's E. A. Poe, but this Poe was a potter), and the eerie remains of the Fayetteville Arsenal. The museum and arsenal site are open for self-guided tours. Visitors receive a guided tour of the 1897 Poe House upon arrival. There is a gift shop in the museum proper. Admission is free. The complex is open from 10 A.M. to 5 P.M. Tuesday through Saturday and from 1 P.M. to 5 P.M. on Sunday. Call 910-486-1330 for information.

■ The *Airborne and Special Operations Museum*, at 100 Bragg Boulevard, is the big excitement in Fayetteville just now. Newly opened in 2000, this is one of the area's premier attractions. It is a state-of-the-art educational facility that houses exhibits and programming that highlight the feats of Airborne and Special Operations units from 1940 to the present day. The museum features graphic coverage of combat missions; extensive displays of uniforms, insignia, and weapons; and information on Airborne songs, marches, and customs. It includes a 250-seat VISTASCOPE theater, a 24-seat VISTADOME simulator, the Hall of Honors, and a main exhibit gallery. Admission is free, though guests must purchase tickets to visit the theater or try the simulator. The museum is open Tuesday through Saturday from 10 A.M. to 5 P.M. and Sunday from noon to 5 P.M. Call 910-483-3003 for more information.

■ The *JFK Special Warfare Museum*, located in Building D-2502 at Ardennes and Marion Streets, offers a behind-the-scenes look at unconventional warfare. The museum houses weapons, military art, and international cultural items with an emphasis on Special Operations units from World War II to the present. Visitors will find displays covering the evolution of the unconventional warrior beginning with the Indian scouts of the American West. Exhibits from World War II, Korea, and Vietnam explain the development of the modern Green Berets. The majority of the exhibits are related to Vietnam. The heart of the collection is a model of the Son Tay prisoner-of-war camp. In 1970, Colonel Arthur D. "Bull" Simons organized and led a daring attempt to rescue 107 POWs held there. Sadly, the prisoners had been moved before the rescuers arrived. The display explains that the attempt was not in vain, though; the prisoners were still years away from freedom, but their living conditions did improve after the raid. A gift shop is on the premises. Admission to the

82nd Airborne Division War Memorial Museum
COURTESY OF FAYETTEVILLE CONVENTION AND VISITORS BUREAU

museum is free. It is open from 11 A.M. to 4 P.M. Tuesday through Sunday. Call 910-432-4272 or 910-432-1533 for information.

■ The **82nd Airborne Division War Memorial Museum**, at Ardennes and Gela Streets, houses over 3,000 artifacts from World War I through Operation Desert Storm. The exhibits include weapons, helmets, uniforms, photographs, aircraft, parachutes, and other items. A film is shown each hour. Visit the gift shop for an out-of-the-ordinary present. Admission to the museum is free. It is open Tuesday through Saturday from 10 A.M. to 4:30 P.M. and Sunday from 11:30 A.M. to 4 P.M. Call 910-432-5307 or 910-436-1735 for information.

CULTURAL OFFERINGS

■ The award-winning **Cape Fear Regional Theatre**, at 1209 Hay Street, has been in existence for nearly four decades. It presents premieres, elaborate musicals, classic dramas, comedies, and children's favorites, performed by local, regional, and national talent in an intimate 325-seat theater. The theater's Studio Performing Arts Program offers courses in acting, voice, and audition technique for ages eight through adult. This theater company is a jewel. Call 910-323-4234 for more information.

▪ The **Gilbert Theater**, at 301 Hay Street, has been in existence for nearly a decade. During its lifetime, it has provided quality theatrical productions for children, the elderly, minorities, and the economically disadvantaged while at the same time giving local artists a venue for displaying and producing their diverse talents. In the past six seasons, the company has produced classics, thought-provoking works such as *How I Learned to Drive*, a children's puppet show, and original local and regional plays. The Gilbert Theater works to involve students whenever possible both on stage and off. Call 910-678-7186 for more information.

▪ The **Fayetteville Symphony Orchestra** performs several concerts a year at Reeves Auditorium. Call 910-433-4690 for information.

RECREATION

▪ **Fort Bragg Riding Stables**, located at Reilly Road and Butner Road, offer open riding, pony rides, riding lessons, trail rides, and hayrides. Advance notice is required for groups of 10 or more. Call 910-396-4510 for fees and information.

▪ Fishing is popular around Fayetteville. There are a couple of boat ramps on the Cape Fear River, one at the junction of U.S. 301 and Old N.C. 87 and the other at **Riverside Sports Center**, at 1122 Person Street. Fort Bragg has 13 lakes that are open to the public, including Muddy Lake, Little Muddy Lake, and Mott Lake; call 910-396-7506 for information. **Lakeview Park Fishing Pier and Campground**, at 377 Waldo's Beach Road, features a 500-foot pier; call 910-424-4814.

SEASONAL EVENTS

▪ The **Dogwood Festival**, held every April, includes an array of activities, the premier event being a drive along the 18-mile Dogwood Trail, which winds through the downtown historic district and among beautiful residential areas. Symphony performances, rodeos, and street dancing take place all around Fayetteville to celebrate the thousands of blooming dogwoods, azaleas, daffodils, and camellias.

- The *Incredible Bed Race* takes place in June on Green Street, with proceeds going to the North Carolina Burn Center. Participants get four pushers to propel their "incredible beds"—creatively decorated contraptions whose only common ground is that they have four wheels and a mattress. The accompanying street fair and entertainment have turned this unusual fund-raising event into a real fun affair. Call 910-433-2191 for information.

Places to Stay

RESORTS, HOTELS, AND MOTELS

- *Clarion Plaza Hotel*. Moderate. 1965 Cedar Creek Road (800-253-7808 or 910-323-8282). If you want to stay near Interstate 85, this is absolutely your best bet. The Clarion Plaza offers golf packages, a lounge, a spa, and indoor and outdoor pools.

- *Comfort Inn Cross Creek*. Moderate. 1922 Skibo Road (800-537-2268 or 910-867-2268). Located near the mall, the Comfort Inn offers 176 rooms and suites, a Jacuzzi, airport transportation, an outdoor pool, and complimentary breakfast. It has been awarded a Three-Diamond rating by AAA.

- *Holiday Inn Bordeaux*. Moderate. 1707 Owen Drive (800-325-0211 or 910-323-0111). This hotel features over 300 rooms with king or twin double beds. Children stay free. Amenities include a concierge, complimentary continental breakfast, evening hors d'oeuvres and cocktail service, a full-service restaurant, a nightclub, and an outdoor pool. It is located near Fayetteville's mighty mall area.

■ **Radisson Prince Charles**. Moderate. 450 Hay Street (910-433-4444). If you want to stay downtown or near the new museum, your choice is pretty much limited to the Radisson. Built in 1924, this beautiful building is listed on the National Register and is a member of the Historic Hotels of America. It's just around the corner from many of the city's historic sites and is a good base if you're interested in a walking tour.

Places to Eat

■ **De Lafayette Restaurant**. Expensive. 6112 Cliffdale Road (910-868-4600). Housed in an old gristmill on McFayden Lake, this restaurant offers one of the finest dining experiences in Fayetteville. Now in its second decade, it serves sophisticated "New American" cuisine in a greenhouse overlooking the lake. De Lafayette does all its own baking, as well as the gardening of its vegetables, herbs, and flowers. It is famous for its "Occasion Martini," built hot and peppery and served with a pickled green tomato. Thanks to its recently added ballroom, this is a popular spot for special events and private functions. Dinner is served Tuesday through Saturday.

■ **Trio Café**. Expensive/Moderate. 201 South McPherson Church Road (910-868-2443). Recently added lunch service will just add to the allure of this Fayetteville favorite, whose uptown look and fine food have garnered it several notable awards. The rack of lamb and veal chops are favorites here. The restaurant also offers a slew of side dishes such as garlic mashed potatoes, Spanish rice, green beans, and roasted red peppers. And don't forget to try the fabulous desserts. Lunch is served Monday through Friday and dinner nightly. Sunday brunch is also offered.

■ **The Cross Creek Brewing Company**. Moderate/Inexpensive. 4150 Sycamore Dairy Road (910-867-9223). Recommended to me by an art collector as the best place to eat in town, this bustling establishment serves everything from steaks to pizza, though it is most famous for its garlic mashed potatoes and Irish beer. My artsy friend recommended the steak and, yes, the garlic mashed potatoes, but the vegetarian fare was also delicious, and the bread was freshly baked. The air was festive and the young clientele in high spirits. Patio dining is available. Lunch and dinner are served daily.

▪ **Hilltop House Restaurant.** Moderate/Inexpensive. 1240 Fort Bragg Road (910-484-6699). This restaurant is located in historic Haymount right across from the Cape Fear Regional Theatre. It offers steaks, seafood, and Greek specialties. Lunch and dinner are served seven days a week. Sunday brunch is also offered.

▪ **Huske Hardware House.** Moderate/Inexpensive. 405 Hay Street (910-437-9905). This place is worth the trip just to see the building. The 100-year-old structure holds rich significance for the town of Fayetteville. At the time it was built, it was called "Major Huske's Folly" because it was so far from the Market House. Proving his critics wrong, the major went on to open six hardware stores, all bearing the initials *HHH*. Now a brewery and restaurant, Huske Hardware House sits in a prime location for a visit after a day at the new Airborne and Special Operations Museum. It offers such dishes as filet tips and tomato-basil shrimp, as well as some vegetarian fare, preferably served alongside its signature "Airborne Ale." Live music is offered on weekend nights. Lunch is served daily and dinner Monday through Saturday.

▪ **New Korea House.** Inexpensive. 4608 Yadkin Road (910-864-2772). This place offers some fine Korean specialties, including hot pork sliced paper-thin and "Skate Hye" (raw fish). This is one of the many Eastern restaurants in Fayetteville that offer genuine house specialties in addition to the usual Chinese fare. Lunch and dinner are served daily.

▪ **Tung Sing.** Inexpensive. 5548 Yadkin Road (910-864-5885) and Raford Road (910-678-8878). Voted a winner of the Reader's Choice Award from the *Fayetteville Observer-Times*, Tung Sing offers dozens of choices, including Mandarin- and Szechuan-style foods. Lunch and dinner are served daily.

Nearby

▪ **Bentonville Battlefield** is located approximately one hour northeast of Fayetteville; take U.S. 701 to S.R. 1008. This is the site of the last great Confederate charge of the Civil War and the largest battle ever fought in North Carolina. The Battle of Bentonville, contested in March 1865 between General Joseph Johnston's Confederate troops and General William T. Sherman's Union men, ended with 2,500 casualties for the South and 1,500 for the North.

The battlefield is now a State Historic Site that includes a Confederate cemetery, Union trenches, a visitor center, and plaques. It is open Monday through Saturday from 9 A.M. to 5 P.M. and Sunday from 1 P.M. to 5 P.M. Admission is free. Call 910-594-0789 for more information.

Golf in the Sandhills
COURTESY OF NORTH CAROLINA DIVISION OF TOURISM, FILM AND SPORTS DEVELOPMENT

PINEHURST
AND SOUTHERN PINES
by Deb Baldwin

*T*he county of Moore gets its name from Alfred Moore of Brunswick County, who, at 29, had already served as attorney general of North Carolina. A well-known militia colonel in the Revolutionary War, he went on to become an associate justice of the United States Supreme Court.

The early Moore County was home primarily to sandy soil and a lot of longleaf and loblolly pines—which continue to define the area today. The area's Scottish farmers harvested the pines first for lumber and later for resin for turpentine. The need for a means of transporting the trees brought the plank roads that the area became famous for and the railway that is still a centerpiece of Southern Pines.

But it wasn't the railroad that changed the town. That honor might be laid at the feet of John T. Patrick, the state's commissioner of immigration, who fixed his attention on lower Moore County as a potential tourist destination. Patrick heard one—one!—visitor tell the story of how his doctor had sent him to the area because it might help his tuberculosis. Recognizing an opportunity, Patrick sought a publishable statement from a doctor. New York physician G. H. Saddleson complied: "Where the long leaf pine exists ozone is generated largely and it has been demonstrated that persons suffering with throat and pulmonary diseases are much benefited when living in an atmosphere impregnated with this gas." A sanitarium was thus conceived.

One noteworthy man who came to the area because of ill health was entrepreneur James Tufts. Though Tufts, too, believed in the health benefits of the Sandhills, he refused to encourage an influx of consumptives. Rather, he set about the business of building a resort on 5,000-plus acres he bought at a price averaging $1.25 an acre. Locals jeered, saying the land wasn't worth it. Tufts invited in the landscaping firm of Olmsted, Olmsted, and Eliot, which had designed New York's Central Park. The firm planted over 200,000 trees and bushes. Tufts's first hotel in the Pinehurst complex, the Holly Inn, opened in 1895.

It was Tufts's son Leonard who brought in the then-Scottish sport of golfing as an antidote to residents' boredom. Leonard invited famed golfer Donald Ross over from Scotland to design a course, and by 1903, activities had begun at the Pinehurst Golf Club. The cast of stars who have visited through the years includes such names as H. J. Heinz, General George C. Marshall (who bought a home here), Amelia Earhart, Henry and Clare Boothe Luce, too many golf greats to mention, and Annie Oakley, who stayed to give gun exhibitions and lessons for years.

Today, the club is home to one of the top 10 courses in the world. Moore County is such a successful resort area that Japanese businessmen have been known to fly their favorite clients here for complimentary rounds.

The residents of this extraordinarily wealthy area have also brought culture to the Sandhills. The Weymouth Center for the Arts and Humanities nurtures hopeful writers. Sandhills Community College and the Sandhills Horticultural Society have created the extraordinary Sandhills Horticultural Gardens. The arts are cherished here, as the number of local galleries attests. History is preserved as well; the district of Cameron, a row of antique stores and vintage homes and churches, is listed on the National Register. You'll see miles of opulent horse farms on your way to Pinehurst and Southern Pines. Indeed, this area is more formal than much of North Carolina, so don't be surprised if you are asked to don a tie and jacket even at lunchtime.

Just the Facts

Southern Pines is approximately four miles south of the intersection of U.S. 1 and U.S. 15/U.S. 501. Pinehurst is four miles to the west, close to the intersection of N.C. 5 and N.C. 2.

Moore County Regional Airport, located at Airport Road and N.C. 22 near Sandhills Community College, offers commuter air service, including daily connecting flights to Charlotte. Call 910-692-3212 for information.

Amtrak reservations can be made by calling 800-872-7245. The train stops in Southern Pines on the tracks right in the middle of town.

The twice-weekly newspaper in Southern Pines is called *The Pilot*. The local magazine is *Pinehurst: The Magazine of the Sandhills*.

The number for the local chamber of commerce is 910-692-3926. You can contact the Pinehurst Area Convention and Visitors Bureau at P.O. Box 2270, 1480 U.S. 15/U.S. 501, Southern Pines, N.C. 28388 (800-346-5362; www.homeofgolf.com).

Things to Do

MUSEUMS AND SCIENCE CENTERS

■ **Weymouth Woods Nature Preserve**, at 1024 Fort Bragg Road in Southern Pines, offers a museum, interpretive programs, and nature trails to allow visitors to observe and better understand the natural history of the region. Development within the natural area has been limited to those facilities concerned with its study, interpretation, and protection. No provisions have been made for camping or other recreational activities.

The nearly 500 plant species in the preserve range from primitive ferns, lichens, and mosses to brilliantly hued wildflowers, shrubs, and trees. British soldier lichen, cinnamon fern, Indian pipe, trailing arbutus,

Weymouth Center for the Arts and Humanities
COURTESY OF WEYMOUTH CENTER FOR THE ARTS AND HUMANITIES

wild orchids, dwarf iris, fall gentian, blueberries, and wild azalea may be found here. Insectivorous plants are located in the moist areas. Gray squirrels and fox squirrels can be seen around the hiking and bridle trails that wind through the preserve, as can deer, red and gray foxes, raccoons, opossums, and rabbits. Among the less common species are mink and otter. Bird life is abundant at Weymouth Woods. Large numbers of migrating songbirds spend the winder in the preserve. Quail, mourning doves, hawks, and owls can be seen throughout the year.

The preserve's natural-history museum has a number of exciting exhibits. A naturalist provides illustrated lectures for groups. Guided tours are offered along the four miles of hiking trails; a self-guided nature trail is located near the visitor center. Sunday-afternoon programs are scheduled spring through fall. The preserve is open from 9 A.M. to 6 P.M. every day except Christmas. Admission is free. Call 910-692-2167 for more information.

CULTURAL OFFERINGS

▪ The **Sandhills Theatre Company** performs dramas, musicals, and comedies at the Sunrise Theater, located at 250 Northwest Broad Street in Southern Pines. The building, which dates to 1898, is also used for concerts and other arts-council programs. For information, call 910-692-3340; the number for the box office is 910-692-3799.

- The **Weymouth Center for the Arts and Humanities**, at 555 East Connecticut Avenue in Southern Pines, has flourished as a full-fledged cultural center since 1979. Thanks to its wild landscaping and airy presence, the center seems almost out of place (refreshingly so!) in a town of carefully manicured lawns.

The center, once the home of North Carolina author James Boyd and his wife, Katharine Lamont Boyd, is a portion of the home built by the author's grandfather. Upon the elder Boyd's death, grandsons James and Jackson split the house in two. They hauled the main portion by mule across the road, where it became the Jackson Boyd House; now known as the Campbell House, it serves as the home of the Arts Council of Moore County. The portion that became the Weymouth Center was redesigned and enlarged in the 1920s by Aymar Embury II, a friend of the Boyds who went on to become the official architect of Princeton. Then, as now, the building served as a center for literary activity, hosting visits from such friends as F. Scott Fitzgerald, Thomas Wolfe, Paul Green, and Sherwood Anderson. James Boyd himself went on to become a well-known author of historical novels, including *Drums, Marching On, Bitter Creek*, and others.

Today, the center hosts a writers-in-residence program that offers writers and composers stays of up to two weeks to pursue their work. Over 600 artists have taken advantage of the opportunity; many testify that they accomplished their most creative work in the tranquil, inspiring atmosphere of the Boyds' former home. All phases of the arts and humanities are included in Weymouth's programming. The concerts offered by the center feature artists from the music facilities at North Carolina's universities, supplemented by nationally and internationally known chamber musicians; local youth are provided an opportunity to participate in a young musicians' competition. The center hosts frequent readings by acclaimed North Carolina writers and a lecture series that brings in a diverse group of speakers. Call 910-692-6261 for more information.

Special Shopping

- Over 90 pottery studios are located in northern Moore County. The traditional handcrafted work remains virtually the same as pottery produced in the 1700s; the oldest known local piece dates back to 1750. You can find fine hand-thrown, high-fired stoneware and porcelain, traditional low-fired pottery, and innovative and decorative art pottery. A variety of different firing techniques are used here, including salt glazing, raku, and wood firing in groundhog kilns.

Some of the Moore County potters are following a four- or five-generation family tradition. As word spreads about the area, other artists are coming in, too. The studios are open year-round, mostly Monday through Saturday. A map of the location of the pottery studios is available at most shops.

Recreation

Moore County, known as the "Golf Capital of the World," has over 720 holes of golf (with 54 more on the drawing board), covering more than 270,000 yards. That's over 153 miles (or 2,700 football fields) of fairways, which are in constant use by the thousands of visitors who come to follow the little white ball. The density of golf-related activities here is said to be the highest in the world. Indeed, the village of Pinehurst and Pinehurst Resort have been awarded National Historic Landmark status for their significant role in golf history. This is the only golf-related designation of its kind in the United States.

Tradition abounds in a land where legends like Nicklaus, Palmer, Hogan, Snead, and Zaharias have tested their skills on the finest golf courses in the world. Nearly 40 championship courses are located in the Sandhills; there is a course for every golfer, regardless of handicap. Designers of the courses include names like Donald Ross (who designed seven local courses), Tom Fazio (who designed four), Robert Trent Jones, Jack Nicklaus, Arnold Palmer, and Gary Player. The area has hosted dozens of major competitions, including the U.S. Women's Open, the U.S. Open, the PGA Championship, the Ryder Cup, and the World Open, among many others. Most of the major competitions are staged at Pinehurst No. 2.

What follows is a very brief overview of a few of the finest courses. For more extensive information, try www.sandhills.org/golf.

- **Pinehurst Country Club**, on Carolina Vista Drive, features eight premier courses. The mecca of Pinehurst golf has long been the glorified Pinehurst No. 2, built by golf master Donald Ross. Ross, who always considered it his home course, once called it "the fairest test of championship golf I have ever designed." This course hosted the 1999 U.S. Open; it will also serve as the site of the U.S. Open of 2005. The course is open only to members and members' guests. For more information, call 800-487-4653 or 910-295-6811, or visit their website at www.pinehurst.com.

- **Pine Needles Lodge and Golf Club**, at 1005 Midland Road, opened in 1927. It was also designed by Donald Ross. This was the site of the 1996 U.S. Women's Open; it will host the event again in 2001. The course is open to the public, based on availability. For more information, call 800-747-7272 or 910-692-7111.

- **The Carolina**, at 277 Avenue of the Carolinas, is an 18-hole course

Pinehurst Country Club
COURTESY OF NORTH CAROLINA DIVISION OF TOURISM, FILM AND SPORTS DEVELOPMENT

designed by Arnold Palmer. It opened in 1997 and is available to the public. For more information, call 888-725-6372 or 910-949-2811, or visit their website at www.thecarolina.com.

SEASONAL EVENTS

- The entire Moore County area, with its beautiful greenery and rolling terrain, is wonderful for biking. It is used to train and qualify Olympic bicycle teams as well as for the now-famed *Tour de Moore*, which draws cyclists from around the world each April. The feature race is 100 miles around Moore County. Several levels of competition are offered. Call 910-692-4494 for information.

- The *Stoneybrook Steeplechase Races* are back! After a few years' hiatus, the fabulous weekend of activities has returned to Five Points Horse Park in Southern Pines in early April. Call 910-245-3100 for more information on this festive affair.

- The *Carolina Carriage Classic* is held at the Pinehurst track in May. A parade takes place on the Sunday after the classic. Call 910-295-4446 for information.

- One of the most immediately noticeable facets of this area is the great abundance of horse farms. Green fields and black and white fences serve as backdrop to creamy Arabians and grazing, gleaming thoroughbreds. For years, Moore County has been a center for the training of the country's best Standardbred harness horses, trotters, and pacers, in addition to thoroughbreds. A training ground for Olympic contenders, the county is home to five past Olympic equestrian champions.

Places to Stay

RESORTS, HOTELS, AND MOTELS

■ **Pine Needles Lodge and Golf Club**. Deluxe. On N.C. 2 just off U.S. 1 in Southern Pines (910-692-7111; www.golfnc.com/PineNeedles). For three generations, the legendary Peggy Kirk Bell and her family have been welcoming guests to Pine Needles Lodge and Golf Club. Here, in one of golf's most peaceful settings, you'll find the ideal atmosphere in which to improve your game, vacation with family and friends, or hold a business function. *Golf Digest* has awarded this resort a Four-Star rating as a golfing destination. You'll play on a Donald Ross course that was the site of the U.S. Women's Open in 1996 and will be again in 2001. And when you're not on the course, you'll enjoy the at-home feeling of the rustic lodge, the elegant dining room, the comfortably intimate guest rooms, and the state-of-the-art meeting facilities. The resort offers a bed-and-breakfast option or a package that includes all meals in the elegant dining room presided over by award-winning chef Chris Currier.

■ **Pinehurst Resort Hotel**. Deluxe. Carolina Vista Drive, Pinehurst (800-487-4653 or 910-295-6811). This is where it all began in Pinehurst, and it doesn't get any more luxurious. The resort encompasses The Carolina, The Holly Inn, The Manor, and The Villas, all of which offer nightly turndown service, in-room mini-bars, bell staff, room service, express checkout, and data ports for internet usage. Each has access to the concierge desk at The Carolina, which can arrange a host of services. Handicapped-accessible and nonsmoking rooms are available. The resort offers meeting spaces and health and fitness facilities. Recreation options include swimming, fishing, windsurfing, and canoeing. The *Pinehurst Post*, issued weekly to all guests, gives a rundown of the many activities and services at the resort.

■ **Comfort Inn**. Expensive/Moderate. 9801 U.S. 15/U.S. 501, Pinehurst (800-831-0541). This recently built hotel has 80 comfortable rooms at reasonable rates. Golf packages are offered, as are an outdoor pool, a fitness room, complimentary welcoming beverages, and a continental breakfast buffet.

- **Residence Inn by Marriott**. Expensive/Moderate. 105 Brucewood Road off U.S. 15/U.S. 501, Southern Pines (888-702-GOLF or 910-693-3400). This friendly all-suite hotel is just right for the casually inclined. Its quiet, comfortable suites include a living room and a fully equipped kitchen. The inn offers an outdoor pool, a fitness center, complimentary continental breakfast, and packages to over 20 local golf courses. The professional, helpful staff will give you advice on anything in town, including activities and restaurants. The inn is centrally located between Southern Pines and Pinehurst.

INNS AND BED-AND-BREAKFASTS

- **The Knollwood House**. Deluxe/Expensive. 1495 West Connecticut Avenue, Southern Pines (910-692-9390; www.sandhills.org/knollwood). This gracious and stately home, built in 1927 as a holiday retreat for a wealthy Philadelphia family, has been totally renovated and artfully restored by its present owners, Dick and Mimi Beatty, who opened the Knollwood House as a bed-and-breakfast in 1992. Since then, it has become one of the area's premier "experiences." Set on five acres amid azaleas, holly trees, longleaf pines, and towering magnolias, this English manor–style home is as beautifully decorated inside as it is landscaped without. It is within easy range of the lovely Southern Pines shopping district as well as the area's horse farms. Dick and Mimi have traveled extensively, collecting 18th- and 19th-century antiques; these and select family heirlooms are showcased against the soft pastels, bright stripes, and colorful chintzes of the living and dining rooms. The engaging, sunlit garden room, filled with flowering plants and wicker furniture, offers a view of the back lawn and the gazebo and a glimpse of the 14th and 15th fairways of the famous Donald Ross course at Mid-Pines. Golf packages are available through the Knollwood House.

- **Magnolia Inn**. Deluxe/Expensive. Magnolia Road, Pinehurst (800-526-

5562 or 910-295-6900). This 100-year-old mansion has 11 guest rooms furnished with period antiques. It offers an English pub and an outdoor pool. The location is perfect for a downtown stroll. Golf packages are available that give guests access to over 20 courses in the area.

■ **The Old Buggy Bed-and-Breakfast Inn.** Moderate. 301 McReynolds Street in Carthage (910-947-1901; www.oldbuggyinn.com). This is a lovingly restored Victorian bed-and-breakfast in the heart of the Sandhills region. W. T. Jones, president of the Tyson-Jones Buggy Manufacturing Company, built this 6,000-square-foot home for his wife, Florence, in 1897. Today, it stands at the entrance to Carthage's beautiful historic district, only minutes away from the Pinehurst and Southern Pines golf resorts. You'll enjoy the inn's fanciful gingerbread trim, extravagant woodwork, old-fashioned wraparound porch, private swimming pool, verandas, and gardens. A gourmet breakfast and afternoon refreshments are provided. The inn offers special Murder Mystery Weekends and Romance Weekends.

Places to Eat

As you might expect, there are many top-shelf dining establishments in Southern Pines and Pinehurst. Each of the resorts features its own first-class restaurant; if you have the wherewithal and the proper attire, you will find fine food and service at any of them. Here are just a few of the towns' more personable restaurants.

■ **Chef Warren's.** Expensive. 215 Northeast Broad Street, Southern Pines (910-692-5240). Chef Warren's has a cozy, open kitchen and a mouthwatering menu. It offers nightly specials, a seasonal menu, and an extensive wine list. Vegetarians can find something to suit. Dinner is served Monday through Saturday.

■ **The Magnolia Inn.** Expensive. At the corner of Magnolia and Chinquapin Streets in Pinehurst (800-526-5562 or 910-295-6900). Graceful longleaf pines and fragrant magnolias surround this stately 100-year-old mansion, which lies within easy walking distance of Pinehurst's galleries and shops. Guests have the choice of informal dining in the pub or more formal fare in the restaurant proper, where they can enjoy the culinary creations of the world-traveled "Cheffy" and his sous-chef, Kim Folken, who turn out such fare as "Crab Cakes with Curry Ginger Beurre Blanc Sauce and Fruit Salsa" and "Grenadine of Veal." This inn, like most of the area, is not known primarily for its vegetarian fare. Dinner is served seven nights a week.

- **Squire's Pub**. Moderate/Inexpensive. 1720 U.S. 1 South, Southern Pines (910-695-1161). A 25-year tradition in Southern Pines, Squire's serves Irish fare in a casual pub atmosphere. It offers the usual entrées—shepherd's pie and corned beef and cabbage—and a very limited menu for the vegetarian. It also has a delicious, light trifle. Lunch and dinner are served Monday through Saturday.

- **Vito's Ristorante and Pizzeria**. Moderate/Inexpensive. 615 Southeast Broad Street, Southern Pines (910-692-7815). Vito's is perfect for the younger set, though they are not the primary clientele in this area. The food is simple southern Italian—manicotti, cannelloni, and "Scaloppines al Marsala," as well as classic spaghetti, calzones, and pizza. Vegetarians can find something to enjoy here. Vito's offers imported beer and a wine list. Note that the restaurant does not accept credit cards. Dinner is served Monday through Saturday.

Nearby

- The **House in the Horseshoe**, on Alston House Road off Carbonton-Carthage Road 10 miles north of Carthage, is so named because of its location in a bend of the Deep River. It is now a State Historic Site. Built by Phillip Alston in 1772, this was one of the first big houses along North Carolina's frontier.

During the American Revolution, irregular warfare was waged in the

House in the Horseshoe
COURTESY OF STATE OF NORTH CAROLINA, DEPARTMENT OF CULTURAL RESOURCES

back country by bands of Whigs and Tories. Two of the North Carolina Piedmont's more notable adversaries were Whig colonel Alston and Tory guerrilla David Fanning. After numerous altercations, one encounter left Fanning's compatriot Kenneth Black beaten dead. Fanning, at his friend's deathbed, heard Black name Alston as the man responsible. On Sunday, August 5, 1781, Fanning and his men surrounded Alston's house, trapping the colonel, his family, and about two dozen of Alston's militia. When a British officer in the company of Fanning tried to lead a charge, he was shot dead. The direct approach having proved fatal, Fanning's men remained well covered. Shots were fired back and forth for hours, neither side gaining an advantage. As the day wore on, Fanning tried another approach. His men pushed a cart filled with hay to the side of the house, the intent being to set the hay on fire and burn Alston's home down around him. The Patriots frantically debated how they might surrender without being shot down in the process. Mrs. Alston, confident that no one would fire upon a woman, took matters into her own hands. Bravely stepping into the yard, she told Fanning that the men inside would lay down their arms if Fanning agreed not to harm them or the house. Fanning agreed upon the promise that they would not again take up arms in support of the Revolution.

The house is still riddled with bullet holes today. A reenactment of the skirmish is conducted each summer. From April through October, the site is open from 9 A.M. to 5 P.M. Monday to Saturday and from 1 P.M. to 5 P.M. on Sunday. From November through March, it is open from 10 A.M. to 4 P.M. Tuesday to Saturday and from 1 P.M. to 4 P.M. on Sunday. Admission is free. For more information, call 910-947-2051.

■ *Town Creek Indian Mound* is about an hour west of Pinehurst on N.C. 731 off N.C. 73, near Mount Gilead. This is one of the best reconstructions of pre-white civilization in the country and the oldest State Historic Site in North Carolina.

During the first half of the 16th century, Indian immigrants from the south replaced the Siouan-speaking tribes in the upper Pee Dee basin. At Town Creek, they selected a bluff overlooking the Little River as the site for their tribal ceremonial center.

Since the Indians left no written records, archaeology was a vital key to Town Creek Indian Mound. Excavations began in 1936 under Joffre L. Coe of the University of North Carolina at Chapel Hill. During the early years, artifacts, burial vaults, and post holes for a palisade were uncovered.

Today, the site includes a visitor center, a museum, two temples, a burial house, and a reconstructed palisade wall. From April through October 31, it is open Monday to Saturday from 9 A.M. to 5 P.M. and Sunday from 1 P.M. to 5 P.M. From November through March, it is open Tuesday to Saturday from 10 A.M. to 4 P.M. and Sunday from 1 P.M. to 4 P.M. Admission is free. Call 910-439-6802 for more information.

The Triad

Winston-Salem

Greensboro

High Point

Triad Nearby

To people who are not North Carolina residents, it can sometimes be confusing to keep the Triad and the Triangle straight. The Piedmont Triad actually covers an area greater than the three cities—Greensboro, High Point, and Winston-Salem—that are usually associated with the name. Technically, the Triad covers a 12-county area that runs from the Yadkin River on the west to the Haw River on the east and from the Virginia border on the north to the start of the Sandhills to the south.

The concept of a Triad region came to light in the mid-1960s, when a group of elected officials from the area's county and municipal governments met to discuss common concerns. They adopted the name Piedmont Triad Committee. As best as can be determined, this was the first time the word *Triad* was used to describe the area. In 1987, the name of the airport was changed to Piedmont Triad International Airport. The name seems to have caught on with the people. The Greensboro telephone book lists over 130 businesses or organizations with Triad in their names; the Winston-Salem telephone book lists over 120. Although local governments and chambers of commerce try to work together on issues of mutual concern, old rivalries die hard. The cities have been pitted against each other in recruiting wars for too long. So much friction exists between Greensboro and High Point that at one point High Point wanted to secede from Guilford County and form a new county. Fortunately, the newcomers who are arriving in the area in droves don't know about the old battle lines, so cooperation among the communities seems to be on the rise. Thousands of Triad couples have one partner working in one city and the other in another, further diminishing the old lines.

Today, due to the state's prosperity and its increasing visibility in technology-related industries, the Piedmont Triad is drawing more and more people and businesses. Greensboro, its largest city, has a population of 205,000. A city that owes much of its economic base to textiles, Greensboro is now home to several colleges and universities. Boasting a population of 187,000, Winston-Salem is the second-largest city in the region. Although it owes much of its prosperity to tobacco, Winston-Salem has now become a leader in the medical field. The home of both the country's first arts council and the North Carolina School of the Arts, it is also known as a city of the arts. High Point has a population of 74,900. Known internationally as a furniture capital, High Point attracts thousands of people to its showrooms. Altogether, the entire 12-county area claims a population of approximately a million.

With the mountains less than two hours distant and the beaches only four hours away, this region becomes more attractive with each passing year.

by Ed Southern

and

Carolyn Sakowski

The Winston-Salem Skyline
COURTESY OF WINSTON-SALEM CONVENTION AND VISITORS BUREAU

WINSTON-SALEM

by Ed Southern

Winston-Salem has seen better days, of that there is no question. Once the largest city in the state, once the most important industrial center south of Richmond, once the home of two international companies that were entirely homegrown, Winston-Salem has lost much of its industry, revenue, and standing to Charlotte and the cities of the Research Triangle.

But if you will pardon a highfalutin' quote from Tennyson's "Ulysses," "Tho' much is taken, much abides."

As is reflected in its hyphenated name, Winston-Salem has always been a city of the philosophical progression: thesis, antithesis, synthesis. In other words, you take pious Salem, throw in raw Winston, and you get a city remarkable for its civility, its commitment to education, and its culture both classical and folk.

The Moravians who came to the area they named *Die Wachau* (later Latinized to Wachovia) in 1753 were sober, thrifty, disciplined, and peaceful. After establishing the villages of Bethabara and Bethania, they began building their main city, Salem, in 1766.

The Salem Moravians belonged to one of the first Protestant sects. They came mostly from German-speaking areas of Bohemia, Poland, and, of course, Moravia. Arriving in America to escape persecution, they settled first in Pennsylvania, then sent colonists into their new land in the back country of North Carolina. They organized themselves—they were nothing if not organized—into congregational towns in which just about everything was owned and controlled by the church. For several decades, no non-Moravians were allowed to live in Bethabara or Salem.

The Moravians were frequently envied and mistrusted by their neighbors, most of whom were small farmers leading hardscrabble lives on the frontier. These farmers struggled all their lives just to eat. By contrast, the Moravians essentially finished building Salem—complete with church, meeting house, and a running-water system—in five years.

Despite this mistrust, Salem quickly became the trading center of northwest North Carolina and southwest Virginia. Nearby was the only safe place to cross the Yadkin River for 50 miles, so all the major thoroughfares in the area (including the Great Wagon Road from Pennsylvania) ran by Salem.

When Forsyth County was created out of Stokes County in 1849, Salem was the logical choice for the county seat. The Moravian leaders, however, wanted no truck with the rabble that came with a county courthouse, so they agreed to sell the new county 51 acres for a town a mile north of Salem Square.

For almost two years, the Forsyth County seat was known only as "that place north of Salem." In 1851, the North Carolina General Assembly named the town after a local Revolutionary War hero, and Winston was born.

While Salem built textile mills, Winston was known for selling dried berries. Not until after the Civil War and Reconstruction did it begin to capitalize on the area's major crop and pledge fealty to King Tobacco. Factories for making plug tobacco and tobacco auction houses and warehouses sprang up around the young town, but those were lemonade stands compared to what a 24-year-old former traveling tobacco salesman had in mind.

Just as his statue outside city hall suggests, Richard Joshua Reynolds arrived in Winston on horseback. He was drawn from his Virginia home in 1874 by Winston's new rail line, by which, the young Reynolds realized, he could ship his tobacco anywhere and permanently retire his salesman's wagon.

Reynolds built his tobacco company and Winston at the same time. He was phenomenally hardworking and uncommonly canny. A decent man, he was also one of the first industrialists to realize how closely his own fortunes were tied to his workers'. He paid his (mostly black) employees well by the day's standard, instituted profit-sharing plans, and provided drinking water, lunchrooms, day nurseries, and a medical department. His wife, Katharine, encouraged and continued his philanthropy, and the leaders who followed him, at R. J. Reynolds Tobacco Company and elsewhere, placed a high value on giving back to the community.

Winston officially merged with Salem in 1913, although they had been called the "Twin City" for years. The two combined, in the words of longtime *Winston-Salem Journal* writer Chester Davis, "the Salem conscience with the Winston purse."

Most of the 20th century was a heyday for Winston-Salem. Reynolds tobacco and Hanes hosiery were sold around the world. Piedmont Airlines, started at what would become Z. Smith Reynolds Airport, grew into one of the best-run airlines in the country. In the 1950s, Wake Forest College moved from its home near Raleigh to a new campus in Winston-Salem donated by R. J. Reynolds's daughter and son-in-law. A new limited-access highway was begun to relieve downtown traffic; the planned east-west expressway became, before its completion, part of Interstate 40. Winston-Salem founded the first municipal arts council in the nation. In the 1960s, the Twin City beat out several other communities to become the home of the North Carolina School of the Arts.

As the century drew to a close, however, so did Winston-Salem's period of startling growth. Population declined in the 1980s, for the first time since Salem's founding. Piedmont Airlines was bought by USAir. The AT&T plant on Lexington Road shut down in 1988. Most devastating of all was the move of the headquarters of R. J. Reynolds Tobacco—now RJR Nabisco—to Atlanta. RJR Nabisco president and CEO F. Ross Johnson became the most hated man in town when he justified the move by calling Winston-Salem too "bucolic."

But as the poet put it, "Tho' much is taken, much abides." The mis-

Trees shade restored turn-of-the-century homes in Winston-Salem's West End.
<small>PHOTOGRAPH BY ED SOUTHERN</small>

fortunes that beset Reynolds and other local giants forced the city to diversify its economy. The sudden absence of patriarchal industry captains led the city to learn how to run itself. Winston-Salem still has the cultural legacy left by its forebears. Wake Forest University, Winston-Salem State University, Salem College, and the North Carolina School of the Arts call the city home. So do two major art museums—Reynolda House Museum of American Art (housed in the country estate of R. J. Reynolds) and the Southeastern Center for Contemporary Art. The Stevens Center for the Performing Arts plays host to outstanding productions of dance, music, and drama.

Just as the Moravians learned to co-exist with their rural neighbors, and staid Salem with boisterous Winston, the high culture in Winston-Salem co-exists with the rowdy, working-class legacy of the city's industrial past. Much of the current downtown revitalization effort, for example, makes use of Winston-Salem's tradition of mountain bluegrass and gospel and Piedmont blues, the music of the farmers and sharecroppers who brought their crops to town to sell or labored in the mills and factories.

Winston-Salem boasts as much culture as any city in the state, while retaining a blue-collar earthiness that has been glossed over elsewhere beneath tides of Northern transplants and slick prosperity. It's a Jeffersonian combination—a combination that reflects the industriousness, piety, and simplicity of the Moravian pioneers. It's a combination that suggests that Winston-Salem will indeed thrive again.

JUST THE FACTS

Winston-Salem is the county seat of Forsyth County, which has a population of more than 290,000. The Winston-Salem Visitors Center, at 601 North Cherry Street, can provide information on the city; call 336-777-3796.

Located in the northwest corner of the North Carolina Piedmont, Winston-Salem is less than two hours from the heart of the Blue Ridge Mountains and less than an hour from the Virginia border. Interstate 40 runs east and west just south of town; Interstate 40 Business cuts straight through downtown. U.S. 52 connects Winston-Salem with the Virginia mountains and the Blue Ridge Parkway to the north and the Yadkin River Valley to the south. U.S. 52 is slated to become part of Interstate 73/Interstate 74, which will run between Detroit and Charleston, South Carolina.

The city's Greyhound bus station is at 250 Greyhound Court; call 800-231-2222 or 336-724-1429 for details. The nearest Amtrak station is in Greensboro, but a connector is available; call 800-872-7245 for information.

Piedmont Triad International Airport, located off Interstate 40 just across the Guilford County line, is the major airport for Winston-Salem. Seven major carriers provide 86 daily flights. Call 336-665-5600 for general airport information. Z. Smith Reynolds Airport, 10 minutes north of downtown Winston-Salem, is a base for commuter and corporate aircraft; call 336-767-6361 for information.

Things to Do

HISTORIC PLACES, GARDENS, AND TOURS

■ **Old Salem**, on Old Salem Road at Academy Street, is where most

Home Moravian Church in Old Salem
COURTESY OF WINSTON-SALEM CONVENTION AND VISITORS BUREAU

visitors will want to begin—on the spot where Winston-Salem itself began. The Moravians' town has been carefully restored into a "living-history town," where costumed interpreters lead tours, demonstrate traditional crafts, and chat with visitors as if the 19th century had just turned, rather than the 21st.

Tickets may be purchased at the visitor center, which is open Monday through Saturday from 9 A.M. to 5 P.M. and Sunday from 12:30 P.M. to 5 P.M. The hours for various buildings and shops within Old Salem may vary slightly. Most shops—including the Moravian Book and Gift Shop, T. Bagge Merchant, J. Blum Printer, and the highly recommended and aromatic Winkler Bakery—do not require tickets. Nor does the Salem Tavern, which is described in the Places to Eat section. Nor does God's Acre, the burial ground used by original settlers and modern-day Moravians alike; it is to God's Acre that worshipers march from Salem Square at dawn during the traditional Easter Sunrise Service, celebrated since 1773. A ticket gains the purchaser unlimited two-day admission to all gardens and restorations, including the Single Brothers House, where you will see early trades demonstrated; the Miksch House and Manufactory; the Vierling House, home of an early physician; the Boys School; and the John Vogler House. At each stop, interpreters tell about the building, the town, and the orderly, pious life of the Moravians. Also available at the visitor center is an all-in-one ticket that includes admission to the Old Salem buildings, the Museum of Early Southern Decorative Art, the Gallery at Old Salem, and the Children's Museum; these museums are covered in the Museums and Science Centers section. For more information, call 888-348-5420 or 336-721-7300, or visit their website at www.oldsalem.org. Old Salem is closed Thanksgiving, Christmas Eve, and Christmas Day. It will take you at least a half-day to see Old Salem thoroughly. You should enjoy it at a leisurely 18th-century pace anyway.

The 1990s saw the addition of an overdue look at the lives of African-Americans, whether slave or free, within antebellum Salem. A special walking tour called "African-Americans in Salem," is offered, along with an audiovisual presentation. African-American sites on the south end of Salem, such as St. Philips Moravian, have been restored. The Moravians were uncomfortable with slavery—but not uncomfortable enough to do anything about it.

Old Salem adjoins the campus of Salem College and Academy, one of the oldest women's schools in the country and a testament to the Moravians' belief that both sexes deserved an education.

■ *Historic Bethabara Park*, at 2147 Bethabara Road, is a restoration of the Moravians' first settlement in Wachovia. The men who came to scout out the site spent their first night in an abandoned trappers' cabin. The town was never intended to be a permanent settlement; in fact, its name means "House of Passage." Bethabara soon became a trading center for the region. A palisade was built to protect against raiding parties during the French and Indian War. The town, however, was largely abandoned

Historic Bethabara Park
COURTESY OF WINSTON-SALEM
CONVENTION AND VISITORS BUREAU

when Salem was established in 1772.

The palisade, the Potter's House, and the Gemeinhaus (or Congregation House) are still standing and are open to the public. Several foundations unearthed at the town site have been studied by archaeologists, and gardens have been re-created. The restored site is surrounded by a 175-acre park and nature preserve that includes trails to the site of Bethabara's mill, a beaver pond, and a picnic ground overlooking the village.

Bethabara does not take as long to explore as Old Salem, but a visit here should certainly not be rushed. A visitor center is located across Bethabara Road. The exhibit buildings are open for guided tours from April 30 through November 30 except for Thanksgiving. Tours run Monday through Friday from 9:30 A.M. to 4:30 P.M. and Saturday and Sunday from 1:30 P.M. to 4:30 P.M. A modest admission fee is charged. The grounds are open all day, every day, all year. For more information, call 336-924-8191, or visit their website at www.co.forsyth.nc.us/beth.

■ **Reynolda Gardens** occupies 20 acres adjacent to Reynolda House on Reynolda Road. Owned by Wake Forest University, the property includes formal flower and vegetable gardens, a greenhouse, and several acres of woods and streams with marked trails. For more information, call 336-758-5593.

Next to the gardens is **Reynolda Village**, created to house and educate the workers on the Reynolds estate. Katharine Reynolds planned the village as a model farm where area farmers could learn the latest

Left: A row of gazebos in Reynolda Gardens
Above: a detail from a fountain
PHOTOGRAPHS BY ED SOUTHERN

agricultural techniques. It has been renovated to house upscale shopping, galleries, and restaurants. For more information, call 336-758-5584.

MUSEUMS AND SCIENCE CENTERS

■ **Reynolda House Museum of American Art**, at 2250 Reynolda Road, was the country home of tobacco magnate R. J. Reynolds. Devoted to building his tobacco company, Reynolds married late. He took as his bride his distant cousin Katharine. She was many years his junior, but he had long admired her intelligence and bearing. For most of their married lives, they lived in a mansion on Fifth Street, where they had four children: Richard Jr., Mary, Nancy, and Zachary Smith.

In 1912, they began work on what they called a "bungalow" on their country estate about three miles north of town. The house was designed by Philadelphia architect Charles Barton Keen. But the driving force behind the development of the estate was unquestionably Katharine. That it was given the name *Reynolda*, the female Latin version of the family name, was no accident.

By the time the house was finished in 1917, R. J. was near death. Katherine did not long outlive him. The house was left to the children, who tended to use it as a holiday house as they grew older. In 1936, however, Mary and her husband, Charles Babcock, renovated the property for use as their family home.

In 1964, Charles Babcock donated the house and 20 surrounding acres to be used as a nonprofit institution dedicated to the arts and education. His daughter, art historian Barbara Babcock Millhouse, and executive director Nicholas Bragg set about turning Reynolda House Museum of American Art into one of the country's finest facilities for the study of American art, architecture, and design. Thomas Cole, Georgia O'Keeffe, Grant Wood, Frederick Remington, Mary Cassatt, Thomas Hart Benton, Alexander Calder, Jacob Lawrence, and Jasper Johns are all represented in the museum's permanent collection. You'll also find a number of quietly magnificent works by lesser-known artists. I highly recommend *The Old Hunting Ground* by Worthington Whittredge. A collection of vintage clothing from the Reynolds family is housed in the attic.

Reynolda House is itself a museum. It is a classic of the Arts and

Reynolda House Museum of American Art
Photograph by Ed Southern

Crafts Movement of the late 19th and early 20th centuries, which encouraged simplicity and rustic craftsmanship in design and decor. The most impressive feature is an Aeolian organ with 2,566 pipes, some of which are visible in the attic. All rooms are furnished with period decor, including many Reynolds family originals. Children (and many adults) are just as impressed by the bungalow's indoor swimming pool, bowling alley, shooting range, squash court, and mirrored Art Deco bar.

Reynolda House Museum of American Art is open from 9:30 A.M. to 4:30 P.M. Tuesday through Saturday and from 1:30 P.M. to 4:30 P.M. on Sunday. It is closed Thanksgiving, Christmas, and New Year's. Admission is charged. Students with valid identification are admitted free. For more information, call 336-725-5325, or visit their website at www.reynoldahouse.org.

■ The *Southeastern Center for Contemporary Art* (SECCA), at 750 Marguerite Drive, not far from Reynolda House, is housed in the 1929 English-style home of Hanes Hosiery industrialist James G. Hanes. Twenty thousand square feet of exhibit space have been added to the original house. None of this space is used for a permanent collection; instead, SECCA hosts as many temporary exhibits as possible, bringing some of the Southeast's most impressive and up-to-the-minute work to Winston-Salem. Like Reynolda House, SECCA hosts a variety of programs and performances in the house and on the grounds. Unlike Reynolda House, it rents out some of its space for private functions.

SECCA is open Tuesday through Saturday from 10 A.M. to 5 P.M. and Sunday from 2 P.M. to 5 P.M. Admission is charged except for children under 12 and SECCA members. For more information, call 336-725-1904, or visit their website at www.secca.org.

■ The *Museum of Anthropology of Wake Forest University* is located behind Ketner Stadium on Wake Forest's main campus. Founded in 1963 by the faculty of Wake Forest's Department of Anthropology, it was originally intended for Wake's students but is now a favorite of Triad residents and visitors.

The permanent collection features artifacts from the Americas, Africa, Asia, and Oceania. Some of the most interesting pieces, however, are prehistoric artifacts found here in the Yadkin River Valley. The museum also hosts a wide range of special exhibits and programs.

The Museum of Anthropology and its museum shop are open from 10 A.M. to 4:30 P.M. Tuesday through Saturday. Admission is free. For more information, call 336-758-5282, or visit their website at www.wfu.edu/MOA.

While you're here, the campus of Wake Forest University is well worth a quick stroll. Wake Forest College was founded by Baptist ministers in the town of Wake Forest, just north of Raleigh, in 1834. In the 1940s, the Reynolds family invited the college to move to Winston-Salem, offering land on R. J. Reynolds's country estate and a sizable endowment. In 1953, President Harry Truman turned the first shovelful at the groundbreaking ceremony. Five years later, classes began on the new campus.

Built of local red bricks in the Colonial Revival style, the campus is dominated by Wait Chapel, located at the north end of the quad. A popular site for weddings and an annual Christmas Lovefeast, as well as the sanctuary for Wake Forest Baptist Church, Wait Chapel was host to presidential debates in 1988 and 2000.

■ *SciWorks*, at 400 West Hanes Mill Road, has been a children's favorite going back to its original incarnation as the Nature Science Center.

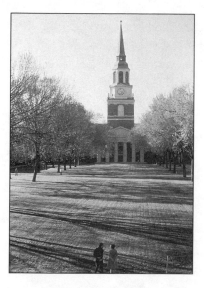

The quad and Wait Chapel on the campus of Wake Forest University
COURTESY OF WINSTON-SALEM CONVENTION AND VISITORS BUREAU

SciWorks boasts 45,000 square feet of exhibits, a 15-acre environmental park, and a 120-seat planetarium. The emphasis is on hands-on, interactive exhibits and programs. Kids can gawk at dinosaur fossils or tease a river otter. SciWorks also offers nature trails and guided walks.

SciWorks is open Monday through Saturday from 10 A.M. to 5 P.M. Admission is charged; the price includes a planetarium show. For more information, call 336-767-6730, or visit their website at www.sciworks.org.

- The *Museum of Early Southern Decorative Art* (MESDA), at 924 South Main Street in Old Salem, is the only museum in the South dedicated to preserving, exhibiting, and researching regional decorative arts. Covering the years from colonization to 1820, MESDA exhibits furniture, paintings, textiles, ceramics, and silver in 24 period rooms and seven galleries.

Visitors here will note the marked cultural differences within the colonial and early federal Southeast; the region was anything but a "Solid South." The Scots-Irish on the frontier lived very different lives from their German neighbors, who in turn existed a world apart from the Englishmen and French Huguenots in the cities of the coastal plain. MESDA takes as its geographical area a region that includes the Chesapeake, the low country, and the back country. This encompasses all of the Carolinas and Virginia and wide swaths of Maryland, Kentucky, Tennessee, Georgia, and what is now West Virginia.

MESDA is open to visitors Monday through Saturday from 9:30 A.M. to 5 P.M. and Sunday from 1:30 P.M. to 5 P.M. Guided tours begin on the hour and half-hour and last 90 minutes. Admission is charged. For more information, call 888-348-5420 or 336-721-7300, or visit their website at www.oldsalem.org.

MESDA shares the Frank L. Horton Museum Center in Old Salem with the *Gallery at Old Salem* and the *Children's Museum*. The Gallery at Old Salem is the museum center's changing exhibit space; contact Old Salem to find out current exhibit and ticket prices. The Children's Museum features hands-on exhibits and activities for children ages four to nine. Admission is charged for children who enter and play and the adults who accompany them; note that the number of adults who may enter is limited. Included are a two-story climbing sculpture, period costumes that kids can try on, a miniature version of the Miksch House, and a secret tunnel.

Visitors admire a sculpture in the Diggs Gallery at Winston-Salem State University
COURTESY OF WINSTON-SALEM CONVENTION AND VISITORS BUREAU

CULTURAL OFFERINGS

■ **Diggs Gallery**, on the campus of Winston-Salem State University, brings in traveling exhibits and artists of national renown. The concentration is on traditional and contemporary African-American art. Artists who have appeared or spoken here in recent years include Jacob Lawrence and Barbara Chase-Riboud.

Diggs Gallery is open Tuesday through Saturday from 11 A.M. to 5 P.M. Admission is free. For more information, call 336-750-2458, or visit their website at www.wssu.edu/diggs.

■ The **North Carolina Black Repertory Company** has its offices at 610 Coliseum Drive. The company sponsors the week-long National Black Theatre Festival every other year. Professional theater groups from around the world come to Winston-Salem for the festival, as do celebrities from theater and film. Call 336-723-7907 for more information.

■ The **Stevens Center for the Performing Arts**, at 405 West Fourth Street, was a vacant 1920s theater until the early 1980s, when the North Carolina School of the Arts turned it into one of the finest performance venues in the Southeast.

The center has a seating capacity of 1,400. It hosts events year-round,

North Carolina Gets a "Toe-Dancin' School"

"A faith in our youth and the talent of our youth. A realization of the place art has in our civilization."

This was the answer Vittorio Giannini gave whenever he was asked what characteristics a city should have to be home to the North Carolina School of the Arts (NCSA). This was in the early 1960s, when the question of the School of the Arts' existence, much less its location, was far from settled. Giannini, an internationally renowned composer from Philadelphia who had long spent his summers in the North Carolina mountains, was an early advocate who would become NCSA's first president.

The North Carolina School of the Arts was the brainchild of novelist and Asheville native John Ehle. In 1961, Ehle wrote an article for the *News and Observer* of Raleigh entitled "What's the Matter with Chapel Hill?" The article was a wide-ranging critique of the failure of the University of North Carolina at Chapel Hill, and liberal-arts colleges in general, to provide the proper environment and training for creative and performing artists.

The article caught the eye of Governor Terry Sanford. Sanford made education a cornerstone of his administration, going so far as to bring Ehle on board his staff as special assistant for new projects. Ehle and Sanford accomplished a number of initiatives, including the Governor's School and the North Carolina Film Board, but the School of the Arts was by far their most original, unortho-

dox, and controversial project.

Unlike liberal-arts colleges, NCSA gives students at both the high school and college levels an intensive and rigorous program in their chosen art. Unlike traditional conservatories, it also provides a solid general education.

The School of the Arts met with opposition from two sides. One side consisted of proponents of traditional liberal-arts colleges and their existing music, art, and drama programs. The second consisted of those who objected to spending tax dollars on a "toe-dancin' school."

Ehle argued, as he had in his 1961 article, that while liberal-arts colleges were superbly equipped to teach the study of the arts, they were inadequate for teaching the techniques of creation and performance.

The second argument was finally defeated on the floor of the North Carolina General Assembly by Representative John Kerr, who took to task for their shortsightedness those who opposed government support of the arts. Kerr closed his speech with this: "Now, some of you have ridiculed this legislation as a toe-dancin' bill. Well, if there's going to be toe-dancin', I want to be there." At that, he assumed a ballet pose, which was photographed for the state's newspapers.

Once the bill for the creation of the School of the Arts passed, the work of selecting a site began in earnest. Biltmore House in Asheville and Reynolda House and Graylyn in Winston-Salem were considered. Several cities expressed some degree of interest, but in the end, only three were judged to have viable claims to being the best location: Raleigh, Charlotte, and Winston-Salem.

Winston-Salem had a tradition of supporting the arts that went back to its founding. The Moravians who built Salem made music an integral part of their worship and culture. The industrialists who built Winston had long supported education. Winston-Salem was the first city in the country with its own arts council. It had at its disposal the facilities of Salem College, Wake Forest College, and Winston-Salem State University.

Tradition, however, was not going to bring the School of the Arts to Winston-Salem. Two city leaders, Smith Bagley and Philip Hanes, spearheaded a drive to prove the Twin City's eagerness and worthiness to host the school. More than 200 volunteers worked the phones in a "Dial for Dollars" campaign that raised nearly $600,000 in two days. A plan was drawn up to convert Gray High School into a campus for the School of the Arts.

But according to Leslie Banner's *A Passionate Preference: The Story of the North Carolina School of the Arts*, the deciding factor was not just that Winston-Salem had better-laid plans and a more successful fund drive. Winston-Salem simply wanted the school more than the other cities did.

John Ehle had a strange thought: to start a school, far from the world's cultural centers, that would teach students to be professional artists of the highest caliber. Unimaginable to most, scoffed at and threatened with extinction, the North Carolina School of the Arts is now known around the world for the quality of its training, faculty, students, and alumni.

The Stevens Center for the Performing Arts in downtown Winston-Salem
COURTESY OF WINSTON-SALEM CONVENTION AND VISITORS BUREAU

ranging from student productions by the North Carolina School of the Arts to performances by such local and regional groups as the Piedmont Triad Symphony, the Piedmont Opera Theatre, the North Carolina Dance Theatre, and the North Carolina Shakespeare Festival. It also brings in national acts such as Emile Pandolfini, touring productions of Broadway shows, and children's performances as part of its popular "Something for Everyone" series.

Call 336-723-6320 for information about ticket prices and upcoming events.

- The city of Winston-Salem sponsors downtown parties every Thursday, Friday, and Saturday night from April to October. *Alive after Five*, held Thursdays from 5 P.M. to 8 P.M. at Corpening Plaza, brings in pop and alternative acts aimed at young professionals. *BellSouth Jazz & Blues*, held every Friday from 6 P.M. to 10 P.M. in the revitalized Fourth Street area, offers funk and soul in addition to jazz and blues. *Summers on Trade*, billed as "Winston's Roots Revival," is held in the arts district on Trade and Sixth Streets on Saturday from 7 P.M. to 10 P.M. It draws on the musical heritage of the Piedmont and the Blue Ridge and has featured performers such as Doc Watson. For more information, call Winston-Salem Events at 336-725-1083, or visit their website at www.wsevents.com.

SEASONAL EVENTS

- The *Dixie Classic Fair*, the regional fair for northwest North Carolina, is the last big fair before the State Fair in Raleigh. Originally a chance for the region's farmers to show off their crops and livestock, the Dixie Classic still shows its agricultural and community roots. Concession stands are operated by local nonprofit organizations such as Boy Scout troops, Little Leagues, and the Kiwanis Club; prizewinning student artwork is displayed in the exhibit hall; and one of the most popular events is the pig race. A re-created folk village offers demonstrations of blacksmithing and woodcarving; bluegrass bands play on the front porch of one of the log cabins. The mile-long Midway, meanwhile, is filled with ample opportunities to lose your money on games of skill and chance. Rides are available for all ages and courage levels. The Dixie Classic Fairgrounds are behind Lawrence Joel Veterans Memorial Coliseum, which is on the corner of University Parkway and Deacon Boulevard. The fair is held in late September and early October. Call 336-727-2236 for more information.

- The *Piedmont Crafts Fair*, held each November in the M. C. Benton Convention Center downtown, brings in more than 100 regional craftsmen to display and (they hope) sell their wares. The fair is sponsored by the Piedmont Craftsmen organization, which operates a separate gallery in Winston-Salem year-round. You can reach the gallery at 336-725-1516 or learn about it on the web at www.webfresco.com/pci.

▪ The **Crosby National Celebrity Golf Tournament** is a pro-am event held each year in the spring or early summer. It pairs players from participating corporate sponsors with celebrity entertainers or athletes (not pro golfers). The tournament is played at Bermuda Run Country Club, which is actually in the town of Advance, 11 miles southwest of Winston-Salem in Davie County. A number of events connected to the Crosby, however, take place in Winston-Salem, including the popular Crosby Clambake at Groves Stadium on Deacon Boulevard. The Crosby is named after the late entertainer Bing Crosby.

▪ Old Salem is renowned for its Moravian Christmas celebrations. *A Salem Christmas*, which includes strolling brass bands and seasonal decorations, is capped by the **Christmas Candle Tea**, in which a Lovefeast of buns, coffee, and hymns is held by candlelight in the Single Brothers House.

Places to Stay

RESORTS, HOTELS, AND MOTELS

In earlier times, Winston-Salem boasted two of the finest hotels in the South: the Hotel Zinzendorf and the Hotel Robert E. Lee. The Zinzendorf stood on the hill overlooking the West End, near the present intersection of Fourth and Glade Streets. It burned in its prime on Thanksgiving Day 1892; among the diners who had to be evacuated were R. J. Reynolds and William A. Blair, whose son John founded the company that publishes this book. The Hotel Robert E. Lee suffered a long period of decline after World War II. It was imploded in 1972 to make way for a succession of fine hotels.

Most of Winston-Salem's hotels are representatives of national chains.

The following, however, feature distinctive accommodations with a definite local flavor.

- **Brookstown Inn**. Deluxe. 200 Brookstown Avenue (800-845-4262 or 336-725-1120). Located in the historic Brookstown Mill area on the edge of the even more historic Old Salem, Brookstown Inn is listed on the National Register of Historic Places. It is housed in what was one of Salem's first textile mills. Each of the 71 guest rooms and suites is furnished with what the inn says are "authentic early American Pieces," including poster beds and handmade quilts. A complimentary continental breakfast is served every morning; a complimentary wine-and-cheese reception is offered each evening. Complete business services (fax, copiers, etc.), an exercise room, meeting space, and banquet facilities are available.

- **Adam's Mark–Winston Plaza**. Expensive/Moderate. 425 North Cherry Street (800-444-ADAM or 336-725-3500). Standing on the block bounded by Marshall, Cherry, and Fifth Streets, the site of the Hotel Robert E. Lee, the Winston-Salem location of the Adam's Mark chain features 605 excellent rooms and 19 suites. It offers an indoor pool, a health club, a gift shop, and 24-hour room service. The Trattoria Carolina Restaurant, the Pasta Bar, the Cherry Street Bar, and Player's Sports Bar are on the premises. The M. C. Benton Convention Center is across Fifth Street; an underground walkway connects the two. A number of special package rates are available.

- **The Hawthorne Inn and Conference Center**. Expensive/Moderate. 420 High Street (800-972-3774 or 336-777-3000). Located just off Interstate 40 Business, the Hawthorne is convenient to downtown, Old Salem, and Wake Forest University Baptist Medical Center. In fact, it is owned and operated by North Carolina Baptist Hospitals, Inc., which means that those in town because of the medical center can receive especially good rates. Particularly suited to business travelers, the Hawthorne combines the cozy comfort of an inn with the facilities of a business hotel. It offers a fitness center, meeting space, an amphitheater, and the Bayberry Restaurant.

• **Wingate Inn**. Moderate. 125 South Main Street (336-714-2800). The first franchise of the Wingate chain to open in the Triad, this inn is considered a key part of the effort to revitalize downtown Winston-Salem. Designed to attract business travelers, the Wingate employs the latest technology in its 24-hour business center and in its rooms, which include cordless keyboards for Web TV, free high-speed internet access, and cordless phones. The lobby features a mural of Old Salem. Valet parking and a breakfast buffet are included in the room rate. A restaurant is scheduled to open next to the hotel in the summer of 2001.

INNS AND BED-AND-BREAKFASTS

• **Henry Fries Shaffner House**. Deluxe/Expensive. 150 South Marshall Street (800-952-2256 or 336-777-0052). In the shadow of Winston-Salem's skyscrapers and just off the bustle of Interstate 40 Business sits the expansive Henry Fries Shaffner House. Built for one of the city's early industrialists, the home is located on what was once called "Millionaire's Row," the stretch of fine houses constructed just south of Winston during the post–Civil War boom. Each of the nine guest rooms has a different decorative theme and name taken from Winston-Salem's history; all have cable television and a phone. A hot breakfast is included. The Shaffner House serves dinner nightly and has recently added a Sunday brunch.

• **The Augustus T. Zevely Inn**. Expensive. 803 South Main Street (800-928-9299 or 336-748-9299). Not to be confused with the Zevely House restaurant in the West End, the Zevely Inn sits in the heart of Old Salem. Each of its 12 rooms is named for a member of the Zevely family. Room rates include a "continental-plus" breakfast during the week and a full gourmet breakfast on weekends, nonalcoholic drinks throughout the day, and wine and cheese at night. Pets can be accommodated if arrangements are made at the time of reservation.

• **Colonel Ludlow Inn**. Expensive. 434 Summit Street (800-301-1887 or 336-777-1887). The Colonel Ludlow occupies two adjacent Victorian houses in the West End neighborhood. It offers more modern amenities than many large hotels, including an exercise room with Nautilus equipment, a billiards room, and a golf practice cage.

■ **Lady Anne's: A Victorian Bed-and-Breakfast Home.** Expensive/Moderate. 612 Summit Street (336-724-1074). Lady Anne's gets bonus points for being in my favorite Winston-Salem neighborhood, the West End Historic District. The West End, Winston's first suburb, was noted for the grand Victorian homes of R. J. Reynolds and all the men he made rich. Many of those homes still stand, though a great many have been divided into apartments. The first time I was able to decide for myself where in Winston-Salem to live, I headed straight to the West End. Lady Anne's is listed on the National Register. Each room is individually decorated with Victorian antiques and includes a private bath, cable television, a phone, a modem, an alarm clock, robes, and a hair dryer. The suites have private entrances, a stereo, a VCR, a coffee maker, a refrigerator, a microwave; some have two-person whirlpools. Guests receive a full breakfast in the dining room or on one of the porches and evening dessert in their rooms. To counter the calories, they have limited privileges at the Central YMCA, just down the hill on Sunset Avenue. The innkeepers ask that guests not bring small children or pets.

■ **Idlewilde Heath 1200 Bed-and-Breakfast.** Moderate. 1200 Idlewilde Heath Drive (336-723-6615). This bed-and-breakfast is within walking distance of Wake Forest University, Reynolda Village and Gardens, and the Reynolda House Museum of American Art. It is located in a pleasant residential neighborhood occupied mostly by faculty, staff, and a few students from Wake Forest. Visitors stay in either the guest house (which includes a living room, a full kitchen, a balcony, a bathroom, a laundry, and a bedroom) or a two-bedroom suite in the main house (which includes a sitting room and a separate bath). The innkeepers host a complimentary wine tasting for their guests. A late check-out time of 1 P.M. is offered.

When in Rome . . .

An apocryphal story, repeated by Frank Tursi in his book *Winston-Salem: A History*, shows the power and the pride displayed by Winston-Salem's leading industrialists in the 20th century. The men who ran R. J. Reynolds Tobacco Company and Hanes Hosiery effectively ran the city as well.

In the 1920s, a state highway commissioner came to town to meet with the mayor and the captains of industry at the Hotel Robert E. Lee. "The highway commissioner lit a cigarette that wasn't made in Winston-Salem, and a hush settled on the room," Tursi writes. "Someone finally slid a pack of Camels across the table and told the commissioner that he would be expected to smoke them while in town.

"The state man stood up and began to undress.

"'What in the world are you doing, man?' one of the astonished city representatives asked.

"'I just remembered,' the commissioner replied, 'I don't have Hanes underwear on either.'"

Places to Eat

- **Michael's on Fifth**. Expensive. 848 West Fifth Street (336-777-0000). One of the most elegant restaurants in town, Michael's is located in a renovated mansion in the West End, near downtown. Open since 1986, it has recently revised its menu, adding a "Leisure Luncheon" on weekdays and a few more continental items to its dinner menu. The paella is excellent. Michael's is open for lunch Monday through Friday and for dinner Monday through Saturday.

- **Ryan's Steaks, Chops, and Seafood**. Expensive. 719 Coliseum Drive (336-724-6132). Ryan's occupies a pastoral setting (complete with a bubbling brook) in an odd location; it is tucked off two of Winston-Salem's busiest roads, Coliseum Drive near the intersection with University Parkway. The name more or less sums up the menu. What Ryan's lacks in surprise it makes up for in execution. Dinner is served Monday through Saturday.

- **Salem Tavern**. Expensive. 736 South Main Street (336-748-8585). The restaurant known as the Salem Tavern is actually located in the Salem Tavern Annex. The original Salem Tavern burned in 1784 but was rebuilt that same year; the brick structure located next to the annex, it hosted a visit from President George Washington in 1791 and serves as a museum today. The highlight of the restaurant's menu is the authentic Moravian chicken pie, though more contemporary food is also served. The restaurant is open for lunch daily and for dinner Monday through Saturday. Reservations are recommended.

- **Staley's Charcoal Steak House**. Expensive. 2000 Reynolda Road (336-723-8631). A Winston-Salem tradition, Staley's once encompassed a number of restaurants throughout town with various price ranges and specialties. Staley's Charcoal Steak House is the finest, most expensive, and last of the line. Its old-fashioned sophistication is one of dark colors, candlelight, and chairs so heavy and deep they're almost intimidating. Don't look for the latest continental trends here; Staley's is a red-meat steakhouse, the kind where your grandparents celebrated their anniversary. Staley's is open for dinner Monday through Saturday. Reservations are recommended.

- **South by Southwest**. Expensive/Moderate. 241 South Marshall Street (336-727-0800). South by Southwest has been bringing the best Southwestern cuisine to Winston-Salem since 1993. The menu here ignores the usual Tex-Mex clichés in favor of more creative items like pineapple-jalapeño salsa and blue corn enchiladas. South by Southwest serves dinner Monday through Saturday.

- **Zevely House Restaurant**. Expensive/Moderate. 901 West Fourth Street (336-725-6666). Located in one of the oldest West End homes, Zevely House offers excellent food in a casual atmosphere. Fireplaces glow in the winter. In spring, summer, and fall, the patio provides cool breezes and a great view of the West End. Zevely House serves dinner Monday through Saturday and offers an outstanding brunch on Sunday.

- **Fourth Street Filling Station**. Moderate. 871 West Fourth Street (336-724-7600). One of Winston-Salem's newest restaurants, Fourth Street Filling Station features outdoor dining (weather permitting) and occasional live music. Young professionals are the targeted clientele here, but not so much so as to intimidate families or those wanting a relaxed, casual meal. Lunch and dinner are served Monday through Saturday.

Hot Doughnuts Now

Fine, don't smoke Winston-Salem's cigarettes. The Twin City now has another delicious, satisfying, addictive, and incredibly unhealthy export sweeping the nation.

Lines in New York and Los Angeles circled city blocks for the opening of the first Krispy Kreme doughnut shops in those cities. Celebrities have been spotted responding to the call of the red neon "Hot Doughnuts Now" sign, lit whenever the "Hot Glazed Originals," the basic and best Krispy Kreme doughnuts, are made.

Technically, Krispy Kreme was not born in Winston-Salem. Its founder, Vernon Rudolph, started a doughnut business in Paducah, Kentucky, where in 1933 he bought a shop and a secret recipe from a French chef. According to the official Krispy Kreme website, Rudolph, looking for a larger market for his doughnuts, moved his operation to Nashville, Tennessee. Relatives opened shops in Charleston, West Virginia, and Atlanta, Georgia. Their primary sales came from delivering doughnuts to area grocery stores.

In 1937, Rudolph decided to leave Nashville and his partners and start over on his own. Eventually, he settled in Winston-Salem. He had two young assistants, a 1936 Pontiac, and $25 in cash. Rudolph used that last $25 to rent a building across from Salem College and Academy, in the middle of what is now Old Salem. He had to convince a grocer to lend him the ingredients for the first batch of doughnuts. To deliver those doughnuts, he took out the backseat of his Pontiac and installed a rack.

As word of Rudolph's yeast-raised doughnuts spread around town, people began to stop by the shop to buy them hot and fresh. So many people came, in fact, that Rudolph cut a hole in the shop's wall to sell the doughnuts as customers motored by, predating Krispy Kreme's current drive-through windows and open viewing of the doughnut-making process.

For decades, Krispy Kreme was just a Winston-Salem—then a Carolinas, then a Southeastern—institution. The expansion into "foreign" markets such as New York, Los Angeles, and Las Vegas has happened only in the past 10 years. Thirty states now have Krispy Kreme franchises.

Krispy Kreme artifacts were placed in the Smithsonian Institution in 1997. Nationwide, Krispy Kreme produces more than 3 million doughnuts a day and more than 1.3 billion a year.

■ **Midtown Café and Dessertery**. Moderate. 151 South Stratford Road (336-724-9800). This restaurant began life as the Dessertery but grew to include breakfast, lunch, and dinner entrées. Don't let those entrées' late arrival fool you, though; the menu here is wonderful. Try the "Banana Crunch Pancakes" and thank me later. Many entrées have Italian and continental overtones. The desserts are original and mouth-watering. Breakfast, lunch, and dinner are served daily.

■ **Noble's Grill**. Moderate. 380 Knollwood Street (336-777-8477). The interior here is very open; most tables have a view of the open-flame grill in the kitchen. A favorite for weekday lunches and weekend dinners, Noble's is run by a longtime Winston-Salem chef who raises his own herbs, vegetables, and rabbits. The pizzas are highly recommended. Noble's serves lunch Monday through Saturday and dinner all week.

■ **Ichiban**. Moderate/Inexpensive. 270 South Stratford Road, Thruway Shopping Center (336-725-3050). This small storefront restaurant offers excellent Japanese food in a setting quieter than typical Japanese steakhouses. No one performs for you, but the teriyaki steak and chicken are not to be missed. There is also a sushi bar in back. Ichiban serves lunch and dinner daily but is closed during the midafternoon.

■ **Village Tavern**. Moderate/Inexpensive. Reynolda Village (336-748-0221) and 2000 Griffith Road (336-760-8686). The Village Tavern began in Reynolda Village and has spread across the state. The patio in the original location has become famous; the atmosphere is upscale but relaxed enough for college students. The second Winston-Salem location is just off Hanes Mall Boulevard at the intersection with Stratford Road; it offers a somewhat classier ambiance and is more spacious. Both locations serve lunch and dinner daily and a brunch on Sunday.

■ **Vincenzo's Italian Restaurant**. Moderate/Inexpensive. 3449 Robinhood Road (336-765-3176). Winston-Salem's oldest Italian restaurant has been heaping on the helpings since 1964. Located near the corner of Robinhood and Polo Roads, Vincenzo's is decorated with framed photographs of local celebrities, sports heroes, and just about every football player to have ever suited up for Wake Forest. The place is packed on Monday nights for the all-you-can-eat lasagna or spaghetti, a favorite for generations of Wake students. Lunch and dinner are served daily.

- **West End Café**. Moderate/Inexpensive. 926 West Fourth Street (336-723-4774). West End Café bills itself as the place "where lunch never ends and dinner is spectacular." It doesn't, and it is. The menu offers everything from sandwiches to Italian entrées; the grinders in particular are excellent. The food is rivaled only by the ambiance; businessmen, families with small children, and young people are all comfortable here. The ambiance is rivaled only by the setting, in the West End just across from beautiful Grace Court. Lunch and dinner are served Monday through Saturday.

- **Bear Rock Café**. Inexpensive. 205 South Stratford Road (336-723-2511). This regional chain has nine locations throughout the Carolinas. It makes some of the best and most original sandwiches around. Lunch and dinner are served daily.

- **Little Richard's Barbecue**. Inexpensive. 4885 Country Club Road (336-760-3457). Winston-Salem's barbecue is often overshadowed by the world-famous barbecue in Lexington, only 20 minutes south on U.S. 52. (The barbecue you'll find in Winston is, in fact, "Lexington-style," which means

Grace Court in Winston-Salem's West End
PHOTOGRAPH BY ED SOUTHERN

that it has a tomato base, unlike its vinegar-based Down East cousin.) The Twin City has seen more than its share of excellent chopped pork barbecue over the years, a tradition carried on by Little Richard's. The original location on Country Club Road serves the best barbecue in town. Two other Little Richard's use the same name and logo but are under different ownership. Little Richard's is open for lunch and dinner Monday through Saturday. On a side note, wherever you eat barbecue in Winston-Salem, don't ask for Tabasco sauce. Use Texas Pete, a hot sauce made right in town. (No, it has nothing to do with Texas. The makers just liked the name.) And for God's sake, do not shorten *barbecue* to *'cue*. Only Yankees and Charlotteans do that.

Skyline of Greensboro at night
COURTESY OF GREENSBORO AREA CONVENTION AND VISITORS BUREAU

GREENSBORO

By Carolyn Sakowski

Greensboro and Guilford County have a long tradition of valuing education. Prior to the formation of the county, a staunchly religious group of settlers arrived around 1750. These settlers were members of the Religious Society of Friends, a group commonly known as Quakers. The Quakers named their first settlement New Garden. These settlers would have a lasting influence on educational standards and moral decisions in the area.

In 1767, David Caldwell started a local school known as the Log College. Serving as a Presbyterian minister in what was then the wilderness, Caldwell established the school to educate young men for the ministry. Five of his students went on to become governors of their states; one of them, John Motley Morehead, was governor of North Carolina from 1841 to 1845.

In 1771, North Carolina's colonial assembly created Guilford County in order to gain more administrative control over the growing Piedmont population. Named after the earl of Guilford, a friend of King George III, the county had a sparse population of about 10,000. By 1774, a log courthouse and jail were built at a place known as Guilford Courthouse.

On March 15, 1780, Guilford Courthouse played an important role in the Revolutionary War. The battle that raged in the woods and over the fields would prove the beginning of the end for Lord Cornwallis's campaign to squelch the Patriot forces in the South. When the county courthouse was ready in 1809, the new town needed a name. The commissioners chose to honor Nathanael Greene, the leader of the American forces at the Battle of Guilford Courthouse. Somehow, the final e on the name got lost, so the town was named Greensborough.

In 1837, the Society of Friends opened New Garden Boarding School to train teachers. In 1887, this school became Guilford College, the first coeducational institution in the South. In 1863, the Methodist Church founded a school for girls named Greensboro Female College, which came to be called Greensboro College. In 1905, its new leader, Lucy H. Robertson, became the first woman to serve as a college president in North Carolina. In 1873, the Freedmen's Aid Society established Bennett Seminary, a normal school. In 1889, the Methodist Church began to support the school, which eventually became Bennett College.

In the 1820s, young lawyer John Motley Morehead, who augmented his law practice with a dry-goods and grocery business, began to push for a railroad to come to Greensboro. He became the first president of the North Carolina Railroad. By July 1851, construction began on the railroad, which was to have its western terminus in Charlotte and its eastern terminus in Goldsboro. Thanks to Morehead, the railroad would pass through Greensboro. The line was completed in 1856.

When war clouds threatened, Morehead and other powerful men in Greensboro did not readily embrace secession. These conservative businessmen realized what war would do to economic progress. In 1861, the citizens of Guilford, including the antislavery Quakers, defeated a proposal to call a convention to consider secession; the margin was 2,771 to 113.

But Guilford benefited from the war when the Confederate government built the Piedmont Railroad to connect Greensboro with Danville, Virginia. The railroad proved the missing link in the supply line from Columbia, South Carolina, to the Army of Northern Virginia.

After the war, industrialization reached Greensboro in a big way when Moses and Ceasar Cone began construction on their Proximity Mill. It was in 1891 that the Cone brothers decided to enter the textile business. Previously, they had been wholesale grocery and tobacco distributors. Oftentimes, they were paid in bolts of cloth from small local mills, which they turned around and sold. They thought they could produce a better-quality product and create a strong marketing organization. By the mid-1890s, the Cones' company was offering services to 90 percent of the South's textile mill owners and getting about five cents on each dollar of the gross receipts. This company would evolve into Cone Mills.

In 1896, the first denim rolled off the looms of the Proximity Mill. Four years later, the Cones joined with the Sternberger brothers in building the first cotton flannel mill in the South. The Revolution Cotton Mill's production allowed the owners to boast that they were the world's leader in flannel production. In 1905, the White Oak plant began to produce denim; it still claims to be the world's largest denim mill. Cone Mills combined with other textile companies to make Greensboro one of the nation's leading textile manufacturing centers.

In the 1890s, the city's civic leaders again showed their enthusiasm for education when the state announced plans to establish two new colleges—one for women and one for African-Americans. In 1891, the state selected Greensboro as the location for the Agricultural and Mechanical College for the Negro Race; to win the bid, the city came up with $8,000 in cash and a suitable site. This college would go on to become North Carolina A & T State University. Also in 1891, Greensboro was selected as the site for the Normal and Industrial School for Women, which would become the University of North Carolina at Greensboro. To receive this bid, the city raised $30,000 through a bond issue and donated a suitable location.

Thanks to the vision of its forefathers, Greensboro is a thriving business and educational center for the vibrant North Carolina Piedmont today. Its revitalization efforts in the Old Greensborough Downtown Historic District and its well-planned Cultural District are a tribute to the continued vision of its leaders.

Just the Facts

Greensboro is located at the intersection of Interstate 40 and Interstate 85, which skirt the southeast section of town.

Piedmont Triad International Airport, which is served by major carriers including US Airways, Delta, Continental, Northwest, American, United, and AirTran, is centrally located among Greensboro, High Point, and Winston-Salem. Many hotels offer free transportation to and from the airport.

The Amtrak station is located at 2603 Oakland Avenue. Call 336-855-3382 for information.

The Greyhound/Trailways bus terminal is located at 501 West Lee Street. Call 336-272-8950.

For visitor information, contact the Greensboro Area Convention and Visitors Bureau, 317 South Greene Street, Greensboro, N.C. 27401-2615 (800-344-2282 or 336-274-2282; www.greensboronc.org). The bureau is located across the street from the Carolina Theatre.

The *Greensboro News and Record*, the city's daily newspaper, publishes a comprehensive calendar in its "City Life" section every Thursday. You can also check the calendar of events in *Triad Style*, the *Rhinoceros Times*, and *ESP*, three free weekly tabloids.

Guilford County's Quaker Heritage

Much of Guilford County's heritage is tied to the Religious Society of Friends, more commonly known as the Quakers.

In 1740, Quaker pioneers from Pennsylvania, Virginia, and Nantucket Island began to settle in northwestern Guilford County. By 1754, the New Garden Meeting was established. It quickly became a center for Quakerism in North Carolina. The Battle of Guilford Courthouse, which raged around Quaker homes and farms in New Garden in 1781, saw the meeting house turned into a hospital for soldiers from both sides. Many of the dead were buried in the Friends' burial ground. Even the leader of the American forces at this battle, Nathanael Greene, was a Quaker. One historical figure from Guilford County with a Quaker connection was Dolley Madison, born in 1768 to parents who were members of the New Garden Meeting.

In 1818, some young people from the New Garden Meeting organized a "Sabbath School House." By 1821, Levi Coffin, Jr., was teaching slaves to read the Bible there. Levi and his wife, Catherine, became leaders in giving assistance to fugitive slaves. In 1826, they followed friends and relatives to a settlement in Indiana. It was there that their efforts to hide runaway slaves earned Levi the title of president of the Underground Railroad.

Since fugitive-slave laws provided severe penalties for anyone who interfered with the recovery of slaves, the efforts of these men and women had to be secretive. The Underground Railroad helped slaves escape to the Northern states and Canada by setting up "stations" every 10 to 20 miles along the way. The wagons and carriages used to transport the slaves were called "trains." The runaway slaves usually traveled at night in groups of two or three. The drivers who assisted them were called "conductors." One Quaker couple who were a vital link in the North Carolina segment of the Underground Railroad were Joshua and Abigail Stanley, who lived in the Centre community. Levi Coffin and Abigail Stanley had grown up together in the New Garden community.

Today, a wagon with a false bottom used to transport fugitive slaves on the Underground Railroad is on display at the Mendenhall Plantation in Jamestown. A nearly identical wagon is housed at the Levi Coffin House and Museum in Fountain City, Indiana. At both the Mendenhall Plantation and the nearby Museum of Old Domestic Life, you can see artifacts left by the Quakers.

The New Garden Friends Meeting still holds worship services at 801 New Garden Road near Guilford College, which also has its roots in the Society of Friends.

Statue of Nathanael Greene
COURTESY OF GREENSBORO AREA
CONVENTION AND VISITORS BUREAU

Things to Do

HISTORIC PLACES, GARDENS, AND TOURS

■ *Guilford Courthouse National Military Park* is six miles north of downtown off U.S. 220 (Battleground Avenue) on New Garden Road.

After a three-year standoff in the North, Lord Charles Cornwallis, the British commander, decided to conquer the South. By 1780, the British controlled Georgia and South Carolina. After Cornwallis suffered a setback in October 1780 at Kings Mountain, he moved to Charlotte just as Nathanael Greene took command of the Americans' Southern forces.

Greene divided his forces into two segments. To counter, Cornwallis divided his troops into three columns. In January 1781, the British were defeated at Cowpens, but Cornwallis pursued Greene's forces into North Carolina. By March, Greene had received reinforcements that brought his strength to 4,400 men. He chose Guilford Courthouse as the site for the battle. Greene wanted a location that would be easy for the militia to find, a place where the British would have to move through woods and make their final assault up a hill across a clearing, and a place where the Americans would not be trapped by water as they departed.

Cornwallis led his force of 1,900 men into the trap on March 15, 1781. The first exchange came just after one o'clock in the afternoon. The militiamen waiting in the woods were under orders to fire three rounds before retreating. A second line of militia deeper in the woods was reinforced with cannon and cavalry. A third line was on a rise above the clearing. After two hours of fighting, the British drove the Americans from the field and claimed the day. But it was to be a Pyrrhic victory. Cornwallis lost one-fourth of his men. And nearly 30 percent of his officer corps was down. Cornwallis later said, "I never saw such fighting since God made me. The fighting was furious."

Too weak to pursue the rebels, Cornwallis began his seven-month journey that would finally end with the British surrender at Yorktown.

In 1886, David Schenck, a Greensboro-based attorney for the Richmond and Danville Railroad, wrote that he was going to "save the battlefield." He helped form the Guilford Battleground Company, which purchased more than 125 acres where the battle was fought. In 1911, Congress appropriated $30,000 to erect an equestrian monument to General Greene; the statue was dedicated on July 3, 1915. Two years later, on March 2, 1917, the Guilford Battleground Company ceded the battleground to the United States government. Today, the park preserves 220 acres of historic fields and forests and 28 monuments.

Among the interesting statues on the grounds is one to Kerenhappuch Turner, a woman who rode on horseback from Maryland to care for her son, who had been wounded in the battle. Another interesting participant is memorialized at the battlefield. Peter Francisco stood six-foot-six when he joined the Continental Army at age sixteen. He was a foot taller and a hundred pounds heavier than the average American soldier. The story goes that Francisco earned fame at Guilford Courthouse when he slew 11 soldiers with his sword in one brief encounter. A tablet that pays tribute to Francisco stands next to the Cavalry Monument. You can also see one of Francisco's immense shoes on display in the visitor center. The battlefield is home to the graves of William Hopper and John Penn, signers of the Declaration of Independence, and Joseph Winston, the Revolutionary War hero for whom the town of Winston (now part of Winston-Salem) was named.

Guests can tour the park on foot, by bicycle, or by automobile. The visitor center includes exhibits, military memorabilia, films, and a bookstore. The battlefield is open from 8:30 A.M. to 5 P.M. daily except for Christmas and New Year's. Admission is free. For more information, call 336-288-1776, or visit their website at www.nps.gov./guco.

▪ Adjacent to the Guilford Courthouse battlefield is *Tannenbaum Park*. This eight-acre park is the site of the restored 1778 Hoskins House. During the Battle of Guilford Courthouse, the house served as a staging area for British troops under Cornwallis. The North Carolina Colonial Heritage Center is located at the park; there, guests can enjoy a diorama of the battle, a gallery of original maps, a museum store, and hand-on exhibits depicting colonial life. They can also stand in a pillory and feel the weight of a musket.

The park is open daily; hours vary according to the season. Regular tours of the Hoskins House are available Tuesday through Sunday. Admission is free. For more information, call 336-545-5313, or visit their websites at www.ci.greensboro.nc.us/leisure/tannenbaum or www.home.interpath.net/history.

Blandwood Mansion
COURTESY OF GREENSBORO
AREA CONVENTION AND
VISITORS BUREAU

▪ *Blandwood Mansion*, at 447 West Washington Street, was the home of former North Carolina governor John Motley Morehead. Now a National Historic Landmark, it began as a clapboard farmhouse in the 1790s. In 1844, Morehead hired Alexander Jackson Davis to design an Italianate addition. Today, Blandwood is the oldest example of Italianate architecture in the United States. Restored to its mid-1800s appearance, it contains many of the original furnishings selected by the Moreheads. Blandwood is open from 11 A.M. to 2 P.M. Tuesday through Saturday and from 2 P.M. to 5 P.M. on Sunday. A small admission fee is charged. For more information, call 336-272-5003, or visit their website at www.blandwood.org.

The city offers three special public gardens sponsored by Greensboro Beautiful, Inc., in partnership with the Greensboro Parks and Recreation Department. The gardens are open daily. Admission is free. For information, call 336-373-2199.

- The **Bicentennial Gardens and David Caldwell Property** feature 7.5 acres of flowering and deciduous trees, shrubs, and annual beds with mass plantings that bring color throughout the year. Located on Hobbs Road just north of Friendly Avenue, the gardens are open daily.

- The **Bog Garden**, located adjacent to the Bicentennial Gardens, offers a half-mile elevated wooden walkway. Visitors can see more than 8,000 individually labeled trees, shrubs, ferns, bamboos, wildflowers, and other plants that thrive in swampy conditions.

- **Greensboro Arboretum** is located on a 17-acre site within Lindley Park, near Wendover Avenue at West Market Street. It features nine permanent plant collections and a number of special garden areas and structural features. The woody plants are labeled and grouped according to type and growing conditions.

MUSEUMS AND SCIENCE CENTERS

The city planners have done an excellent job of putting many of Greensboro's museums and other cultural offerings together in a compact few blocks identified by street signs as the "Cultural District." Here, you'll find the Greensboro Historical Museum, the Greensboro Children's Museum, the central branch of the Greensboro Public Library, the Greensboro Cultural Center at Festival Park (discussed in the "Cultural Offerings" section of this chapter), and the downtown branch of the Y.W.C.A.

- The **Greensboro Historical Museum**, at 130 Summit Avenue, has just undergone a major renovation to update its heating and air-conditioning systems. Its exhibits focus on early settlement, military history (there's an interesting display of weapons used during the Civil War), Native Americans, and transportation. Located in a building that dates to the turn of the 20th century, the museum is listed on the National Register of Historic Places. Some of the more popular displays show items—a snuffbox, a collection of fine china, and French gowns—once owned by Greensboro native Dolley Madison, the wife of President James Madison. Another display features items owned by Greensboro native Wil-liam Sydney Porter, better known as O. Henry. These items include photographs, letters, and early editions of his books, as well as sketches he made when he worked at his uncle's drugstore. A reproduction of that drugstore is also featured. One exhibit highlighting a more recent historical event includes stools and the countertop from the local Woolworth's where four local college students staged a sit-in demonstration that sparked the nation.

Greensboro Historical Museum
PHOTOGRAPH BY CAROLYN SAKOWSKI

Behind the museum, you can walk through a small cemetery where several Revolutionary War soldiers rest. You can also see examples of early Guilford County homes and a bust commemorating another local native, Edward R. Murrow.

The museum is open from 10 A.M. to 5 P.M. Tuesday through Saturday and from 2 P.M. to 5 P.M. on Sunday. Admission is free. For more information, call 336-373-2043, or visit their website at www.greensboro.lib.nc.us/museum.

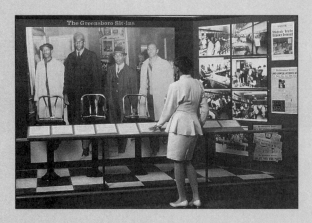

An exhibit at the Greensboro Historical Museum showing the original lunch counter
COURTESY OF GREENSBORO AREA CONVENTION AND VISITORS BUREAU

The Greensboro Four

On February 1, 1960, four students from North Carolina A & T State University—David Richmond, Franklin McCain, Jibreel Khazan (Ezell Blair, Jr., before his conversion to Islam), and Joseph McNeil—paid a visit to the F. W. Woolworth Store in downtown Greensboro that would change the world. Though they knew that Jim Crow laws prohibited an integrated lunch counter, the four men took seats and politely requested coffee around 4:30 P.M. After being told that "coloreds" were not served at the counter, the four remained seated in silence until the store closed at 5:30.

They returned the next day around 10:30 A.M. with a group of 20 students. The students made small purchases elsewhere in the store, then sat at the lunch counter in groups of three or four as spaces became

- Across from the new Greensboro Public Library at 220 North Church Street is the **Greensboro Children's Museum**. This active place offers hands-on exhibits and activities for children ages one to 12. The "Our Town" section has a grocery store complete with check-out registers, a bank, a theater, a media studio, a house under construction, and a post office. A craft room and exhibits about the continents, the furniture industry, and the textile industry are also on the premises. But the section that excites children the most is the transportation area. Here, they can climb in the cockpit of an airliner and slide down the escape shoot or sit

available. They sat there until noon without being waited on, while white customers were served.

Sit-in demonstrations had been tried previously in other cities. No one knows exactly why the spontaneous actions of four students in Greensboro sparked a movement. They were soon joined by more students from A & T, as well as students from Bennett College and from what is now the University of North Carolina at Greensboro. Within two weeks, sit-ins were staged in 11 other cities. Eventually, 54 cities in nine states saw similar demonstrations.

It took the Greensboro students six months before Woolworth's relented on its policy of respecting "local custom." The actions of these young students played a vital role in the early days of the national civil-rights movement that changed our nation's policies and laws regarding racial segregation.

When the F. W. Woolworth Company announced the closing of its Elm Street location in 1993, a group of citizens organized to preserve the architecturally significant Art Deco building and its historically significant lunch counter. Work is now under way to convert the building

into the International Civil Rights Center and Museum. Plans for the center include a museum, a computer center, a library and reading area, classrooms, workrooms, conference rooms, an auditorium, and the centerpiece—the original lunch counter, restored as a working café. In the meantime, you can look at the architectural drawings posted on the window of the building or contact the temporary office on Elm Street, which is open Monday through Friday. Call 336-334-3209.

In 1998, the Greensboro Public Library and The Depot (which is associated with the *Greensboro News and Record*) joined forces to launch an impressive website about the sit-ins. By visiting www.sitinmovement.org, you can hear nearly 100 audio clips in which the participants themselves describe what happened. You can also read the original news articles and see historic photographs.

A portion of the lunch counter and four of the original stools are currently on display at the Greensboro Historical Museum. A display of the faded Formica lunch counter and four 1950s stools is featured in the Smithsonian in Washington, D.C.

in a NASCAR automobile, a police car, or a fire truck. They can also place objects on a Bernoulli blower, which demonstrates how an airplane flies; although the blower teaches the four forces of aerodynamics and Newton's Third Law, most children just have a ball watching the air pressure shoot objects toward the ceiling. The museum is open from 9 A.M. to 5 P.M. Tuesday through Saturday and from 1 P.M. until 5 P.M. on Sunday; during the summer, it stays open until 9 P.M. on Friday and is open on Monday. An admission fee is charged; discounted rates are available for groups of 10 or more. For more information, call 336-574-2898, or visit their website at www.gcmuseum.com.

■ The *Mattye Reed African Heritage Center* is located in the Dudley Building on the campus of North Carolina A & T State University at 1601 East Market Street. It houses one of the best collections of African culture in the country. You can see over 3,500 art and craft items from more than 30 African nations, New Guinea, and Haiti. The museum offers lectures, seminars, workshops, slides, and films. It is open from 10 A.M. to 4:30 P.M. Monday through Friday. Admission is free. Call 336-334-3209 for information. The center has a satellite gallery at the Greensboro Cultural Center.

■ The *Natural Science Center* is located at 4301 Lawndale Drive, northeast of the downtown area. This is a hands-on museum, zoo, and planetarium. You can come face to face with a 36-foot model of a *Tyrannosaurus rex*; see endangered lemurs; look directly at sunspots over 200,000 miles across in size; pet a variety of small wildlife in the 30-acre zoo; and tour the herpetarium and the gem-and-mineral gallery. The center is open from 9 A.M. to 5 P.M. Monday through Saturday and from 12:30 P.M. to 5 P.M. on Sunday. The zoo has shorter hours; call for planetarium show times. A nominal admission fee is charged. For more information, call 336-288-3769, or visit their website at www.greensboro.com/sciencecenter.

CULTURAL OFFERINGS

■ The *Greensboro Cultural Center at Festival Park*, at 200 North Davie

Street in the Cultural District, comes close to providing one-stop shopping for Greensboro's visual and performing arts. The center is open from 8 a.m. to 10 p.m. Monday through Friday, from 9 a.m. to 5 p.m. on Saturday, and from 2 p.m. to 5 p.m. on Sunday. Admission is free. Hours for the individual offices and galleries are the same as listed above, unless otherwise noted. All told, the center includes four levels of galleries, studios, classrooms, and rehearsal halls. It has a sculpture garden, a privately operated restaurant with outdoor café-style seating, and the Price Bryan Performance Place, an outdoor amphitheater. Call 336-373-2712 for information.

▪ Let's start with the visual arts. One of the organizations headquartered in the Greensboro Cultural Center is the **Green Hill Center of North Carolina Art**, which offers nine to 12 annual exhibits and events featuring works by emerging and nationally recognized artists from across the state. It also offers artists' talks, conferences, panel discussions, workshops, performances, and a great gift shop. In 1996, Green Hill expanded its programs to include ArtQuest, the state's first interactive art gallery for children and families. ArtQuest features hands-on exhibits designed by North Carolina artists and studio space where children and adults can experience the arts together. For more information, call 336-333-7460, or visit their website at www.ncart.org/artquest.org.

▪ The **Guilford Native American Art Gallery** is the only gallery of its kind in the Southeast. It offers four or five exhibitions annually, featuring local, state, regional, and international Native American artists. The gallery's gift shop carries authentic Native American art, including jewelry, pottery, baskets, prints, and music. Admission is free. Call 336-273-6605.

▪ **African American Atelier** is an organization of local artists and their supporters committed to providing a showcase for African-American art. The organization's gallery exhibits original artwork by local, regional, and national African-American and ethnic artists. The gift shop offers African-American gifts, cards, and prints. Admission is free. Call 336-333-6885.

- The satellite gallery of the **Mattye Reed African Heritage Center** provides exhibits drawn from the collection. The center sponsors traveling exhibits from other museums as well. Call 336-334-7108.

- The **Greensboro Artists League** represents over 400 local artists and makers of fine crafts whose works are exhibited here and displayed for sale in the adjacent sales gallery. Admission is free. For information about events and gallery hours, call 336-333-7485.

- The **Community Theatre of Greensboro** offers studios, theatrical classes, and workshops for children and adults. It also presents original pieces in its Studio Theatre and full-scale musicals at the Carolina Theatre. For several years, it has presented *The Wizard of Oz* at the Carolina Theatre; this is quickly becoming a Thanksgiving tradition. The office number is 336-333-7470; the box office number is 336-333-7469.

- Despite concern in the summer of 2000 that financial difficulties might halt the **Eastern Music Festival**, the show will go on. This internationally acclaimed classical music festival, founded in 1962, is headquartered at the Greensboro Cultural Center. For several weeks from late June to early August, 200 exceptionally talented students combine with a faculty of outstanding musicians from leading symphony orchestras and music schools for an intensive training program on the campus of Guilford College. They stage more than 40 orchestral concerts and chamber music performances per week. These concerts offer some of the best classical performances you can get for the money. Top guest artists are even brought in to perform with the professional ensembles. For more information, call 336-333-7450, or visit their website at www.easternmusicfestival.com.

- The **Greensboro Ballet** provides three performances each season, including *The Nutcracker* during December. It has over 300 students and offers classes to all ages. For information, call 336-333-7480.

- The **Greensboro Symphony Orchestra** performs eight masterworks and three pops concerts a year. Each features guest artists. The symphony also offers three chamber orchestra concerts. For more information, call 336-335-5456, or visit their website at www.greensborosymphony.com.

■ The final organization in the Greensboro Cultural Center is the *United Arts Council of Greensboro*, a coalition of 15 funded member arts agencies. The council produces three events each year: CityStage (see the "Seasonal Events" section); the African American Arts Festival, a two-month, citywide celebration of African heritage; and Karamu, an evening celebration that transforms the Greensboro Cultural Center into an African marketplace. Call 336-373-7523 for information.

■ Although Guilford College, Greensboro College, and North Carolina A & T State University all have galleries that host touring exhibits, the *Weatherspoon Art Gallery* at the University of North Carolina at Greensboro is special, primarily because of Etta Cone's donation in 1949. Miss Cone was a part of the intellectual scene in Paris that included Gertrude Stein and company. Her bequest of a remarkable collection of lithographs and bronzes by Henri Matisse helped form the core for this collection. Today, the Weatherspoon boasts one of the best university collections of 20th-century American art. Located at the corner of Spring Garden and Tate Streets on the university campus, it is housed in a building that won architectural awards for its design. The structure contains six galleries and a sculpture courtyard. The gallery is open from 10 A.M. to 5 P.M. Tuesday, Thursday, and Friday, from 10 A.M. to 8 P.M. on Wednesday, and from 1 P.M. to 5 P.M. on Saturday and Sunday. For more information, call 336-334-5770, or visit their website at www.uncg.edu/wag.

■ One of Greensboro's enduring landmarks is the *Carolina Theatre*. Since it opened in 1927 as a vaudeville theater, it has continued to be one of

Carolina Theatre
COURTESY OF GREENSBORO
AREA CONVENTION AND
VISITORS BUREAU

Greensboro's principal performing-arts centers, offering theater, dance, concerts, and films. The impressive structure, listed on the National Register of Historic Places, is located downtown at 310 South Greene Street. For more information, call 336-333-2600, or visit their website at www.carolinatheatre.com.

SPECIAL SHOPPING

In recent years, the **Old Greensborough Downtown Historic District** has become a revitalized turn-of-the-20th-century commercial area. The district is located in and around South Elm Street from the 100 block to the 600 block south. It also includes blocks of South Davie, South Greene, and East and West Washington Streets. The area has come alive with antique shops, antiquarian book dealers, chic restaurants, and art galleries. Sandwiched among them are old retail establishments that never closed when the area hit hard times. Being so close to downtown Greensboro, this area is ripe for even more activity in the coming years. You can pick up a free brochure for a self-guided tour at the Greensboro Area Convention and Visitors Bureau, located in the district across from the Carolina Theatre. For information, check out the downtown Greensboro website at www.greensboro.com/downtown.

▪ **State Street Station**, located north of downtown between Church and Elm Streets one block south of Cornwallis Drive, is a group of unique boutiques and restaurants that cater to a decidedly upscale clientele. The buildings were once part of a small mill village, so the shops have the feel of a village within a city. For information, call 336-230-0623, or visit their website at www.statestreetstation.com.

▪ For something entirely different, check out **Replacements, Ltd**. This is the world's largest retailer of old and new china, crystal, flatware, and collectibles. Founded in 1981, the warehouse has over 6 million pieces of china, crystal, silver, and collectibles, all of which are entered in the company's state-of-the-art computer system. The facility is the size of four football fields. The 12,000-square-foot showroom includes new stock and over 2,000 unique pieces of china, crystal, and silver. Located on

Knox Road, east of Greensboro off Interstate 85/Interstate 40 at Mount Hope Church Road (Exit 132), the facility is open from 8 A.M. to 9 P.M. daily. For information, call 800-737-5223 or 336-697-3000, or visit their website at www.replacements.com.

▪ If you're looking for fresh fruit and vegetables, try the **Piedmont Triad Farmers Market**. Customers come to the several buildings at this state-owned facility to purchase fresh produce, baked goods, preserves, flowers, and ornamentals. The retail farmers' building has over 10,000 square feet of space, where local growers come daily to sell their wares. The market is located on Interstate 40 west of Greensboro at Sandy Ridge Road (Exit 208). It is open from 6 A.M. to 6 P.M. Monday through Saturday and from 1 P.M. to 6 P.M. on Sunday. For information, call 336-605-9157, or visit their website at www.agr.state.nc.us/markets/facilit/farmark/triad/index.htm.

RECREATION

Greensboro has a wide variety of public parks. Couple these with the more than 200 acres available for walking, running, or biking at Guilford Courthouse National Military Park and you have a lot of green space. What follows is a description of a few of the parks; you can get a complete listing from the Greensboro Area Convention and Visitors Bureau.

▪ The **Bryan Park Complex** and **Lake Townsend** offer two 18-hole championship golf courses. The Players Course, designed by George Cobb and modified by Rees Jones, opened in 1974. The Champions Course, which opened in 1990, was designed by Rees Jones; seven holes of this course border scenic Lake Townsend. The park offers a conference center, horseshoe pits, picnic shelters, tennis and volleyball courts, and an 11-field soccer complex. Sailing, boating, and fishing are popular on Lake Townsend. Located off U.S. 29 North at 6275 Bryan Park Road in Browns Summit, the park is open daily from 8 A.M. to sunset; the golf courses have seasonal hours. For more information, call 336-375-2222, or visit their website at www.bryanpark.com.

▪ **Country Park** offers two stocked fishing lakes, pedal boats, picnic shelters, and trails for jogging, hiking, and cycling. It is located adjacent to the Natural Science Center off Lawndale Drive. It hosts several regional bike races. Country Park is open from 8 A.M. to sunset. Call 336-545-5343.

▪ **Greensboro Jaycee Park** is adjacent to Country Park on Forest Lawn Drive off Pisgah Church Road. It has a variety of sports facilities, including Stoner-White Stadium, Spec Evatt Field, the J. Spencer Love Tennis Center, and two volleyball/badminton courts. Fees may be charged for some events. Call 336-545-5310.

▪ The centerpiece of the 409-acre **Hagan-Stone Park**, located south of Greensboro off U.S. 421 in Pleasant Garden, is its campsites for trailers and tents. The park also offers horseshoe pits, softball fields, pedal boats, nature trails for hiking and bicycling, and cross-country courses. An admission fee may be charged for some activities. Call 336-674-0472.

▪ Prominent among Greensboro's commercial recreational offerings is **Wet 'n Wild Emerald Pointe Water Park**, which bills itself as the largest water park in the Carolinas. Thunder Bay is one of only four tsunami (giant wave) pools in the country. Among the 34 different rides are enclosed slides, drop slides, tube rides, and cable glides. Located south of Greensboro off Interstate 85 at Holden Road (Exit 121), the park is open during the summer months. Admission rates change according to the length of your stay. For fees and operating hours, call 800-555-5900 or 336-852-9721.

▪ **Celebration Station** offers miniature golf, go-carts, water bumper boats, arcade games, and batting cages. It is located off Interstate 40 at the Wendover Avenue exit. Hours and rates vary, so call 336-316-0606 for information.

▪ If you like golf, you'll feel you've died and gone to heaven in North Carolina. You might experience culture shock when you read our sports pages. We give a lot of space to college basketball, but the rest of the year, the focus seems to be on golf and NASCAR. The Greensboro area offers over 20 public golf courses. For a complete list, contact the Greensboro Area Convention and Visitors Bureau at 800-334-2282 or 336-274-2282, or visit their website at www.greensboronc.org.

- If you like minor-league baseball, you'll enjoy the **Greensboro Bats**, a class-A farm club for the New York Yankees. They play in historic War Memorial Stadium, which gives fans a real feel for old-fashioned baseball. The stadium is located at the corner of Lindsay and Yanceyville Streets, east of the downtown area. For information, call 336-333-BATS, or visit their website at www.greensborobats.com.

SEASONAL EVENTS

- *A reenactment of the Battle of Guilford Courthouse* is held every year at Country Park on the weekend closest to the March 15 anniversary of the battle. Hundreds of reenactors portray British and American soldiers who fought in the American Revolution. The battle is staged at 2 P.M. Admission is free. Call 336-545-5343 for information.

A reenactment of the Battle of Guilford Courthouse
COURTESY OF GREENSBORO AREA CONVENTION AND VISITORS BUREAU

- On the first weekend in October, Greensboro closes its downtown streets and holds it annual *CityStage* street festival. The two-day event features local and nationally known musicians performing on several outdoor stages, as well as booths selling crafts and food. Activities are offered for children and a beer garden is open for adults. Admission is free, though a fee may be charged for some activities. Call 336-373-7523.

- The **Greater Greensboro Chrysler Classic** is the third-oldest event on the PGA tour. A fund-raiser for the Greensboro Jaycees, the tournament is held in mid-April at Forest Oaks Country Club, south of Greensboro on U.S. 421. For dates and ticket prices, call 800-999-5446, or visit their website at www.pgatour.com.

Places to Stay

RESORTS, HOTELS, AND MOTELS

Every major chain is represented somewhere in the Greensboro area. Most hotels are grouped at the various exits off Interstates 85 and 40. The greatest concentration is at the N.C. 68 exit off Interstate 40 west of town; this is the exit for Piedmont Triad International Airport, so the crowd of hotels makes sense. The accommodations listed below tend to be deluxe or expensive. If you are looking for a more moderate price, the budget chains are your best bet.

- **The Grandover Resort and Conference Center**. Deluxe. 1000 Club Road (800-472-6301 or 336-294-1800; www.grandover.com). Located just southwest of town, this new resort is nestled among 1,500 acres of land. One big draw is its two 18-hole golf courses, located just outside the lobby. The lobby evokes an Old World feel, with contrasting floor patterns of Italian travertine, Tasmanian gold limestone, and black granite. Several types of guest rooms are available at this AAA-rated Four-Diamond resort. The basic rooms offer color television, two dual-line telephones with voice mail, a data jack, a refrigerator, a wet bar, a complimentary newspaper, a hair dryer, an iron and ironing board, and a coffee maker. The suites have Jacuzzis, private balconies, and separate parlor areas. The two bedroom bi-level suite offers a dining/conference table for eight. The resort includes a spa, tennis and racquetball courts, a whirlpool, a pool, a fitness center with sauna and steam room, a billiards room, and dining rooms.

- **O. Henry Hotel**. Deluxe. 624 Green Valley Road (800-965-8259 or 336-854-2000; www.o.henryhotel.com). Located off Wendover Avenue at Benjamin Parkway near Friendly Shopping Center, this 131-room grand hotel has an intimate feel. It is the brainchild of the same folks who gave the Triad the Lucky 32 restaurants. The O. Henry earned a Four-Diamond rating from AAA in its first year, and you'll see why the minute you enter the wood-paneled lobby. The regular room amenities include color television, a dressing room with two vanities, an in-room safe, an iron and ironing board, in-room movies and video games, a coffee maker, a microwave, a refrigerator, a hair dryer, a makeup mirror, two-line speaker phones with modem hookups, a complimentary morning newspaper, direct-dial telephone access, and voice mail. In the suites, you get all these amenities plus a gas-burning fireplace in the separate sitting area, a stereo, a VCR, and a huge dressing room. The hotel offers a fine restaurant, afternoon tea and cocktails in the lobby, a business center, an exercise facility, and an outdoor pool. Guests often remark about the lack of bedspreads in their room. The beds are triple-sheeted, so all the bed coverings can be cleaned on a daily basis. And of course, each room has a collection of O. Henry short stories to remind guests of a local boy who made good.

- **Greensboro Hilton**. Expensive. 304 North Greene Street (800-HILTONS or 336-379-8000; www.hilton.com). This is the only full-service hotel in the downtown area. It has 281 guest rooms, including three luxury suites. One of these, the Presidential, claims to be the largest hotel suite in Greensboro. You'll find the usual Hilton amenities: color television, coffee makers, and desk phones with data ports. The hotel has a 16,000-square-foot athletic club, which includes an indoor heated pool, a sauna, a whirlpool, and tanning beds. It offers meeting space for conferences.

- **Sheraton Greensboro Hotel at Four Seasons**. Expensive. 3121 High

Point Road (800-242-6556 or 336-292-9161; www.kourycenter.com). The Joseph S. Koury Convention Center, which connects with this hotel, calls itself the largest hotel and convention center in the Carolinas. Located at the High Point Road exit off Interstate 40, this hotel has 1,017 guest rooms and access to 250,000 square feet of meeting and banquet space. As a result, it attracts numerous conventions. Amenities include data ports, satellite television, pay-per-view movies, hair dryers, and voice mail. It offers a full-scale business center, a health club, a pool, a whirlpool, a sauna, and a racquetball court. Because the same developers own the Grandover Resort, the Sheraton staff can make reservations for you on the Grandover golf courses. Greensboro's major shopping mall, Four Seasons Town Centre, is next door.

INNS AND BED-AND-BREAKFASTS

▪ *The Biltmore Greensboro Hotel.* Expensive. 111 West Washington Street (800-332-0303 or 336-272-3474; www.members.sol.com/biltmorenc/index.html). This hotel, which bills itself as "a unique European boutique hostelry," is located in the Old Greensborough Downtown Historic District. You enter an elegant walnut-paneled lobby through crystal front doors. In the morning, a deluxe continental breakfast is served in this lobby; in the evening, a reception featuring informal wine tasting and hors d'oeuvres is held here. The rooms have king-sized four-poster canopy beds and 16-foot ceilings. Amenities include color television, telephones with data ports, a refrigerator, a hair dryer, and an iron and ironing board. Free parking and free airport pickup are provided. Some small pets are accepted.

▪ *Greenwood Bed-and-Breakfast.* Expensive. 205 North Park Drive (800-535-9363 or 336-274-6350; www.greenwoodbb.com). The Greenwood is a 23-room, turn-of-the-20th-century Craftsman-style home. Located just off Elm Street, this AAA-rated Three-Diamond bed-and-breakfast is owned by Bob and Dolly Guertin. Bob is a former New Orleans chef and Dolly a former custom decorator. Each of the five guest rooms has a private bath. The abundant breakfasts, served at a time of your choosing, have a New Orleans flare. Upon request, you can enjoy evening desserts such as bread pudding with whiskey sauce, bananas Foster, cherries jubilee, and crêpes suzette. One amenity that is unusual for a bed-and-breakfast is the in-ground pool. The Greenwood also offers terry cloth robes, remote-controlled ceiling fans, fireplaces, in-room telephones, and access to a fax and a copy machine.

■ **The Troy-Bumpas Inn**. Expensive. 114 South Mendenhall Street (800-370-9070 or 336-370-1660; www.troy-bumpasinn.com). Built in 1847, this home is listed on the National Register of Historic Places. Close to the campuses of the University of North Carolina at Greensboro and Greensboro College, it offers four rooms with telephones, private baths, hair dryers, and robes. All of the rooms are furnished with antiques or antique reproductions. Cable television is available in the sitting room.

Places to Eat

Because of space constraints, some very good restaurants are not mentioned here. I have tried to balance the number of offerings in each price category, but most of the exceptional restaurants fall within the expensive and moderate categories. I have also tried to list restaurants that continually appear on everyone's list of favorites. A good source for recent restaurant reviews is food critic John Batchelor of the *Greensboro News and Record*; you can find some of his more recent reviews at www.thedepot.com.

■ **Gate City Chop House**. Expensive. 106 South Holden Road, near the intersection with West Market Street (336-294-9977). This is the place to go for your standard big hunk of beef. In addition to the Angus beef selections, Gate City Chop House offers grilled seafood, chicken, and pasta dishes. Lunch is served Monday through Friday and dinner Monday through Saturday.

■ **George K's**. Expensive. 2108 Cedar Fork Drive (336-854-0007). This establishment serves northern Italian, French, and Greek cuisine. It is noted for its seafood, lamb, veal, beef, poultry, and pasta dishes and its good wine selection. It is open for dinner Monday through Saturday.

■ **Leblon**. Expensive. 4512 West Market Street (336-294-2605; www.yp.bellsouth.com/sites/leblon/index.html). In 1996, the Vanuccis brought the food of their native Brazil to the Piedmont. The cuisine at Leblon ranges from spicy dishes from northern Brazil to the more European style of the southern part of that country. Delectable paella and beef selections and fresh seafood, pork, and chicken dishes (some with spicy Brazilian sauces) are offered. On Tuesdays and Thursdays only, the restaurant serves feijoada, a traditional Brazilian dish of black bean stew with sausage, pork, dry beef, and a side dish of Brazilian-style collard greens. Lunch is served Monday through Friday and dinner Monday through Saturday.

■ **Lo Spiedo Di Noble**. Expensive. 1720 Battleground Avenue (336-333-9833). Jim Noble has an exceptional restaurant in each of the Triad's three main cities. Greensboro's offering has a Tuscan and Mediterranean slant with a French flair. The rotisserie grill and brick ovens use hickory and oak. *Wine Spectator* gave the wine list here its Award of Excellence. Dinner is served Monday through Saturday.

■ **Paisley Pineapple**. Expensive. 345 South Elm Street (336-279-8488). Located in Old Greensborough, the Paisley Pineapple has drawn praise since 1988. Beef, game, fowl, seafood, and pasta are offered. Live jazz is sometimes performed in the upstairs sofa bar. This restaurant also received *Wine Spectator*'s Award of Excellence for its wine list. Dinner is served Tuesday through Saturday. Reservations are recommended.

■ **Market Street West**. Expensive/Moderate. 5340 West Market Street (336-294-0575). This restaurant has had a strong following for a long time. It offers good ingredients served in a straightforward, traditional way. Prime rib, steaks, roast duck, and chicken cordon bleu are all mainstays. The ambiance is enhanced by a live pianist playing a grand piano. Dinner is served daily.

■ **Mark's on Westover**. Expensive/Moderate. 1310 Westover Terrace (336-273-9090). This establishment looks and feels like a Paris bistro. Food critic John Batchelor gave it one of his rare Five-Star ratings. Mark's serves contemporary American cuisine with regional specialties. If crab cakes are featured as an off-menu special, you'd be well advised to try them. Lunch is served Tuesday through Friday and dinner Tuesday through Saturday.

- **Undercurrent Restaurant.** Expensive/Moderate. 600 South Elm Street (336-370-1266; www.undercurrentrestaurant.com). Undercurrent is located in Old Greensborough, which is quickly becoming the in place to open a restaurant. The decor in this small bistro is elegantly simple and tasteful. The current owner and chef, formerly the chef at Winston-Salem's City Club, offers "New American" and classical cuisine combined with Asian influences. The *New York Times* called this a "smart restaurant." Lunch is served Tuesday through Friday and dinner Tuesday through Saturday.

- **Bert's Seafood Grille.** Moderate. 2419 Spring Garden Street (336-854-2314). This establishment has set the standard for seafood in Greensboro since it opened in 1988. Its Four-Star rating from John Batchelor is well deserved. Bert's offers the widest variety of seafood in the Triad. One sign that it takes its claim of serving fresh seafood seriously is that it does not own a freezer. Its wine list is another winner of *Wine Spectator*'s Award of Excellence. Dinner is served daily.

- **Green Valley Grill.** Moderate. 622 Green Valley Road (336-854-2015). The restaurant wing of the O. Henry Hotel, this establishment comes from the same team that created the Lucky 32 restaurants that are so popular all over North Carolina. The look is very upscale, as befits a Four-Diamond hotel. The restaurant uses a wood-fired oven for pizzas and a wood-fired grill to roast chicken and beef on a spit. The open kitchen allows diners to watch the process. Lunch and dinner are served daily.

- **Mudbugs.** Moderate. 309 State Street (336-273-0683; www.mudbugs.net). Located in the State Street Station complex, this restaurant offers Cajun-style cuisine. If you like shrimp or crawfish, this is the place. Dinner is served Tuesday through Saturday; brunch is offered on Saturday.

■ *Nikita India*. Moderate. 4612-A West Market Street in the Price Place Shopping Center (336-852-2077; www.nikitaindia.com). Nikita India's restaurant on Tate Street, near the UNC-G campus, was a local staple for years but has now closed. Fortunately, the tradition continues at the new location. Don't worry if you don't know anything about Indian food; the menu describes every dish in easy-to-understand English. And you can always order one of the combination dinners to sample a little of everything. Vegetarians will find Nikita's especially inviting. Lunch is served Tuesday through Sunday and dinner daily.

■ *Rearn Thai*. Inexpensive. 5109 West Market Street (336-292-5901). This gem of a place offers reasonably priced traditional Thai dishes. Lunch and dinner are served Monday through Saturday.

■ *Stamey's Barbecue*. Inexpensive. 2206 High Point Road (336-299-9888) and 2812 Battleground Avenue (336-288-9275). You can't come to North Carolina and not try the barbecue the natives pine for when they have to move away. Stamey's serves what is called Lexington-style barbecue, which has a vinegar-and-tomato sauce. The dining rooms are large and busy; you can also use the drive-through line. Both places serve barbecue cooked the old-fashioned way in a smokehouse behind the High Point Road location. Lunch and dinner are served Monday through Saturday.

The "World's Largest Chest of Drawers"
Courtesy of High Point Convention And Visitors Bureau

HIGH POINT

by Carolyn Sakowski

When John Motley Morehead brought the North Carolina Railroad to Guilford County, a survey revealed that the tracks would intersect with the existing plank road that connected Fayetteville to Salem. That intersection, located 912 feet above sea level, would be the highest point on the rail line. It was obvious that this transportation hub would draw speculators. By 1859, the new village had 525 people, two hotels, two churches, and seven stores. In May of that year, the two-mile-square town was chartered under the name High Point.

High Point has been linked with the furniture industry since the 1880s. Today, its 79,400 residents are proud to call their city the "Home Furnishings Capital of the World."

If you're looking for a fun photo opportunity to capture the furniture feel, check out the "World's Largest Chest of Drawers," located at 508 North Hamilton Street. Built in 1926 and recently restored, it is actually the facade of a building shaped like an 18th-century chest of drawers. The building houses the offices of the High Point Jaycees.

Just the Facts

High Point is southwest of Greensboro. It may be reached via Interstate 85 Business or U.S. 311.

Piedmont Triad International Airport is centrally located among High Point, Greensboro, and Winston-Salem. Its carriers include US Airways, Delta, Continental, United, American, AirTran, and Northwest. Some local hotels offer free transportation from the airport. Call 336-665-5666 or 336-665-5600 for airport information.

The Amtrak station is located at 100 West High Street. For information, call 336-841-7245.

The Trailways bus station is located at 100 Lindsay Street. For information, call 336-882-2000.

For visitor information, contact the High Point Convention and Visitors Bureau, 300 South Main Street, High Point, N.C. 27260 (800-720-5255 or 336-884-5255; www.highpoint.org).

The city's daily newspaper, the *High Point Enterprise*, publishes an "Entertainment" section with listings of local events. You can also check *Triad Style* and *ESP*—two free weekly tabloids—for events listings.

Things to Do

Historic Places, Gardens, and Tours

Tours of furniture manufacturers' market showrooms are available to groups of 15 or more. Reservations must be made in advance with the High Point Convention and Visitors Bureau by calling 800-720-5255. No tours are available in April and October, when the furniture markets are held.

"Showplace"
COURTESY OF HIGH POINT CONVENTION AND VISITORS BUREAU

The Furniture Industry and High Point

Drawing on the nearby hardwood forests, local furniture factories owned and run by Northern industrialists were shipping their products out of High Point by the trainload in the 1880s. In 1889, High Point Furniture Company became the first locally owned furniture manufacturer. Others soon followed. Local entrepreneurs realized that the quality of their furniture exceeded that produced in the North. They just needed to come up with some way to display their wares. In 1905, the High Point Exposition Company opened its first furniture show. In 1909, the city's furniture manufacturers began hosting biannual expositions, but they couldn't compete with the ones held in the North.

In 1911, J. J. Farris, editor of the *High Point Enterprise*, suggested that High Point construct a large display building. The Southern Furniture Manufacturers' Association led the movement to create a central display building that would make High Point

the center for Southern furniture. In June 1919, construction began on a 10-story, $1 million structure that would house 261,000 square feet of exhibit space. When the building opened in 1921, more than 700 furniture buyers showed up to view the 149 exhibits. By 1924, the building's exhibit space was completely rented.

Over the years, the Southern Exposition Building underwent repeated expansions. When the first postwar market was held in January 1947, some 5,147 retail furniture buyers came to town. By 1955, the display area increased to 500,000 square feet. Now known as the International Home Furnishings Center, the showrooms have completely taken over downtown High Point. In 1990, the city boasted 8.5 million square feet of display space.

Today, approximately 60 percent of all the furniture in the United States is manufactured within a 200-mile radius of High Point. The city has more than 100 furniture factories and 170 showrooms. It plays host to "the market" twice a year—in April and October. In 1999, the market attracted 1,800 manufacturers. The trade show, which is not open to the public, draws more than 80,000 visitors to High Point from every state and 65 countries; these guests spend an estimated $312 million locally. Because accommodations are scarce during these times, many local residents rent their homes to people coming for the markets and use the money to go on a vacation.

Although the markets are not open to the public, the city's huge furniture retailers are. People from all over the country come to High Point to take advantage of prices 40 to 50 percent off the national retail. When you are shopping, remember that these retailers do not have huge warehouses stocked with ready-to-ship furniture. Rather, the retailers place orders with the manufacturers; it usually takes from eight to 12 weeks for customers to receive their shipment. Some manufacturers require local retailers to exhibit complete collections in order to get volume discounts. This means that customers have a better selection in High Point than in traditional stores. Giants like Furnitureland South, Boyles, and Rose Furniture have immense showrooms with professional designers on staff as sales associates.

In addition to full-service stores, there are several clearance centers in High Point. The area around South Main Street near Interstate 85 Business could be called "Clearance Row." These stores stock unclaimed merchandise, discontinued items, and pieces that have been moved out of the galleries to make room for new collections. Items that were originally 40 to 50 percent off the retail price in the main stores are discounted even further.

When you come to High Point, you will see that this is indeed the "Home Furnishings Capital of the World."

■ *Mendenhall Plantation* is located at 603 West Main Street (U.S. 70 Alternate) in neighboring Jamestown. James Mendenhall, a Pennsylvania Quaker, received a land grant in 1762. The settlement that grew up around his farm was called Jamestown in his honor. In 1811, his grandson Richard built the original part of what is now known as Mendenhall Plantation.

This wonderful example of early-19th-century Quaker architecture has been enlarged several times yet retains its simple character. The grounds feature a "bank barn" built into a hillside in the tradition of the Pennsylvania settlers. One of the nation's few surviving false-bottomed wagons, used to help slaves to freedom on the Underground Railroad, is on the site. The house and grounds are open from 11 A.M. to 2 P.M. Tuesday through Friday, from 1 P.M. to 4 P.M. on Saturday, and from 2 P.M. to 4 P.M. most Sundays. Admission is free, though donations are encouraged. For information, call 336-454-3819.

Mendenhall Plantation
COURTESY OF HIGH POINT CONVENTION
AND VISITORS BUREAU

MUSEUMS AND SCIENCE CENTERS

▪ *High Point Museum and Historical Park* is located at 1859 East Lexington Avenue. The park contains the 1786 Haley House, listed on the National Register of Historic Places, and a blacksmith shop and weaving house from the mid-1700s. The recently renovated museum features furniture displays, military artifacts, pottery, and more. The facility is open Tuesday through Saturday from 10 A.M. to 4:30 P.M. and Sunday from 1 P.M. to 4:30 P.M. Call 336-885-6859.

▪ The *Museum of Old Domestic Life* is located at Springfield Friends Meeting at 555 East Springfield Road. More than 500 antique household and farm artifacts are housed in the Springfield Friends' third meeting house, which was used for worship from 1858 to 1927. Items from the old plank road, a rock from the Underground Railroad, and many implements for tanning, shoemaking, cloth making, cooking, farming, and everyday Quaker life can be seen here. The adjacent cemetery dates from 1780. The museum is open by appointment; call 336-882-3054.

▪ The *Furniture Discovery Center*, located at 101 West Green Drive, is designed to simulate a modern furniture factory, so visitors can see how furniture is made. Exhibits include a talking tree, 15 hand-carved miniature bedrooms, and a display of more than 40 pieces of ⅛-scale hand-carved furniture pieces that were used to create full-sized furniture. You can see how wood veneers are created and how textile furniture upholstery is made. You can try out tools on an assembly line and enjoy the

The talking tree exhibit at the Furniture Discovery Center
COURTESY OF HIGH POINT CONVENTION AND VISITORS BUREAU

American Furniture Hall of Fame, which gives details about High Point's growth in the industry. The center is open from 10 A.M. to 5 P.M. Monday through Friday, from 9 A.M. to 5 P.M. on Saturday, and from 1 P.M. to 5 P.M. on Sunday; it is closed Mondays from November to March. Hours are extended during the furniture markets. An admission fee is charged. Call 336-887-3876 for information.

▪ Located at 101 West Green Drive in the same building as the Furniture Discovery Center is the *Angela Peterson Doll and Miniature Museum*. Approximately 1,700 dolls make this one of the most extensive collections of its type in the country. You'll see antique dolls made of china, wood, bisque, wax, papier-mâché, and tin. You'll see Pilgrims, witches, Eskimos, Amish, a doll made of seaweed, and an extensive display of paper dolls. One large case features over 100 tiny figures less than six inches high. You'll also find three couples of fully dressed "fleas" that can be seen only under a magnifier. The Shadow-Box Room features scenes from a Danish farm, a Caribbean basket shop, a tea party, and a Mexican bullfight. Among the items on display are original Barbies, a Pillsbury Doughboy, Chatty Kathy, a 60-year-old Charlie McCarthy puppet, 120 Shirley Temple dolls, dolls from 53 different countries, and dozens of dollhouses. The museum is open from 10 A.M. to 4:30 P.M. Monday through Friday, from 9 A.M. to 4:30 P.M. on Saturday, and from 1 P.M. to 4:30 P.M. on Sunday; it is closed Mondays from November through March. An admission fee is charged. Call 336-885-3655.

CULTURAL OFFERINGS

■ The **North Carolina Shakespeare Festival** is headquartered in High Point. This professional troupe performs three or four plays—usually by Shakespeare—at different venues in the Triad during the late summer and fall. It also stages *A Christmas Carol* in December. You can contact the festival at P.O. Box 6066, High Point, N.C. 27262 (336-841-2273).

■ The **Bernice Bienenstock Furniture Library**, at 1009 North Main Street, holds 7,000 volumes, making it the world's largest collection of books on the history of furniture. The library is open to the public Monday through Friday from 9 A.M. to noon and from 1 P.M. to 5 P.M. Admission is free. Call 336-883-4011.

■ ***Theatre Art Galleries***, at 220 East Commerce Avenue, offers three exhibition areas with changing art shows. It is open Monday, Tuesday, Thursday, and Friday from noon to 5 P.M., Wednesday from noon to 7 P.M., and weekends by reservation. It is closed in April and October for the market shows. Call 336-887-2137.

SPECIAL SHOPPING

Although High Point has about 70 retail stores that feature a vast array of home furnishings to suit every taste and budget, I will highlight only a few because of their unique qualities.

■ ***Furnitureland South***, located on Interstate 85 Business, is phenomenal. Its 500,000-square-foot showroom is billed as the largest retail furniture showroom in the world. Couple this with a 104,000-square-foot distribution center and you have a major source for furniture. From the moment you enter the building, you'll know you're not in your ordinary furniture store. It's so big that they even give you a map. You are free to browse the several floors, where furniture is shown in gallery settings and grouped according to type and style. When you need assistance, just pick up the nearest telephone. For information, call 336-841-4328, or visit their website at www.furniturelandsouth.com.

- **Rose Furniture Company** has been in business for 75 years. Its 175,000-square-foot showroom has three floors, a large resource/catalog room, and more than 65 salespeople to help you. It carries over 700 lines of furniture. The address is 916 Finch Avenue. From Interstate 85 Business, take the Surrett Drive exit and turn right; you will see where to turn right again to reach Finch Avenue. The store is open Monday through Friday from 8:30 A.M. to 5 P.M. and Saturday from 8:30 A.M. to 4 P.M. For information, call 336-886-6050, or visit their website at www.rosefurniture.com.

- The **Atrium Furniture Mall,** located in the downtown area at 430 South Main Street, houses over 20 different furniture stores in one location. It is open Monday through Friday from 9 A.M. to 6 P.M. and Saturday from 9 A.M. to 5 P.M. For information, call 336-882-5599, or visit their website at www.atriumfurniture.com.

RECREATION

- **Oak Hollow Lake Park and Marina**, located at 3431 North Centennial Street, has an 18-hole Pete Dye–designed golf course with a practice range and a clubhouse. The 1,500-acre park offers boating, water-skiing, and sailing; small sailboats can be rented for use on the lake. The park has tennis courts and 90 campsites with full hookups. Call 336-883-3486.

- **City Lake Park**, at 602 West Main Street in Jamestown, is a 969-acre site with a 340-acre lake. Visitors enjoy the fishing, the paddleboats, and the fishing boat and canoe rentals. The park has amusement rides, a train, a water slide, the largest outdoor swimming pool in the state, a miniature golf course, a gymnasium, a playground, and an excursion boat. Call 336-883-3498.

- **Piedmont Environmental Center** was founded in 1972 to provide environmental education through outdoor experiences. Located at 1220 Penny Road adjacent to High Point Lake, its 375 acres of protected land offer 11 miles of trails for jogging and hiking. The Bicentennial Greenway, a 10-foot-wide, 6.5-mile-long paved trail, also runs through the site. The

Playing at City Lake Park
COURTESY OF HIGH POINT CONVENTION AND VISITORS BUREAU

center has a nature preserve; a nature store; small-animal exhibits including a red fox, a white-tailed deer, hawks, raccoons, and owls; and a large "walk-on" relief map of North Carolina that demonstrates the state's geology, geography, and physiography. The center is open Monday through Saturday from 9 A.M. to 5 P.M. and Sunday from 1 P.M. to 5 P.M. The trails are open from sunrise to sunset seven days a week. Admission is free. For information, call 336-883-8531, or visit their website at www.highpointnc.com/pec.

SEASONAL EVENTS

▪ Say no more—the big events in High Point are the two *International Home Furnishings Markets,* held in April and October. Other than that, you have the *North Carolina Furnishings Festival,* which doesn't really have anything to do with the furniture markets. It is held in early August in the downtown area. The festival offers activities for children and adults; several stages feature live entertainment. Call 336-956-1888.

▪ *Day in the Park* is held on a Saturday in September at City Lake Park. Music, food, crafts, and children's crafts are included. Call 336-889-2787.

Places to Stay

Good locally owned accommodations are few in High Point. Most of the major chains are represented around the intersections of Interstate 40 and N.C. 68 (the airport exit) and Interstate 40 and High Point Road. Both of these areas are within a quick drive of downtown High Point. See the listings under Greensboro, because the two cities have virtually run together.

RESORTS, HOTELS, AND MOTELS

▪ **The Radisson Hotel High Point**. Expensive. 135 South Main Street (336-889-8888). Located next to the largest of the furniture showroom buildings, this is the best you'll find in High Point proper. It has 252 rooms, a restaurant, a bar, a fitness room, an indoor pool, and meeting space. The hotel provides free airport transportation.

INNS AND BED-AND-BREAKFASTS

▪ **The Bouldin House Bed-and-Breakfast**. Expensive. 4332 Archdale Road in Archdale (800-739-1816 or 336-431-4909; www.bouldinhouse.com). This lovely old farmhouse sits on three acres of a former tobacco farm. The fine country home has been beautifully restored. It has wainscoting in the hallways, crafted oak paneling in the dining room, and decorative patterns in the hardwood floors. Each guest room has a king-sized bed, a ceiling fan, an alarm clock/radio, a fireplace, and a private bath. Your stay includes early-morning coffee and tea service, a gourmet breakfast, and home-baked goodies in the evening. A guest telephone and a color television with a VCR and videotapes are located in the gathering room; televisions are also available in select guest rooms. Children over 10 are welcome.

■ **Westwood House Bed-and-Breakfast**. Expensive. 814 Westwood Avenue (336-886-2177; www.webs4you.com/westwood). Westwood House is located in downtown High Point close to the furniture showrooms. Your stay here includes complimentary morning coffee and newspaper, a full country breakfast from the menu, and complimentary afternoon and evening refreshments. The rooms are air-conditioned and have private baths, ceiling fans, and cable television. Data-port access is also available.

Places to Eat

With one notable exception, your best bet is to go to Greensboro to dine.

■ **J Basul Noble's**. Expensive. 101 South Main Street (336-889-3354). Jim Noble, the proprietor of this restaurant and two other top restaurants in Greensboro and Winston-Salem, has recently moved his first venture to a new location. Jim Noble's restaurants all get rave reviews from the critics. This one received a rare Five-Star rating from John Batchelor, the food critic for the *Greensboro News and Record*. Dinner is served Monday through Saturday.

North Carolina Zoological Park
COURTESY OF NORTH CAROLINA DIVISION OF TOURISM, FILM AND SPORTS DEVELOPMENT

TRIAD NEARBY

by Ed Southern and Carolyn Sakowski

■ *North Carolina Zoological Park* is the largest walk-through natural-habitat zoo in the country. Covering more than 500 acres in the Uwharrie Mountains just south of Asheboro, it features animals living in conditions as close to their natural habitats as possible. The zoo has nearly 1,000 undeveloped acres waiting for future expansion.

Five miles of trails take visitors through the zoo's two continental regions, North America and Africa; other such regions are planned. Indoor exhibits include the African Pavilion, the R. J. Reynolds Forest Aviary, and Streamside. The usual animals are here—lions, tigers, elephants, gorillas, giraffes, and chimpanzees. Among the most recent and most popular attractions are the polar bears. Bison (not buffalo) also make their home here.

A restaurant, picnic areas, some handicapped access, and trains for those who don't feel like hoofing it are available. The zoo is open every day except Christmas; it also closes during severe weather. The hours are 9 A.M. to 5 P.M. from April 1 to October 31 and 9 A.M. to 4 P.M. from

November 1 to March 31. Admission is charged. Half-price tickets are available from December through February. No rain checks are given. To get to the zoo, take U.S. 220 south from Asheboro and follow the signs. For more information, call 800-488-0444, or visit their website at www.nczoo.org.

- **Chinqua-Penn Plantation**, located near Reidsville, is named after the chinquapin tree, a dwarf chestnut common in the Southeast, and the Penn family, who built the home. Thomas Jefferson "Jeff" Penn started on the West Coast as a tobacco salesman for his father's company. He later moved to Buffalo, New York, where he became a partner in an investment firm. He married and fathered four children, but illness eventually took all of his children and, finally, his wife. After her death, Penn focused his attention on his dairy farm in North Carolina. He married heiress Beatrice "Betsy" Schoellkopf in 1923. The two devoted the rest of their lives to their passions for traveling, collecting, and working on Chinqua-Penn.

Today, the plantation house at Chinqua-Penn, listed on the National Register of Historic Places, is open to the public for guided tours and special events. The collection features everything from ancient Egyptian art to 1960s Americana, with a healthy dose of Asian and religious art mixed in. The house has been used as a set for a number of movies and was featured on the Arts & Entertainment Network's *American Castles* series.

The house is open Tuesday through Saturday from 9 A.M. to 5 P.M. and Sunday from noon to 5 P.M. The final tour of the day begins at 4 P.M. The house is closed Thanksgiving, Christmas, and all of January and February. Admission is charged. Garden-only passes, 12-month passes, and group rates are available. From the Triad, take either U.S. 29 or U.S. 158 to Reidsville and follow the brown signs. For more information, call 800-948-0947, or visit their website at www.chinquapenn.com.

- **Seagrove** is a small town 30 miles south of the Triad, at the north end of the Uwharries. Twenty potteries lie within a five-mile radius of the town, carrying on a tradition more than 200 years old. Some families have been Seagrove potters for five generations or more, but as Seagrove's fame has spread, so have the newcomers practicing the craft.

A Seagrove potter displays his wares.
COURTESY OF NORTH CAROLINA DIVISION OF TOURISM, FILM AND SPORTS DEVELOPMENT

Signs directing travelers to the potteries are easy to find along U.S. 220 and N.C. 705. Be advised that the potteries are packed on Saturdays and closed on Sundays. Seagrove is home to the North Carolina Pottery Center, at 250 East Avenue, an interpretive and educational facility devoted to researching and preserving the potter's craft. The center can help plan a visit; call 336-873-8430 or visit www.ncpotterycenter.com.

- **Tanglewood Park** was once the plantation estate of William Neal Reynolds, R. J.'s brother and an executive at R. J. Reynolds Tobacco Company. He bequeathed his estate to the citizens of Forsyth County—actually, his will left it to the "white citizens" of Forsyth County, but that stipulation has been ignored for a few decades now.

Perched on the banks of the Yadkin River, Tanglewood has been turned into a premier recreation area. It boasts two 18-hole golf courses designed by Robert Trent Jones, Jr., as well as a par-three course. Canoes and paddleboats are available to rent during the summer months. Picnic facilities abound, including several shelters that can be reserved for large parties. Horseback riding and fishing are also popular pastimes here.

Tanglewood hosts special events throughout the year, including *Music at Sunset* during the summer, and the *Festival of Lights* during the holiday season. Each year, the Championship Course at Tanglewood hosts the *Vantage*, one of the top events on the Senior PGA circuit.

The entrance to Tanglewood, on U.S. 158 about 10 miles southwest of Winston-Salem, is easily accessible from Interstate 40. Admission is charged. Call 336-778-6300 for hours and information.

■ **Korner's Folly**, billed as the "strangest house in the world," is the former home of Jule Gilmer Korner, the man for whom the town of Kernersville is named. Korner made a small fortune traveling the country and painting "Bull Durham" signs on the sides of buildings. Those classic signs became a well-known symbol of James B. Duke's American Tobacco Company.

In the late 19th century, Korner designed his dream house, one that combined bachelor's quarters, an artist's studio, an office, a billiards room, a ballroom, a carriage house, and stables. He worked the rest of his life on the house, which eventually included 22 rooms spread over three floors and seven levels. Korner packed those rooms with exquisite tiles, frescoes, and decorative pieces and turned his attic into a private theater. The ceiling height was six feet in some rooms and 25 feet in others.

Since Korner's death in 1924, Korner's Folly has been used as a family home, a summer home, an architect's office, an antique store, and even a funeral home. It now serves as a museum celebrating Korner's eccentricity and impeccable taste. The home is located at 413 South Main Street in Kernersville, which is off Interstate 40 between Winston-Salem and Greensboro. Tours are offered from 10 A.M. to 3 P.M. on Thursday, from 10 A.M. to 1 P.M. on Saturday, and from 1 P.M. to 5 P.M. on Sunday. Admission is charged. Call 336-996-7922 for more information.

■ **Alamance Battleground State Historic Site** is located off N.C. 62 near Burlington, which is east of Greensboro. This is the site of a 1771 battle between Royal Governor William Tryon's militia and the rebellious backcountry farmers known as Regulators. The Regulators objected to the control exercised over the colonial government by the merchants and planters to the east; their dissatisfaction eventually led to the short-lived War of Regulation. They were crushed by Tryon here at Alamance, which ended the Regulator movement. On the other hand, many interpret the battle and the Regulators' grievances as a warmup for the American Revolution.

From April through October, the battleground is open from 9 A.M. to 5 P.M. Monday through Saturday and from 1 P.M. to 5 P.M. on Sunday. From November to March, it is open from 10 A.M. to 4 P.M. Tuesday through Saturday and from 1 P.M. to 4 P.M. on Sunday. Admission is free. Call 336-227-4785 for more information.

- **Lexington**, approximately 25 miles south of Winston-Salem on U.S. 52, is the county seat of Davidson County. This city used to be known almost exclusively for its barbecue. Here in Lexington, a unique style was developed that used a tomato-based sauce for cooking pork shoulders. This led to a barbecue with a more mellow, less spicy taste than that from the eastern part of North Carolina, where a vinegar-based sauce is used. Every October, the many, many barbecue joints in town get together for the **Barbecue Festival**, a nightmare for both dieters and hogs. Call 336-956-1880 for more information.

In recent years, Lexington has also become known as the home of Bob Timberlake, the extraordinarily successful painter. Inspired to take up painting as an adult by an article about Andrew Wyeth, Timberlake has since branched out into furniture making, clothing design, and, most recently, architecture. Almost anything Timberlake puts his name on sells like hot cakes, and it can all be found at the **Bob Timberlake Gallery**, located on the East Center Street Extension in Lexington. Call 336-249-4428 for more information.

- **Westbend Vineyards** uses 40 acres of fertile Yadkin River Valley bottom land to grow traditional European grape varieties, which are made into award-winning vintage wines. The vineyards and winery are open for tours, tastings, and wine sales Friday and Saturday from noon to 6 P.M. and Sunday from 1 P.M. to 6 P.M. The vineyards are located outside Lewisville, a small town just west of Winston-Salem. Call 336-945-5032 for more information.

- The town of **Mount Airy** is a must for those who love *The Andy Griffith Show*. If you're a fan, you probably already know that Mount Airy is Griffith's hometown and the model for Mayberry. Located on U.S. 52 northwest of Winston-Salem, Mount Airy is very visibly proud of its most famous son.

- Speaking of Mayberry, **Pilot Mountain State Park**, also on U.S. 52 in Surry County, is located next to the town of Pilot Mountain, which was the basis for "Mount Pilot" on *The Andy Griffith Show*. Though many visitors think Mount Pilot is the correct name, it's not. And don't go looking for any "fun girls" here either. Pilot Mountain, in fact, is the most distinctive peak in the Sauratown range and a well-known image of the Triad. The state park offers picnic grounds, campsites, bridle paths, and plenty of hiking trails. The quartzite dome that sits atop the mountain, however, is a fragile ecosystem unto itself; climbing it is not allowed. Call 336-325-2355 for more information.

■ *Hanging Rock State Park*, located about 15 miles east of Pilot Mountain on N.C. 89, is the largest state park in the Piedmont. Three sheer rockfaces—Cooks Wall, Moores Knob, and Hanging Rock itself—dominate the park. Climbing is allowed (and is very popular) on the first two but not on Hanging Rock. Campsites, cabins, picnic areas, swimming, fishing, and 20 miles of hiking trails are offered. Many visitors like to canoe on the Dan River, a gentle, slow-moving river except after storms. Call 336-593-8480 for more information.

The Old Mill of Guilford
COURTESY OF GREENSBORO AREA
CONVENTION AND VISITORS BUREAU

■ The *Old Mill of Guilford* offers a great photo opportunity. This working, water-powered gristmill is located on N.C. 68 at Oak Ridge, five miles north of Piedmont Triad International Airport. Listed on the National Register of Historic Places, the mill was in operation as far back as 1745. In fact, Lord Cornwallis's troops ground meal here on their way to the Battle of Guilford Courthouse.

Today, the mill offers a gift shop that sells cornmeal, whole-wheat flour, buckwheat, rye, and other stone-ground meals. It also sells mixes for hush puppies, buckwheat pancakes, and Scotch shortbread, as well as country hams, honey, molasses, and North Carolina pottery and crafts. It is open daily from 9 A.M. to 6 P.M. Admission is free. Call 336-643-4783 for information.

- **Charlotte Hawkins Brown Memorial State Historic Site** was North Carolina's first State Historic Site honoring the contributions of African-American citizens. Located off Interstate 85 at Exit 135 about 10 miles east of Greensboro in Sedalia, this was also the first State Historic Site to honor a woman.

Charlotte Hawkins Brown was born in North Carolina but grew up in Cambridge, Massachusetts. Dissatisfied with the lack of educational opportunities for blacks in the Jim Crow South, she returned to North Carolina in 1901 to teach African-American youth in Sedalia. When the school closed after she had taught only one term, Charlotte raised money in New England to found her own school, which she named Palmer Memorial Institute. In its early years, the day and boarding school emphasized agricultural and industrial education for rural living. During her 50-year presidency, Dr. Brown saw more than 1,000 students graduate from her school.

The historic site focuses not only on Palmer Memorial Institute but on the larger themes of educational and social history in North Carolina as well. It offers exhibits, tours of historic structures, and audiovisual presentations. Winter hours are from 10 A.M. to 4 P.M. Tuesday through Saturday; summer hours are 9 A.M. to 5 P.M. Monday through Saturday and 1 P.M. to 5 P.M. on Sunday. Admission is free. For more information, call 336-449-4846, or visit their website at www.netpath.net/-chb.

Charlotte

There is no reason on God's green earth for Charlotte to be here. Charlotte has no advantage of nature to justify its location, its geographical presence. It has no port like New York or New Orleans, no confluence of rivers like Charleston or Pittsburgh, no navigable river like Wilmington, no commanding heights like Memphis.

So as the first white men moved west from the coast and south down the Great Wagon Road, why did they stop there? When Thomas Spratt, the first European to settle, walked into what is now the heart of Uptown Charlotte, what made him decide to stay and (literally) set up shop?

The land Spratt came to was unquestionably beautiful. Green hills swelled gently from ridge to red-clay field to ridge; pines grew in stands thick as jungles with brush and briars and berries; and throughout ran clear, fast creeks that fed the Catawba River to the west.

But the land that would be Charlotte and Mecklenburg County had more going for it than just beauty. The soil was more fertile than in the Uwharries to the east or the Blue Ridge to the west. Close at hand were several of the best fords for crossing the Catawba River. For centuries, the Cherokee and Catawba tribes had directed their trading routes towards these fords, so that in time two main paths had developed, one running northeast and southwest, the other northwest and southeast.

So when Thomas Spratt made his way to the top of the low hill where Trade Street now crosses Tryon Street, the thought that has occurred to thousands since when gazing upon Charlotte may have come to his mind: *I could do all right for myself here.*

Stand at Trade and Tryon on any weekday and picture the courthouse here at the corner, which is where it stood until the mid-19th century (and which is why the intersection is still referred to as "the Square," as in Courthouse Square). Look up at the steel and glass around you and imagine the fine Victorian houses that once lined both streets as far as the city limits. Now watch the traffic speed by and try to see the intersection of two dusty Indian trading paths, traveled by foot or mule or horse.

Spratt opened a trading post here in 1753. Small farms already dotted the area, farms that would coalesce into townships mostly remembered now by street names: Providence, Sharon, Berryhill, Mallard Creek. Charlotte has been growing, of course, since the very beginning, and growing aggressively. As one longtime Charlottean has said, "Charlotte's always been a chamber-of-commerce town." The colonial city fathers built a courthouse and jail before their community was named the county seat, then used said construction as proof that Charlotte deserved to be the county seat.

The new county—Mecklenburg—and Charlotte itself took their names from the German queen of England's King George III, a rather blatant attempt to curry favor. This proved ironic, since Mecklenburg County was one of the earliest communities to call for independence from Great Britain, and since guerrilla opposition was so fierce when Cornwallis came through that he called Charlotte "a damned hornet's nest of rebellion," inadvertently naming an NBA basketball team.

The boom really began when the railroad came through in 1852. Suddenly, the cotton grown in all those surrounding townships no longer needed to be hauled in wagons all the way to Cheraw or Camden in South Carolina for boats to take it to market in Charleston. Now, farmers could have their crop weighed, graded, and loaded onto rail cars right in Charlotte. Business prospects, and population growth, took flight in the county seat.

Two sides of Charlotte:
Left: On one corner of the Square,
a prospector pans for gold,
on the other, a woman lifts her baby.

The Civil War left Charlotte, safely tucked away in the back country, surprisingly intact. The town subsequently experienced another boom in wealth and population. Country boys and newly freed blacks rushed in from the countryside to take advantage of the opportunities created first by the railroads and then by that emblem and icon of the New South: the textile mill.

Charlotte and the rest of the South joined in the fashion of mill building in the 1880s. The first local operation, Robert Oates's Charlotte Cotton Mill, opened in 1880 just a block off West Trade Street in the Fourth Ward. Three more—the Alpha, the Ada, and the Victor—opened within the city limits by the end of the decade. As the railroads had done a generation earlier, the mills lured thousands to Charlotte, some seeking opportunity, some just a steady paycheck.

Textile mills were trumpeted by men like Charlotte's D. A. Tompkins as the means by which the New South would rise. Looking at Charlotte, which is more of a New South city than even Atlanta, one would have to agree. By 1930, the mills and the other industry they brought with them made Charlotte once and for all the largest city in the Carolinas, laying the groundwork for the prosperity Charlotteans enjoy today.

But they also indirectly hardened barriers of race and class. Read the letters to the editor of the *Charlotte Observer* today, with their concerns over busing, unequal opportunity, and Uptown versus the suburbs, and you find the long-term effects of sudden industrialization.

Economically, cotton mills carried Charlotte through the onset of the 20th century and both World Wars. The spun and woven cotton from the mills had to be transported. Luckily, Charlotte sat astride the "Main Street of the South"—J. P. Morgan's Southern Railway line from Washington, D.C., to New Orleans. By the second decade of the 20th century, three more major railroads ran through Charlotte, making the Queen City the center of the Carolina Piedmont's vast network of textile mills. Rather than simply shipping Mecklenburg's own cotton crop, Charlotte brought crops in by rail from as far away as Mississippi and Alabama. The railroads continued to grow until after World War II, when new highways and then the Eisenhower Interstate System—specifically Interstates 77 and 85—brought the trucking industry up to speed.

The opening of the 20th century saw tobacco magnate James B. Duke ready to experiment with the newfangled science of harnessing electrical power. Charlotte, having a strong industrial base and having the Catawba River nearby, seemed the logical place for the project's headquarters. In 1904, Duke sent engineer Bill Lee to Charlotte to form the Catawba Power Company, the forerunner of Duke Power.

In contrast to their counterparts in other areas of the South, Charlotte's business leaders did a remarkable job of diversifying industry while riding the crest of the cotton wave. Everything from cars to crackers was made here. Historian Thomas Hanchett, in his book *Sorting Out the New South City*, said that by the 1920s, "if you went to a movie or wrote a check or bought a bottle of cough syrup anywhere from Charleston to Raleigh, you were probably doing business indirectly with some resident of the Queen City."

Which was a good thing, because by the postwar years the mills were slowly dying, vulnerable as they were to foreign production. But although no one knew it at the time, the mills had left Charlotte in position for another economic and population boom, a boom greater and richer and grander than even D. A. Tompkins, much less Thomas Spratt, could have imagined.

All the money that the mills generated, you see, had to be managed, had to be kept and nurtured and used wisely. Banks sprang up around town to receive the deposits of mill owners and mill hands alike. The Federal Reserve opened its regional master bank in Charlotte. In the 1890s, textile men from the North joined with some local magnates and formed Charlotte National Bank, which in time became North Carolina National Bank, which in time became NationsBank, which in 1999 became Bank of America, the first coast-to-coast bank. Through the textile mills, Charlotte and the New South did in fact rise again.

Charlotte's current leaders are different from their predecessors in looking beyond the bottom line. Having built their companies, they are now working to build their community into all that the word *city* implies. Charlotte in the last two decades has seen not only an economic boom, but a cultural one as well. The downtown area, which most Charlotteans call "Uptown" because they like the sound better, has undergone an extensive revitalization that has brought in restaurants, nightclubs, and facilities such as Spirit Square, the Tryon Center for the Visual Arts, Discovery Place, and the Mint Museum of Craft + Design. Charlotte has even recognized and mostly stopped what was once its most pernicious habit—tearing down anything old, regardless of historic value, to make way for the new. Finally interested in more than doing well, Charlotte concentrates more and more today on doing good.

JUST THE FACTS

Charlotte sits just this side of the North Carolina–South Carolina border in the Piedmont region. It has 500,000 people within its city limits, 1.3 million within its metro area, and 6 million within a 100-mile radius.

Having seen most of its growth in the late 20th century, Charlotte is easy to get to and around by car. Interstates 85 and 77, which intersect in North Charlotte, are major thoroughfares through the west side of Charlotte and Mecklenburg County. U.S. 74 runs east and west to connect Charlotte to the coast and the mountains, while N.C. 16 runs north and south through Charlotte along the Catawba River Valley.

Charlotte is serviced by Greyhound buses and Amtrak trains. The bus station is at 601 West Trade Street; call 704-372-0456 for information. The train station is at 1914 North Tryon Street; call 800-USA-RAIL or 704-376-4416.

Charlotte/Douglas International Airport sees more than 500 flights daily and offers nonstop service to 160 cities; call 704-359-4000 for information.

For more facts on Charlotte, contact INFO!Charlotte, run by the Charlotte Convention and Visitors Bureau. The bureau is at 330 South Tryon Street in Center City. Call 800-231-4636, or visit their website at www.charlottecvb.org.

by Ed Southern

The Legend of the Meck Dec

Despite naming themselves for King George III's queen, Charlotte and Mecklenburg County were among the earliest supporters of the Continental Congress's effort to break free of Great Britain.

Exactly how early this support came has been a cause for debate for more than two centuries.

The crux of the debate is the Mecklenburg Declaration of Independence. Since seemingly everything in Charlotte has to have a perky nickname, this document has long been known as the "Meck Dec." The story goes that on May 20, 1775, the leading citizens of Mecklenburg County met at the county courthouse, just east of the Trade and Tryon intersection, to decide on a course of action in response to the British occupation of Boston Harbor. According to Meck Dec believers, this meeting ended with the writing and signing of a declaration of independence announcing that British law no longer held effect in Mecklenburg County, and that Mecklenburg's citizens would henceforth be responsible for their own governance.

A copy of the document was given to someone recorded in history as Captain Jack, the son of a local tavern keeper. Captain Jack was supposed to carry the Meck Dec to Philadelphia to present to the Continental Congress. Records show that he stopped in Salisbury and Salem, but he never arrived in Philadelphia. What the good citizens of Mecklenburg learned from this was that, while a man called Captain Jack may be absolutely trusted to make popcorn shrimp, he should not be trusted with history-making political documents.

The original was kept in the home of one of the signers and was destroyed in a house fire. No other copies existed.

Many outside the Carolinas soon began to question the authenticity of the Meck Dec. One of these was Thomas Jefferson, who found the version of the Meck Dec pieced together from the signers' memories to be remarkably similar to his Declaration of Independence. Meck Dec supporters retorted that the similarities in language resulted from the strong influence of John Locke on both statements.

Regardless of whether the Meck Dec existed, or existed in the form its supporters claim, Mecklenburg County deserves recognition for being quick to take up the cause of liberty. Three weeks after the meeting that produced the Meck Dec, another such meeting indisputably produced the Mecklenburg Resolves, a less strongly worded denunciation of British injustices in America. And Mecklenburg men were present in April 1776 when North Carolina issued the Halifax Resolves, the first official recommendation by a colonial government that the colonies declare their independence from Great Britain.

Many in Charlotte and Mecklenburg County continue to insist on the authenticity of the Meck Dec. May 20, "Meck Dec Day," was an official county holiday until the 1960s, celebrated with parades and speeches by local and even national leaders. Some sites in Charlotte, such as the Hezekiah Alexander Homesite and Rosedale Plantation, still celebrate Meck Dec Day, though it draws much less attention than in times past.

The Rock House on the Hezekiah Alexander homesite
PHOTOGRAPH BY ED SOUTHERN

Things to Do

HISTORIC PLACES, GARDENS, AND TOURS

▪ The *Charlotte Museum of History* and the *Hezekiah Alexander Home-site*, both at 3500 Shamrock Drive, together tell Charlotte's story from its earliest pioneers to its boom as a manufacturing center to its current heyday as a banking powerhouse.

The Charlotte Museum of History is housed in a new, four-wing, multi-gallery structure that replaced the cramped quarters it had occupied since 1976. Its displays include artifacts from pre-colonial times, historic flags, a re-created gold mine, a replica of the original Mecklenburg County Courthouse, and household items from throughout Charlotte's history that were either found by historians or donated by Mecklenburg families. The museum also houses a research library and an archive.

Located atop a small hill behind the museum, the Hezekiah Alexander House is Mecklenburg County's oldest surviving structure. A member of one of Mecklenburg's earliest and most prominent families, Alexander supposedly signed the Mecklenburg Declaration of Independence, co-founded Queens College, and helped frame North Carolina's first state constitution. His rock house is three miles from what was then the hill-top village of Charlotte; the area in between was so wild that Alexander's brother always carried two loaded pistols whenever he came to visit. The house is open for guided tours led by costumed interpreters who tell about life in the colonial back country and the American Revolution in the South. A re-created log kitchen sits behind the house, and a recon-structed stone springhouse is alongside the creek at the bottom of the hill. The wooded homesite has picnic tables spread across its seven acres.

The Charlotte Museum of History and the Hezekiah Alexander Homesite are open Tuesday from 10 A.M. to 9 P.M., Wednesday through Saturday from 10 A.M. to 5 P.M., and Sunday from 1 P.M. to 5 P.M. Admission is charged for both sites. Call 704-568-1774 for more information.

▪ Historic **Latta Plantation**, at 5225 Sample Road in neighboring Huntersville, is the 1800 Catawba River plantation home of merchant and planter James Latta. The house and immediate grounds are now a living-history farm owned and run by the Mecklenburg County Depart-ment of Parks and Recreation. The house is furnished with antiques from 1790 to 1840, roughly the time period in which the Latta family occu-pied the property. The grounds contain 13 outbuildings, which are used as interpretive centers to tell about work on the plantation and the lives of the plantation's slaves and the area's yeoman farmers. The fields are planted with crops appropriate to the period and place, and farm animals roam the barnyard. Volunteer docents dressed in period costumes lead guided tours through the house, fields, and grounds. Tours are of-fered Tuesday through Saturday at 1 P.M., 2 P.M., and 3 P.M. and Sun-day at 2 P.M., 3 P.M., and 4 P.M. from March through December. In January and February, they are offered Saturday at 1 P.M., 2 P.M., and 3 P.M. and Sunday at 2 P.M. and 3 P.M. Admission is charged. For information, call 704-875-2312, or visit their website at www.lattaplantation.org.

▪ Historic **Rosedale Plantation**, at 3427 North Tryon Street, is one of the finest examples of Federal architecture in North Carolina. Built in 1815 by merchant Archibald Frew, Rosedale was the plantation home of Dr. D. T. Caldwell and his family in the 1830s. Three miles from what is now Uptown Charlotte, Rosedale was part of the farming community known as Sugaw Creek, from which present-day Sugar Creek Road gets its name.

Rosedale hosts special events including lectures and exhibits. Along with the Hezekiah Alexander Homesite, it is one of the last places in Charlotte to celebrate Mecklenburg Declaration of Independence ("Meck Dec") Day. Visitors can take a guided tour of the home, gardens, and grounds every hour on the hour from 1 P.M. to 4 P.M. on Thursday and Sunday. Groups of 15 or more need to call at least two weeks in advance. The grounds are open Monday through Friday from 9 A.M. to 4 P.M. Rosedale is closed in January. Admission is charged for anyone over eight. Call 704-335-0325 for more information.

▪ The Charlotte Convention and Visitors Bureau publishes a brochure for a **Center City Walking Tour**, which leads visitors to several Uptown sites, including places for shopping, Thomas Polk Park, Settlers Cemetery, the Victorian Fourth Ward neighborhood, and Ericsson Stadium, home of the NFL's Carolina Panthers. Call the bureau at 800-231-4636 for more information.

▪ The **James K. Polk Memorial**, at 308 South Polk Street in nearby Pineville, marks the birthplace of the United States' 11th president. Born here in 1795, Polk spent most of his childhood in Mecklenburg County before moving with his family to Tennessee. He later returned to North Carolina to study at the state university in Chapel Hill. Polk accomplished more in his single term as president than many others have in two, including the creation of an independent treasury, the creation of the Department of the Interior, the settlement of the Oregon boundary, the annexation of Texas, and the acquisition of California, which provoked the unpopular Mexican War. Polk had promised not to seek a second term, and he kept his word. He died three months after he left the presidency in 1849.

The farm where he was born is now a State Historic Site. The log cabin and farm buildings and their furnishings are not the Polk family originals, but period pieces from the early 1800s that create a strong impression of what life must have been like for the young Polk. Mecklenburg County was still very much the back country in those days, and the memorial accurately depicts the work required to succeed on the frontier.

The James K. Polk Memorial is open year-round except for major holidays. From April to October, it operates Monday through Saturday from 9 A.M. to 5 P.M. and Sunday from 1 P.M. to 5 P.M. From November through March, it is open Tuesday through Saturday from 10 A.M. to 4 P.M. and Sunday from 1 P.M. to 4 P.M. Admission is free. For more information, call 704-889-7145, or visit their website at www.ah.dcr.state.nc.us/hs/polk/polk.htm.

■ The **UNCC Botanical Gardens and Sculpture Garden**, on the campus of the University of North Carolina at Charlotte, offers a green respite from the traffic and development of the surrounding University City area. The McMillan Greenhouse features orchids, cacti, carnivorous plants, and a small rain forest. The Van Landingham Glen is a cool and shady place for a stroll. Call 704-547-2364 for more information.

The University of North Carolina at Charlotte was begun in 1947 to handle the sudden increase in college applicants created by the GI Bill. UNCC has since grown into a premier regional university. It has a nationally recognized faculty and students from all over the country.

■ **Wing Haven Gardens and Bird Sanctuary**, at 248 Ridgewood Avenue, has four acres of woodlands and formal gardens in Myers Park, one of Charlotte's most genteel neighborhoods. Pools, fountains, and baths are available for the birds and special events and an upscale gift shop for the people. Call 704-331-0664 for more information.

MUSEUMS AND SCIENCE CENTERS

■ The **Mint Museum of Art**, at 2730 Randolph Road, is the oldest art museum in North Carolina. The story of how it came to be is an unusual one. In 1799, a 12-year-old found a shiny rock on his father's farm 25 miles east of Charlotte. Gold miners from as far away as Europe flocked to the area. If you're wondering what this has to do with an art museum, trust me. I'm getting there. To take advantage of the ready gold supply, the United States Mint built a Charlotte branch in 1837. The mint thrived until the gold began to run out and until the Charlotte gold rush was overshadowed by the California gold rush in 1849. The mint closed in 1913. By 1933, the building was slated for demolition. Instead, it was merely dismantled and moved brick by brick to its present location in the genteel Eastover neighborhood. In 1936, the Mint Museum of Art opened.

The museum's permanent collection focuses on American art from pre-Columbian to contemporary. It includes not only works by masters such as Andrew Wyeth and Thomas Eakins, but also pottery from nearby Seagrove, ceramics, and even some of the gold coins made during the building's former life. Also in the permanent collection are artworks from Europe and Africa, including ceremonial masks. The museum also hosts impressive traveling exhibits year-round.

The Mint Museum of Art is open Tuesday from 10 A.M. to 10 P.M., Wednesday through Saturday from 10 A.M. to 5 P.M., and Sunday from noon to 5 P.M. Admission is charged except on the second Sunday of each month and on Tuesday from 5 P.M. to 10 P.M. Children under 12 are always admitted free. For more information, call 704-333-6468, or visit their website at www.mintmuseum.org.

- The **Mint Museum of Craft + Design**, at 220 North Tryon Street, is the museum's Uptown branch. Housed in the old Montaldo's department store building, the Mint Museum of Craft + Design is itself an impressive design work. Opened in 1997, it houses the extensive crafts collection that was becoming cramped at the Randolph Road location, as well as contemporary studio crafts. The collection is divided according to the materials used: ceramics, fiber, glass, metal, and wood.

Both museums host educational programs and traveling exhibits. Hours and fees for the Mint Museum of Craft + Design are the same as those for the Mint Museum of Art, including the free admission on the second Sunday of each month and Tuesday from 5 P.M. to 10 P.M. One ticket covers admission to both museums if used on the same day, unless otherwise noted. For more information, call 704-333-6468, or visit their website at www.mintmuseum.org.

- The **Museum of the New South**, at 324 North College Street, is currently undergoing a renovation and expansion that will more than double its space. It is not rescheduled to reopen until the fall of 2001.

The only museum in the country that concentrates on the New South period (1877 to the present), it features hands-on activities and displays that not only tell the history of the New South but also put it in the context of national and world history. The concentration, of course, is on Charlotte and the Piedmont region of the Carolinas. Exhibit pieces include raw cotton, textile-mill equipment, and Jeff Gordon's racing suit.

For information on new hours and admission fees, call 704-333-1887, or visit their website at www.musnew.com.

▪ **Discovery Place**, at 301 North Tryon Street, was one of the first reasons to come back to Uptown Charlotte after the urban blight of the 1970s. It was also one of the first "hands-on" museums, where kids (and adults) could do more than walk, stop, and stare. Its exhibits include the Knight Rain Forest, whose snakes are a favorite among kids; the *Challenger* Learning Center, which re-creates a space station, a space shuttle, and Mission Control; the Life Center, where kids can learn and exercise at the same time; and an aquarium with a wave tank and an ocean touch pool. Discovery Place also has a planetarium and the *Charlotte Observer* OMNIMAX theater for IMAX films.

Discovery Place operates daily except for Thanksgiving and Christmas. From September through May, the exhibit halls are open from 9 A.M. to 5 P.M. Monday through Friday, from 9 A.M. to 6 P.M. on Saturday, and from 1 P.M. to 6 P.M. on Sunday. From June through August, the hours are 9 A.M. to 6 P.M. Monday through Saturday and 1 P.M. to 6 P.M. on Sunday. Admission is charged except for children under three. Times and ticket prices for the planetarium and OMNIMAX shows vary. For more information, call 704-372-0471, or visit their website at www.discoveryplace.org.

▪ The **Carolina Raptor Center**, at 6000 Sample Road in Huntersville, is on the grounds of Latta Plantation Park and Nature Preserve. A facility dedicated to the rescue, care, and treatment of birds of prey, the center also has an exhibit building, the only eagle aviary in the Carolinas, and a nature trail on which visitors can view the eagles, falcons, owls, vultures, and hawks that the center has treated but cannot rerelease into the wild.

It is open Tuesday through Saturday from 10 A.M. to 5 P.M. and Sunday from noon to 5 P.M. Admission is charged. For more information, call 704-875-6521, or visit their website at www.birdsofprey.org.

■ The *Charlotte Nature Museum*, at 1658 Sterling Road, is a small nature center familiar to generations of Charlotte schoolchildren. Recently refurbished, it features a live animal room, a butterfly pavilion, a nature trail, and a puppet theater. It is open Monday through Friday from 9 A.M. to 5 P.M., Saturday from 10 A.M. to 5 P.M., and Sunday from 1 P.M. to 5 P.M. It is closed Thanksgiving, Christmas Eve, Christmas Day, New Year's, and Easter. A modest admission fee is charged for those over age three. Call 704-372-0471 for more information.

■ The *Carolinas Aviation Museum*, at 4108 Airport Drive, is located near Charlotte/Douglas International Airport, a World War II training field that has become one of the busiest hubs in the country. The museum, housed in an old hangar, offers guided tours and aviation "artifacts" from the early days of flight. Most people, however, come for the historic aircraft: a World War II F-84G fighter, a Vietnam-era UH-1 "Huey" helicopter, an A-4D-1 jet fighter, and a DC-3, built in 1942 and restored to flight-ready condition in 1987. The museum is open Monday through Saturday from 10 A.M. to 5 P.M. and Sunday from 1 P.M. to 5 P.M.; its brochure, however, says that hours are subject to change and asks that visitors call beforehand. Admission is charged. Call 704-359-8442 for more information.

CULTURAL OFFERINGS

■ The *North Carolina Blumenthal Center for the Performing Arts*, at 130 North Tryon Street, opened in 1992 adjacent to the Bank of America Corporate Center and Founders' Hall. The Blumenthal Center contains three performance spaces: the Belk Theater, the Booth Playhouse, and the intimate Studio Theater. National touring productions of Broadway shows and performances by the Charlotte Symphony Orchestra, the Charlotte Repertory Theatre, Opera Carolina, and the North Carolina Dance Theatre are all staged here. For information on upcoming perfor-

Founders' Hall on the corner of Trade and Tryon
PHOTOGRAPH BY ED SOUTHERN

mances and ticket prices, call 704-372-1000, or visit their website at www.performingartsctr.org.

- Adjoining the Blumenthal Center is the massive **Bank of America Corporate Center**, the tallest skyscraper in the Carolinas. Designed by renowned architect Cesar Pelli (who also designed the Blumenthal Center), the tower is a welcome break from the glass-and-steel boxes that dominated the Charlotte skyline for decades. In its lobby are three frescoes by world-famous artist (and North Carolina native) Ben Long. Finishing up the city block is **Founders' Hall**, a two-story indoor plaza offering upscale shopping and dining and a box office for the Blumenthal Center.

- **Spirit Square Center for Arts and Education**, at 345 North College Street, came under the auspices of the Blumenthal Center in 1997. Spirit Square was built in 1909 as First Baptist Church; the facade facing Tryon Street still features the church's Byzantine design and stained-glass windows. The church moved in the 1970s, at which time the property was turned into a community arts center. The former sanctuary is now the McGlohon Theatre, named after Charlotte native and jazz composer and pianist Loonis McGlohon. Spirit Square also houses the Duke Power Theatre, home to the Actor's Theatre of Charlotte, and five galleries run by the Tryon Center for Visual Art. The focus of Spirit Square, however, is

Spirit Square Center for Arts and Education
PHOTOGRAPH BY ED SOUTHERN

education. The site hosts numerous workshops and programs sponsored by most of Charlotte's cultural institutions. For more information, call 704-372-1000, or visit their website at www.performingartsctr.org.

■ It will probably take at least two more generations before the *Tryon Center for Visual Art*, at 721 North Tryon Street, will no longer be called "the Burned-Out Church." Once a gutted hulk at the north end of Uptown, easily visible from the Brookshire Freeway, the former church was restored in the late 1990s to house two large, open-flow galleries that make dramatic use of the Neo-Gothic architecture. The Tryon Center sponsors and organizes educational programs and exhibits here and throughout Charlotte and also hosts meetings and special events. Call 704-332-5535 for more information.

■ Like Spirit Square and the Tryon Center, the *Afro-American Cultural Center*, at 401 North Myers Street, is housed in a former church. It takes a multidisciplinary approach to education and programming, hosting art exhibits, film series, and performances of music, drama, and dance to preserve Charlotte's rich African-American heritage. It also maintains two galleries, one housing a permanent display of African artifacts and the other hosting traveling exhibits by local, state, and national artists. For more information, call 704-374-1565, or visit their website at www.aacc-charlotte.org.

RECREATION

▪ The property beyond the immediate grounds of Latta Plantation is now *Latta Plantation Park and Nature Preserve*. Picnic tables and shelters, nature trails, bridle paths, canoe rentals, and fishing on Mountain Island Lake are all available to visitors. The grounds are open Tuesday through Friday from 8 A.M. to 4 P.M., Saturday from midnight (for fishermen) to 4 P.M., and Sunday from 1:30 P.M. to 5 P.M. Admission is free except during special events. For more information about the house and grounds, call 704-875-2312, or visit their website at www.lattaplantation.org.

▪ Across a wooden footbridge from the Charlotte Nature Museum is *Freedom Park*, the largest public park within the Charlotte city limits. Tennis courts, basketball courts, volleyball sand pits, baseball fields, soccer fields, playgrounds, picnic tables and shelters, an old locomotive for kids to play on, a pond, and a band shell for outdoor concerts can all be found in Freedom Park. You might even find a little solitude here, five minutes from Uptown.

The pond at Freedom Park
PHOTOGRAPH BY ED SOUTHERN

A Bankers' Town

Anyone who follows the world of banking and finance, or even just glances at the *Wall Street Journal* occasionally, should know that, for years now, Charlotte has been a financial center in the same league with New York and San Francisco.

In 1999, Charlotte became home to Bank of America—America's first coast-to-coast bank—the result of a merger between San Francisco's Bank America and Charlotte's hometown NationsBank.

The question is obvious: How did Charlotte, once a hinterland settlement in the backwoods of a backwater region, become an international financial power?

Charlotte has not traditionally been a banker's town. It began as a courthouse town and a trading center for the region's farmers. After the Civil War, it was a textile town. In the 20th century, Charlotte has had a thriving trucking and transportation industry.

But whatever the means, Charlotte has always been comparatively prosperous. This was one of several conditions that began to come together in the 1950s and 1960s to turn two local banks into international powerhouses. North Carolina has long had banking laws favorable to expansion and a progressive, pro-business attitude. But this only begins to explain Charlotte's meteoric ascent.

In an article for *Charlotte Magazine* that was reprinted in his book *The Heart of Dixie*, Charlotte writer Frye Gaillard describes the rise of North Carolina National Bank, now Bank of America, and First Union National Bank. Both are headquartered within spitting distance of the intersection of Trade and Tryon Streets, where Charlotte began more than 200 years ago. Both have aggressively bought other banks and expanded into other states. Both have created a legacy beyond making money, by contributing resources, energy, and leadership to their community. Both banks are led by driven, ambitious men with visions not just for their banks, but for Charlotte and the South as well. First Union has Ed Crutchfield, a native of Albemarle, North Carolina, who played college football at Davidson but went north to the University of Pennsylvania for his master's degree. Bank of America is led by Hugh McColl, a graduate of the University of North Carolina at Chapel Hill and, according to Gaillard, "perhaps more importantly, of the U.S. Marines." McColl and Crutchfield began their banking careers at a time when Northern financial institutions regarded the South—whose banks were still recovering from the Civil War, Reconstruction, and the Great Depression—with disdain. A large part of their ambition, Gaillard says, comes from regional pride in being the underdog. McColl, who keeps a glass hand grenade on his desk, is fond of the motto of ancient Scottish warrior-kings: "No one provokes me with impunity."

▪ The *Carolinas' Carrousel Parade* is a lot like an old small-town Christmas parade, only bigger. So much of Charlotte's communal history has been lost to development that the holdovers, like the Carrousel Parade, have become more attractive through sheer nostalgia. Held on Thanksgiving Day, the parade proceeds down Tryon Street through Uptown. Onlookers enjoy the floats, the marching bands, and, of course, Santa and his sleigh bringing up the rear.

▪ *Festival in the Park* has been bringing arts, crafts, music, food, and crowds together in Freedom Park since 1964. More than 200 artists and craftsmen from across the region and nation display their work in tents set up around the pond. Nearly 1,000 entertainers perform in the band shell and at sites set up across the park. Workers string lights around the park so activities can continue after dark. The festival is held over a weekend in September. Admission is free. Contact the Charlotte Convention and Visitors Bureau at 800-231-4636 for dates.

▪ The *NOVELLO Festival of Reading*, sponsored by the Public Library of Charlotte and Mecklenburg County, brings some of the most renowned authors in the world for lectures, readings, discussions, and signings. More than 20 authors and illustrators participate in events held throughout the city; there is also a downtown street festival for families. Past guests

The main branch of the Public Library, host of the NOVELLO Festival of Reading
PHOTOGRAPH BY ED SOUTHERN

have included Pulitzer Prize winner Frank McCourt and Nobel laureate Toni Morrison. NOVELLO is held in October; call 704-336-2020 for more information.

▪ **Winston Cup racing**, the major leagues of NASCAR, comes twice a year to Lowe's Motor Speedway, formerly Charlotte Motor Speedway. Two races are held in May—the Winston Select, an all-star race run at night under the lights, and the Coca-Cola 600, the longest and most grueling race on the NASCAR circuit. October brings the UAW/GM Quality 500, one of the last races of the Winston Cup season.

▪ **Lowe's Motor Speedway**, which is actually north of Charlotte in Concord, is so big it looks more like an army installation than a racetrack. On the premises are a gift shop, the Carolinas Boxing Hall of Fame, condominiums, and the upscale Speedway Club. In addition to the Winston Cup races, Lowe's Motor Speedway hosts events throughout the year, including Busch Grand National racing, Legends and World of Outlaws racing, classes of the Richard Petty Driving Experience, car-club meetings, and the Food Lion Auto Fair, a gathering of hot rods and vintage automobiles. Lowe's Motor Speedway is located at the intersection of U.S. 29 and Speedway Boulevard. You can reach the ticket hot line at 800-455-FANS. For information about other events, call 704-455-3200, or visit their website at www.charlottemotorspeedway.com.

▪ The **Southern Christmas Show**, the **Southern Spring Show**, the **Southern Ideal Home Show**, and the **Southern Women's Show** are held at various times through the year at the Charlotte Merchandise Mart on Independence Boulevard. Each features fashions, crafts, and tips on design and decorating appropriate to its theme and season. For exact dates and ticket prices, contact Southern Shows, Inc., at 704-376-6594, or visit their website at www.southernshows.com.

▪ The **Loch Norman Highland Games**, sponsored by the Catawba Valley Scottish Society, are held each year in April at Rose Hill, the former Davidson family plantation overlooking the Catawba River. The site is rolling, grassy, and partially wooded. With all the kilted lads strolling about, the more imaginative (or drunk) members of the crowd might come to

The bustle of uptown Charlotte at night
COURTESY OF NORTH CAROLINA DIVISION OF TOURISM, FILM AND SPORTS DEVELOPMENT
(ALSO USED ON PAGE 365)

believe they're actually in old Caledonia. Sanctioned competitions in High-land dancing, fife-and-drumming, and, of course, Scottish athletics like caber tossing are held. You'll also find dart throwing, archery, and demonstrations of Scottish crafts and artwork. The clans erect tents around the main competition field, where visitors can check to see if they're related to William Wallace or Robert the Bruce. A food-and-drink area is on the grounds. Yes, you can get haggis, but why would you?

Admission is charged, as is a parking fee. For more information, call 704-875-3113.

▪ The *Carolina Renaissance Festival* is held weekends from late September until mid-November in a field off Poplar Tent Road in Huntersville. The festival seeks to re-create a medieval European village, but without the stench, filth, and Black Death. Instead of serfdom and subsistence farming, visitors get excellent food; I highly recommend the gigantic turkey legs. Rather than the Inquisition and rampant superstition, the festival offers the pomp of fake jousts and corny jokes. Make sure you see the Comic Duellists before you leave. A remarkable variety of crafts and gifts for all ages can be purchased at the tents. Admission is charged. The festival is open Saturday and Sunday from 10 A.M. to 5:30 P.M.; call 704-896-5555 for exact dates and other information.

Places to Stay

RESORTS, HOTELS, AND MOTELS

▪ **The Park Hotel.** Deluxe. 2200 Rexford Road (704-364-8220). Located in the *über*-swank South Park area, the *über*-swank Park Hotel has a reputation as Charlotte's finest. This, after all, is where the Rolling Stones stay when they come to town. The Park Hotel has 194 of Charlotte's most well-appointed rooms, furnished in 18th-century style, along with plenty of space for meetings, banquets, and receptions. Amenities include an outdoor pool, a health club, and an ever-helpful concierge.

▪ **Adam's Mark Hotel.** Deluxe/Expensive. 555 South McDowell Street (704-372-4100). Its 613 units make the Adam's Mark one of the largest hotels in Charlotte. Offering lovely views of the city and Marshall Park from its lavish, oversized rooms, the Adam's Mark is known for its amenities, which include large meeting rooms, two heated pools, an exercise room, and a jogging track.

▪ **Charlotte Marriott City Center.** Deluxe/Expensive. 100 West Trade Street (704-333-9000). The Marriott boasts a heated indoor pool, an exercise room, valet parking, airport transportation, one of the biggest ballrooms in town, and an exceptional staff. Its Cutters Cigar Bar was recently featured in *Bon Appétit* magazine.

▪ **The Dunhill Hotel.** Deluxe/Expensive. 237 North Tryon Street (704-332-4141). Tucked among the towering buildings of downtown Charlotte, the Dunhill, built in 1929, offers elegant charm in the manner of a stylish European hotel. The richly and traditionally decorated rooms include well-stocked refrigerators. In the lobby are a comfortable seating area and the Monticello restaurant.

▪ **Hilton at University Place**. Deluxe/Expensive. 8629 J. M. Keynes Drive (704-547-7444). This 12-story hotel is the most visible landmark of the University City area, off Interstate 85 at Harris Boulevard. The service here is exceptional.

▪ **Hilton Charlotte and Towers**. Deluxe/Expensive. 222 East Third Street (704-377-1500). The Uptown location of the Hilton offers 407 rooms, each with two telephones and a refreshment center, and the Uptown YMCA, which guests may use as an unusually large fitness center.

▪ **Omni Charlotte Hotel**. Deluxe/Expensive. 2 Bank of America Plaza (704-377-0400). This was Charlotte's first luxury hotel Uptown. Amenities include concierge service, an exercise room with a sauna, free parking (a gold mine in Uptown), and airport transportation.

▪ **South Park Suites**. Deluxe/Expensive. 6300 Morrison Boulevard (704-364-2400). In a city full of hotels that cater to business travelers, South Park Suites may be the best. Each suite includes a living room, a dining area, a kitchen, a bathroom, and a spacious bedroom. The on-site business center has all the latest equipment. The hotel offers 13 meeting and banquet spaces. The suites, by the way, are exceedingly comfortable.

▪ **Holiday Inn Woodlawn**. Expensive/Moderate. 212 West Woodlawn Road (704-525-8350). Convenient to the airport and the interstates, the Holiday Inn is ideal for business travelers. Completely renovated in 1998, it offers a pool and complimentary airport transportation. O'Hara's, the hotel's nightclub, has been known for its nightly live entertainment (primarily beach music) over the past 25 years.

INNS AND BED-AND-BREAKFASTS

▪ **The Homeplace Bed-and-Breakfast**. Deluxe/Expensive. 5901 Sardis

Road (704-365-1936). Unlike most Charlotte accommodations, the Homeplace is set in a quiet residential neighborhood that is nonetheless convenient to South Park and other business districts. A buff-colored 1902 Victorian home with a wraparound porch overlooking a shaded yard, it offers two guest rooms and one two-bedroom suite. Full breakfast in the morning and beverages in the evening are included. Small children are not allowed.

- **The Morehead Inn**. Deluxe/Expensive. 1122 East Morehead Street (704-376-3357). Located near Uptown and the growing South End district, this 1917 residence was transformed into an 18th-century farmhouse-style country inn in 1984. Each room has a phone and a television; one includes a coffee maker and a refrigerator. An extended continental breakfast is included, as are privileges at the nearby Central YMCA. Meeting rooms are available.

- **The Elizabeth Bed-and-Breakfast**. Expensive/Moderate. 2145 East Fifth Street (704-358-1368). Located in the historic and charming Elizabeth neighborhood, this bed-and-breakfast offers four guest rooms with brass beds, ceiling fans, and private baths. Guests can choose between a continental and a full breakfast.

Places to Eat

Part of Charlotte's energy comes from its ever-changing, ever-evolving, ever-expanding restaurant scene. Two months after I finished my research, I found two brand-new restaurants in Uptown alone. The following list is only a sampling of some of the fixtures—eateries that have been around awhile and expect to be around awhile longer.

- **La Bibliothèque**. Expensive. 1901 Roxborough Road (704-365-5000). French and American cuisine share a creative menu in this restaurant in the South Park neighborhood. Have *escargot* if you want, but you can also order a spiffy tuna salad sandwich. The patio, open during the summer months, accents the European feel. Reservations are recommended. Lunch is served Tuesday through Friday and dinner Monday through Saturday.

■ **The LampLighter Restaurant**. Expensive. 1065 East Morehead Street (704-372-5343). Fine American cuisine can be found at this longtime Charlotte establishment. Housed in a 1925 Mediterranean-style house between Midtown and Dilworth, the LampLighter offers a quiet, refined dinner. The veal and duck come highly recommended, as do reservations. Dinner is served nightly; the cocktail bar opens at 5:30 P.M.

■ **Bistro 100**. Expensive/Moderate. 100 North Tryon Street (704-344-0515). Located in Founders' Hall overlooking the intersection of Trade and College Streets, Bistro 100 offers good food in a relaxed, yet definitely classy, setting. Its secret is the wood-burning oven; the aromas are dangerous. The menu's wide range—from excellent sandwiches to more elaborate entrées—suits most every taste and checkbook. The Mother's Day brunch here has become famous. Bistro 100 is open Monday through Saturday for lunch and dinner and Sunday for brunch and dinner.

■ **Pewter Rose Bistro**. Expensive/Moderate. 1820 South Boulevard (704-332-8149). The Pewter Rose has long been one of the most exciting restaurants in Charlotte, offering a menu as imaginative as the decor. Almost all the entrées are outstanding, the wine list is expansive, and the occasional live music accentuates the slightly eccentric ambiance. It's one of the best places in Charlotte to take a first date. The Pewter Rose is open daily for lunch and dinner.

■ **300 East**. Expensive/Moderate. 300 East Boulevard (704-332-6507). East Boulevard runs from the edge of Myers Park past Freedom Park, then through the heart of Dilworth before ending at South Boulevard. Located toward the South Boulevard side, 300 East is convenient to Uptown, Midtown, the South End, and the South Boulevard business district. It's great for a business lunch, a nice dinner, or a late-night drink. Lunch and dinner are served Monday through Saturday; brunch and dinner are served Sunday.

■ **Alexander Michael's**. Moderate. 401 West Ninth Street (704-332-6789). Located in the historic Fourth Ward, Alexander Michael's is one of the few true "hangouts" in Charlotte that isn't a sports bar. The food here is excellent, but this is also a welcoming place to stop by and join the young professionals from Uptown for a drink. Lunch and dinner are served daily.

■ **Sir Edmund Halley's**. Moderate. Park Road Shopping Center (704-525-2555). Sir Edmund Halley's comes as close as you're going to find to a real English pub—unless you're in England, of course. Located in a basement space in the back of a shopping center, it has the low ceilings and dark ambiance of a real pub; the price of this feel and Sir Edmund Halley's success is the occasional sardine-can night. The only thing that's not authentic is the food; it's much better than the real thing. Fish and chips and bangers and mash coexist on the menu with ostrich meat loaf and grilled kangaroo. Dedicated alcoholics can get not just a pint but a whole yard of stout, ale, or lager. Lunch is served Monday through Friday; dinner is served nightly. The kitchen is open until midnight, while the pub stays open until 2 A.M.

■ **Zarelli's**. Moderate. 1801 South Boulevard (704-335-7200). The place burned down a couple of years ago, but a little thing like fire won't stop Neil Zarelli. Though Zarelli's is known for its pizza, the traditional Italian entrées leave nothing to be desired either. And you might get to hear Mr. Zarelli, a former opera singer and a national-anthem favorite at Charlotte Hornets games, belt out a song while you eat. Lunch is served Monday through Friday and dinner Monday through Saturday.

■ **Athens Restaurant**. Inexpensive. 101 East Independence Boulevard (704-375-3597). Athens is the king of Charlotte's late-night dining. Sit in your booth long enough and you'll see every variation of *Homo sapiens*. Truckdrivers, ambulance drivers, nurses and doctors off their rotation at one of the nearby hospitals, faculty and students from Central Piedmont Community College next door, Uptown business people, punk-rock kids coming down or riding out the night: these folks and more are drawn by the restaurant's mix of down-home cooking and Greek dishes. The souvlaki and the desserts are outstanding, and the iced tea may be the best in town. Athens is open all day, every day.

- **Fat City**. Inexpensive. 3127 North Davidson Street (704-343-0240). One of the pioneers of the North Davidson Street arts scene, Fat City makes some of the best sandwiches in town; its club sandwich goes places most sandwiches never dream. And it definitely serves the best pasta salad; don't even try to argue. To call the place "funky" would be an understatement, and a cheesy one to boot; Fat City has an underground style all its own. But even Uptown bankers in suits and ties are irresistibly drawn by a Fat City sandwich. If you eat inside, be prepared for the wall-to-wall music and the big pterodactyl hanging from the ceiling. This is also a great late-night hangout and music venue, though perhaps not for the faint of heart. It is open daily from lunchtime until whenever.

- **The Landmark Diner**. Inexpensive. 4429 Central Avenue (704-532-1153). A roomy diner in the classic style, the Landmark boasts a number of all-American menu items. It earns its listing here, however, on the strength of its "Challa French Toast," a crispy concoction that makes the finest gourmet breakfast taste like Pop-Tarts by comparison. Kids aren't the only ones who enjoy the little jukeboxes at each table. The Landmark is open 24 hours on Friday and Saturday and until 3 A.M. the rest of the week.

- **Laurel Market**. Inexpensive. 114 Cherokee Road (704-347-4989). There's no seating on the premises, so the advice here is to take Laurel Market sandwiches to one of Charlotte's many parks for a picnic. The soups and sandwiches are earthy and imaginative. Every sandwich is made to order right in front of the customer, so you can control the amount of each ingredient. Laurel Market also has a terrific selection of drinks, chips, wine, and beer. The deli is open for lunch Monday through Saturday.

- **Lupie's Café**. Inexpensive. 2718 Monroe Road (704-374-1232). In a city full of bankers, Lupie's is the most economical spot in town. The quantity of food you get for the money is staggering. A different special is offered each night. The meat loaf on Mondays is a personal favorite, but Lupie's is just as famous for its chili, served any day of the week. The side dishes run the gamut and are a meal unto themselves. Even the children's portions are huge. If physically possible, save room for the banana pudding. The atmosphere is loud but relaxed, and the wait staff is friendly and easygoing, making Lupie's a great place to bring kids. The walls are decorated with work by local artists and photographers, along with a big poster of John Wayne near the kitchen. Lupie's does not take reservations, so be prepared to wait in line at lunchtime and most weekend nights. Lunch and dinner are served Monday through Saturday.

■ *Price's Chicken Coop*. Inexpensive. 1614 Camden Road (704-333-9866). Fried chicken and fried fish from Price's Chicken Coop are as much a Charlotte tradition as bank takeovers. A little over a mile distant but a world away from the slick bistros of Uptown, Price's is as Southern as it gets. Call for directions if you're new to town. Otherwise, you'll likely get lost, and Price's isn't in the best neighborhood in town. The chicken is worth the search, however. Lunch and dinner are served Monday through Saturday.

■ *South 21 Curb Service*. Inexpensive. 3101 East Independence Boulevard (704-377-4509). Those of us raised after the era of drive-in service should make sure we go to South 21 before we die. This ranks with the Varsity in Atlanta as one of the last of the great Southern drive-ins, serving milk shakes guaranteed to freeze your brain, hamburgers that shouldn't be eaten by anyone wearing a white shirt, and onion rings you'll still be wanting even after your coronary. Lunch and dinner are served Tuesday through Sunday.

■ *Spoon's*. Inexpensive. 415 Hawthorne Lane (704-376-0974) and other locations. Spoon's began as an ice-cream parlor down the street from Presbyterian Hospital and has grown into an ice-cream parlor and burger joint with locations all over Charlotte. The original is still in the same Hawthorne Road spot, though it has undergone extensive remodeling inside and out. The burgers, hot dogs, and ice cream are great, but the real draw at Spoon's is the biggest cup of iced tea you've ever seen. Lunch and dinner are served daily.

■ *Wolfman Pizza*. Inexpensive. Selwyn Corners Shopping Center (704-377-4695) and other locations. When Barry Wolfman (yes, that's his name) came to town to make California-style pizzas, folks were a little skeptical. I guess four locations throughout Charlotte have put that skepticism

Lake Tillery and the Pee Dee River form the border between Morrow Mountain State Park and the Uwharrie National Forest
PHOTOGRAPH BY ED SOUTHERN

to rest. You can get a basic pepperoni or sausage pizza here, but where's the fun in that? Try the Thai or the barbecue chicken pizza. Lunch and dinner are served daily.

Nearby

■ **Waxhaw**, a small town 13 miles south of Charlotte on N.C. 16, is known for its turn-of-the-century architecture and its large number of antique shops. Shopping here is leisurely; shopkeepers rarely keep to a set schedule. Each February, the Waxhaw Women's Club hosts an antique show at the American Legion hut. Waxhaw is also where Andrew Jackson spent his childhood.

■ The **Reed Gold Mine**, in Cabarrus County northeast of Charlotte, saw the beginning of the short-lived Charlotte gold rush, one of the first in the United States. It is now a State Historic Site. The mine and the legacy of the gold rush are preserved through a museum, a film, a guided underground tour, a stamp mill, and walking trails. For a small fee, you can even learn how to pan for gold (but don't get your hopes up). From April through October, the site is open from 9 A.M. to 5 P.M. Monday through

Saturday and from 1 P.M. to 5 P.M. on Sunday. From November to March, it is open from 10 A.M. to 4 P.M. Tuesday through Saturday and from 1 P.M. to 4 P.M. on Sunday. For more information, call 704-721-4653, or visit their website at www.itpi.dpi.state.nc.us/reed.

- **Morrow Mountain State Park** is a beautiful and tranquil piece of the Uwharrie Mountains only 45 minutes from Charlotte, seven miles east of the town of Albemarle. A modern swimming pool, a bathhouse, vacation cabins, and tent and trailer campsites are available. Visitors also enjoy fishing, picnicking, and renting canoes and boats. The Kron House is the reconstructed cabin of one of the area's earliest doctors. The hiking trails here are challenging and scenic. An admission fee is charged, as are rental fees for some activities. Call 704-982-4402 for more information.

- **Uwharrie National Forest** lies just across the Pee Dee River from Morrow Mountain State Park. Campgrounds, boat ramps, nature trails, and the strenuous 20-mile Uwharrie Trail are all within the forest's 50,000 acres. Call 910-576-6391 for more information.

- Straddling the border of North and South Carolina, **Paramount's Carowinds** is the largest theme park in the Carolinas. It has evolved far beyond the wooden Thunder Road roller coaster. Current attractions include the Top Gun Jet Coaster, the Zoom Zone children's area, and the WaterWorks water park. Musical revues and concerts are held at the park. Visiting Carowinds can easily use up an entire day; be sure to wear sunscreen. The park is located at 14523 Carowinds Boulevard; take Exit 909 off Interstate 77. It is open from early spring to early fall. For hours and admission prices, call 800-888-4386, or visit their website at www.carowinds.com.

- The **Schiele Museum of Natural History**, on Garrison Boulevard in Gastonia, is the area's largest nature museum. The exhibition galleries showcase North American habitats and wildlife. The half-mile nature trail takes visitors through 16 acres of Piedmont forest to a re-created 18th-century backwoods farm and a Native American village. The Schiele Museum also houses a state-of-the-art planetarium. The museum is open Monday through Saturday from 9 A.M. to 5 P.M. and Sunday from 1 P.M.

to 5 P.M. Admission is charged. Call 704-866-6908 for more information.

■ **Crowders Mountain State Park** lies just west of Gastonia, near the South Carolina line and Kings Mountain National Military Park. In addition to hosting the normal state-park activities, Crowders Mountain is popular as one of the best rock-climbing sites east of the Appalachians. Admission is charged. Call 704-853-5375 for information.

■ **Duke Power State Park** sits on the shores of Lake Norman, a man-made "inland sea" created when Duke Power put Cowan's Ford Dam on the Catawba River. **Lake Norman** is the largest lake in North Carolina, yet still manages to be the most crowded. Very little of the shoreline is undeveloped; in fact, the area around the southern end of the lake is Mecklenburg's fastest-growing neighborhood.

Such concerns can be left behind at the park, which offers a full range of activities including camping, hiking, picnicking, and, of course, fishing and boating. Canoeists are advised not to take their craft out into the main channel, especially on weekends and summer holidays.

The park office is in Troutman in Iredell County; call 704-528-6350 for more information.

■ **McDowell Park and Nature Preserve**, located on Lake Wylie south of Charlotte, encloses 1,000 acres off N.C. 49. Camping, hiking, fishing, picnicking, and boating are all available here. Lake Wylie, one of a series of lakes formed by the damming of the Catawba River, is the last lake before the Catawba leaves North Carolina. Admission is charged. Call 704-588-5224 for more information.

■ **Salisbury** was once a rough frontier town where Daniel Boone stocked up on provisions and Andrew Jackson practiced law with pistols tucked in his belt. During the Civil War, the city was home to one of the Confederacy's largest prison camps; the burial of 5,000 Union soldiers outside the camp led to the creation of a National Cemetery.

Now the model of a genteel Southern small town, Salisbury is proud of two of its more recent products: Republican presidential candidate Elizabeth Dole and the delicious soft drink Cheerwine.

Twenty-three blocks near downtown have been designated a National

Historic District. The business district retains the charm of an earlier era; it even has a true general store. The **Rowan Museum**, located at 202 North Main Street in a home dating to 1819, contains artifacts from the Civil War and local history. The museum is open Thursday through Sunday from 2 P.M. to 5 P.M.; call 704-633-5946 for information.

■ Just north of Salisbury on Interstate 85 lies the small town of **Spencer**, home of the **North Carolina Transportation Museum** and the **Historic Spencer Shops**. The museum, housed in a 1924 roundhouse and the largest repair facility for J. P. Morgan's Southern Railroad, tells the story of inland transportation in North Carolina from the 19th century to the present. It offers train rides for visitors and guided tours for school groups. The museum and the Historic Spencer Shops are open Monday through Saturday from 9 A.M. to 5 P.M. and Sunday from 1 P.M. to 5 P.M. from April through October. From November through March, they are open Tuesday through Saturday from 10 A.M. to 4 P.M. and Sunday from 1 P.M. to 4 P.M. For more information, call 704-636-2889, or visit their website at www.nctrans.org.

■ **Davidson**, a college town just off the banks of Lake Norman, is remarkable for its old-timey Main Street, maintained in the face of

Main Street in Davidson
PHOTOGRAPH BY
ED SOUTHERN

Mecklenburg County's astounding growth. Main Street runs alongside the campus of Davidson College, where future president Woodrow Wilson studied. It features a row of shops, coffee houses, and a soda shop, housed mainly in 19th-century buildings.

The Coolest Mill Village Around

Cool, of course, is largely a matter of personal taste, but by most millennial definitions, North Davidson Street is far and away the coolest stretch of road in Mecklenburg County.

A four-block section of North Davidson Street that lies only two and a half miles from the middle of Uptown was once the main street of the mill village known as North Charlotte. In the early part of the 20th century, the community developed core businesses and services for its residents, almost all of whom worked at the mill. Then the mill closed, and North Charlotte quickly died. North Davidson Street became home to isolated industrial properties, abandoned buildings, vacant lots, and one of Charlotte's poorest residential areas.

Maybe only an artist could see the opportunity. Or more correctly, a pair of artists—Ruth Ava Lyons and J. Paul Sires. In 1985, Lyons and Sires opened the Center of the Earth Gallery in a renovated 1927 office building on North Davidson Street in the heart of the old mill village. Center of the Earth quickly became known as one of the boldest galleries in the Southeast. It remains so today, having won "Best Gallery" awards from 1995 through 1998, as well as the Governor's Award for Businesses in the Arts.

While Center of the Earth drew artistic and daring Charlotteans to North Davidson Street, Fat City provided them with a hangout. Located across and just down the street from the gallery, on a lot that backs up to a truck depot, Fat City became an oasis in a 1990s desert of sports and yuppie bars.

Other galleries and restaurants followed Center of the Earth and Fat City to North Davidson Street, as did bars, coffee shops, and clothing stores. Their proprietors recognized the benefits of the insularity and communal nostalgia of the old mill village. The Neighborhood Theatre, located on 36th Street just off North Davidson, has hosted plays such as *Under Milk Wood* by Dylan Thomas and *The Life and Times of Malcolm X*, as well as musicians such as Doc Watson and Robert Earl Keen. Twice a month, the street is host to a "Gallery Crawl," in which all doors are opened and a drum circle is formed in an open space down the street from Fat City.

Inevitably, the residential area that stretches southeast from North Davidson Street toward the Plaza is being redeveloped. Neighborhood Realty, which owns and operates the Neighborhood Theatre, has for over a decade bought and renovated former mill houses in the North Davidson Street area and other central Charlotte locations. The company rents or sells the homes to artists, actors, musicians, dancers, teachers, and even bankers who want to avoid the endless Charlotte suburbs and live close to the action.

Just as inevitably, more and more Charlotteans are starting to come to North Davidson Street. These days, Fat City serves lunch to as many bankers as bikers. The area has an official designation as the "Historic North Charlotte Arts District" and a catchy, somewhat cheesy nickname, "NoDa." A play on "North Davidson," it's supposed to echo New York's SoHo and TriBeCa. Get it?

As one of the original *Saturday Night Live* writers once said, "You can only be avant-garde for so long, until you become garde." Tastes change; coolness is diluted by its own success.

But North Davidson Street still offers an edgy alternative to the sanitized entertainment so common these days, a place for independent thought and style to compete with the mainstream.

THE MOUNTAINS

The Blue Ridge Parkway

By Carolyn Sakowski

$\mathcal{T}$he Blue Ridge Parkway is an unusual part of the National Parks system. It's really a linear park, stretching 469 miles from Shenandoah National Park in Virginia to Great Smoky Mountains National Park on the North Carolina–Tennessee border.

The parkway has always been refreshing. Regulations keep the signage to a minimum; what is there is informative and tasteful. A major purpose of the highway's construction was to give men jobs during the Depression. You'll see evidence of their clearly identifiable stonework all along the route. In recent years, the Friends of the Parkway and other interested parties have gone to great lengths to ensure that the pastoral feel of the land is preserved.

One thing you'll notice is that the speed limit is 45 miles per hour. The parkway is designed for leisurely driving, with plenty of overlooks along the way. If you're in a hurry, take the regular roads.

It is legal for you to pull off on the shoulder for a picnic, as long as you make sure your vehicle is completely off the road. On weekends in the summer and fall, you'll see lots of people taking advantage of this opportunity.

This chapter will provide a few details about some of the sites along the Blue Ridge Parkway. The parkway actually begins near Charlottesville, Virginia; the markers start with Milepost 0 at Shenandoah National Park. The North Carolina section starts at Milepost 217 at the North Carolina–Virginia line.

Milepost 217–Cumberland Knob is in Alleghany County. The boundary line that divides North Carolina and Virginia was surveyed in 1749 by a group that included Peter Jefferson, Thomas's father. Just south of the line is Cumberland Knob Recreation Area, where restrooms, water fountains, picnic tables, and hiking trails are available. You can take a short walk to Cumberland Knob or a two-hour hike into Gully Creek Gorge.

Milepost 218.6—Fox Hunter's Paradise recalls a once-popular sport in the mountains. Men would turn loose their dogs to "run" foxes through the night. Catching one was rare—and not the point. Listening to the "music" of fox hounds calling through the deep woods was what mattered. A picnic table and a hiking trail are available at Fox Hunter's Paradise.

Milepost 229—U.S. 21 intersects the parkway here. Sparta is seven miles west and Roaring Gap four miles east.

The Blue Ridge Parkway in Alleghany County
COURTESY OF ALLEGHANY COUNTY CHAMBER OF COMMERCE

Milepost 232.5—Stone Mountain Overlook offers a good view of Stone Mountain State Park, which is covered in the "Recreation" section of the Alleghany County chapter.

Milepost 237.1—Air Bellows Gap is appropriately named; on a windy day, the wind sweeps up from the deep gorge below.

Milepost 238.5—Brinegar Cabin is an original mountain homestead that has been preserved. The farm of Martin and Caroline Joines Brinegar is located to the left. When it is open, you can get a glimpse of old-time life in the mountains. Craft demonstrations are offered at various times. Check at Doughton Park for a schedule.

Milepost 238.5–244.8—Doughton Park, named for Congressman Robert Doughton, is one the parkway's treasures. The park offers the Bluffs Lodge and Restaurant, a campground, a gift shop, excellent hiking trails, and wonderful views.

Milepost 248.1—N.C. 18 intersects the parkway here. It is two miles west to Laurel Springs and 24 miles east to North Wilkesboro.

Milepost 252.5—Jesse Sheets built a small cabin for his family at Sheets Gap around 1815, making it one of the oldest surviving settlers' cabins. An overlook at Sheets Gap is three-tenths of a mile south; from there, a trail leads back to the cabin.

Milepost 259—Northwest Trading Post is described in the "Special Shopping" section of the Alleghany County chapter.

Milepost 261—N.C. 16 intersects the parkway here. It is five miles west to Glendale Springs and 20 miles east to North Wilkesboro.

Milepost 266.9—Mount Jefferson is covered in the "Recreation" section of the Ashe County chapter.

Milepost 270—Until 2002, travelers will be detoured to avoid construction at the Deep Gap entrance. The route is well marked. You will detour at Phillips Gap Road, which meets Idlewild Road; both roads are two-lane highways that were not heavily traveled until this detour. Idlewild Road runs into U.S. 221, which runs south to the Deep Gap community; this is the main route from Boone to Jefferson, so it is busy. The final link of the detour is on U.S. 421, which is very well traveled, hence the need for the four-lane construction now under way. Travelers reenter the parkway at an unnamed but marked entrance near Parkway Elementary School after exactly 11.3 miles.

Milepost 271.9—The Cascades Nature Trail offers a brisk hike through rich pine forests. In late May, the mountain laurel is beautiful here. At the bottom of the trail, a waterfall rolls down the side of the mountain to the lowlands below. Hikers need to exercise caution on the rocks near the waterfall. Even in recent years, people have fallen to their deaths here. Restrooms, water fountains, and picnic tables are available at this site.

Milepost 272.6—Located on the left side of the road are two historic buildings. One is the Jesse Brown Cabin, built in the mid-1800s. Nearby is Cool Spring Baptist Church, an open-air shelter that was already standing when the Civil War ended in 1865; it was typical of the earliest churches in the region. An overlook here offers a short trail back to these early structures.

Milepost 276.4—Until 2002, the entrance at Deep Gap will be closed while construction crews build a second bridge for U.S. 421. Deep Gap is the way into Watauga County from the east. A Civil War entrenchment once stood near where the parkway bridge is today, just before the exit for U.S. 421.

Milepost 281.7—Grandview Overlook is where the detour brings you back onto the parkway—and a grand overlook it is.

Milepost 285.1—Daniel Boone Trace marks the place where Boone regularly camped and hunted in this area in the 1760s, before opening Kentucky to settlers. A monument and a roadside picnic table are located here.

Milepost 289–290—Raven Rocks and Thunder Hill are two exceptional overlooks near Blowing Rock. Raven Rocks offers views of the mountains surrounding the valley of the Watauga River. Thunder Hill's view looks over the valley of the Yadkin River stretching to Lenoir, Hickory, and beyond. Both are popular spots with locals and visitors alike.

Milepost 291.9—U.S. 221/U.S. 321 intersects the parkway here. It is seven miles north to Boone and two miles south to Blowing Rock.

Milepost 293–295—Moses S. Cone Memorial Park is described in the "Special Shopping" section of the Blowing Rock chapter.

Milepost 295–299—Julian Price Park offers a campground, canoe and boat rentals on Price Lake, and a host of trails to hike. The trail around Price Lake is relatively level. The campground's 197 spaces are offered on a first-come, first served basis. Cold water and grills are available, but electricity is not. A dump station is located near the office. This office is normally open from 8 A.M. to 8 P.M.; campers may self-register after hours and at times when no ranger is available. Price Lake offers excellent fishing. It is classified as "general trout waters"; fishermen may use natural or artificial baits but no fresh eggs or live or dead fish or amphibians. A state license is required, but a trout stamp is not.

Julian Price Park
COURTESY OF NORTH CAROLINA DIVISION OF TOURISM, FILM AND SPORTS DEVELOPMENT

Milepost 298–305—Grandfather Mountain is the crown jewel of the parkway. For over 50 years, owner Hugh Morton fought the government over the environmental impact its original road plans would have caused this landmark—and visitors are glad he did. The Linn Cove Viaduct, which almost rivals the mountain itself in beauty, was the compromise the two sides found. The free trail system here links with Grandfather's system, for which a permit is required.

Milepost 304—The Linn Cove Viaduct is one of the engineering marvels of our age, and the view from it is unmatched in the eastern United States. You can hike the Linn Cove Viaduct Trail, which leads beneath the viaduct and gives visitors a true appreciation of this architectural masterpiece. The visitor center here has displays, books, videos, and restrooms.

Milepost 305.9—U.S. 221 intersects the parkway here. It is three miles west to Linville and one mile west to the entrance of Grandfather Mountain.

Milepost 306—Grandfather Mountain Overlook offers a view of the mountain's southern side, which resembles a hawk. That explains why

The Linn Cove Viaduct
PHOTOGRAPH BY CAROLYN SAKOWSKI

the Cherokees called it Tanawha, meaning "Hawk." One of the best trails in the area is the Tanawha Trail, which extends from Milepost 305.5 for 13.5 miles back toward Price Lake.

Milepost 308.2—Flat Rock Overlook has a short nature trail that leads to a view of the Linville Valley and Grandfather Mountain.

Milepost 310—Lost Cove Cliffs Overlook offers one of the best vantage points for seeing the Brown Mountain Lights. In recent years, the haze that appears on most summer evenings prevents visitors from seeing the mysterious lights moving along the ridge in the distance. No one has ever explained what causes these lights, but the tales that have grown up around them make great campfire stories.

Milepost 312—N.C. 181 intersects the parkway here. It is two miles north to Pineola and 32 miles southeast to Morganton.

Milepost 316.3—Linville Falls is covered in the "Recreation" section of the chapter on Banner Elk, Beech Mountain, and Linville.

Milepost 317.4—Linville Falls Visitor Center has a picnic area and a bridge where you can fish in the Linville River. It is three miles south to the Linville Falls community and 24 miles south on U.S. 221 to Marion.

Milepost 331—The Museum of North Carolina Minerals is described in the "Museums and Science Centers" section of the chapter on Spruce Pine and Burnsville. It is six miles north to Spruce Pine and 14 miles south to Marion.

Milepost 334—N.C. 226A intersects the parkway at Little Switzerland.

Milepost 339.5—Crabtree Meadows offers a 250-acre park that includes a picnic area and a comfort station. The focus of the park is a 40-minute hike to Crabtree Falls.

Milepost 344—N.C. 80 intersects the parkway at Buck Creek Gap. It is 16 miles north to Burnsville and 16 miles south to Marion.

Crabtree Falls at Crabtree Meadows
COURTESY OF NORTH CAROLINA DIVISION OF
TOURISM, FILM AND SPORTS DEVELOPMENT

Milepost 355.4—N.C. 128 leads to Mount Mitchell State Park, described in the "Recreation" section of the chapter on Spruce Pine and Burnsville.

Milepost 364.4—Craggy Gardens Visitor Center offers information, exhibits, and self-guided tours. In June, the rhododendron gardens here are spectacular.

Milepost 377.4—N.C. 694 intersects the parkway here. It is eight miles west to Asheville.

Milepost 382—The Folk Art Center is described in the "Special Shopping" section of the Asheville chapter.

Milepost 382.6—U.S. 70 intersects the parkway here. It is one mile to Oteen, five miles to Asheville, and 10 miles to Black Mountain.

Milepost 384.7—U.S. 74A intersects the parkway here. It is three miles west to Asheville. Chimney Rock, Bat Cave, and Lake Lure lie to the east.

Milepost 388.8—U.S. 25 intersects the parkway here. It is five miles north to Asheville and 17 miles south to Hendersonville.

Milepost 393.6—N.C. 191 intersects the parkway here. It is six miles north to Asheville and 20 miles south to Hendersonville.

Milepost 408.6—Mount Pisgah, which was part of the 100,000 acres donated from George Vanderbilt's Biltmore Estate, offers a campground, picnic area, trails, an inn, a restaurant, and a service station. You can see the 5,749-foot peak in the distance.

Milepost 412—U.S. 276 intersects the parkway at Wagon Road Gap. It is 18 miles south to Brevard, eight miles north to Cruso, and 22 miles northwest to Waynesville. On the way to Brevard, you can visit the Cradle of Forestry.

Milepost 417—Looking Glass Rock is a 3,969-foot summit whose sheer cliffs give it its name.

Milepost 418.8—Graveyard Fields Overlook has a 2.3-mile loop trail to Yellowstone Falls.

Milepost 422.4—From the Devil's Courthouse Parking Area, it is a strenuous half-mile hike to the Devil's Courthouse. The Cherokees

Graveyard Fields

believe this 5,462-foot mountain was the location of the giant Judaculla's courtroom.

Milepost 423.2—N.C. 215 intersects the parkway at Beech Gap. It is 24 miles north to Waynesville and 17 miles south to Rosman.

Milepost 431—At the Haywood-Jackson Overlook, visitors can take a 1.5-mile self-guided loop trail to the summit of Richland Balsam, which is the highest point on the parkway, at 6,058 feet.

Milepost 431.4—Richmond Balsam Overlook is located here.

Milepost 443.1—U.S. 74/U.S. 23 intersects the parkway at Balsam Gap. It is seven miles east to Waynesville and 12 miles west to Sylva.

Milepost 451.2—At Waterrock Knob Overlook, you'll find an information center, a comfort station, a trail to the knob, and a four-state view.

Milepost 455.7—U.S. 19 intersects the parkway at Soco Gap. It is 12 miles west to Cherokee and five miles east to Maggie Valley.

Milepost 458.2—From here, Heintooga Ridge Road Spur goes to Mile High Overlook. It is 12 miles to Great Smoky Mountains National Park Campground.

Milepost 461.9—Big Witch Overlook is located here.

Milepost 469.1—Great Smoky Mountains National Park begins at the junction with U.S. 441. It is two miles south to Cherokee and 29 miles north to Gatlinburg, Tennessee.

by Carolyn Sakowski

The High Country

Alleghany County

Ashe County

Boone

Blowing Rock

Banner Elk, Beech Mountain, and Linville

Spruce Pine and Burnsville

This book's definition of the High Country differs slightly from that employed by the High Country Host organization. This section will cover Alleghany, Ashe, Watauga, Avery, Mitchell, and Yancey Counties.

In this northern portion of North Carolina's Appalachian Mountains, you'll find the highest peaks not only in the state but in the entire eastern United States. You'll discover a booming tourism industry thanks to the cool summer temperatures, the vibrant fall foliage, and the winter skiing. All of the places mentioned here are within an easy day's drive of each other.

Although many of the top attractions—Grandfather Mountain, the New River, the Blowing Rock, Linville Falls—have remained the same for millions of years, the last 30 years have brought dramatic changes to the rest of the area. When the tourists began to arrive, they liked what they saw so much that they bought mountain property and built summer or retirement homes. As a result, many of the natural vistas have disappeared. It's a double-edged sword in many ways. While longtime residents lament the influx of "outsiders," they now have amenities they could not have imagined a few decades ago. You not only don't have to drive 30 miles to buy groceries or an alcoholic beverage, you can now get espresso and the Sunday *New York Times*—on the same Sunday they get it in New York—a few minutes from almost anywhere.

Speaking of alcoholic beverages, you'll find that the liquor laws in these mountain counties are vastly inconsistent. Some resorts have been very creative in procuring legislative exemptions that allow them to serve alcohol. Some townships have voted to allow it, while people are unable to purchase even beer or wine a few miles away. If having access to alcoholic beverages is important to your vacation, you might want to check on the liquor laws where you're staying or dining.

You should also know that, even though you may be leaving 90-degree temperatures to come to the mountains, you'll still need a jacket or sweater in the evenings here. The rule of thumb is to expect a five-degree change in temperature for every 1,000 feet of change in elevation. You might also want to throw in rain gear. Many a clear, sunny day has a short, late-afternoon shower here. These cool days and frequent showers ensure that the region's wildflowers and cultivated mountain gardens are prolific. You'll be struck by the abundance of vibrantly colored flowers.

In the last few decades, there has been an explosion of outdoor activities in the mountains. Skiing, golf, whitewater rafting, mountain biking, and hiking have all brought thousands of people. For those who prefer less physical "exercise," the area has also seen a boom in shopping outlets, gourmet restaurants, first-rate resorts, and bed-and-breakfasts in wonderful restored homes. Although I recommend some specific places to stay, all of these counties have scores of individual cabins and condominiums for rent. Contact the appropriate chamber of commerce to be put in touch with realtors.

North toward the Virginia border, you can see how dramatically the times have changed. Those who long for the way things used to be in the mountains may find Ashe and Alleghany Counties more to their liking. For at least the next few years, you can still get the best of both worlds by traveling from one county to the next to find what you seek.

JUST THE FACTS

You can get visitor information from High Country Host, 1700 Blowing Rock Road (U.S. 321), Boone, N.C. 28607 (800-438-7500 or 828-264-1299; www.highcountryhost.com). This regional visitor center promotes tourism in Watauga, Ashe, Avery, Alleghany, Mitchell, and Wilkes Counties. The center is open Monday through Saturday from 9 A.M. to 5 P.M. and Sunday from 10 A.M. to 4 P.M.

This area is served by an excellent free weekly newspaper, the *Mountain Times*. You can access the paper's website and its extensive links at www.mountaintimes.com.

by Carolyn Sakowski

PHOTOGRAPH USED IN THE BACKGROUND ON PAGE 411:
Daniel Boone looking out at the mountains at sunset
PHOTOGRAPH BY JUDI SCHARNS
COURTESY OF BOONE CONVENTION AND VISITORS BUREAU

Waterfall in Alleghany County
COURTESY OF ALLEGHANY COUNTY CHAMBER OF COMMERCE

ALLEGHANY COUNTY
by Carolyn Sakowski

*A*lleghany County was once known as the "Lost Province" because of its early isolation. Even today, the county has a year-round population of only 10,000 people. But it is finally starting to reap the benefits of its former isolation. The local chamber of commerce now touts this county as the "Unspoiled Province," and that's exactly what it is. Here, you'll find scenic views that are still largely unmarred by progress. As you drive along Alleghany County's two-lane highways, you'll be struck by the number of two-story, white clapboard farmhouses with wraparound porches sitting smack dab in the middle of large, working farms. You won't see the clutter of billboards and the urban sprawl that come with the influx of national chain stores and gimmicky roadside gift shops.

Nestled in mountains that reach 3,000 to 4,000 feet, the county is surrounded by 20,000 acres of National and State Parks, including Doughton Park, Stone Mountain State Park, New River State Park, and Grayson Highlands State Park in Virginia. The Blue Ridge Parkway weaves along the edge of the county for 30 miles.

If you want to see the mountains like they used to be, you'd better hurry to Alleghany County before the rest of the world discovers it.

Things to Do

SPECIAL SHOPPING

- You'd be well advised to call for exact directions to **Mangum Pottery**, located at 280 Turkey Hollow Lane in Sparta. It's a bit off the main road but well worth the effort. As you drive up Turkey Hollow Lane, you'll start seeing pieces of interesting pottery and stoneware perched on rocks and peeking from behind foliage. This is just a sample of the creativity that awaits you when you arrive at Robin and Bet Mangum's gallery and workshop. They create stoneware, porcelain, majolica, and raku pieces, many with a special quirkiness. Call 336-372-5291.

RECREATION

- **Stone Mountain State Park** is located in Alleghany and Wilkes

Stone Mountain
PHOTOGRAPH BY
CAROLYN SAKOWSKI

Counties seven miles southwest of Roaring Gap. From U.S. 21, turn on to S.R. 1002, which takes you to the John P. Frank Parkway. If you're coming from the west, take N.C. 18 North and turn right on S.R. 1002.

Located on 13,500 acres, the park offers four easily accessed water-falls, 17 miles of trout streams, two fishing piers for the handicapped, 15 miles of hiking and horseback-riding trails, and a historic mountain home-stead. However, the big attraction is Stone Mountain itself, a 600-foot granite dome. Climbing on the cliffs is permitted in designated areas, but all climbers must register and possess a valid rock-climbing permit.

Campsites are available for a fee. The campground has a wash house with hot showers, but there are no utility hookups. Campers cannot leave the park after the gates are closed. The park is open from 8 A.M. to 6 P.M. November through February, from 8 A.M. to 7 P.M. in March and October, from 8 A.M. to 8 P.M. in April, May, and September, and from 8 A.M. to 9 P.M. June through August. For informa-tion, contact the park at 3042 Frank Parkway, P.O. Box 17, Roaring Gap, N.C. 28668 (336-957-8185).

■ ***Doughton Park***, which is part of the Blue Ridge Parkway, has over 30 miles of hiking trails that range from modest strolls to all-day outings. Horse trails, fishing, camping, and picnicking are all offered. See the chap-ter on the Blue Ridge Parkway for more information.

■ ***New River State Park*** is located in Ashe and Alleghany Counties. The

A scene along the New River
PHOTOGRAPH BY CAROLYN SAKOWSKI

Alleghany County Access Area can be reached only by canoe. (See the chapter on Ashe County and the sidebar about the New River for more information.)

Camping and canoeing on the New are big draws here. Two local campgrounds bill themselves as canoe campgrounds. **River Camp USA** has sites for RVs and tents. It offers full hookups, picnic tables, a country store, a playground, a laundry, and hot showers. The proprietors rent canoes and inner tubes and provide shuttle service. For information, contact the camp at P.O. Box 9, Piney Creek, N.C. 28663 (800-RIVERCAMP or 336-359-CAMP; www.rivercamp.net). **New River Canoe and Campground**, located six miles north of Sparta on U.S. 21, has grassy and shady spots along the river. All sites have a picnic table, a lantern post, and a fire ring. The campground offers RV hookups, camping cabins, a camp store, a restaurant, a playground, and pedal boats for rent. Guests can make arrangements for canoeing instruction and day or overnight canoe trips. For information, contact the campground at Route 2, Box 238-A, Sparta, N.C. 28675 (336-372-8793).

■ **Mountain Music Jamboree** is held every Saturday night from 7 P.M. to 11 P.M. at the Burgiss Barn, located at the junction of U.S. 18 and N.C. 113 in Laurel Springs. Two bands take shifts playing the finest traditional and bluegrass music. The barn has a large wooden dance floor for square dancing and clogging. Patrons can order refreshments, a hot dinner, and sandwiches, but no alcohol is permitted. A fee is charged.

Tom Burgiss, who runs Mountain Music Jamboree, is quite the entrepreneur. He and his wife, Nancy, run the Burgiss Farm Bed-and-Breakfast on the same property. Grapestompers, where he sells winemaking kits, is Tom's latest enterprise. He'll also be glad to show you how to make your own.

- Three Alleghany County golf courses allow nonmembers to play: *New River Country Club* (336-372-4869) in Sparta, *High Meadows Golf and Country Club* (336-363-2622) in Roaring Gap, and *Olde Beau Golf Club* (336-363-3333), also in Roaring Gap.

- Nearby Virginia offers two exceptional places for bicycling. The *Virginia Creeper Trail* and *New River Trail State Park* are both rails-to-trails venues. They are perfect for inexperienced cyclists, children, and even experienced cyclists who want to test their stamina. Unfortunately, Sparta does not have any bike-rental establishments, but you can make arrangements in the Virginia communities of Damascus and Galax.

The New River—North Carolina's American Heritage River

The New River, which some say is 300 million years old, is supposedly the oldest river in North America. It begins in Watauga County and is the only river in the eastern United States that flows northward to the Midwest. The North and South Forks of the river join a few miles south of the North Carolina–Virginia border. From there, the river continues through Virginia and West Virginia.

Archaeological investigations suggest that humans have been in the region for at least 10,000 years. Arrowheads, pottery shards, and stone axes indicate the Canawhay Indian tribe occupied the river valley during the precolonial period. There is also evidence of hunting trails used by Creeks, Shawnees, and Cherokees moving north along the New River to the Ohio River.

The first European to see the river was probably Colonel Abraham Wood, who came seeking trade with the Indians in 1654. Before the 1770s, long hunters were probably the only white men to venture into the region. Originally known as Wood's River, it was renamed the New by Peter Jefferson, the father of Thomas Jefferson, when he surveyed the North Carolina–Virginia boundary in 1749.

In 1752, Bishop Augustus Spangenburg, an early traveler sent by the Moravian Church to find land for a settlement, wrote the following: "For several days we followed the river in the hope that it would lead us out, we found ourselves only deeper in the wilderness, for the river ran now north, now south, now east, now west, in short to all points of the compass! Finally, we decided to leave the river and take a course between east and south, crossing the mountains as best we could." If you look at the course of the river on a modern map, you'll see exactly why Bishop Spangenburg was so frustrated.

In 1965, the Appalachian Power Company applied for a license to dam the river. In response to unprecedented grassroots opposition, the North Carolina General Assembly declared a 26.5-mile stretch from the river's confluence with Dog Creek to the Virginia state line a State Scenic River. In April 1976, the New was designated a National Wild and Scenic River, thus ensuring that it will remain untouched. On July 30, 1998, President Bill Clinton and Vice President Al Gore showed up with a group of dignitaries to proclaim the New an American Heritage River.

The centerpiece of the New River State Park, the river is a popular spot for camping, canoeing, picnicking, and fishing. The easy flow and mild rapids make it perfect for inexperienced paddlers. The best months for high water levels are May and June; August and September are usu-

ally the low-flow periods. Those wishing to canoe can leave their vehicles at the Wagoner Road Access Area, located at River Mile 26, eight miles southeast of Jefferson; the access area can be reached via S.R. 1590 off N.C. 88 some 1.2 miles east of the intersection of N.C. 16 and N.C. 88. The other parking area is at the U.S. 221 Access Area, located at River Mile 15, eight miles northeast of Jefferson; it may be reached via U.S. 221. The Alleghany County Access Area, at River Mile 1, may be reached only by canoe. Canoes can also be launched from several bridges and roads that cross the river.

Picnic areas and primitive campsites with tables and grills are located at the three access areas. Pit toilets and drinking water are nearby. The South and North Forks offer excellent smallmouth and redeye bass fishing. The South Fork downstream from the U.S. 221 bridge has been stocked with muskellunge. Trout fishing is excellent in the smaller tributaries, most of which are stocked regularly with rainbow and brown trout. Make sure you get that fishing license!

For information, contact the chamber of commerce in Ashe County or Alleghany County. Or you can contact New River State Park at P.O. Box 48, Jefferson, N.C. 28640 (336-982-2587).

Places to Stay

RESORTS, HOTELS, AND MOTELS

■ **Station's Inn on the Parkway**. Inexpensive. N.C. 18 at Milepost 248 on the Blue Ridge Parkway, Laurel Springs (877-528-7356). This 1950s motor lodge has been wonderfully restored. Guests get to stay in wood-paneled rooms with 1950s-style furniture, but they also enjoy modern bathrooms and cable television. On the premises are a country store and Station's Restaurant, which offers pizza, barbecue, wings, burgers, beer, and wine. On Sundays from 3 P.M. to 6:30 P.M., the inn offers free bluegrass music. On Saturday nights, it shows classic movies that feature cars (such as *Thunder Road* and *American Graffiti*) on the side of the building; everyone brings lawn chairs and watches the movie. Everywhere you look, you'll see old gas station memorabilia and old photographs of Laurel Springs and the Blue Ridge Parkway. Station's Inn caters to motorcyclists, but they're not the Hell's Angels variety. You're liable to sit next to a doctor from Charlotte who rode up on his Harley for the day.

INNS AND BED-AND-BREAKFASTS

■ **Harmony Hill**. Expensive. 1740 Halsey Knob Road, Sparta (336-372-6868). Located eight miles from Sparta, this beautifully restored Victorian home has an incredible view of the surrounding countryside. It offers three bedrooms and a carriage house. Each bedroom is air-conditioned and has its own private bath. Some rooms have Jacuzzis; most have fireplaces with gas logs; all have ceiling fans, televisions, and telephones. Breakfast is served in the dining room, in the gazebo, or on the porch. Pets and children under 12 are not allowed.

■ **Bald Knob Farm House**. Moderate. Bald Knob Road, Sparta (336-372-4191). To reach this place, go north on N.C. 18 for four miles from the intersection with U.S. 21 in Sparta. Turn left on Pleasant Home Road, then take the first left on to Bald Knob Road. It is the first house on the right. The owners have lovingly restored this old family home, which

Doughton-Hall
Bed-and-Breakfast
Photograph by
Carolyn Sakowski

dates to 1918. It offers four large bedrooms furnished with antiques. Color television, a VCR, a telephone, a microwave, and a washer and dryer are all available for sharing, as is the bathroom. The owners also operate the Rock House, a 1950s stone house, and The Barn, a refurbished milk barn, both of which are available for rent. Credit cards are not accepted here.

▪ *Doughton-Hall Bed-and-Breakfast*. Moderate. 12668 N.C. 18 South, Laurel Springs (336-359-2341). This is the historic residence of former congressman Robert L. Doughton, who served in the House of Representatives from 1911 to 1953, during which time he was the powerful head of the House Ways and Means Committee. It was Doughton who was largely responsible for bringing the Blue Ridge Parkway to this area. Located 13 miles from Sparta and 1.7 miles from the intersection of the Blue Ridge Parkway and N.C. 18, his Queen Anne–style home dates to 1898. It is listed on the National Register of Historic Places. It has four guest rooms, three with private baths and Jacuzzis. Wine and hors d'oeuvres are served nightly, and a full country breakfast is served each morning.

Places to Eat

▪ *The Senator's House*. Moderate. 360 North Main Street, next to Sparta Elementary School (336-372-7500). Excellent American cuisine is served in the historical home of former state senator Eugene Transou. Hours vary seasonally; dinner is usually served on the weekends only. Reservations are required.

■ **Blue Ridge Café**. Inexpensive. 38 South Main Street, Sparta (336-372-7400). Housed in the old Smithey's Department Store, this café is part of Blue Ridge Plaza, which houses 50 vendors under the same roof; antiques, art, and collectibles are sold here on a consignment basis. The café offers sandwiches and subs for lunch and chicken, pasta, and seafood dishes for dinner. Lunch is served Monday through Saturday and dinner Wednesday through Saturday.

■ **The Pizzeria**. Inexpensive. Trojan Village Shopping Center, Sparta (336-372-8885). This restaurant serves pizza, subs, and sandwiches, but what it's really known for is its great chicken pie, which comes with the luncheon buffet on Sunday and Wednesday. A regular buffet is served from 11 A.M. to 2 P.M. Tuesday through Sunday. Dinner is served Tuesday through Sunday as well.

ASHE COUNTY
by Carolyn Sakowski

The farther south you travel from the Virginia line, the more you'll see tourist development and the proliferation of vacation homes. Ashe County lies between Alleghany and Watauga Counties not only geographically but developmentally as well. Here, you'll see more chain motels and urban sprawl than in Alleghany, but it's nothing like you'll get in Watauga.

Thanks to its cheese factory and its frescoes, Ashe County has long been a great day trip from anywhere in the High Country. Because of its two canoe access areas for New River State Park, it has also been a logical place for outfitters to spring up. This is also one of the major areas for the growing of Fraser fir Christmas trees, so the landscape is dotted with picturesque farms of uniform rows of evergreens growing along the hillsides.

The town of Jefferson, the county seat, was founded in 1800 at the base of Mount Jefferson. In 1917, a group of investors founded West Jefferson, which attracted the railroad. Jefferson subsequently went into decline, leaving West Jefferson as the economic center of the county.

Just the Facts

To reach Ashe County's twin cities of Jefferson and West Jefferson, take U.S. 221 from Deep Gap, U.S. 421 from the Blue Ridge Parkway, or N.C. 194 or N.C. 16 from Virginia.

For visitor information, contact the Ashe County Chamber of Commerce, 6 North Jefferson Avenue, P.O. Box 31, West Jefferson, N.C. 28694 (888-343-2743 or 336-246-9550; www.ashechamber.com).

The *Jefferson Post* is the area's weekly newspaper. Its website is www.jeffersonpost.com. *Mountain Times*, a free weekly, is distributed in Ashe County.

Things to Do

Historic Places, Gardens, and Tours

■ In downtown West Jefferson at Main and Fourth Streets, you can tour North Carolina's only cheese manufacturer, **Ashe County Cheese Company**. This company has been producing cheese for over 60 years. You can see cheese being made and stop at the wine and cheese shop. The store is open every day; it opens at 1 P.M. on Sundays. The plant is open Monday through Saturday. For information, contact Ashe County Cheese Company, P.O. Box 447, West Jefferson, N.C. 28694 (336-246-2501).

▪ Just outside West Jefferson, you'll see signs directing you to the frescoes at **St. Mary's Episcopal Church** in Beaver Creek. Less than 10 miles to the east on N.C. 16 in Glendale Springs, you can see the larger fresco at **Holy Trinity Episcopal Church**. All were created by North Carolina native Ben Long and his helpers. While at Holy Trinity, be sure to see the columbarium, located downstairs. If you've ever wondered where you might put your cremated ashes, the columbarium provides an interesting option.

The Last Supper at Holy Trinity Episcopal Church
PHOTOGRAPH BY
CAROLYN SAKOWSKI

The Frescoes

Though St. Mary's Episcopal Church now houses one the area's main tourist attractions, it was not always the focus of community pride

Milnor Jones was an Episcopal minister and active missionary who organized the first Episcopal church in Ashe County, the Church of St. Simon the Zealot. On June 21, 1896, Bishop Joseph Blount Cheshire came from Raleigh to conduct services. He was met at the church by an unexpected greeting committee. Cheshire wrote, "I was assaulted and forcibly prevented from entering this building by a mob of between fifty and one hundred men which had been gotten together for the express purpose of preventing our service that day. And the reason they gave

St. Mary's Episcopal Church
PHOTOGRAPH BY CAROLYN SAKOWSKI

Holy Trinity Episcopal Church
PHOTOGRAPH BY CAROLYN SAKOWSKI

for this action was that they 'did not like Mr. Jones' doctrine' and they understood that I taught the same doctrine." Cheshire further noted that he "met with the most violent opposition, accompanied with bitter abuse from Methodists and Baptists, especially the latter."

Milnor Jones went on to organize a school at Beaver Creek. His quaint Church of St. Simon the Zealot was later renamed St. Mary's. It was eventually abandoned for lack of funds until a different sort of notoriety came its way.

In the summer of 1980, artist Ben Long returned to the United States to train others in a dying art form. For seven years, he had studied fresco painting in Italy with a master of Renaissance technique. Long took on as many as 20 apprentices at one time in Ashe County and used two Episcopal churches in the area as his studios.

Fresco painting is a tedious and complicated process, which explains its rarity in today's world. Natural ground pigment is mixed with distilled water, thinned with lime, and painted on damp plaster. As the plaster dries, the lime and pigment bind chemically, so that the wall literally becomes the painting. This unusual technique produces an interesting effect—many say that fresco walls seem to glow. The drawback is that the pigment is absorbed the moment brush touches plaster, so a mistake can necessitate the removal of an entire section of wall.

Ben Long imported lime from the same site in Florence, Italy, that Michelangelo used when working on the Sistine Chapel. He mixed it with North Carolina sand to make his plaster. Local people served as models for the characters in his frescoes; Long himself took the role of Doubting Thomas. The results are so impressive that thousands of people a year visit the out-of-the-way chapels to view the frescoes. Those at St. Mary's are *Mary, Great with Child; John the Baptist;* and *The Mystery of Faith.* At the Church of the Holy Trinity, you can see Long's interpretation of the Last Supper, which occupies the entire front wall. Despite frequent busloads of tourists, both churches are worthwhile stops.

Special Shopping

- The **Northwest Trading Post**, located at Milepost 259 on the Blue Ridge Parkway, is a quaint gift shop sponsored by the Northwest Development Association. Its mission is to keep alive the old mountain crafts. The shop sells over 250 types of handmade crafts made by over 500 craftsmen from 11 northwestern North Carolina counties. You'll find woodcarvings, baskets, woven materials, handmade toys, pottery, baked goods, jellies, jams, musical instruments, bird feeders, and even country hams. The shop is open from 9 A.M. to 5:30 P.M. from April to October. Call 336-982-2543.

- The **New River General Store** is located on U.S. 221 halfway between West Jefferson and Sparta. Here, you can browse antiques, buy old-fashioned candies, and purchase gifts, groceries, and cheese. It even offers a deli serving pizza and subs. The store is open daily from 8:30 A.M. to 6 P.M. New River Outfitters runs its canoeing trips out of this store. For information, call 336-982-9192.

Recreation

- **Mount Jefferson State Natural Area**, located on Mount Jefferson Road off U.S. 221 at West Jefferson, is a relatively undeveloped park covering 539 acres. It offers picnicking and a few short trails, but the big attraction is the view. Mount Jefferson rises abruptly more than 1,600 feet above the surrounding landscape. Visitors can see the farms and forests of a great part of the county from its summit. For information, contact Mount Jefferson State Natural Area, P.O. Box 48, Jefferson, N.C. 28640 (336-246-9653).

- See the sidebar about the New River for information on **New River State Park**.

  The big pastimes in Ashe County are canoeing and tubing on the New River. Because the water flows so gently, the river is safe even for young children. Local outfitters give lessons and provide inner tubes, canoes, safety equipment, and shuttle service. Contact *Zaloo's Canoes* (800-535-4027; www.zaloos.com) near Jefferson, *New River Outfitters* (800-982-9190; www.canoethenew.com) near Jefferson, or *Appalachian Adventures* (336-877-8800; www.appalachianadventures.com) in Todd.

SEASONAL EVENTS

■ *Christmas in July* is held in downtown West Jefferson during the weekend nearest the Fourth of July. Workers in the area's Christmas tree industry challenge each other for cash and prizes in a variety of competitions. You can hear live music and purchase crafts and other items from the vendors who line the streets. Call 336-246-9550 or visit www.ashechamber.com.

Places to Stay

INNS AND BED-AND-BREAKFASTS

■ *River House Inn*. Deluxe/Expensive. 1896 Old Field Creek Road, Grassy Creek (336-982-2109; www.riverhousenc.com). Owned by Gayle Winston, a well-known restaurateur and innkeeper, this inn offers eight guest rooms, each with a private bath and a Jacuzzi. Most of the rooms have views of the mountains and/or the river; some have private porches. Two cabins located beside the millpond are also available. The inn is situated on 170 acres with a mile of riverfront; it offers two tennis courts. Coffee and tea are left by guests' doors in the morning. A full breakfast is served. The inn frequently hosts live music in the evenings.

■ *Buffalo Tavern Bed-and-Breakfast*. Expensive. 958 West Buffalo Road, West Jefferson (336-877-2873; www.buffalotavern.com). This Southern Colonial home was originally a tavern. It was the place to go during the 1920s. Today, it offers three guest rooms, each with a private bath, a fireplace with gas logs, and a claw-foot tub. A guest refrigerator, complimentary beverages, and laundry service are available. A two-night minimum stay is required for weekends and holidays. No children are allowed.

■ *French Knob Inn*. Expensive. 133 Ferguson Road, West Jefferson (336-246-5177; www.frenchknobinn.com). Located two miles from West Jefferson and seven miles from the Blue Ridge Parkway, this inn rests in the valley of Frenches Knob. Its six guest rooms have Victorian furniture and private baths; two have Jacuzzis. A full American breakfast is included in the room rate.

■ *Glendale Springs Inn*. Expensive. 7414 N.C. 16, Glendale Springs (800-287-1206 or 336-982-2103; www.glendalespringsinn.com). Located 0.3 mile from Milepost 259 on the parkway, this authentic country inn was built about 100 years ago. The original historic structure contains five guest rooms, all with private baths. The guesthouse contains four rooms; the two first-floor rooms have a fireplace and a Jacuzzi. Amenities include a full breakfast, afternoon tea, cable television, air conditioning, a fax machine, and a copier. A minimum two-day stay is required on certain holidays and weekends.

Places to Eat

■ *Club at Jefferson Landing*. Expensive. At the Jefferson Landing Golf Club near Jefferson (336-982-7378). The clubhouse dining area seats 170. The Jefferson Landing Grille seats 70 for casual dining. Dinner is served in the clubhouse dining area Wednesday through Saturday; brunch is served on Sunday. Reservations are recommended. The grille is open for lunch and dinner every day.

■ *Glendale Springs Inn and Restaurant*. Expensive. 7414 N.C. 16, Glendale Springs (800-287-1206 or 336-982-2103; www.glendalespringsinn.com). This is the place President Bill Clinton and Vice President Al Gore chose for their weekly private "Thursday lunch" while they were in the area to dedicate the New River as an American Heritage River. The inn has three dining areas. The seafood is fresh, and the herbs are grown in the inn's own garden. Beer and wine are offered. Lunch and dinner are served Thursday through Tuesday.

- **River House Inn and Restaurant**. Expensive. 1896 Old Field Creek Road, Grassy Creek (336-982-2109; www.riverhousenc.com). Anyone in Winston-Salem can tell you how good Gayle Winston's restaurants are; she is still the owner of the Salem Tavern in historic Old Salem. At River House Inn, she features Country French cuisine and regional fare. Beer and wine are offered; reservations are required. Dinner is served nightly.

- **Shatley Springs Inn**. Moderate. 407 Shatley Springs Road, Crumpler, off N.C. 16 five miles north of Jefferson (336-982-2236). This is one of those all-the-home-cooking-you-can-eat places. Its fixed-price meals include fried chicken, country ham, tons of vegetables, and homemade cobbler. In the summer and fall, you may have to wait for a table. Luckily, you can try one of the rocking chairs on the front porch, where guests are entertained by occasional bluegrass music. Breakfast, lunch, and dinner are served from May through October.

- **Garden Gate Café**. Inexpensive. 3 East Main Street, West Jefferson (336-246-2996). This café features homemade soups, salads, vegetarian dishes, and daily specials. Lunch is served Monday through Saturday.

- **Greenfield Restaurant**. Inexpensive. On Mount Jefferson Road off U.S. 221 in West Jefferson (336-246-9671). Greenfield has been serving family-style meals for years. Now, guests can also order steaks and American, Italian, and seafood dishes from a menu. Breakfast, lunch, and dinner are served daily.

- **Lily and the Three Bears Sandwich and Bakery**. Inexpensive. In Glendale Springs next to Greenhouse Crafts (336-982-4442; www.mtnviewlodge.com/threebears.html). This café features Belgian waffles, home-smoked meats, homemade yeast buns, pies, and sugar-free jellies. Breakfast and lunch are served Tuesday through Sunday; call for winter hours.

A view of Appalachian State University and downtown Boone
PHOTOGRAPH BY JUDI SCHARNS, COURTESY OF BOONE CONVENTION AND
VISITORS BUREAU

BOONE

by Carolyn Sakowski

*B*oone is home to Appalachian State University, a branch of the University of North Carolina that has seen amazing growth in recent years. If you haven't visited the campus in the last 10 years, you won't recognize it. Along with the growth of the university has come predictable urban sprawl. Boone is where everyone who lives in the area does their regular shopping. The town has an indoor mall and several strip shopping centers, as well as all the usual chain motels and eateries.

But there's also a lively downtown area that was recently honored for its revitalization efforts. It was recognized by the National Trust for Historic Preservation as a National Main Street Center, a highly coveted honor.

This chapter also includes the scenic Valle Crucis, North Carolina's only Rural Historic District; for more information, try their website at www.vallecrucis.com. In 1915, local historian John Preston Arthur wrote, "There is a dreamy spell which hangs over this little valley." Although many remember the spell as being stronger a few decades ago, this area still retains its mystique. Much of the history of Valle Crucis revolves around the work of the Episcopal Church. You can still see their historic buildings—a cabin built by Bishop L. Silliman Ives, a conference center, and a small church. The other historic buildings that draw tourists to Valle Crucis are the Mast Farm Inn and the Mast General Store complex.

To get to Boone, you can take either U.S. 321 or U.S. 421. Both N.C. 105 and N.C. 194 terminate here. You can reach Valle Crucis by traveling on N.C. 105 from Boone and turning on to S.R. 1112.

For visitor information, contact the Boone Chamber of Commerce/Boone Convention and Visitors Bureau, 208 Howard Street, Boone, N.C. 28607 (800-852-9506 or 828-2624-2225; www.boonechamber.com), or North Carolina High Country Host, 1700 Blowing Rock Road, Boone, N.C. 28607 (800-438-7500 or 828-264-1299; www.highcountryhost.com).

The *Watauga Democrat* is published three times a week. *Mountain Times*, a free weekly, offers news and events listings; you can access its excellent website at www.mountaintimes.com.

Things to Do

HISTORIC PLACES, GARDENS, AND TOURS

■ *Daniel Boone Native Gardens* is sponsored by the Garden Club of North Carolina. Located in Daniel Boone Park adjacent to the amphitheater where *Horn in the West* is performed, the gardens can be reached by following the signs from U.S. 421, U.S. 321, U.S. 221, and N.C. 105 Extension. The gardens, which opened in 1966, feature a collection of native North Carolina plants. Visitors enjoy a fern garden, a bog garden, a sunken garden, a natural spring, a rhododendron thicket, an arbor, and a meadow. The wrought-iron gates were made by Daniel Boone VI. From May through October, the gardens are open daily from 9 A.M. to 6 P.M.; they remain open until 8 P.M. when *Horn in the West* is in production. An admission fee is charged. Call 828-264-6390.

- The **Appalachian Cultural Museum** was created to foster an understanding of the mountain heritage. The permanent exhibit features objects ranging from fossils to Winston Cup racecars to a section of the yellow brick road from the Land of Oz theme park. You can see exhibits about African-Americans in the Appalachians, the soldiers who fought in the Civil War, moonshining, weaving and quilting, mountain music, Jack tales and the oral storytelling tradition, snowmaking for the ski industry, and the Blue Ridge Parkway. The museum is located on University Hall Drive just off U.S. 321 (Blowing Rock Road) near the university campus. It is open Tuesday through Sunday; an admission fee is charged. For information, call 828-262-3117, or visit their website at www.museum.appstate.edu.

Mast General Store
PHOTOGRAPH BY
CAROLYN SAKOWSKI

SPECIAL SHOPPING

- **Mast General Store**, located on N.C. 194 in Valle Crucis, is the granddaddy of the area's restored general stores. It opened in 1883 and quickly gained a reputation for carrying everything from "cradles to caskets." Even today, you'll find goods ranging from hiking boots to reproductions of antique cooking utensils to mountain toys. The post office inside the store is still used by local residents, as is the huge potbellied stove, which you'll notice as soon as you enter.

The **Mast Store Annex** is located just down the road. Here, you'll find casual clothing and a complete outfitter's shop. The best part is the candy store, where you'll rediscover candies that you haven't seen since childhood.

You can also visit their outlet, **Old Boone Mercantile**, located on Howard Street in downtown Boone.

Mast General Store is open from 7 A.M. to 6:30 P.M. Monday through Saturday and from 1 P.M. to 6 P.M. on Sunday; the Boone store opens at 10 A.M. For information, call 828-963-6511, or visit their website at www.mastgeneralstore.com.

■ The **Todd General Store** is 10 miles south of West Jefferson and 11 miles north of Boone off N.C. 194. It overlooks the South Fork of the New River from its location on Railroad Grade Road, which has turned into one of the most scenic bike routes in the area. Established in 1914, the store features crafts, collectibles, antiques, country ham, baked goods, and an old-time candy shop. Its summer hours are from 7 A.M. to 7 P.M. Monday through Saturday and from 12:30 P.M. to 5 P.M. on Sunday. Call 336-877-1067.

■ **Wilcox Emporium Warehouse** is located at 161 Howard Street in historic downtown Boone. This historic 60,000-square-foot space has more than 180 vendors. You'll find art, antiques, collectibles, furnishings, food, gifts, and even a brewpub. Its summer hours are 10 A.M. to 6 P.M. Monday through Thursday, 10 A.M. to 8 P.M. on Friday and Saturday, and 1 P.M. to 6 P.M. on Sunday. For information, call 828-262-1221, or visit their website at www.wilcoxemporium.com.

■ In the past 10 years, the number of artists in the High Country has grown from a handful to over 200. These are not just your average mountain craftspeople; these artists work in all mediums in traditional, contemporary, and exploratory genres. You can get an excellent brochure listing all the fine craft and art galleries in Boone, Blowing Rock, Valle Crucis, and Foscoe by calling the High Country Host office and asking for their **Gallery Guide**. You can also find listings in the free tabloid **2000 Summer Times**, published by **Mountain Times**; try their website at www.mountaintimes.com.

Tweetsie Railroad
PHOTOGRAPH BY JUDI SCHARNS
COURTESY OF BOONE CONVENTION AND
VISITORS BUREAU

RECREATION

■ Located on U.S. 321 about halfway between Boone and Blowing Rock, *Tweetsie Railroad* is one of North Carolina's earliest theme parks. The centerpiece of this recreated Wild West town is a historic, narrow-gauge, coal-fired steam locomotive that used to carry passengers on a daily 66-mile trip from Johnson City, Tennessee, to Boone. In addition to riding the train (where you might get attacked by robbers), you can take the chairlift up the mountain to pan for gold, pet friendly animals, try the amusement rides, and take in a show that includes music and clogging. From mid-May to mid-August, Tweetsie Railroad is open daily from 9 A.M. to 6 P.M.; from mid-August to the end of October, it is open on weekends; it is also open Labor Day Monday. An admission fee is charged. For information, call 800-526-5740 or 828-264-9061, or visit their website at www.tweetsie.com.

■ Next to Tweetsie is *Mystery Hill*, founded in 1949. A day pass gains you access to four different areas. The main attraction for all these years has been a house where you have to stand at a 45-degree angle to keep from falling over. You can also see water flow uphill and see a swing that defies gravity. In the Hall of Mystery are hands-on experiments where you can lose your shadow, stand inside a giant soap bubble, and see several optical illusions. At the Appalachian Heritage Museum, you'll see antiques and artifacts showing how mountain families lived at the turn of the 20th century; the exhibit is housed in the Dougherty House, which was built by the brothers who were instrumental in the founding of Appalachian State University. The final section exhibits over 50,000 Native American artifacts. Mystery Hill is open daily all year. Hours vary with the season. An admission fee is charged. Call 828-264-2792.

■ The cool summer climate is perfect for golfing. This area has been a golf mecca since the first holes were built in Linville in 1895. Although the really famous mountain courses are private, some excellent courses around Boone are open to the public. Among them are **Blue Ridge Country Club** (828-756-4013), **Boone Golf Club** (828-264-8760), and **Willow Valley** (828-963-6865).

If you want to read brief descriptions of area courses, check out www.mountaintimes.com.

■ A sport that has exploded on the High Country scene in recent years is cycling—whether it be mountain biking or road biking. Sugar Mountain opens 20 miles of trails in and around its ski slopes during the summer months. Both mountain-bike races and road races are held in the area. Here are some of the local shops that offer bike rentals: **Appalachian Adventures** (336-877-8800) in Todd; **Boone Bike and Touring** (828-262-5750); **Magic Cycles** (828-265-2211); and **Rock & Roll Sports** (828-264-0765).

■ Several outfitters offer whitewater rafting trips down the Nolichucky and Watauga Rivers and on Wilson Creek: **Appalachian Adventures** (336-877-8800), **Appalachian Challenge Guide Service** (888-844-RAFT or 828-898-6484), **B-Cliff** (800-592-2262), **Cherokee Adventures** (800-445-7238), **Edge of the World** (800-789-3343), **High Mountain Expeditions** (828-898-9786), **Wahoo's Adventures** (800-444-RAFT or 828-262-5775), and **Watauga Kayak Tours and Outfitters** (888-277-1757).

Some of these same outfitters offer rock-climbing trips. **Footsloggers Outdoor and Travel Outfitters**, with stores in Boone and Blowing Rock, has a climbing tower in Boone. It rents equipment, gives instruction, and offers trips. Call 828-262-5111.

- One activity that doesn't require a guide is hiking. This area is flush with trails that can provide any length or difficulty of hike you're seeking. For information about the parkway trails, see the Blue Ridge Parkway chapter. Pisgah National Forest offers trails in Linville Gorge, Wilson Creek, Lost Cove Cliffs, and Harper Creek. For information about hiking in the National Forest, contact the Grandfather Ranger District, Route 1, Box 110-A, Nebo, N.C. 28761 (828-652-2144).

SEASONAL EVENTS

- Since 1952, Kermit Hunter's outdoor drama, **Horn in the West**, has played on summer nights. The story is set during the American Revolution, when Daniel Boone and the mountain men struggled against the British and the Cherokees led by Dragging Canoe. Who cares about historical accuracy? It's fun to sit outside under the stars and watch the drama unfold. There's lots of whooping and gunfire to keep things lively. From late June through mid-August, the show plays nightly except on Monday. Performances begin at 8 P.M., just as the sun starts to set. An admission fee is charged. You can reach the amphitheater by following the signs from U.S. 421, U.S. 321, U.S. 221, or N.C. 105 Extension. For information, call 828-264-2120.

- *An Appalachian Summer Festival* is a series of music, dance, art, and theater performances that spans the month of July. Past performers have included the Paul Taylor Dance Company, Willie Nelson, the Preservation Hall Jazz Band, Mary Chapin Carpenter, the Duke Ellington Orchestra, and the North Carolina Symphony. Workshops in writing, dance, and art are also offered. An admission fee is charged for most events, which are usually held on the campus of Appalachian State University. For information, call 800-841-ARTS, or visit their website at www.appsummer.appstate.edu.

- *Valle Country Fair* has been held during an October weekend for over 20 years. Since it happens during the height of the fall foliage season, thousands of tourists flock to Valle Crucis. Part crafts fair, part old-time cooking fair, this event attracts top craftsmen and the best canners of preserves in the area. There's old-time music and dancing. One of the highlights is the cooking of apple butter from scratch. For information, call the Mast General Store at 828-963-6511.

Places to Stay

RESORTS, HOTELS, AND MOTELS

▪ **The Broyhill Inn and Conference Center**. Moderate. 96 Bodenheimer Drive, Appalachian State University (800-951-6048 or 828-262-2205; www.highcountryhost.com/nc/broyhill). This inn has 76 guest rooms and seven suites. It is run by Appalachian State University and primarily serves as a conference center. The full-service dining room is quite good; there is also a lounge for guests. During the summer, visitors enjoy great views from the outdoor patios; during the winter, they stay warm by the large native stone fireplace.

▪ **High Country Inn**. Moderate. 1785 N.C. 105 (800-334-5605 or 828-264-1000; www.highcountryinn.com). This inn has 120 recently renovated guest rooms and suites. Each has cable television. Some king-sized rooms have a fireplace. The suites have a Jacuzzi. The efficiency suites have a kitchen, a den, a fireplace, and a Jacuzzi. A sports lounge, a restaurant, an indoor/outdoor pool, a hot tub, a sauna, and a fitness center are on the premises.

▪ **Quality Inn Appalachian Conference Center**. Moderate. 949 Blowing Rock Road at the intersection of U.S. 321 and N.C. 105 (828-262-0020; www.qualityinnboone.com). Quality Inn was one of the first chains to move into the area and for many years was the only show in town if you wanted to have meetings. The rooms here have queen- or king-sized beds and cable television. Guests receive a complimentary newspaper. A heated indoor/outdoor pool, a restaurant and lounge, and meeting space are available.

- **The Inn at Taylor House**. Deluxe. N.C. 194, Valle Crucis (828-963-5581; www.highsouth.com/taylorhouse). Taylor House, built in 1910, has been described as "country elegant." Its seven rooms all have private baths. Two rooms are located in a nearby cottage and one in the innkeeper's house. A two-course gourmet breakfast is served each morning.

- **Lovill House Inn**. Deluxe. 404 Old Bristol Road (800-849-9466 or 828-264-4205; www.lovillhouseinn.com). Housed in an 1875 farmhouse with a wraparound porch, this inn offers a private bath, cable television, a ceiling fan, bathrobes, a hair dryer, a clock radio, and a telephone in each room. Some rooms have gas-log fireplaces. Early-morning coffee and tea are served before the complimentary breakfast. A cottage behind the farmhouse is available for rent.

- **Mast Farm Inn**. Deluxe. 2543 Broadstone Road (S.R. 1112) on the way to Valle Crucis (888-963-5857 or 828-963-5857; www.MastFarmInn.com).

Mast Farm Inn
PHOTOGRAPH BY CAROLYN SAKOWSKI

Mast Farm Inn is a huge, rambling three-story farmhouse with a wrap-around porch. Built in 1885, it began operating as an inn in the early 1900s. The guest rooms, most of which have private baths, are furnished with country antiques and old quilts; some of the nine rooms have their original wood paneling. Four guest cottages are also available for rent, including the farm's old loom house. A wonderful restaurant is on the premises.

■ **The River Farm Inn**. Deluxe. 179 River Run Bridge Road in Fleetwood, about 20 miles northeast of Boone (336-877-1728; www.riverfarminn.com). This inn, housed in a reconstructed 1880s dairy barn, offers two incredible suites. One is French Country and the other Victorian in style. Both have 12-foot Palladian windows offering a view of the river. Each suite has a queen-sized bed, a large Jacuzzi, a gas-log stove, satellite television, a CD player, a full kitchen and bath, central air and heat, ceiling fans, room phones, and hair dryers. A three-bedroom log cabin and a carriage-house suite are also available for rent. Guests receive a welcome basket of beverages, fruit, and baked goods. They enjoy the porches, the sumptuous lawns, the gazebo down by the river, and the Adirondack chairs by the outdoor fireplace. Two-night minimums are required for the weekends and three nights for holidays.

■ **The Baird House**. Deluxe/Expensive. 1451 Watauga River Road, near the Mast General Store in Valle Crucis (800-297-1342 or 828-297-4055; www.bairdhouse.com). This Colonial farmhouse was built in 1790. The inn rests on 16 acres of rolling pasture overlooking the Watauga River. A full country breakfast is served.

■ **Bluestone Lodge**. Deluxe/Expensive. Near the intersection of N.C. 105 and S.R. 1112 (Broadstone Road), which leads to Valle Crucis (828-963-5177; www.bluestone-lodge.com). This is more of an inn than a restored home. It offers two rooms with kitchenettes and full baths and a cozy bungalow with a deck, a whirlpool bath, a kitchenette, and a gas-log stove. The Tree House Suite has vaulted cedar ceilings, huge windows, a large deck, a stone fireplace, a whirlpool bath, and a full kitchen. The main lodge includes a hot tub, a sauna room, and a living area with a fireplace. Guests receive a full breakfast.

Places to Eat

Boone is the High Country town where the chains are best represented. If you're looking for unique dining, you might want to make the short drive to Blowing Rock.

■ *Mast Farm Inn*. Expensive. S.R. 1112 on the way to Valle Crucis (888-963-5857 or 828-963-5857; www.MastFarmInn.com). The restaurant is housed in the same historic farmhouse as the inn. The "Gourmet Country" fare includes interesting items like "Sautéed Shrimp with White Cheddar Grits" and "Artichoke Parmesan-Filled Ravioli." Lunch and dinner are served Tuesday through Saturday; brunch is offered on Sunday. Reservations are suggested.

■ *The Daniel Boone Inn Restaurant*. Moderate. At the junction of U.S. 321 and U.S. 421 (828-264-8657). Opened in 1959, this family-style restaurant is an institution. In the summers, the crowds line up across the porch and down the walk. The fixed-price meals begin with a salad in the summer and soup in the winter; they include three meats, five vegetables, homemade biscuits, a beverage, and desserts. Breakfast, lunch, and dinner are served daily.

■ *Pepper's*. Inexpensive. 240 Shadowline Road in the Shops at Shadowline (828-262-7111). Opened in 1975, Pepper's has been a Boone staple ever since. The menu includes sandwiches, seafood, pasta, and homemade desserts. Lunch and dinner are served daily.

A scene from Blowing Rock
COURTESY OF BLOWING ROCK CHAMBER OF COMMERCE

BLOWING ROCK

by Carolyn Sakowski

*B*lowing Rock began to attract summer residents in the 1880s. At the town's elevation of 4,000 feet, summer temperatures rarely climb over 80 degrees. In the early days, most visitors spent the entire summer. Some built beautiful Victorian summer homes, many of which still stand.

Blowing Rock has always catered to an upscale crowd. Because of this, it's been relatively easy for the town to maintain its quaint character through zoning regulations. Most of what passes for urban sprawl has been consigned to the bypass, while the downtown buildings have gone through constant refurbishing.

The village is an easy drive from Boone. Because Blowing Rock literally hangs on the side of the mountain, you'll find incredible views of the John's River Gorge from various points in the town.

Blowing Rock is located seven miles south of Boone where U.S. 321 and U.S. 221 join and become Blowing Rock Road.

For visitor information, contact the Blowing Rock Chamber of Commerce, P.O. Box 406, Blowing Rock, N.C. 28605 (800-295-7851 or 828-295-7851; www.blowingrock.com). The visitor center is located at 132 Park Avenue, to the side of the park. It has an excellent selection of menus from area restaurants, in addition to all the usual travel brochures.

The *Blowing Rocket* is the weekly newspaper. Events are also covered in *Mountain Times*, a free weekly.

Things to Do

SPECIAL SHOPPING

■ *Parkway Craft Center*, located at Moses S. Cone Memorial Park at Milepost 294 on the Blue Ridge Parkway, has served as a showcase for the Southern Highland Craft Guild for nearly 50 years. In this historic home built by Moses and Bertha Cone, you'll find weaving, basketry, pottery, woodcarvings, and glass and metal work. Craft demonstrations are usually going on. If you're up for a nice walk, ask how to get to the Cones' grave sites. The center is open from late March through November. Call 828-295-7938.

■ The *Shoppes on the Parkway*, located on U.S. 321, are a group of brand-name outlet stores. Some of these stores have real bargains, so the parking lot is usually full. For information, call 800-720-6728 or 828-295-444, or visit their website at www.tangeroutlet.com.

The Parkway Craft Center at Moses S. Cone Memorial Park
PHOTOGRAPH BY CAROLYN SAKOWSKI

RECREATION

▪ The **Blowing Rock** is an immense cliff that hangs 3,000 feet over the John's River Gorge. The rock walls form a flume that sweeps the northwest wind upward with such force that it blows light objects back up the mountain.

There's not much to see at this attraction other than the spectacular view. On clear days, you can see Mount Mitchell, Grandfather Mountain, Table Rock, and Hawksbill. The Blowing Rock is located off U.S. 321 near the Green Park Inn. Call 828-295-7111.

Hiking brochures are available at the Blowing Rock Chamber of Commerce.

▪ Those interested in two-wheel adventures around Blowing Rock may rent bikes from **High Mountain Expeditions** (828-295-4200), **Boone Bike and Touring** (828-262-5750), **Magic Cycles** (828-265-2211), or **Rock & Roll Sports** (828-264-0765).

▪ For those who'd rather get their thrills on skis, **Appalachian Ski Mountain** is located near Blowing Rock. Call 800-322-2373, or visit their website at www.appskimtn.com. More ski slopes are listed in the chapter on Banner Elk, Beech Mountain, and Linville.

SEASONAL EVENTS

▪ For almost 40 years, Blowing Rock Memorial Park has been turned into a crafts festival one Saturday each month from May to October. *Art in the Park* has blossomed into a big attraction, with over 100 juried art and craft exhibits. For information, call the Blowing Rock Chamber of Commerce at 828-295-7851.

▪ Held in late July, the **Blowing Rock Charity Horse Show** has been one of the top equestrian events in the Southeast for almost 80 years. Centered at the Blowing Rock Stables off U.S. 221 west of town, this two-week-long English saddle event features hunters/jumpers and American Saddlebreds in competition. For information, call 828-295-7851 or 828-295-9861, or visit www.blowingrock.com.

Places to Stay

RESORTS, HOTELS, AND MOTELS

Blowing Rock has several small motels that have been locally owned and operated for years. They are all lovingly maintained, and you will rarely go wrong with any of them. You'll find them along Sunset Drive and North Main Street.

▪ **Chetola Lodge and Conference Center**. Deluxe. Just off U.S. 321 on North Main Street (800-243-8652 or 828-295-5500; www.Chetola.com). The manor house here, started in 1846, is the centerpiece of a fabulous former summer estate. The resort now encompasses 87 acres of beautifully landscaped grounds surrounding a lake. The lodge, a modern addition, offers guest rooms. You can also rent one-, two-, and three-bedroom condominiums that have fireplaces, fully equipped kitchens, and outdoor decks. A first-class sports center, an indoor swimming pool, a whirlpool, a sauna, and massage therapy are offered. You can play tennis or racquetball, hike, fish, ride horses, or go mountain biking. Chetola offers meeting space and has a first-class restaurant.

■ *Green Park Inn*. Deluxe. U.S. 321 (800-852-2462 or 828-295-3141; www.greenparkinn.com). Established in 1882, this impressive old 85-room inn is listed on the National Register of Historic Places. It offers golf and tennis packages at the nearby Blowing Rock Country Club. A fine restaurant is on the premises. In recent years, the inn has undergone several management changes and at times has not been up to standards. However, it deserves one more try.

■ *Westglow Spa*. Deluxe. 2845 U.S. 221 South (800-562-0807 or 828-295-4463; www.westglow.com). The historic mansion, built in 1917 as the home of artist Elliott Daingerfield, now offers elegantly restored bedroom suites. Cottages are also available for rent. The prices are high here because the whole focus is the adjoining Life Enhancement Center, a world-class spa that offers a variety of packages including body massages, herbal body wraps, facials, and hair and nail services. If you stay at the mansion, your package will include meals as well as privileges at the spa.

■ *Meadowbrook Inn*. Deluxe/Expensive. 711 North Main Street (800-456-5456 or 828-295-4300; www.meadowbrook-inn.com). This 61-room inn is a few blocks from Blowing Rock Memorial Park, the town's center. Each room has a terrace, a gas fireplace, and a whirlpool tub for two. Some suites have a wet bar, a refrigerator, and a microwave. The top-of-the-line pool suites are unique. What appears to be a closet leads down a spiral staircase into your own private swimming pool. These are not Jacuzzis, but rather eight-foot-wide, 14-foot-long, four-foot-deep in-room swimming pools. A fully equipped fitness center, a full-sized swimming pool, bicycles, and a Jacuzzi are available for all hotel guests. A full-service restaurant, a bar, and meeting rooms are on the premises.

■ *Azalea Garden Inn*. Expensive. North Main Street (828-295-3272). The first thing that strikes you about this inn is its landscaping. The owners go all out in covering the one-acre setting with flowering perennials. The rooms have either two full-sized beds or one king-sized bed, air-conditioning, and cable television. An authentic log cabin on the premises is also available for rent; it has a log-burning fireplace, a kitchen, and two queen-sized beds. Guests enjoy complimentary morning coffee on the veranda, where they have a view of the abundant flowers.

- **Cliff Dwellers Inn.** Expensive. 116 Lakeview Terrace, one mile south of the Blue Ridge Parkway off U.S. 321 (800-322-7380 or 828-295-3121; www.cliffdwellers.com). All the rooms here have king- or queen-sized beds, cable television, telephones, coffee makers, refrigerators, air conditioning, and ceiling fans. Some suites have gas-log fireplaces and Jacuzzis. A heated pool and a hot tub are located at the gazebo. The grounds feature beautiful rock walls and a large perennial garden.

INNS AND BED-AND-BREAKFASTS

- **Gideon Ridge Inn.** Deluxe. 202 Gideon Ridge Road near the Blowing Rock (828-295-3644; www.ridge-inn.com). Housed in an elegant former summer home, this 10-room inn offers a spectacular view of the John's River Gorge—the same view you'll pay a lot to see at the nearby Blowing Rock attraction. *Country Inns Magazine* called this "one of the ten best inns in America." Stone terraces are everywhere, most with incredible views of the mountains or the perennial gardens. The library has a lovely stone fireplace. Breakfast is served in a room that offers a wonderful view of the surrounding mountains. Some rooms have Jacuzzis and fireplaces; all have first-class amenities.

- **The Inn at Ragged Gardens.** Deluxe. 203 Sunset Drive (828-295-9703; www.ragged-gardens.com). Here is a fully restored summer home built in the early 1900s. It sits in the center of an acre of colorful gardens just a block from Blowing Rock Memorial Park. The chestnut siding is a distinctive aspect of local architecture; unfortunately, it is no longer used, since the chestnut blight destroyed the source. Local granite was used in the entry columns, the flooring, and the staircase. Inside, you'll find chestnut-paneled walls and beams and a large rock fireplace. The rooms have goose-down comforters and pillows, fireplaces, private baths, and ceiling fans. Most offer balconies, sitting rooms, and one- or two-person whirlpools. Breakfast is served in a dining room that overlooks the rock-walled garden.

▪ *Maple Lodge Bed-and-Breakfast*. Expensive. On Sunset Drive a short walk from Blowing Rock Memorial Park (828-295-3331; www.maplelodge.net). The 11 rooms here are furnished with a blend of antiques and family heirlooms. Each has a goose-down comforter on a four-poster or lace-canopy bed. Each also has a private bath. The library has a stone fireplace. A full breakfast is served in the dining room, which overlooks a wildflower garden.

Places to Eat

▪ *The Best Cellar*. Expensive. Off U.S. 321 Bypass (828-295-3466; www.thebestcellar.com). This place is difficult to find, so you may want to call for directions. The Best Cellar has been one of the top restaurants in the area for over 20 years. The original part of the restaurant is a 60-year-old log cabin. Among the favorites here are the raw oyster bar, the Angus beef, and the fresh seafood. Dinner is served Monday through Saturday from May to November and Thursday through Monday the rest of the year. Reservations are recommended.

▪ *Crippen's Country Inn and Restaurant*. Expensive. 239 Sunset Drive (877-295-3487 or 828-295-3487; www.crippens.com). Crippen's has consistently received glowing reviews from food critics across the country, including those at *Southern Living* and the *New York Times*. The menu changes daily, but the restaurant's website will give you a feel for what to expect. How about "Applewood-Smoked, Bacon-Wrapped Grilled Loin of Venison with Acorn Squash, Summer Vegetables, and Mango Chutney"? Or "Almond-and-Peppercorn-Crusted Chilean Salmon with Golden-Raisin Couscous, Pineapple Relish, and Crispy Fried Leeks"? Not your typical restaurant fare, huh? All desserts are made on the premises. Dinner is served nightly from June through October and Thursday, Friday, and Saturday the rest of the year; an expanded schedule is offered between Christmas and New Year's.

- **The Manor House Restaurant at Chetola**. Expensive. Just off U.S. 321 on North Main Street (828-295-5505; www.chetola.com). This restaurant occupies a restored 1846 manor house. It serves mountain specialties in the dining rooms and on the patio overlooking the lake. Breakfast, lunch, and dinner are served daily; Sunday brunch is offered during the summer. Dinner reservations are recommended.

- **Navelli's Italian Chop House and Seafood Grille**. Expensive/Moderate. U.S. 321 near the Blue Ridge Parkway (828-295-0802). The name pretty much says it all. Navelli's serves seafood and Italian-style steaks and chops. Dinner is served seven days a week; lunch is offered on Sunday. The restaurant shares an entrance with the New River Inn.

- **The Riverwood**. Expensive/Moderate. 7179 Valley Boulevard off U.S. 321 (828-295-4162; www.theriverwood.com). The cuisine here includes grilled fresh fish, marinated beef tenderloin, fresh pasta, sautéed shrimp and chicken, and mountain trout. The dressings and desserts are homemade. Dinner is served Monday through Saturday in the summer and Wednesday through Saturday during the winter. Reservations are recommended.

- **The Original Emporium Restaurant**. Moderate/Inexpensive. 8960 U.S. 321 Bypass (828-295-7661). This restaurant started out as a wine-and-cheese shop but now caters to those who want good burgers, sandwiches, and salads. One of the main attractions is the fabulous view. While enjoying a reasonably priced meal, you'll get to see the John's River Gorge and stare straight into the profile of Grandfather Mountain. Lunch and dinner are served daily year-round.

- **Woodlands BBQ**. Inexpensive. U.S. 321 Bypass (828-295-3651; www.woodlandsbbq.com). This establishment has been a Blowing Rock staple for years. It smokes its own ribs, chicken, beef, and pork (sliced or chopped) and offers a variety of sandwich and plate options. It also serves burritos, tacos, and nachos. A full-service lounge is on the premises. Entertainment is offered nightly. Lunch and dinner are served daily.

The Scottish Clans gather at the foot of Grandfather Mountain.
PHOTOGRAPH BY HUGH MORTON
COURTESY OF BOONE CONVENTION AND VISITORS BUREAU

BANNER ELK,
BEECH MOUNTAIN,
AND LINVILLE

by Carolyn Sakowski

*A*very County offers several distinctly different communities.

The area around Newland, the county seat, is where many of the longtime, year-round residents live. You won't find much evidence of a tourism boom here.

The community of Linville, established in the late 1880s, was planned as an exclusive resort area. It remains that today. Its lovely old homes have a distinctive architectural flavor, largely because of the chestnut siding found on many of them. This community is still very private, as are the Grandfather Golf and Country Club and Linville Ridge Club. When these exclusive clubs came to the area, so did wealthy summer residents.

At 5,506 feet, Beech Mountain claims to be the highest town in eastern North America. Because this community is a year-round tourist mecca, this is where you'll find the bulk of the county's high-end accommodations.

Linville Gorge
Wilderness Area in
Pisgah National Forest
PHOTOGRAPH BY
CAROLYN SAKOWSKI

At the foot of Beech Mountain is Banner Elk. Because it is home to Lees-McRae College, the village has a bit of a college-town flavor. Here, you'll find quaint bed-and-breakfasts and excellent restaurants. Since the arrival of skiing as a winter draw, Banner Elk also claims many of the county's year-round citizens.

Today, retirees are discovering that the climate in the North Carolina mountains is not as severe as they had previously thought. Thanks to improved road conditions and crews that keep the roads open to serve the area's ski resorts, more and more people are coming to the area to live year-round.

Avery County still has some of the strangest liquor laws in the country. Some clubs have become quite creative about getting exemptive legislation passed that allows them to serve alcoholic beverages. Visitors find it illogical when they walk into one convenience store and learn that beer and wine are not sold there, then visit another store owned by the same chain just a mile down the highway and find those items stocked.

When you're traveling through the county, note the strange building atop one of the region's most prominent peaks. Although this structure spoils the view from all over the county, the good news is that it caused everyone throughout western North Carolina to wake up and pass a "ridge law" to prevent multistory buildings from being constructed on the ridge tops.

In Avery County, you'll find excellent accommodations and restaurants and attractions such as Grandfather Mountain, Linville Falls, and Linville Caverns. The county can also claim more ski slopes than any other in the Southeast.

JUST THE FACTS

Banner Elk is less than 20 miles southwest of Boone at the intersection of N.C. 194 and N.C. 184.

To reach Beech Mountain, go to Banner Elk and turn onto Beech Mountain Parkway; follow the signs to the ski resort.

Linville is located at the intersection of U.S. 221, N.C. 105, and N.C. 181 three miles west of Milepost 305.9 on the Blue Ridge Parkway.

For visitor information, contact the Avery–Banner Elk Chamber of Commerce. Its office is in the Shoppes at Tynecastle, located at the corner of N.C. 104 and N.C. 184. The mailing address is P.O. Box 335, Banner Elk, N.C. 28604. Call 800-972-2183 or 828-898-5605, or visit www.banner-elk.com. You can contact the Beech Mountain Chamber of Commerce at 403-A Beech Mountain Parkway, Beech Mountain, N.C. 28604. Its office is in Beech Mountain Town Hall near the top of the mountain. Call 800-468-5506 or 828-387-9283, or visit www.beechmtn.com.

The weekly newspaper is the *Avery Journal*. The county is also covered by *Mountain Times*, a free weekly that has a separate edition for this area.

Things to Do

SPECIAL SHOPPING

■ *Old Hampton Store and Grist Mill* is located off N.C. 181 on Ruffin Street in Linville. This old country store offers corn and wheat products ground right on the premises in a gristmill. The big draw here is hickory-smoked pork, beef, and chicken barbecue, served on homemade sourdough bread. The store is open Monday through Saturday from 10 A.M. to 5:30 P.M. and Sunday from 11 A.M. to 5 P.M. Call 828-733-5213.

▪ **Gardens of the Blue Ridge** is located off N.C. 181 on Pittman Gap Road; it is just off the Blue Ridge Parkway between Mileposts 312 and 313. This is North Carolina's oldest licensed nursery. Since 1872, this family-owned business has been selling wildflowers, trees, shrubs, and ferns. It ships native plants and wildflowers to customers all over the world. If you visit, you'll enjoy a variety of wildflowers seldom seen in one place. For information, call 828-733-2417, or visit their website at www.gardensoftheblueridge.com.

RECREATION

▪ The biggest attraction in Avery County, and perhaps the whole High Country, is **Grandfather Mountain**. The private part of this majestic mountain offers a wide range of activities. Be forewarned that admission is charged by the person, not the carload, and is fairly expensive.

After paying at the front entrance, you'll drive to the top of the mountain. Along the way, you can stop at the nature museum, which offers a short film about the mountain and exhibits about the area's flora, minerals, wildlife, and history; a gift shop and a snack bar are also on the premises. Next to the nature museum is the animal habitat, one of the top attractions on the mountain. Here, you can see black bears (there are usually some cubs around in the summer), rare cougars, a golden eagle, an American eagle, otters, deer, and other wildlife. It is best to arrive soon after the park opens because the best time to see the elusive cougars is right after they've been fed. The park maintains over 30 miles of hiking trails, some so steep that they employ ladders; those who don't wish to pay the whole admission fee can purchase a hiking permit to venture on to the trails. One of the biggest highlights is the famous Mile-High Swinging Bridge, straddled between two of Grandfather's peaks. You can glimpse this bridge from all over the area, but it's a whole new experience to walk across it and look into the gorge below.

The mountain itself stands 5,964 feet in the midst of the privately owned park. The park has been named a biosphere because of the 47 rare and endangered species found within its boundaries. It is open from 8 A.M. to 7 P.M. during the summer, from 8 A.M. to 6 P.M. in the spring and fall, and from 8 A.M. to 5 P.M. in the winter. Grandfather Mountain is located on U.S. 221 two miles northwest of Linville, just off Milepost 305.9 on the Blue Ridge Parkway. For information, call 800-468-7325 or 828-733-4337, or visit their website at www.grandfather.com.

▪ **Linville Caverns** is located on U.S. 221 between Linville and Marion, just four miles south of the Blue Ridge Parkway; take the Linville Falls Village exit off the parkway and turn left on U.S. 221. The cave was discovered in 1822 when some fishermen decided to follow trout that seemed to be swimming in and out of the mountain. Once inside the mountain, the fishermen discovered various rooms dripping with stalactites and stalagmites that had been forming for centuries.

New rock continues to form in the limestone cave today. The temperature is a constant 52 degrees year-round, so take a sweater. Linville Caverns is open daily from 9 A.M. to 6 P.M. June through Labor Day, from 9 A.M. to 4:30 P.M. during November and March, and from 9 A.M. to 5 P.M. during April, May, September, and October. It operates weekends only during December, January, and February. An admission fee is charged. For information, call 800-419-0540 or 828-756-4171, or visit their website at www.linvillecaverns.com.

▪ **Linville Falls** cascades 90 feet into Linville Gorge, a National Wilderness Preserve. Located at Milepost 317.4 on the Blue Ridge Parkway, the falls are accessible by a series of trails that can accommodate all types of hikers or walkers. You can take the 2.1-mile round-trip Linville Falls Trail to see the upper and lower falls. The hike to the upper falls is the easy one. Viewing the lower falls is more strenuous, but these falls are the ones you usually see on postcards.

▪ **Linville Gorge Wilderness Area**, located in the Grandfather Ranger District of Pisgah National Forest, is a favorite hiking, camping, fishing, and hunting area for locals as well as tourists. Because the trails here are not well marked, it is important to take topographical maps and a compass with you. For information about trails in the gorge, contact the Pisgah National Forest office at 828-652-2144, or consult the published hiking and mountain-biking books on the area's trails.

▪ If you want to see some relatively accessible, stunning views, consider

Linville Falls
PHOTOGRAPH BY CAROLYN SAKOWSKI

a trip to **Table Rock** or **Wiseman's View**. To get to both, you'll have to drive on gravel forest-service roads. You won't need a four-wheel drive, but you may not want to take your brand-new car. To get to Table Rock, take N.C. 181 to Gingercake Acres, where you'll see signs directing you to Table Rock Picnic Area. You'll drive through a residential area until you reach F.R. 210, where the pavement ends. It's about four miles on F.R. 210 to Table Rock. The route is well marked with signs. To reach Wiseman's View, take N.C. 183 North from Milepost 316.3 on the Blue Ridge Parkway. It is 0.7 mile from the town of Linville Falls to a road that runs four miles to the parking area.

▪ Additional opportunities for fishing, hiking, camping, and hunting are available in the **Lost Cove, Wilson Creek**, and **Harper Creek** areas of Pisgah National Forest.

▪ In the winter months, the big attraction is the area's ski slopes. Many now offer snowboarding and skating, as well as skiing; some even offer night skiing. You can rent equipment at the various slopes or at a number of area stores that have set up rental operations. The following slopes are located in Avery County: **Ski Beech** (800-438-2093; www.skibeech.com), **Ski Hawksnest** (888-429-5763; www.hawksnest-resort.com), and **Ski Sugar Mountain** (800-784-2768; www.skisugar.com).

▪ Among Avery County's golf opportunities are **Hawksnest Golf and**

Ski (828-963-6561), *Mountain Glen* (828-733-5804), and *Sugar Mountain* (828-898-6464).

■ *Appalachian Ski Center* (828-898-9701), located in Banner Elk, and *Beech Mountain Biking Center* (828-387-2795) offer bike rentals.

SEASONAL EVENTS

Two annual events take place on Grandfather Mountain.

■ *Grandfather Mountain Highland Games and Gathering of Scottish Clans* takes place the second full weekend in July. This event has been held for over 45 years. Although plenty of proud Scots in full regalia attend the event, you don't have to be of Scottish descent to enjoy the games. Traditional track and field events are held, but the real draws are the tossing of the caber (which resembles a telephone poll) and the throwing of sheep sheaves. The track is rimmed by brightly colored tents that house representatives from each clan. You can see Highland dancing, bagpipe competitions, and sheep dog demonstrations. The festivities begin with a Torchlight Ceremony on Thursday, when all the clans march in. The events on Friday focus on music; a Ceilidh (a concert of Scottish music) is held Friday evening. Saturday sees more competition, a Scottish dance, and another Ceilidh. Sunday closes out with the Parade of

The throwing of the caber at the
Grandfather Mountain Highland Games
PHOTOGRAPH BY HUGH MORTON
COURTESY OF BOONE CONVENTION AND VISITORS BUREAU

Tartans. Parking is restricted to certain areas off the mountain, so you'll have to use the shuttle buses to get to the games. An admission fee is charged. Unlike years past, alcoholic beverages and pets are no longer allowed. For information, call 828-733-1333.

- The other event on top of Grandfather Mountain is the **Singing on the Mountain**. This all-day gospel sing has been held since 1924 on the fourth Sunday in June. It started out as a modest gathering of families and friends from local churches. Today, thousands show up to hear the best in gospel music from all races and to hear such well-known ministers as the Reverend Billy Graham. At the 50th Singing on the Mountain, a record crowd of 100,000 people showed up to hear Johnny Cash and see Bob Hope. Admission is free. Bring your own lawn chairs or blankets. Call 828-733-2013 for information.

- The **Woolly Worm Festival** is held during a weekend in October. The woolly worm is actually a furry caterpillar with black and brown bands. Mountain folklore says you can predict what kind of winter lies ahead by examining the bands on these caterpillars right before the first frost.

  The festival includes food, live music, and crafts, but the real center of attention is the woolly worm races. You can bring your own or purchase a woolly worm, name it, and enter it in one of the heats. Several worms are placed side by side at the bottom of long strings. The winner is the worm that reaches the top of its string first. It's fun to watch, and kids love it. The winners of the heats compete until there is a grand champion. It's the champion worm that is used to predict the forthcoming winter. For information on the festival, call 828-898-5605.

Places to Stay

RESORTS, HOTELS, AND MOTELS

- **4 Seasons at Beech.** Expensive/Moderate. 608 Beech Mountain Parkway, Beech Mountain (828-387-4211; www.4Seasons.Beech.net.) Located at the top of Beech Mountain, 4 Seasons offers one- and two-room units, each with a telephone, a television, and a kitchen with a microwave, a refrigerator, and a dishwasher. Special packages are available during ski season.

▪ **Pinnacle Inn**. Expensive/Moderate. Beech Mountain Parkway, Beech Mountain (800-438-2097 or 828-387-4276). You can rent a one- or two-bedroom villa or a ski suite at this resort. The villas have well-equipped kitchens, fireplaces, telephones, and color television. The inn offers an indoor heated pool, a sauna, a steam room, hot tubs, an exercise room, and opportunities for tennis, shuffleboard, and golf.

INNS AND BED-AND-BREAKFASTS

▪ **Eseeola Lodge**. Deluxe. 175 Linville Avenue in Linville, near the intersection of U.S. 221, N.C. 105, and N.C. 181 (800-742-6717; www.eseeola.com). This resort has received a Four-Star rating from Mobil and has been recognized by *Golf Magazine* as a Silver Medalist Resort. Because of the chestnut siding and Tudor look, the lodge and its surrounding buildings remind one of an English inn. Eseeola Lodge has been welcoming vacationers since 1892. In recent years, the rooms have been renovated and spacious suites have been added. Guests can arrange to play tennis or golf. A regulation croquet lawn is even located across the street. The inn is open from mid-May to the end of October.

▪ **Archer's Mountain Inn**. Expensive. 2489 Beech Mountain Parkway, Banner Elk (828-898-9004). This inn has 15 rooms. All accommodations have a native stone fireplace, a full private bath, and a color television. You can rent a Jacuzzi suite, a room with a mountain-view balcony, an efficiency suite, rooms with vaulted ceilings, and traditional bed-and-breakfast-style rooms. The inn offers a full bar and the Jackalope's View restaurant, which serves fresh seafood, certified Angus beef, and exotic wild game.

▪ **The Azalea Inn**. Expensive. Located behind the Village Shops in Banner Elk (888-898-2743 or 828-898-8195; www.azalea-inn.com). Built in 1937, this inn has seven guest rooms, each with its own tiled bath and cable television. The carriage-house cottage has an upstairs and can accommodate four people; it has a bedroom, a bath with a whirlpool, a living room with a sofa bed and a fireplace, and a full kitchen. The inn sits behind a white picket fence on a beautifully landscaped lot with a birdhouse collection and brightly colored flowers in summer. Guests enjoy the fireplace in the living room and the wood stove on the sun porch.

- **The Banner Elk Inn**. Expensive/Moderate. 407 Main Street East, Banner Elk (828-898-6223). This cozy historic inn has several rooms filled with antiques. All the rooms have European down comforters; some have private baths. The inn includes a great room, where guests can watch cable television or relax by the stone fireplace. A full breakfast is served each morning.

- **The Beech Alpen Inn**. Expensive/Moderate. 700 Beech Mountain Parkway, Beech Mountain (828-387-2252; www.beechalpen.com). This inn has 25 rooms with exposed beams and views of the mountains and ski slopes. Some rooms have a queen-sized bed and French doors that lead onto a balcony. Others have two double or king-sized beds, easy chairs, and a window seat. Some have stone fireplaces. All have private baths and color cable television. The inn offers a sitting area and a dining room in a fireside setting.

- **Top of the Beech**. Expensive/Moderate. 700 Beech Mountain Parkway, Beech Mountain (828-387-2252; www.beechalpen.com). The main floor of this Swiss-style lodge has a great room with a cathedral ceiling, a ski chandelier, a game table, sofas, and a large stone fireplace. All the rooms have two double beds, a table with seating, a private bath, and color cable television. A restaurant is on the premises.

Places to Eat

- **Eseeola Lodge**. Expensive. Near the intersection of U.S. 221, N.C. 105, and N.C. 181 in Linville (828-733-4311). A coat and tie are required for men at dinner at this grand old resort. The restaurant has won the prestigious Mobil Four-Star Award. It features French and New American cuisine. Breakfast and dinner are served daily. Reservations are required.

■ **Louisiana Purchase**. Expensive. In downtown Banner Elk (828-963-5087). This restaurant has an award-winning wine list to go along with its Cajun, Creole, and classical French fare. Live jazz is offered in the lounge on Friday and Saturday nights. Reservations are suggested. Dinner is served Monday through Saturday.

■ **Morels Restaurant**. Expensive. 1 Banner Street, Banner Elk (828-898-6866). This small restaurant seats only 40, but its intimate bistro style creates a warm ambiance. The chef is an award-winning restaurateur who was selected as one of *Food & Wine Magazine*'s top 60 chefs in America. He's also been seen on the Discovery Channel's *Great Chefs of the South* series. He prepares imaginative dishes featuring locally grown and organic produce, wild game, seafood, and pasta. Dinner is served daily.

■ **Stonewalls**. Expensive. N.C. 184, Banner Elk (828-898-5550). For over 15 years, Stonewalls has been known as a place to get good steak and prime rib. The menu also includes seafood dishes, but this is primarily a meat place. Dinner is served daily.

■ **Corner Palate**. Moderate. At the corner of N.C. 184 and Main Street at Banner Elk's only stoplight (828-898-8668). If you're looking for a good lunch spot, this is it. You'll find an interesting selection of tasty dishes that are reasonably priced. Lunch and dinner are served daily.

■ **Sorrentos**. Moderate. In the Village Shops in Banner Elk (828-898-5214). This restaurant bills itself as "a touch of Italy in the mountains." Sorrentos changes its menu monthly. Its nightly specials are usually excellent. It also has an extensive wine list. Lunch and dinner are served daily.

■ **Fred's Backside Deli**. Inexpensive. 501 Beech Mountain Parkway, Beech Mountain (828-387-4838). Located in Fred's General Mercantile, which serves as a sort of community center for the Beech Mountain community, this deli serves sandwiches, salads, soups, pizzas, and homemade desserts. It also offers meats and cheeses for purchase. Breakfast, lunch, and dinner are served daily.

■ *Italian Restaurant*. Inexpensive. On U.S. 221 at the intersection with N.C. 181 in Pineola (828-733-1401). Located in a building that used to house a Tastee-Freez, this restaurant might not inspire expectations of good food. But diners find themselves pleasantly surprised. The restaurant serves sandwiches, pasta dishes, pizza, calzones, beer, and wine. Lunch is served Saturday and Sunday and dinner Tuesday through Sunday.

■ *Kersh's Old World Bakery*. Inexpensive. In the Shoppes at Mill Ridge on U.S. 105 in Foscoe (828-963-5668). This establishment started out as the area's most popular bakery. The word spread about how good its freshly baked bread was. Soon, people were driving here from all over the area. Now, Kersh's offers a lunch menu and great desserts. Breakfast and lunch are served Monday through Saturday.

Black Mountains
COURTESY OF NORTH CAROLINA DIVISION OF TOURISM, FILM AND SPORTS DEVELOPMENT

SPRUCE PINE
AND BURNSVILLE

by Carolyn Sakowski

ecause the main highways have still not reached Mitchell and Yancey Counties, development here is less than it is around Boone and Blowing Rock. Ironically, it seems this area would attract the most tourists because it has some of the highest peaks in North Carolina. But despite recent road improvements north of Asheville, development is just now starting here. Fortunately, this isolation means you can still find unspoiled vistas.

Prominent in this area are the Black Mountains, where Mount Mitchell sits among a dozen peaks over 6,000 feet high.

Spruce Pine, the largest town in Mitchell County, has a long mining heritage that has evolved into a tourist industry. It is now the site of the annual North Carolina Mineral and Gem Festival. It is also home to many craftsmen, some of whom came to study at Penland School of Crafts and stayed.

A short drive west is Yancey County, where Burnsville is the largest town. Its town square showcases a statue of the man for whom the town is named, Captain Otway Burns, a hero of the War of 1812. Yancey County has a population of only 17,000. It markets itself as a place to escape traffic jams, urban blight, polluted air, and tainted water.

JUST THE FACTS

Spruce Pine is located at the intersection of U.S. 19E and N.C. 226 six miles from Milepost 331 on the Blue Ridge Parkway.

Burnsville is located at the intersection of U.S. 19 and N.C. 197. From Milepost 344 on the parkway, follow N.C. 80 to U.S. 19.

For visitor information about the Spruce Pine area, contact the Mitchell County Chamber of Commerce, 79 Parkway Road, Spruce Pine, N.C. 28777 (800-227-3912; www.mitchell-county.com). For information about the Burnsville area, contact the Yancey County Chamber of Commerce, 106 West Main Street, Burnsville, N.C. 28714 (800-948-1632 or 828-682-7413; www.yanceychamber.com).

The weekly newspaper in Mitchell County is the *Mitchell News Journal*. In Yancey County, the weekly newspaper is the *Yancey Common Times Journal*.

Museum of North Carolina Minerals
COURTESY OF MITCHELL AREA CHAMBER OF COMMERCE

Things to Do

MUSEUMS AND SCIENCE CENTERS

- The *Museum of North Carolina Minerals*, located at Milepost 331 on the parkway, is part of the Blue Ridge Parkway Visitor Center. This is also the location of the Mitchell Area Chamber of Commerce. Here, you can see exhibits on the wide range of minerals found in North Carolina. The gift shop carries books about gems and mining. The museum is open from 9 A.M. to 5 P.M. daily year-round. Admission is free. Call 828-765-2761.

CULTURAL OFFERINGS

- *Penland School* is open from mid-April to early December. The hours for the Penland Gallery are 10 A.M. to noon and 1 P.M. to 4:30 P.M. from Tuesday through Saturday and noon to 4:30 P.M. on Sunday. To reach the school, take Penland Road off U.S. 19E between Spruce Pine and

The Penland School of Crafts
COURTESY OF MITCHELL AREA CHAMBER OF COMMERCE

COURTESY OF NORTH CAROLINA
DIVISION OF TOURISM, FILM AND
SPORTS DEVELOPMENT

The Penland School of Crafts

The Penland School of Crafts has been described as one of the leading shapers of the American crafts movement and a producer of some of the best artisans in the country.

In 1914, Rufus Morgan founded the Appalachian School. Morgan wanted to include handicrafts in his program of instruction. In visiting area homes, he discovered high-quality woven articles that had been discarded when store-bought cloth became available. He convinced his sister, Miss Lucy Morgan, to return to Penland from Chicago and learn weaving from a local woman, Aunt Susan Phillips, so that she could teach the skill at his school.

Miss Lucy went on to instruct girls at the school and women in the community. She founded the Penland School with the goal of perpetuating the art of weaving and providing a source of income for local people. Miss Lucy also began collecting her students' wares and selling them to the outside world. In 1928, a pottery department was added to the school. By 1929, the sale of student-made goods totaled $18,000.

Today, the Penland School campus has over 40 buildings. It is open to students during the spring, summer, and fall. Terms last one, two, or eight weeks, and the courses vary from year to year. The curriculum usually includes work in wood, glass, fiber, clay, metal, photography, and weaving. All are studied in rustic, yet professionally equipped, studios. Penland School has approximately 1,200 students a year studying in 10 craft media.

Visitors can browse the Penland Gallery to get an idea of how important the Morgans' contribution was in preserving and encouraging traditional mountain crafts.

Burnsville. It is 2.9 miles to a left turn on to S.R. 1164, then 1.8 miles down the winding road to the school. See the sidebar about Penland School for information on the school itself, or call 828-765-6211.

RECREATION

■ **Emerald Village** is on McKinney Mine Road and Crabtree Creek Road in Little Switzerland. Located at the site of the Big McKinney and Bon Ami Mines, this attraction offers an underground museum in a former mine, where you can see equipment and learn about methods used for mining gems a century ago. You can also mine for your own gems—for a price. The mine offers enriched gravel and claims that visitors will "find a gem every time." This is good if you have children, because they get pretty excited about finding a "jewel." You can also see artisans at work cutting and mounting gems. The attraction is open from 9 A.M. to 6 P.M. from Memorial Day to Labor Day and from 9 A.M. to 5 P.M. during May, September, and October. Fees are charged for the mine tour and mining buckets. Call 828-765-6463.

■ The **Orchard at Altapass** is located at Orchard Road at Milepost 328.3 on the Blue Ridge Parkway, near Spruce Pine. This working orchard grows Heritage apples. The best time to visit is the early fall, when the apples are ripe. The orchard offers hayrides, storytelling, mountain music, hand-made crafts, jams, apple butter, cider, mountain honey, and dried fruits. It even has a geologist and botanist who give guided walking tours. It is open daily from 10 A.M. to 6 P.M. from Memorial Day through October. For information, call 888-765-9531 or 828-765-9531, or visit their website at www.altapassorchard.com.

■ **Mount Mitchell State Park**, accessible at Milepost 355 of the Blue Ridge Parkway, boasts the highest peak east of the Mississippi River. The park has picnic areas, nature trails, a lookout tower offering spectacular mountain views, camping areas, a concession stand, and a ranger station. The park and the ranger station are open year-round except for Christmas; the concession stand is open May through October. For information, call 828-675-4611.

Elisha Mitchell

It was not until Dr. Elisha Mitchell arrived in 1827 that anyone had much of an idea how tall the Black Mountains really were.

In 1825, Mitchell took charge of the North Carolina Geological Survey, the first statewide survey anywhere in the nation. In the course of fulfilling his duties, he made his first visits to the western part of the state. In an 1829 geological report, Mitchell stated his belief that the Black Mountains contained the highest land between the Gulf of Mexico and the White Mountains of New Hampshire.

When he returned to the Blacks in 1835, the first peak he climbed to take measurements was Celo Knob, elevation 5,946. There, he noted "peaks considerably more elevated farther South." Mitchell took measurements of barometric pressure and temperature and compared them to measurements taken at his base in Morganton. He then used a formula to determine that the peak that later became known as Mount Mitchell stood 6,476 feet above sea level. He proclaimed it "the Highest Peak of the Black." Eventually, it turned out that Mount Mitchell is actually 208 feet higher than Mitchell thought. He made the wrong measurements at his base. If those had been correct, he would have been off by only six feet.

General Thomas L. Clingman, a member of Congress and a man of scientific tastes, was taking measurements in the area at that same time. Clingman published a statement claiming that he had found a peak higher than the one measured by Mitchell.

Mitchell became obsessed with proving that he was right and Clingman was wrong. He returned to the Blacks in 1857 to settle the matter. He set out alone. When he failed to meet his son as scheduled, a search party was organized. Ten days later, the frustrated group enlisted the aid of Big Tom Wilson, a legendary hunter and tracker who lived in the Cane River area, at the foot of the Blacks. The writer Charles Dudley Warner described Big Tom as "six feet and two inches tall, very spare and muscular, with sandy hair, long gray beard, and honest blue eyes. He has a reputation for great strength and endurance; a man of native simplicity and mild manners." The searchers agreed to let Wilson take the lead. Following seemingly invisible clues—broken limbs and faint impressions in the earth—Big Tom brought the group to a 50-foot waterfall. There, in a pool at the foot, was the perfectly preserved body of Dr. Mitchell. It was surmised that he must have become lost in the fog and fallen over the edge while following the stream. His body was buried in Asheville and later moved to the top of the peak that now bears his name.

■ A popular summer activity in this area is tubing on the South Toe River. At **Carolina Hemlocks Recreation Area** on N.C. 80, you'll see crowds of people bobbing along the river on rubber inner tubes. The slow-moving current and gentle cascades lend just enough excitement to make the activity exhilarating but not too dangerous. You'll see signs for tube rentals at the stores near the recreation area.

■ The **North Carolina Mineral and Gem Festival** is held the first week of August in Spruce Pine. It includes exhibits and demonstrations about gems, of course. For information, call 828-765-9483.

Places to Stay

RESORTS, HOTELS, AND MOTELS

■ **The Clear Creek Guest Ranch**. Expensive. 100 Clear Creek Drive off N.C. 80 South, Burnsville (800-651-4510 or 828-675-4510; www.clearcreekranch.com). This is a little different from your typical accommodation because it's a dude ranch. The rates include three full meals a day, lodging, horseback riding, and all ranch activities. Guests stay in cabins (one-, two-, and three-bedroom units are available) that have porches with rocking chairs. All meals are served family-style in the main lodge. Lots of activities are available for children. The ranch is open from April to Thanksgiving.

■ **Switzerland Inn**. Expensive. N.C. 226A at Milepost 334 on the Blue Ridge Parkway, Little Switzerland (828-765-2153; www.switzerlandinn.com). This popular retreat has chalet-style architecture, paintings of storks on the chimney, and a magnificent panoramic view. An entire wall of the fieldstone-floored lobby is a window that frames the Black Mountain Valley below. All the rooms have hand-painted murals that make you think of the Swiss Alps. Most have balconies; all have cable television, telephones, and baths. Cottages are also available, as are large suites with air conditioning and separate sleeping and living areas. All rooms include a full breakfast and use of the swimming pool and tennis and shuffleboard courts.

■ **Pinebridge Inn and Executive Center**. Moderate. 207 Pinebridge Avenue, Spruce Pine (800-356-5059 or 828-765-5543; www.pinebridgeinn.com). This AAA Three-Diamond hotel is located in a converted schoolhouse, which allows for large rooms. Guests have free use of the Pinebridge Center, which includes an indoor heated pool, a sauna, exercise equipment, a steam room, a whirlpool, an indoor walking track, and the largest ice-skating rink in the Southeast.

INNS AND BED-AND-BREAKFASTS

■ **Castle Inn on English Knob**. Deluxe. 638 Castle Way, Spruce Pine (800-925-2645; www.CASTLE-INN.com). To reach this inn, go 2.25 miles north on U.S. 19E from the intersection with U.S. 226 at Spruce Pine. Turn left on Gouges Creek Road and go one mile to Castle Way. Opened in 1997, Castle Inn offers five rooms, each differing in style and theme. Some have fireplaces or private balconies. The towers, the observation balcony, the courtyard, the library, and the great room may be used by all guests. The inn also has three dining rooms open to the public.

■ **The Nu Wray Inn**. Moderate. On the town square in Burnsville (800-368-9729 or 828-682-2329; www.NuWrayInn.com). Already in business when Burnsville was established in 1833, this is the oldest continuously operating inn in western North Carolina. Guests can rent standard or deluxe rooms or a two-room suite. Room rates include a hearty country breakfast and afternoon refreshments.

Statue of Otway Burns in front of Nu Wray Inn in Burnsville
PHOTOGRAPH BY CAROLYN SAKOWSKI

■ **Richmond Inn**. Moderate. 51 Pine Avenue, Spruce Pine (877-765-6993 or 828-765-6993; www.richmond-inn.com). This half-century-old inn is shaded by towering white pines and landscaped with native trees and shrubbery. You almost forget that the town of Spruce Pine is only three blocks away. The inn's terrace overlooks the valley of the North Toe River. Your night's stay comes with a full breakfast.

■ **Terrell House Bed-and-Breakfast.** Moderate. 109 Robertson Street, Burnsville (828-682-4504; www.TerrellHouseBandB.com). Built in the early 1900s as a girls' dorm for Stanley McCormick School, this Colonial-style home has six guest rooms, each with a private bath. A full breakfast is provided. Credit cards are not accepted. Children must be 12 or older to stay here.

■ **Wray House Bed-and-Breakfast**. Moderate. Just off the town square in Burnsville (877-258-8222 or 828-682-0445; www.wrayhouse.net). Built in 1902, this beautifully restored old home offers two rooms. The one across from the library has a bath with a shower and a claw-foot tub. The Rush Wray Room has a four-poster canopy bed. An additional two rooms are in the carriage house, one upstairs and one down. They both have courtyard entrances and private baths (one with a claw-foot tub). The downstairs room has brick floors and a fireplace.

■ **The Bicycle Inn**. Inexpensive. 319 Dallas Young Road, Bakersville (888-424-5466; www.bicycleinn.com). To reach this inn, make your way to the only traffic light in Bakersville and follow the signs for two miles. As its name implies, the Bicycle Inn was built by bicycling enthusiasts and caters to that same crowd. The four guest rooms and the parlor are named for famous cyclists. The owners also found creative ways to incorporate bicycles into the decor. The inn's economy room has two sets of bunk beds; guests have to share the room and the bath with whoever shows up, but the rate is very reasonable. The rest of the rooms have private baths. Although the inn attracts cyclists, it is open to anyone who wants to get away from the hustle and bustle. It has a café where breakfast and dinner are served; breakfast does not come with the room rate.

Places to Eat

- **The Castle Inn on English Knob**. Expensive. 638 Castle Way, Spruce Pine (828-765-0000). Diners at the Castle Inn have a choice of an à la carte menu or a seven-course prix fixe meal. The à la carte menu includes beef, seafood, lamb, chicken, and pasta dishes. Only adults may dine here; men must wear coats or ties and women dresses or pantsuits. Reservations are required. Dinner is served Wednesday through Saturday; lunch is offered on Sunday.

- **Beam's**. Moderate. On U.S. 19E four miles north of Spruce Pine (828-765-6191). This establishment has been serving great Chinese food since 1938. A recipient of the coveted Silver Spoon Award, it also offers American cuisine, but the Oriental food is what brings everyone back. The Friday-night buffet features most of the menu favorites. Dinner is served Tuesday through Saturday.

- **The Dining Room at Mount Mitchell Golf Club**. Moderate. 7590 U.S. 80 South, Burnsville (828-675-4911). This restaurant offers views of the mountains and the golf course to go with its pasta, chicken, pork, seafood, trout, and beef dishes. You can order dinner from the à la carte menu Wednesday through Friday. A prime rib buffet is offered for Saturday dinner. A breakfast buffet is served on Saturday and Sunday.

- **The Nu Wray Inn**. Moderate. On the town square in Burnsville (800-368-9729 or 828-682-2392). For a fixed price, you get your choice of entrée, rice or potato, two vegetables, homemade soup, biscuits, salad, a drink, and dessert. The menu changes daily. Dinner is served nightly. On Thursday nights during the summer, the inn offers a bluegrass barbecue.

- **Garden Deli**. Inexpensive. On the town square in Burnsville (828-682-3946; www.garden-deli.com). This family-owned and -operated restaurant, in business since 1987, offers sandwiches and salads. Lunch is served Monday through Saturday.

Asheville

$\mathcal{T}$ here is a peace that settles on my soul whenever I get away to the mountains. Driving west on Interstate 40 from my home in the Piedmont, it's easy to be fooled into thinking the blue images in the distance are a line of thunderstorms marching eastward. But as the engine of my car works harder as I climb, the mountains come into clearer view, and that familiar peace welcomes me. I have heard many people remark that coming to the Blue Ridge Mountains is like coming home, even if it's the first time they've visited. These ancient peaks and valleys beckon with a warmth and understanding that comes from their age. In Asheville, as they like to say, "altitude affects attitude."

After what seems a tortuous climb past Old Fort, the mountains are suddenly all around you. The road curves more sharply, but the reward is a new view with every turn. Drivers beware! It's easy to be distracted by the vistas that you'll encounter for the next half-hour on your drive toward Asheville.

The city of Asheville, named for Governor Samuel Ashe, was incorporated in 1797. The influence of the Scots-Irish immigrants who settled this area is apparent. For example, many old bluegrass tunes sound quite similar to Irish jigs.

Asheville was an isolated small town of only 2,600 before the coming of the railroad in the 1880s. Some of the first flatlanders to find their way to Asheville were the wealthy, who came to escape the oppressive heat of summer. They built large summer homes and elaborate resort hotels. Soon, Asheville's population was over 10,000.

In the 1920s, Asheville experienced another growth spurt. The popular Art Deco style of the day can still be seen in many downtown buildings. When city hall was erected, many citizens were disturbed by its opulent domed roof covered with green and pink tiles. The same architect was scheduled to build the county courthouse, but the pendulum swung in the opposite direction, and his contract was canceled. The courthouse looks like the straight-laced sibling of the neighboring city hall.

Asheville continues to attract visitors as well as those who come to settle on this plateau between the Blue Ridge and Great Smoky Mountains. And if the temperate weather and beautiful vistas aren't enough, the city offers a unique regional culture, a longstanding crafts tradition, a wide variety of shops and restaurants, outdoor recreation to suit even the most adventurous tastes, and first-class accommodations. Oh yes, and don't forget a French chateau and a five-star hotel and spa.

A trip to Asheville can be filled with shopping, dining, high culture, hiking, rafting, mountain climbing—the options are endless. Personally, watching sunsets is usually the activity that occupies my time.

by Sue Clark

PHOTOGRAPH ON PREVIOUS PAGE—

Biltmore Estate
COURTESY OF THE BILTMORE COMPANY

Sunset over Asheville against the backdrop of the mountains
COURTESY OF ASHEVILLE CONVENTION AND VISITORS BUREAU

JUST THE FACTS

Asheville is located at the crossing of Interstate 40 and Interstate 26.

It is served by Asheville Regional Airport; for information, call 828-684-2226.

The Greyhound bus terminal is located at 2 Tunnel Road; call 828-253-5353 for information.

The Asheville Visitor Center is at 151 Haywood Street; take Exit 4C off I-240. It is well staffed and open daily. You can contact the center at P.O. Box 1010, Asheville, NC 28802 (828-258-6109).

The daily newspaper, the *Asheville Citizen-Times*, is a great source of information, as is the *Mountain X-Press*, a free weekly.

Biltmore Estate
COURTESY OF THE BILTMORE COMPANY

Things to Do

HISTORIC PLACES, GARDENS, AND TOURS

- **Biltmore Estate** is located on U.S. 25 just north of Exit 50 off I-40. Words do little to describe this 16th-century-styled chateau modeled after those found in France's Loire Valley. This working estate is surrounded by rolling forestland, formal gardens, a winery, and a river. All of this is surprising, considering its proximity to Asheville's center.

Opened as a private home in 1895, Biltmore Estate boasted all the latest innovations, including central heating, indoor plumbing, electric lights, a bowling alley, a gymnasium, and an indoor pool—awe-inspiring features for its time. It has charmed its many visitors with its beauty, luxury, and amenities ever since.

George Vanderbilt, grandson of industrialist Cornelius Vanderbilt, purchased 125,000 acres near Asheville because he loved the mountain views and climate. He promptly hired architect Richard Morris Hunt and landscape architect Frederick Law Olmsted, two of America's leading designers, to plan his estate.

The 250-room mansion took hundreds of workers more than five years to build. The construction site had its own brick kilns and woodworking shops. Limestone was transported on a railroad spur laid just for Biltmore. Artisans and craftsmen were brought from Europe. Many of the men employed in the building of the home also fell in love with Asheville and stayed after construction was finished. They settled easily into the area's strong crafts tradition.

While work was progressing on the mansion, the land was also getting attention. Vanderbilt wanted an estate that would be a productive farm and forest enterprise. His emphasis on land management is evidenced by the fact that most of the property was eventually sold to the federal government and became part of the Blue Ridge Parkway or Pisgah National Forest. Family descendants still own the mansion and 8,000 surrounding acres. Frederick Law Olmsted, most famous for his design of New York's Central Park, planned the gardens and the park surrounding the home, including the three-mile driveway.

After passing the Lodge Gate, you will make that beautiful drive to the visitor center, where you can purchase admission tickets. You may also view a short film about Biltmore, see a relief map of the area, check the menus of the estate's restaurants, and visit the restrooms. Short paths lead through the woods to the mansion.

Your first view of the chateau is across a long lawn with a reflecting pool in the center. The complex exterior features massive carved archways, columns, and gargoyles. This is but the beginning of the wonders to behold here.

Today's visitors enter Biltmore House just as George Vanderbilt's guests did over a century ago—through the main door and into the grand foyer. Here, you can purchase personal headsets that will allow you to tour the house at your own speed. It's well worth the fee, especially since the opening of many new rooms on the third floor. Elevators are available for those who can't negotiate the many staircases. The grand foyer is the hub of the mansion. Groups are often invited to perform in the atrium on the right side of the foyer.

Each room in the mansion has a distinctive style. The medieval-style banquet room has a 70-foot arched ceiling, a table that seats 64, Flemish tapestries, numerous elk and moose heads, and a carved mantel that spans three massive fireplaces. The two-story Baroque library has elaborately carved paneling and an 18th-century painted ceiling imported from Venice.

You should plan on at least half a day at Biltmore. The tour of the mansion lasts at least two hours and covers everything from the third-floor guest suites to basement service areas such as the kitchens, pantries, and laundry. You'll also see the servants' quarters, the bowling alley, the gymnasium, and the indoor pool, complete with private changing rooms.

After touring the mansion, go for a stroll in the formal gardens. You may also want to visit the Biltmore Estate Winery, where a brief tour and a wine tasting are offered. The vintners are understandably proud of their award-winning wines. If you get hungry, your options include sandwiches, drinks, and ice cream at the Stable Café, located next to the main house; baked goods and snacks at the bakery and the candy shop; and upscale dining at Deerpark Restaurant and the Winery Bistro, both located near the winery.

The house is open from 9 A.M. to 6 P.M. daily. The winery is open Monday through Saturday from 11 A.M. to 7 P.M. and Sunday from noon to 7 P.M. Both are closed on Thanksgiving and Christmas. The admission fee seems expensive until you realize that you're paying for at least half a day's entertainment in a place unlike any other in America. For more information, call 800-543-2961 or 828-255-1700.

▪ The **Thomas Wolfe Memorial**, located at 52 North Market Street in downtown Asheville, remained closed for repairs at the time of this writing. The house suffered a fire at the hands of an arsonist on July 24, 1998. Over 85 percent of the personal belongings and artifacts of the Wolfe family escaped harm and have since been in storage or on display in the adjoining visitor center.

Wolfe grew up in this 28-room house yet had no room of his own, since his mother used the majority of the building for a boardinghouse. In 1929, when Wolfe published **Look Homeward, Angel**, the residents of Asheville easily recognized the "Dixieland" boardinghouse in "Altamont." They were not amused by Wolfe's less-than-flattering picture of his hometown. The local public library banned the book for more than seven years. Asheville eventually came to appreciate the talent of its native son. In 1948, only 10 years after Wolfe's death, the Asheville Chamber of Commerce helped purchase the house as a memorial to one of this century's great novelists. In 1976, the memorial was designated a State Historic Site. The memorial and the city of Asheville now stage the *Thomas Wolfe Festival* every year on or around October 3, the author's birthday.

The visitor center is open Monday through Saturday from 9 A.M. to 5 P.M. and Sunday from 1 P.M. to 5 P.M. Hours are shortened in the winter. For a nominal fee, the staff will continue offering tours of the exterior of the home until repairs on the interior are completed. For information, call 828-253-8304.

■ *Botanical Gardens of Asheville*, located at 151 W. T. Weaver Street, is a beautiful setting for the preservation and display of trees, plants, and flowers native to the southern Appalachians. In 1960, several local garden clubs came together to help plant the grounds of this 10-acre preserve on the campus of the University of North Carolina at Asheville. Now operating as a nonprofit organization, the gardens provide a study area and information center for those interested in horticulture, as well as those of us who simply appreciate a place of quiet beauty. Unpaved trails wind through the various areas, including the azalea garden and the garden for the blind. A wheelchair ramp is available. The gardens are open daily during daylight hours. Admission is free. For information, call 828-252-5190.

MUSEUMS AND SCIENCE CENTERS

■ *Pack Place*, located at 2 South Pack Square in downtown Asheville, opened in 1992 at the cost of $14 million. It provides western North Carolina with a premier arts-and-sciences center, housing offices for local arts organizations and galleries and studios for artists. The *Asheville Art Museum* has a collection of contemporary and traditional paintings and some sculptures by Southern artists. The *Colburn Gem and Mineral Museum* displays 1,500 gems, semiprecious stones, fossils, and minerals, many from the surrounding area. Pack Place also houses an interactive gallery called **Health Adventure** and Asheville's African-American cultural center, **YMI Cultural Museum**, as well as a 514-seat performing-arts theater. The complex is open Tuesday through Saturday from 10 A.M. to 6 P.M. and Sunday from 1 P.M. to 5 P.M. from June through October; it is closed Sundays during the winter. For information on performances and events, call 828-257-4500.

▪ **Smith-McDowell Museum of Western North Carolina History** is located at 283 Victoria Road in Asheville's oldest existing house. Built in 1840, the home has three stories with double-tiered full-length porches. It was purchased in a land grant that opened the area to permanent settlement. In 1974, the Western North Carolina Historical Association leased the house and began restoration work. The museum features temporary exhibits in keeping with its Victorian furnishings. It is open Tuesday through Friday from 10 A.M. until 4 P.M. and Sunday from 1 P.M. to 4 P.M. from May through December. From January through April, it is open Tuesday through Friday from 10 A.M. to 4 P.M. A small admission fee is charged. Group tours can be arranged. For information, call 828-253-9231.

▪ **Western North Carolina Nature Center**, located at 75 Gashes Creek Road on the grounds of the former Asheville Zoo, is designed to show the interaction between plants and animals in the southern Appalachian environment. Aimed at family audiences, the exhibits interest both children and adults. One features the underground den of a live chipmunk beneath a tree's roots. The center presents animals in natural-habitat exhibits. It also presents domestic animals at its Educational Farm, where, for example, children can see a cow being milked. A small gift shop features nature books and souvenirs. The center is open daily from 10 A.M. to 5 P.M. A small admission fee is charged. For information, call 828-298-5600. The center's website (www.wncnaturecenter.org) is a great place to learn about current displays and events.

CULTURAL OFFERINGS

▪ The **Asheville Symphony** is a fine regional orchestra founded in 1960.

It offers a series of classical concerts usually featuring an internationally known guest artist. Call 828-254-7046 for information and a schedule of performances.

- **Asheville Community Theater**, located at 35 East Walnut Street, presents six productions annually. These include comedies, dramas, and musicals. The theater also offers a reader's theater, a children's theater, and classes. For information, call 828-254-1320.

St. Lawrence Basilica

The most beautiful building in Asheville may be the Spanish Baroque-style St. Lawrence Basilica on Haywood Street. The most striking feature of the church is its central dome, which is built wholly of tiles and is entirely self-supporting. Measuring 58 feet by 82 feet, it is reputed to be the largest freestanding elliptical dome in North America.

St. Lawrence Basilica is filled with bas-relief and other sculptures, stained-glass windows, ornately carved doors, and glazed tiles from all over the world; some of the carved wooden statues come from Spain and the stained-glass windows from Germany, to name just a few. The beautiful altar is topped with an 1,800-pound block of Tennessee marble.

St. Lawrence Catholic Church was the first Catholic church in North Carolina. It was designated a basilica by Pope John Paul II in April 1993. The basilica designation is given to certain churches because of their antiquity, dignity, historical importance, or significance as a place of worship. At that time, there were only 33 basilicas in the United States. As a basilica, St. Lawrence has the privilege of displaying the pontifical seal. The dominant feature of the seal is a pair of crossed keys, which symbolize the keys to the Kingdom. Basilicas also carry special responsibilities, such as promoting the study of the documents of the pope and the Holy See, especially those concerning the Sacred Liturgy. Additionally, a Basilica has the responsibility to promote the participation of the faithful in the Mass and the Liturgy of the Hours, especially matins (morning prayers) and vespers (evening prayers).

St. Lawrence Basilica is the only church built by the renowned Rafeal Guastavino. The massive stone foundation and the brick superstructure give silent testimony to the architect's desire to build an edifice that would endure for generations. There are no beams of wood or steel in the entire structure.

A visit to St. Lawrence Basilica offers a chance not only to view fine architecture, beautiful stained glass, and wonderful sculptures, but also to witness some of the sacred traditions of the Catholic Church that are not often on display in the modern world.

Special Shopping

■ The **Folk Art Center** is located east of Asheville at Milepost 382 on the Blue Ridge Parkway. It features the work of the Southern Highland Craft Guild, an organization of artisans who make pottery, baskets, quilts, candles, brooms, weavings, furniture, jewelry, dolls, musical instruments, and woodcarvings, among other things. This low-roofed building opened in 1980 in a beautiful setting surrounded by flowering trees and azaleas. It serves as an educational center, a research library, a craft shop, and exhibition space. The guild hosts special events such as folk dancing, demonstrations of traditional crafts, and lecture series. The Allanstand Craft Shop, located on the premises, offers the largest and most diverse collection of high-quality handmade crafts anywhere in the North Carolina mountains. This is definitely a great place for gift shopping, even if the gift is for you! The center is open from 9 A.M. to 6 P.M. daily; it closes an hour earlier during January, February, and March. Admission is free. For information, call 828-298-7928.

■ **Biltmore Village**, across U.S. 25 from the entrance to Biltmore Estate, is a quaint neighborhood of houses built for the artisans and craftsmen who helped construct the mansion. The two-story houses have been turned into restaurants and shops selling gifts, stationery, jewelry, clothing, knitting supplies, and household accessories. The little village is a nice setting for strolling and window shopping.

■ **Western North Carolina Farmer's Market**, on Brevard Road off N.C. 191 and Interstate 40, is a feast for the eye as well as the palate. This modern facility is operated year-round by the North Carolina Department of Agriculture. The feast for the senses begins with the fresh local fruits and vegetables and continues with dried flowers, jams and jellies, and homemade crafts. The market is open Monday through Friday from 8 A.M. to 6 P.M. Admission is free. For information, call 828-253-1691.

■ **Greenwood Gallery** adjoins the Grove Park Inn on Grovewood Road. It used to be called the Biltmore Homespun Shops. Established in 1901 by Mrs. George Vanderbilt, the shops were set up as a school to preserve the dyeing, spinning, and weaving skills that had been passed on to the mountain residents by their English and Scottish ancestors. Today, the shops feature lengths of hand-woven wool, as well as many kinds of handmade crafts and gifts. There's also a small museum where you can see a brief film about the history of the Biltmore weaving industry. The gallery shops are open Monday through Saturday from 10 A.M. to 6 P.M. and Sunday from 1 P.M. to 5 P.M. from April through December; they are open Monday through Saturday from 10 A.M. to 5 P.M. from January through March. The museum is open Monday through Saturday from 10 A.M. to 5 P.M. and Sunday from 1 P.M. to 5 P.M. during the spring, summer, and fall; it is open on Friday and Saturday from 10 A.M. to 5 P.M. during the winter. Admission to the museum is free. For information, all 828-253-7651.

- **Downtown Asheville** has been experiencing a very successful revitalization. The streets are dotted with a wonderful mix of coffee houses, antique shops, boutiques, and restaurants. **Wall Street**, part of which has been blocked off to create a pedestrian mall, has the best concentration of interesting shops and restaurants. Just a short distance away at 55 Haywood Street is **Malaprop's** (828-254-6734), one of those great independent bookstores that are becoming increasingly rare these days. Besides a fine selection of regional books, Malaprop's has a small, trendy café, where you can sip a cappuccino while getting started on your latest literary purchase.

RECREATION

If you like the great outdoors, Asheville's the place for you. Surrounded by three park areas containing more than a million acres, it offers plenty of opportunities for camping, hiking, fishing, whitewater rafting, and mountain biking.

- If you plan to visit **Great Smoky Mountains National Park**, call 423-436-1200 for information. If you'd like to camp in one of the six campgrounds of the **Blue Ridge Parkway**, call 828-298-0398. For camping information concerning **Pisgah National Forest**, call 828-257-4200.

- For hikers, there's the legendary *Appalachian Trail,* which cuts through Pisgah National Forest and Great Smoky Mountains National Park. Check with the park offices listed above.

- Is fishing your passion? Head for *Lake Julian,* south of Asheville on N.C. 280, off U.S. 25; *Lake Powhatan,* on N.C. 191 just off the Blue Ridge Parkway south of Asheville; or *Lake Lure,* on U.S. 74 southeast of Asheville. You'll need a state fishing license. For information about hunting and fishing regulations, call 828-258-6101.

- Whitewater rafting is popular from June through August on the *French Broad River* north of Asheville. If you're a serious rafter and want to try other rivers, see the chapter on Franklin for companies that raft the Nantahala Gorge.

- Skiing doesn't often come to mind when visitors ponder the outdoor activities of North Carolina. However, the highest mountains in the eastern United States are here. *Wolf Laurel Ski Resort* (828-689-4111) is closest to Asheville. *Cataloochee Ski Resort* (828-926-0285) is a short drive away in Maggie Valley. Other ski resorts can be found in the Blowing Rock and Banner Elk/Beech Mountain/Linville chapters.

- Golf in the mountains presents its own special challenges and pleasures. Check out *Buncombe County Golf Club* (828-298-1867), *Black Mountain Golf Course* (828-669-2710), *Reems Creek Golf Club* (929-645-4393), and *Grove Park Inn and Spa* (828-252-2711).

SEASONAL EVENTS

- The *Mountain Dance and Folk Festival,* held the first weekend in August, is the oldest festival of its kind in the nation. It showcases the best mountain crafts, musicians, and dancers—both cloggers and folk dancers. Started in 1927 by Bascom Lamar Lunsford, it is often called the "Granddaddy of Mountain Festivals." For information, call 800-257-1300 or 828-258-6107.

Golf in Western North Carolina
COURTESY OF NORTH CAROLINA DIVISION OF TOURISM, FILM AND SPORTS DEVELOPMENT

■ The *Southern Highland Craft Guild Fair* is held the third weekend in July and the third weekend in October every year. Over 100 craftspeople from the South demonstrate, display, and sell their works. Mountain music and dancing are part of the celebration. Call 828-298-7928 for information.

■ *Bele Chere Downtown Community Celebration*, held the last weekend in July, features bands (many of them nationally known), international food vendors, crafts, and contests. The downtown area is closed to vehicles for the weekend. For information, call 828-259-5800.

■ *Shindig on the Green* is a series of free bluegrass concerts held on Saturday nights throughout the summer. They take place at City-County Plaza and are a great way to spend a Saturday evening in the mountains. For more information, call 800-257-1300 or 828-258-6107.

Places to Stay

Asheville has a great selection of places to stay. It offers 6,000-plus rooms in historic mountain retreats, country inns, bed-and-breakfasts, upscale downtown hotels, economy motels, national chain hotels, and everything in between. Reservations are highly recommended. You'll find Asheville a great home base for your mountain adventure, but don't even think about dropping in for a room during fall leaf season or during one of Asheville's popular festivals, when rooms have been reserved months in advance. Consider visiting in the winter season, when many rates are drastically reduced from the summer and fall.

RESORTS, HOTELS, AND MOTELS

■ *The Grove Park Inn and Spa*. Deluxe. 290 Macon Avenue (800-438-5800 or 828-252-2711; www.groveparkinn.com). There are only a handful of truly grand resort hotels in the United States. This is one of the finest. The attention to details here comes from a long tradition. Back in the early 1900s, staff members used to polish every coin so that no guest would be handed a tarnished piece of currency. While that is no longer the rule, it is an example of the kind of service that is still a part of the Grove Park.

The Grove Park Inn was the dream of E. W. Grove, the owner of a pharmaceutical firm famous for Grove's Tasteless Chill Tonic. Grove visited Asheville and found the climate beneficial to his health. His dream was to build the finest resort hotel in the world. After it opened in 1913, it became a favorite destination for the rich, the famous, and the powerful. One of the long hallways features photos of some of the inn's illustrious guests: Presidents Wilson, Taft, Coolidge, Hoover, and Eisenhower; business tycoons Henry Ford and Harvey Firestone; inventor Thomas Edison; and entertainers Enrico Caruso and Mikhail Baryshnikov. Many of the rooms have brass plaques on the doors that tell the year some famous person stayed there. One of the most requested rooms was used by F. Scott Fitzgerald.

In 1973, the inn was listed on the National Register of Historic Places. That same decade, it added a championship golf course, an indoor pool, a sports center, and a clubhouse. In the 1980s, wings were added to provide 510 deluxe rooms, two ballrooms, and a conference center. The new millennium will bring the most ambitious addition to date—a state-of-

The Grove Park Inn and Spa
COURTESY OF THE GROVE PARK INN AND SPA

the-art spa complete with a Roman bath–style swimming pool. Located below the Sunset Terrace and between the two wings, the spa will be mostly underground, so as not to spoil the view from the main lodge.

The guest rooms are all luxurious, and the service is outstanding. The Grove Park Inn offers wonderful dining, shopping and browsing opportunities, and outdoor activities. Many people who come for a once-in-a-lifetime experience wind up making a stay at the Grove Park Inn a tradition.

■ *Haywood Park Hotel and Promenade*. Deluxe/Expensive. 1 Battery Park Avenue (800-845-7638 or 828-252-2522; www.haywoodpark.com). Haywood Park is an ultrasophisticated suite hotel in the heart of downtown. The feel here is elegant and refined. The lobby, accented by polished brass railings, doesn't overpower guests with a lot of furniture. The huge rooms open into small common areas located on each floor. The Haywood's location makes it the ideal spot to enjoy Asheville's boutiques and restaurants. It's also a popular choice for a front-row seat for the city's summer festivals.

■ *Great Smokies Holiday Inn Sunspree Resort*. Expensive/Moderate. 1 Holiday Inn Drive (828-254-3211; www.sunspree.com). While large chains are generally not listed in this guide, this one is worthy of an exception.

Situated on 120 acres close to downtown, this resort and conference center has some unusual extras. The low-rise buildings allow an unobstructed view of the city and the surrounding mountains. Extensive meeting and banquet facilities are on the premises, but what makes this place unique are the options for play, such as the 18-hole championship golf course, the indoor soccer center, the outdoor tennis courts, and the children's programs.

- **Country Inn and Suites**. Moderate. 845 Brevard Road (828-670-9000; www.countryinns.com) This is part of a small, new chain of inns that succeeds in not looking like your average hotel chain. The feel here is spacious and homey. Rooms are available with separate bedroom areas, large whirlpool tubs, telephones with voice mail and data ports, and large, comfortable sitting areas. Amenities include a swimming pool, a fitness room, and a generous continental breakfast. The lobby looks like a living room, complete with fireplace and comfy chairs. The inn is located within easy reach of all that Asheville has to offer and is a great place to come home to after a day of exploring.

INNS AND BED-AND-BREAKFASTS

- **Richmond Hill Inn**. Deluxe. 87 Richmond Hill Drive (800-545-9238 or 828-252-7313; www.richmondhillinn.com). This elegant mansion, built in 1895, was designed as a private residence for Richmond Pearson, a former congressman and ambassador. It is considered Asheville's finest example of Queen Anne–style architecture. Sitting on top of a hill, the inn commands a 360-degree view encompassing the French Broad River, the Asheville skyline, and mountain peaks. Guest quarters are in the main house, the garden pavilion, and a row of charming cottages. Each individually decorated room includes a private bath, a television, and a telephone. The cottages have fireplaces, porches, and refrigerators. As for the landscaping, it's nothing short of stunning, from the croquet lawn to the parterre garden with its stone-lined brook, terraced walkway, and waterfall. A full-course gourmet breakfast is served, as is afternoon tea. Guests can enjoy dinner at the highly awarded Gabrielle's, which features extraordinary entrées, a vast wine selection, and piano music in an elegant and intimate setting.

- **Cedar Crest Victorian Inn**. Deluxe/Expensive. 674 Biltmore Avenue (828-252-1389; www.cedarcrestvictorianinn.com). Cedar Crest is one of the largest and most opulent residences surviving Asheville's 1890s boom period. Perched on a hill three blocks north of Biltmore Estate, this Queen Anne–style dwelling is positioned on four landscaped acres featuring English perennial gardens and a croquet lawn. Architectural details include a captain's walk, projecting turrets, expansive verandas, carved oak paneling, and leaded glass. The guest rooms are appointed with satin and lace Victorian trappings and feature period antiques, canopied ceilings, clawfoot tubs, and fireplaces. Guests are treated to a sumptuous hot breakfast, afternoon refreshments, evening coffee, and a true spirit of hospitality.

- **Chestnut Street Inn**. Expensive/Moderate. 176 East Chestnut Street. (800-894-2955 or 828-285-0705; www.chestnutstreetinn.com). This large Colonial Revival home is located in the Chestnut Hill National Historic District. Its large porches are a beautiful accent to the mellow red-brick exterior. The high ceilings and ornate mantels together with the antique furnishings and decorations transport guests back to a time when life had a relaxed quality. Amenities include private baths, down comforters, bathrobes, and fresh flowers. A full gourmet breakfast is served each morning. Late-afternoon tea is often enjoyed on the veranda. If you're lucky, Mr. Bently, the inn's canine butler, may lead you through the English-style flower garden.

- **The Lion & the Rose**. Expensive/Moderate. 276 Montford Avenue (800-546-6988 or 828-255-7673; www.lion-rose.com). Comfort and elegance abound in this wonderful bed-and-breakfast, where no detail is overlooked. A Georgian mansion built around 1895, it has five elegant guest rooms including a bridal suite with a balcony. Located in the Montford historic district, the inn has beautiful gardens perfect for strolling and a veranda perfect for relaxing. A full gourmet breakfast is served each morning. Afternoon tea is a great time to come together with other guests and share the day's adventures. The Lion & the Rose is the place to come for a little pampering.

- **Blake House Inn**. Moderate. 150 Royal Pines Drive. (888-353-5227 or 828-681-5227). Blake House was built in 1847 in the Italianate-Gothic style. It originally served as the summer home of a wealthy lowland rice planter. The restored mansion boasts 22-inch-thick granite walls, heart-pine floors, original English plaster moldings, seven fireplaces, covered porches, and a patio. Each room offers fine linens, cable television, a telephone, and a private bath. This is also one of the few bed-and-breakfasts that welcomes children.

Places to Eat

- **Gabrielle's at Richmond Hill**. Expensive. 87 Richmond Hill Drive (828-252-7313 or 800-545-9238). Fine dining in an elegant setting is the order of the day at Gabrielle's. Guests have their choice of two areas in which to dine: the dining room, which recalls the formality of traditional Victorian dining, and the sun porch, which has wicker furniture and ceiling fans. Gabrielle's features American cuisine and *nouvelle cuisine*. The emphasis is on fresh foods available locally. A six-course set-price dinner with a few choices is available, or you can order from the menu. Whatever your choice, you'll be treated to a fine evening in a magical setting. Dinner is served daily.

- **Zambra's**. Expensive. 85A Walnut Street (828-232-1060). *Zambra* is arabic for *flute*, and it is an apt description for the "music" of this menu. This is exquisite food—exotic, roughly beautiful, and delicious. Zambra's makes generous use of sherries, ports, and madeiras. Herb pastas and nut mixtures are blended in unusual combinations. The menu features the tastes of Spain, Morocco, and the Mediterranean. While trying to decide their edible journey, diners are treated to fire-roasted tomatoes with just a touch of tangerine flavor, along with thick bread for dragging in the juice. The menu changes each night, according to the available foods and the whim of the chef. And don't forget the wines; there are over 150 to choose from, as well as homemade sangria. Dinner is served Monday through Saturday.

- **23 Page Restaurant and the New French Bar**. Expensive/Moderate. 1 Battery Park (828-252-3685). These two downtown restaurants draw a large local following. The smart visitor would do well to follow the locals' lead. For a casual experience, try the New French Bar, which features espresso, pastries, and café fare. On nice days, you may choose to sit at one of the outdoor tables. For a more formal evening, try the American cuisine with European accents at 23 Page. Lunch is offered daily at the New French Bar. Dinner is served daily at both restaurants.

- **American Bistro and Bakery**. Moderate. 1636 Hendersonville Road (828-277-2253). Don't let the name fool you—we're not talking just hamburgers here. The extensive menu is truly American; foods of different ethnic origin come together like a true melting pot. With choices such as quesadillas, pizzas, salmon linguine, and chicken scallopine, all complemented by the bakery's fine breads and desserts, every taste or craving can be satisfied. And don't discount the hamburgers—they're the best anywhere. Lunch and dinner are served daily; a large and delicious brunch is offered on Sunday.

- **Café on the Square**. Moderate. 1 Biltmore Avenue (828-251-5565). Overlooking historic Pack Square in the heart of downtown Asheville, this open, airy café is casual, yet elegant. It offers the freshest in produce, seafood, and meats. Lunch includes salads and a variety of sandwiches. Shrimp étouffée and chipotle with pork tenderloin are among the dinner entrées. The café has an extensive wine list. Catering is available. Lunch is served Monday through Saturday and dinner daily.

- **Charlotte Street Grill and Pub**. Moderate. 157 Charlotte Street (828-253-5348 or 828-252-2948). Built in the early 1920s, this was North Asheville's first drugstore. "The Pub" opened in 1976; the offerings in this festive, intimate setting lean toward appetizers and sandwiches. Eventually, the building was enlarged to include fine dining upstairs in a Victorian setting. This is now the Charlotte Street Grill, which offers an extensive menu featuring meats, seafood, pastas, and tofu. Whatever your preference, you can enjoy a unique and tasty dining experience here. Lunch and dinner are served Monday through Saturday.

▪ **Yesterdays Classic Diner**. Moderate. 290 Underwood Road (828-654-7660). Located south of Asheville, this diner is everything you'd expect from its name. From the gleaming chrome exterior to the jukebox to the waitresses on roller skates, this is the place to come for nostalgia. The extensive menu is a treat to read; the text for almost every food item includes references to the 1950s. The salad dressings are made fresh, the sandwiches come with fries and a kosher pickle, and the entrées are called "Momma's Meals." And of course, you can get a milk shake, a float, or a malt prepared the old-fashioned way in just about any flavor you can dream of. The diner serves breakfast, lunch, and dinner daily.

▪ **The Laughing Seed**. Moderate/Inexpensive. 40 Wall Street (828-252-3445). This popular downtown restaurant features a vegetarian menu that is innovative and delicious—and this from an author who is an avowed meat lover. Pastas, pizzas, sandwiches, and daily specials are offered. You'll find Mexican, Indian, Asian, Mediterranean, and New American accents in the cuisine. Outdoor dining is available when weather permits. The atmosphere is open and casual. This is a great place to take a break from exploring Asheville's downtown shops and boutiques. Lunch and dinner are served Wednesday through Monday.

▪ **Mountain Smoke House**. Moderate/Inexpensive. 802 Fairview Road (828-298-8121). Classic Southern cooking is the draw here. Popular buffet and menu items include hoppin' John, macaroni and cheese, thinly sliced sweet potato chips, greens, okra, corn, string beans, fried green tomatoes, hush puppies, apple dumplings, sweet potato pie, lemon meringue pie, cobblers, and freshly baked rolls and cookies. And you don't have to worry about calories, because you can burn them off when the music starts. Some of the area's best bands are regulars. Somehow, the fiddle playing always manages to get even the most fervent non-dancers on the floor. Lunch and dinner are served Tuesday through Saturday.

Nearby

▪ **Black Mountain** is a small community about 10 miles east of Asheville in the Swannanoa River Valley. The town has a history of attracting nonconformists and freethinkers. Oddly enough, it is also the center of the largest concentration of religious retreats in the United States; there are 20 in a 35-mile radius. Black Mountain, once a spiritual center for the Cherokee Indians, was home of the experimental Black Mountain College from 1933 to 1956. Today, the town draws visitors who come to see the beautiful Montreat Conference Center and to enjoy shopping for crafts and antiques.

Along Cherry Street, you'll find a number of shops selling antiques and collectibles. When you're ready for a bite to eat, try lunch at **Pepper's** at 122 Cherry Street (828-669-1885), noted for its remarkable display of Dr. Pepper memorabilia; you can even order a Dr. Pepper served steaming hot. After a day of shopping, there's no better way to unwind and ponder your purchases than an overnight stay at the **Red Rocker Inn** (828-669-5991; www.bbdirectory.com/inn/redrockr.html), located at 136 North Dougherty Street. This old-fashioned inn, open from mid-February through December, features a wide porch that looks out onto a beautiful, tree-shaded yard.

▪ **Craggy Gardens**, located between Milepost 363 and Milepost 369 on the Blue Ridge Parkway, isn't really a garden at all. Instead, it's an ideal place for viewing wide slopes bursting with mountain laurel and rhododendron in June and the incredible display of fall color in October. Trails wind among trees, shrubs, and flowers. The picnic area commands a striking view of the Blue Ridge. The visitor center has displays on the area's geology. The rangers occasionally present interpretive programs. For information, call 828-298-0398.

▪ **Zebulon B. Vance Homestead** is located in Weaverville, about 12 miles north of Asheville. A State Historic Site, it features a reconstruction of the mountain home of one of North Carolina's preeminent statesmen. Vance is best known as North Carolina's governor during the Civil War.

The two-story pine-log home has period furniture, some of it from the original house, built in 1790. Among the log outbuildings are a corn-crib, a springhouse, a loom house, a slave house, a smokehouse, and a toolhouse. A guide is on hand to explain what life was like in the mountains for the Vances and other homesteaders. The visitor center offers displays that further illustrate life at that time. You are welcome to bring a picnic lunch to enjoy on the grounds. The homestead is open Tuesday through Saturday from 10 A.M. to 4 P.M. from November to March. It is open Monday through Saturday from 9 A.M. to 5 P.M. and Sunday from 1 P.M. to 5 P.M. from April to October. Admission is free. For information, call 828-645-6706.

The Southern Mountains

Hendersonville

Brevard

Highlands

Franklin

The southern mountains are an area of stark contrasts and rich beauty. Don't be deceived by what looks like a highway on your road map—it could just as easily be a winding, twisting way to get from one town to another. But arduous drives are rewarded by some wonderful surprises. Within easy walking distance of those "highways," you'll encounter waterfalls to slide down, waterfalls to walk behind, and even a waterfall to drive under. In this four-county area south of Asheville, you'll find the home of one of America's greatest poets, a world-class music festival, boutiques, golf courses, and gem mines. Each trip here seems to provide many reasons for a return visit.

Connemara, Carl Sandburg's Home
COURTESY OF NORTH CAROLINA DIVISION OF TOURISM, FILM AND SPORTS DEVELOPMENT

HENDERSONVILLE

by Sue Clark

*E*stablished in 1840, Hendersonville is ideally situated on a plateau between the Blue Ridge Mountains and the Great Smoky Mountains. Thanks to its mild climate and moderate altitude (2,200 feet), many people find this the perfect place to live and vacation. What's not to like? You can play golf 11 months of the year; there is little crime or pollution; you'll find lots of friendly people. The area attracts many retirees.

Apples are the mainstay of Henderson County's economy. The North Carolina Apple Festival takes place in Hendersonville on Labor Day weekend. This county produces 70 percent of the state's leading fruit crop. Regional farmers produce about 8 million bushels of Red and Golden Delicious, Rome Beauty, and Stayman apples each year.

Downtown Hendersonville is great for walking. Small shops, boutiques, and restaurants line the main streets.

Things to Do

HISTORIC PLACES, GARDENS, AND TOURS

■ **Carl Sandburg Home National Historic Site** is located south of Hendersonville in the town of Flat Rock. This 240-acre farm is where the Pulitzer Prize–winning poet and biographer spent the last 22 years of his life. In 1945, Sandburg bought the farm, called Connemara, and moved here with his wife, Paula, who was herself renowned for raising champion goats. In 1967, shortly after Sandburg's death at age 89, Connemara became a National Historic Site.

You'll immediately get a sense of Connemara's peacefulness as you walk up the trail from the information center to the white three-story house. Built around 1838, the home is surrounded by trees and situated with a lovely view of the rolling countryside. Nearby are several outbuildings. About a quarter-mile away is the barn, where the goats were housed and tended. A few goats are still kept there.

In the reception area of the house, you can see a filmed interview of

Sandburg conducted by Edward R. Murrow. The furnishings, family pictures, shelves of books, and huge stacks of papers and magazines in the living room and Sandburg's study have been left just as they were when he was in residence. On the dining-room table are his thermos and a handful of letters to be opened.

In the summer, actors and actresses from the nearby Flat Rock Playhouse dramatize tales from Sandburg's *Rootabaga Stories*, a book of children's folk tales, in a small outdoor amphitheater located on the grounds. Performances of *World of Carl Sandburg* and *Sandburg's Lincoln* are also given. Shows are offered Tuesday through Saturday; admission is free.

The Carl Sandburg Home is open daily except Christmas from 9 A.M. to 5 P.M. Admission to the grounds is free. Adults are charged a small fee for the house tour, but children under 17 are admitted free. The tour lasts about 30 minutes, after which you may enjoy walking the two marked trails on the property. For more information, call 828-693-4178.

▪ **Oakdale Cemetery** on U.S. 64 West is the site of "Wolfe's Angel." Thomas Wolfe's first novel, *Look Homeward, Angel*, contained numerous references to an angel statue carved from Italian marble. The statue in Oakdale Cemetery served as the inspiration. The author's father, W. O. Wolfe, sold it to the Johnson family to mark the family plot here. The angel holds a lily in her left hand while she extends her right hand upward. The statue is protected by a wrought-iron fence. A historical marker is located on the highway.

CULTURAL OFFERINGS

▪ **Flat Rock Playhouse**, located on U.S. 25 in Flat Rock, is the state theater of North Carolina. It is a professional summer theater that presents eight or nine comedies, mysteries, and musicals from late May to mid-October. Periodically, Thomas Wolfe's **Look Homeward, Angel** is presented in honor of the local boy. Call 828-693-0731 for information, or visit their website at www.flatrockplayhouse.org.

Special Shopping

- **Henderson County Farmers Mutual Curb Market**, at 221 North Church Street, offers home-grown flowers, fresh fruits and vegetables, baked goods, handmade crafts, and an impressive array of pickles, relishes, jellies, and jams. It's also a great place to chat with the locals. The market is open Tuesday, Thursday, and Saturday from 8 A.M. to 2 P.M. from May to December. It is open Tuesday and Saturday from January through April. For more information, call 828-692-8012.

- **Downtown Hendersonville** has experienced a revitalization over the last few years. Within easy walking distance are antique shops, art galleries, and specialty stores. Visitors can go back in time at an old-fashioned soda shop located in an old pharmacy that has occupied the same spot since the turn of the century. Downtown shoppers will find everything from boutiques filled with local crafts to galleries featuring modern art exhibits.

- My favorite downtown spot is **Kilwin's Chocolate Shoppe** (828-698-9794), located on Main Street. My son and I consider ourselves fudge experts, so when a friend recommended a new place in Hendersonville as the home of the best fudge she'd ever tasted, we knew we had to check it out. Imagine my delight upon discovering that the "new" place was actually a beacon of my childhood. You see, the original Kilwin's is in Petoskey, Michigan, where my family had a summer home when I was a child. The owners assured me it truly was the same Kilwin's; in fact, they had to travel to Petoskey to learn to make fudge the Kilwin's way. Don't limit yourself to just the fudge. There's also ice cream, caramel corn, brittle, taffy, and candies, all of which live up to Kilwin's reputation for quality.

Recreation

- **Holmes State Forest**, located eight miles southwest of Hendersonville on Crab Creek Road, is a managed forest offering picnic areas, hiking trails, and sites for tent camping. Some of the trees have button-activated recordings describing aspects of the forest. Holmes State Forest is open for visitors Tuesday through Sunday from mid-March to the Friday before Thanksgiving. For more information, call 828-692-0100.

SEASONAL EVENTS

▪ The *North Carolina Apple Festival*, held Labor Day weekend, celebrates the apple harvest with street dancing and crafts for sale. The King Apple Parade rolls through downtown on Labor Day. For more information, call 828-697-4557.

▪ The *Garden Jubilee* is held the Saturday and Sunday of Memorial Day weekend. The emphasis here is on plants and garden advice. Arts and crafts are available for sale. Call 800-828-4244.

▪ The *Sidewalk Art Show*, held the first full weekend in August, features regional artists displaying and selling their framable artwork. Call 828-696-7926.

▪ Those interested in the display and sale of new and old quilts will enjoy the *Annual Quilt Fest*, held in October. It is sponsored by the Tar Heel Piecemakers and the Western North Carolina Quilters Guild. Boutiques sell associated merchandise. Call 800-828-4244.

Places to Stay

INNS AND BED-AND-BREAKFASTS

▪ *Mélange Bed-and-Breakfast*. Expensive. 1230 Fifth Avenue West, Hendersonville (800-303-5253 or 828-697-5253; www.melangebb.com). This beautiful old mansion, restored in 1996, offers Old World charm and tradition and European flair. High ceilings, marble fireplaces, ornate mirrors, Mediterranean porches, crystal chandeliers, and antique furnishings make the place elegant and warm. The large guest rooms and the two-room suite feature either solid brass, old plantation oak, or French canopy beds; each has a private bath. Room rates include a gourmet breakfast served in the rose garden, on the covered porches, or in the formal dining room.

- **Woodfield Inn**. Expensive/Moderate. U.S. 25, Flat Rock (800-533-6016 or 828-693-6016; www.woodfieldinn.com). Woodfield Inn has been receiving guests since 1852. It is a landmark establishment with a long tradition of Southern hospitality. A three-story frame hotel with a huge front lawn, it has an enormous entrance hall, a large sitting room, and three dining rooms downstairs. On the upper floors, which slant slightly, are Victorian bedrooms with high ceilings and French doors opening onto a veranda. Only three of the guest rooms have private baths. Throughout the inn are antique furnishings, some of which have been here since the Civil War. Continental breakfast is included.

- **Claddagh Inn**. Moderate. 755 North Main Street, Hendersonville (800-225-4700 or 828-697-7778; www.claddaghinn.com). This three-story frame house with a wraparound veranda has been an inn for 90 years. It lends the same feeling you might get if you were visiting your grandmother. Each of the 14 guest rooms and two suites is graciously appointed and has a private bath. A full country breakfast is served in the dining room.

- **The Waverly Inn**. Moderate. 783 North Main Street, Hendersonville (800-537-8195 or 828-693-9193; www.waverlyinn.com). This three-story frame house has a porch full of rocking chairs extending across the front, which sets a casual mood and creates a pleasant ambiance. All of the guest rooms are comfortably decorated and have private baths. Room rates include a sumptuous home-cooked breakfast.

Places to Eat

- **Highland Lake Inn**. Expensive. Highland Lake Road, Flat Rock (828-

696-9094). This restaurant is part of a conference center at Highland Lake that was once a Catholic camp. The French chef is a true gourmet. The restaurant prides itself on fresh ingredients, including vegetables from its own garden. Dinner is served Tuesday through Saturday, and brunch is offered on Sunday. Reservations are requested.

▪ *Expressions*. Expensive/Moderate. 114 North Main Street, Hendersonville (828-693-8516). Expressions offers continental dining in a renovated storefront. Plum wallpaper, dark green carpeting, and brass lamps on the tables set the mood for the sophisticated menu and the restaurant's seasonal specialties. The chef-owned Expressions has received many accolades and awards. Dinner is served Monday through Saturday.

▪ *Woodfield Inn*. Expensive/Moderate. U.S. 25, Flat Rock (828-693-6016). This inn has been a dining tradition since 1852, when it was a stop on the stagecoach line. Warm muffins are brought to your table for you to enjoy while reading the menu, which includes fried chicken, baked ham, prime rib, and trout amandine. After one of the delicious homemade desserts, you'll want to linger on the veranda. The restaurant is open for dinner Wednesday through Sunday and for brunch on Sunday.

▪ *McGuffey's*. Moderate. Blue Ridge Mall, Hendersonville (828-697-0556). This is an amusing restaurant with a schoolhouse theme based on the McGuffey readers. Its tasty offerings will appeal to everyone in the family. They include several varieties of hamburgers, chicken sandwiches, pasta, vegetable stir-fry, and steaks. Lunch and dinner are served daily.

▪ *Jimmy's Italian Villa*. Moderate/Inexpensive. 1903 Asheville Highway, Hendersonville (828-693-0980). This has been Hendersonville's most popular restaurant since opening its doors in 1977. The interior has a pleasant Mediterranean decor. The pizza and the Italian dishes are excellent, as are Jimmy's famous garlic rolls. Dinner is served Tuesday through Saturday.

▪ *Hannah Flanagan's Pub*. Inexpensive. 300 North Main Street, Hendersonville (828-696-1665). As in any good pub, the bar is the focus in this local hangout. Recently expanded to offer more table seating,

Flanagan's is also a great place to stop and take stock of your shopping expedition. Patrons enjoy the hearty soups, sandwiches, and other traditional pub fare, as well as the fine selection of imported beers. This is one of those great pubs that makes you feel comfortable the minute you walk in the door. Lunch and dinner are served daily.

Chimney Rock
COURTESY OF NORTH CAROLINA
DIVISION OF TOURISM, FILM AND
SPORTS DEVELOPMENT
(ALSO USED IN THE BACKGROUND
OF PAGE 493)

Nearby

■ To reach **Chimney Rock Park** from Hendersonville, take U.S. 64 East to Bat Cave, then turn right on U.S. 74. Located 15 miles east of Hendersonville, this private park includes a massive rock formation known for its tall, narrow shape. Chimney Rock rises 225 feet above the entrance to Hickory Nut Gorge and provides a 75-mile panoramic view of Lake Lure and the Blue Ridge Mountains. Visitors cross the Rocky Broad River just past the entrance to the park and from there begin a three-mile drive to the base of the rock formation. Visitors are transported to the top via an elevator that runs up a 26-story shaft hewn in the granite. For the more adventurous, a trail of plank steps also leads to the top. Once on top, you can enjoy the view from the fenced-in overlook or from inside the Sky Lounge, which has a gift shop and a snack bar. The park also offers picnic areas with grills, a playground for children, an interpretive nature center, and hiking trails. Chimney Rock Park is open daily except for Thanksgiving, Christmas and New Year's. An admission fee is charged. The ticket office is open from 8:30 A.M. to 4:30 P.M. during daylight saving time; otherwise, it's open until 5:30 P.M. The park closes 90 minutes after the ticket office. For more information, call 800-277-9611 or 828-625-9611.

■ If you'd like to stay in the area, you can't go wrong with the *Lake Lure Inn* (828-625-2525), on U.S. 64 in neighboring Lake Lure, or the famous *Esmeralda Inn* (828-625-9105; www.esmeraldainn.com), on U.S. 74 between Bat Cave and Lake Lure. The famous visitors at the Esmeralda over the years have included the likes of Mary Pickford, Gloria Swanson, Douglas Fairbanks, and Clark Gable.

■ *Saluda*, located on U.S. 176 approximately 12 miles southeast of Hendersonville, is a small community where a number of craftspeople live and work. You can see some of their work and an array of regional country antiques in Saluda's old train depot, which has been converted to shops. Saluda is also home to the famous Saluda Grade, the steepest main-line railroad grade in America.

■ A noteworthy local hostelry is the *Orchard Inn* (828-749-5471), located on U.S. 176. It occupies an old vacation retreat built for the Brotherhood of Railway Clerks.

■ *Tryon*, on U.S. 176 east of Saluda, is named for the British governor of the North Carolina colony. Tryon has a pretty main street with a steep slope to it. Visitors come for its gift and craft shops and to see works by local artists and craftspeople at the *Tryon Fine Arts Center* (828-859-8322). The area is well known for its steeplechase races, held in April and October.

■ If you're staying in Tryon, try the *Pine Crest Inn* (828-859-9135), at 200 Pine Crest Lane, a former tuberculosis sanitorium transformed into a rustic inn in 1918, or the *Mimosa Inn* (877-646-6724 or 828-859-7688; www.carolina-foothills.com) on Mimosa Lane.

■ To reach *Pearson's Falls*, look for the sign to turn off U.S. 176 approximately three miles from Saluda. You'll then travel one mile on S.R. 1102 and an easy quarter-mile trail to the 90-foot falls. The area is maintained by the Tryon Garden Club. A small admission fee is charged.

Connestee Falls
COURTESY OF NORTH CAROLINA DIVISION OF TOURISM,
FILM AND SPORTS DEVELOPMENT

BREVARD
by Sue Clark

On the edge of Pisgah National Forest sits the pretty little town of Brevard. Its permanent population of 7,000 swells to many times that number during the annual Brevard Music Festival. Brevard is in the heart of an area called the "Land of Waterfalls." It is the county seat of Transylvania County, whose name means "Across the Woods."

Brevard's downtown, about four blocks long, has shops, restaurants, a movie theater, antique malls, and a picturesque brick courthouse. Beyond downtown, you'll see attractive homes with big porches on shaded residential streets. Given the size of the town, Brevard's many cultural offerings come as a surprise to many visitors. The mild climate and attractive landscape draw a large number of retirees, summer residents, and tourists. Brevard is an ideal place to stay if you enjoy driving through the mountains and stopping at waterfalls.

Things to Do

HISTORIC PLACES, GARDENS, AND TOURS

■ The **Cradle of Forestry in America**, on U.S. 276 in Pisgah National Forest, is another legacy of George W. Vanderbilt (see the chapter on Asheville). When Vanderbilt bought property in 1889 to create Biltmore Estate, he hired Gifford Pinchot to manage the forestland. Pinchot was the first man in America to practice selective timber cutting, which did not do wholesale damage to the forest. Pinchot's successor, Dr. Carl Schenck, started the first school of forestry in America, the Biltmore Forest School, which lasted from 1898 until 1913. In 1968, Congress established the 6,400-acre Pisgah National Forest.

The Cradle of Forestry in America is a national historic site commemorating the birthplace of scientific forestry and forestry education in America. The visitor center has exhibits, an 18-minute film outlining the history of the forestry school, a gift shop, and a snack bar. Two interpretive trails are on the property. The Biltmore Forest School Campus Trail visits restored and reconstructed buildings that depict the life of the first forestry students at the turn of the 20th century. The Forest Festival Trail features early forestry equipment such as a 1915 logging locomotive and a steam-powered sawmill. The Cradle of Forestry is open daily from 9 A.M. to 5 P.M. from May through October. A small admission fee is charged. Call 828-877-3130 for more information.

Brevard Music Center
COURTESY OF NORTH CAROLINA DIVISION OF TOURISM, FILM AND SPORTS DEVELOPMENT

CULTURAL OFFERINGS

▪ Held for seven weeks each summer, the **Brevard Music Festival** presents a smorgasbord of more than 70 performances ranging from symphony and pops to Broadway musicals and grand opera.

In 1936, Davidson College in Davidson, North Carolina, began a summer music camp. In 1943, the operation moved to an abandoned summer camp in Brevard. Three years later, the director and a few local students started the Brevard Music Festival, which at that time was a one-week series of performances by those attending the camp. The Brevard Music Camp subsequently built an 1,800-seat open-sided auditorium.

The camp offers private lessons, a concerto competition, an opera workshop, and performance experience with the Transylvania Symphony, the Brevard Music Center Orchestra, brass, wind, and woodwind ensembles, and a chamber choir. Students can earn college credit; during the festival, they have the opportunity to perform with guest artists.

Each summer, more than 400 of the nation's finest musicians gather to teach and perform. Guest artists have included Boston Pops conductor Keith Lockhart, vocalist Frederica von Stade, and the Louisiana Jazz Ensemble. Each season also promises four beautifully staged operas or musical theater productions, such as Lerner and Loewe's **Brigadoon**, Strauss's **Die Fledermaus**, and Verdi's **Aida**. It's a good idea to purchase tickets in advance; the festival has many devoted followers who buy season tickets and attend every performance. If you intend to stay in the area during the festival, make room reservations well in advance. Some performances are free; a fee is charged for others. For more information, call 800-405-8338 or 888-384-8682, or contact their website at www.brevardmusic.org.

SPECIAL SHOPPING

▪ **Downtown Brevard** is brimming with boutiques, galleries, specialty shops, restaurants, and coffee houses. Visitors can also find numerous outfitters' shops in the area, as well as guide services for mountain climbing, mountain biking, canoeing, and other outdoor pastimes.

▪ **Southern Expressions Gallery and Studios**, on U.S. 64 five miles east of Brevard, is one of the best places in the mountains for contemporary crafts. Showcasing the work of only the finest craftspeople, this shop sells ceramics, pottery, beautifully polished wooden boxes, baskets, brooms, weavings, quilts, toys, and musical instruments. Call 828-884-6242.

RECREATION

▪ **Pisgah National Forest** is a land of mile-high peaks, cascading waterfalls, and heavily forested slopes. It is an ideal place for recreational enjoyment. The forest gets its name from Mount Pisgah, a prominent peak in the area. In the 1700s, a Scots-Irish minister saw the peak and named it for the biblical mountain from which Moses saw the Promised Land after 40 years of wandering in the wilderness.

The national forest is managed to provide the best combination of uses to benefit the general public while protecting the long-term quality of the forest. Some of the many uses include the harvesting of timber products, camping, hiking, hunting, fishing, and wildlife observation. If you plan to fish, you'll need a license, which can be obtained at many of the outfitters' shops. For more information on facilities, hiking, and biking, stop at the information center, located in the ranger station about a mile into the forest on U.S. 276 from U.S. 64. Or you can contact the Pisgah National Forest supervisor at 828-257-4200.

■ Waterfall viewing is one of the favorite activities in the area. The most popular drive goes north from Brevard on U.S. 276 through Pisgah National Forest to **Looking Glass Falls**. You can see the waterfall from the road, but parking your car and walking to get a closer view is a much better way to experience this breathtaking natural wonder. U.S. 276 continues to **Sliding Rock**. Be sure to pack your bathing suit, because the best way to experience this water wonder is on your behind. A lifeguard is on duty in the summer, and a bathhouse is provided. There's no better way to cool off on a hot summer day. Another popular option is to drive west out of Brevard on U.S. 64 between Highlands and Franklin. You'll pass **Dry Falls**, where you can take an easy walk behind a 75-foot wall of water. Also west on U.S. 64, just past the town of Highlands, is **Bridal Veil Falls**, which cascades over the road. Cars can actually drive behind the veil of water. In Brevard you can pick up a guide to area waterfalls. Connestee Falls and Graveyard Fields are two of the most picturesque.

■ Hiking opportunities abound in the area. If you take U.S. 276 to the Blue Ridge Parkway, a right turn will take you to Mount Pisgah, and a left will lead you past the Devil's Courthouse. Both areas offer hikes with

Graveyard Fields
Courtesy of North Carolina
Division of Tourism, Film and
Sports Development

breathtaking views. Information on hiking trails can be obtained at the outfitters' shops.

▪ Fly-fishing on Transylvania County's Davidson River is an obsession to many. *Trout Unlimited* magazine ranks the Davidson as one of America's top 10 trout streams. The Davidson and other area streams are stocked with brook, brown, and rainbow trout from the Pisgah Fish Hatchery.

Places to Stay

INNS AND BED-AND-BREAKFASTS

▪ **Greystone Inn**. Deluxe/Expensive. Greystone Lane in Lake Toxaway, 17 miles west of Brevard (800-824-5766 or 828-996-4700; www.greystoneinn.com). The magnificent mountains, beautiful Lake Toxaway, a charming historic mansion, and fine cuisine are just a few of the superlatives that apply to the Greystone Inn. A spectacular array of activities—golf, tennis, hiking, skiing, canoeing, and fishing, among others—are only steps away. The Greystone Spa offers an opportunity to be pampered and replenished. Built in the early 1900s, this mansion was converted to a luxury resort in 1984. The 33 guest rooms are decorated with antiques. Each has a view of the lake and the surrounding forest. A heated pool is on the premises. Boats and gear for fishing and water-skiing are available. Room rates include breakfast, afternoon tea, and an elegant dinner.

▪ **Earthshine Mountain Lodge**. Expensive/Moderate. Golden Road in Lake Toxaway (828-862-4207). Situated on a 70-acre farm, this lodge is built entirely of logs and is decorated with log furnishings throughout. The eight guest rooms all have private baths and sleeping lofts. The real attraction, however, is the activities available for guests. The rope-climbing area resembles those at Outward Bound. There are also opportunities for horseback riding, hiking, and rock climbing. A barnyard on the premises is filled with animals for the children. And there's always entertainment for guests after dinner. Room rates include all three meals.

- **The Pines Country Inn**. Moderate. 719 Hart Road in the town of Pisgah Forest (828-877-3131; www.pinescountryinn.bizonthe.net). This inn, located a short distance from Brevard, is in a peaceful farming area overlooking the Little River Valley. Guests here can see horses grazing and wake to the songs of the birds. The house, built in 1883, has been an inn since 1905. The atmosphere is homey and comfortable. The 18 guest rooms include some separate cottages. Room rates include breakfast.

- **The Womble Inn**. Moderate. 301 West Main Street (828-884-4770; www.thewombleinn.com). This New Orleans–style house three blocks from the middle of town is where guests at the music festival often stay. Each room has a private bath. Continental breakfast is provided; a full breakfast is also available for an additional fee. The inn serves lunch Monday through Friday and will pack a picnic basket for a takeout lunch.

- **The Red House Inn**. Inexpensive. 412 West Probart Street (828-884-9349). The Red House Inn sits on a corner shielded from traffic by high hedges. Porches extend across the front of the two-story house, built in 1851 as a trading post. The oak woodwork is polished to a high gloss, and the comforters are fluffed on the antique beds. Room rates include a full breakfast served in the dining room.

Places to Eat

- **Chianti's Italian Café and Bar**. Moderate. At the intersection of U.S. 64 and N.C. 280 in the town of Pisgah Forest (828-862-5683). Chianti's has a reputation for serving tasty, authentic Italian cuisine ranging from classic entrées to New York–style hand-tossed pizzas. Dinner is served seven nights a week. Entertainment is provided on weekends.

- **Falls Landing**. Moderate. 23 East Main Street (828-884-2835). This restaurant specializes in fresh seafood such as grilled salmon, broiled trout, swordfish, mahi-mahi, live Maine lobster, fresh clams and oysters, jumbo shrimp, and steamed mussels. The menu also includes pasta dishes, top-grade steaks, chicken, and homemade soups and desserts. Falls Landing is open for lunch Monday through Saturday and dinner Tuesday through Saturday.

- **Corner Bistro**. Moderate/Inexpensive. At the corner of Main and Broad Streets (828-862-4746). This casual restaurant offers deli and gourmet sandwiches, tortilla wraps, black bean and veggie burgers, turkey chili, fresh salads, quesadillas, vegetarian fare, soups, and daily specials. The Corner Bistro is open for lunch Monday through Saturday and dinner Tuesday through Saturday.

- **Bracken Mountain Bakery**. Inexpensive. South Broad Street (828-883-4034). This bakery specializes in European crusty breads and American sandwich breads. Breads and pastries are made from scratch and baked fresh daily on the premises. While the bakery is primarily a takeout operation, tables are available for those who wish to dine in. Flatbreads and filled pocket breads are available for a delicious lunch treat. The bakery serves lunch Monday through Saturday from May to October and Tuesday through Saturday the rest of the year.

- **Essence of Thyme**. Inexpensive. 37 East Main Street (828-884-7171). This restaurant is a unique place to take a break from downtown shopping. The menu features a variety of espresso beverages, coffees, teas, root beer floats, fresh fruit smoothies, and a nice selection of wines by the glass. In the morning, you can get New York bagels with a selection of toppings. Lunch and dinner feature deli-style sandwiches and salads. Pastries, pies, and cheese cakes are also available. Essence of Thyme serves breakfast from Monday through Saturday and lunch and dinner every day.

HIGHLANDS
by Sue Clark

*T*he unique mountain town of Highlands has a rich history, a wonderful climate, and an enviable way of life. Highlands stands tall in the high country. Its average altitude is 4,118 feet, making it one of the highest incorporated towns east of the Mississippi River. The surrounding mountains soar to over 5,000 feet. During July, the average temperature is a cool 67 degrees, making this a haven for those escaping the heat of the flatlands. Surrounded by Nantahala National Forest, the plateau on which Highlands rests is botanically and geologically unique.

Founded as a summer resort in 1875 by Samuel T. Kelsey and Clinton C. Hutchinson, Highlands has from its beginnings been a retreat from the fast pace of city life. While the year-round population is about 4,000, the summer population is over 20,000. Highlands has become a place of renewal for professionals and executives, who purchase land here and build beautiful summer homes. The cultural amenities during the summer season include live theater, chamber-music concerts, cabarets, and special dinners. Educational seminars and informative lectures are also offered. And did I mention shopping? The shopping in Highlands encompasses boutiques, specialty shops, antiques, jewelry, and handmade crafts and furniture.

JUST THE FACTS

Highlands is located at the intersection of N.C. 106/N.C. 28 and U.S. 64, which makes a 90-degree turn at Main Street. The roads to Highlands from Brevard and Cashiers—and from anywhere else, for that matter—are twisting and demanding of drivers' attention. Leave the sightseeing to passengers.

The Highlands Chamber of Commerce is located at the town hall on Main Street; call 828-526-2112 for information.

The semiweekly newspaper for the area is called the *Highlander*.

Things to Do

MUSEUMS AND SCIENCE CENTERS

■ **Highlands Nature Center** is on East Main Street half a mile east of downtown. This small but informative center offers exhibits that interpret the flora and fauna of the area's forests. It has a small botanical garden with trails and a display of mineral samples and Cherokee artifacts. The center is open Monday through Saturday from 10 A.M. to 5 P.M. from May 15 to Labor Day; variable hours continue through October. Admission is free. For more information, call 828-526-2623.

CULTURAL OFFERINGS

■ **Highlands Playhouse**, located on Oak Street, presents a summer season of professional theater featuring contemporary dramas and comedies. Call the ticket office at 828-526-2695 for the current schedule.

■ The **Highlands Chamber Music Festival**, which takes place from mid-July to the first weekend of August, features several concerts by renowned artists. The concerts are held in different venues, including local churches. For information, call 828-526-9060.

RECREATION

Since the main attraction in this area is the scenery, one of the favorite local pastimes is driving tours. Two routes are particularly scenic.

■ From Highlands to Franklin, U.S. 64 follows the Cullasaja River Gorge. The river cascades over falls and ripples over rapids, all within sight of the road. The drive toward Franklin is downhill. The road starts out twisting and winding, then widens and curves more gently. Along the route, you may want to stop to photograph **Bridal Veil Falls**, where you can actually drive behind the 75-foot veil of water. The most spectacular waterfall on this route is **Lower Cullasaja Falls**, a dramatic series of cascades dropping more than 250 feet in a quarter-mile. It is difficult to find a parking space here because the narrow road hangs on a cliff. Drive past the falls and hike back to see them. It's worth the effort.

▪ From Highlands to Cashiers, U.S. 64 is sharply curved but well paved and marked. The trees and rhododendron are thick and close to the road except where a great valley vista opens to the south, revealing a bird's-eye view of nearby **Whiteside Mountain**, which rises 2,100 feet from the valley floor. Its summit has an elevation of 4,930 feet. Both the north and south faces feature stunning, sheer cliffs ranging from 400 to 750 feet in height. This route continues to the town of **Cashiers**, where you'll find several pottery shops, gift shops, and resorts.

▪ Highlands is surrounded by **Nantahala National Forest**. You can enjoy the forest on foot or by car. If you're interested in hiking, contact the district ranger at 828-526-3765, or write U.S. Forest Service, District 2010, Flat Mountain Road, Highlands, N.C. 28741.

▪ Located seven miles south of Highlands on N.C. 106, **Ski Scaly** is North Carolina's southernmost ski area. It has four slopes and a vertical drop of 225 feet. The lodge offers cafeteria meals. Rental equipment and instruction are available. For more information, contact Ski Scaly, Box 339, Scaly Mountain, N.C. 28775 (828-526-3737).

Places to Stay

RESORTS, HOTELS, AND MOTELS

▪ **High Hampton Inn and Country Club**. Deluxe/Expensive. N.C. 107 just south of Cashiers (800-334-2551 or 800-334-2551; www.highhamptoninn.com). This warm, family-oriented resort has a rustic style it has preserved since it was built in 1932. The exterior is covered with chestnut-bark shingles. Inside, the inn has log banisters in the stairwells and wood paneling on the walls and ceilings.

The enormous lobby has four stone fireplaces around a central chimney and baskets of magazines and jigsaw puzzles for guests to relax over. The inn's 235 rooms have private baths but no telephones or televisions, so you can truly get away from it all. Meals are served buffet-style in the large dining room; it sounds casual, but men are expected to wear coats and ties for dinners and ladies to dress appropriately. The inn has an 18-hole golf course, outdoor tennis courts, and a lake with a sand beach. Canoes, sailboats, and fishing boats are available for rent. The inn offers planned activities for children and teens and a long list of special seminars, golf and fishing schools, and art workshops. The room rates include three meals. The inn is open from April to Thanksgiving.

■ **Fairfield Sapphire Valley**. Expensive/Moderate. U.S. 64 (828-743-3441). This top-rated resort offers a range of activities year-round. Set on green, forested slopes, it looks like an attractive housing development with rows of townhouses behind stands of trees. The lodgings range from luxurious hotel rooms to efficiency rooms with kitchens to one-, two-, and three-bedroom condos with separate living areas. All are comfortably furnished and attractively decorated; some have splendid views of the surrounding mountains. The kitchens are fully stocked, but if you prefer not to cook, the restaurant on the premises is open for lunch and dinner. Recreation facilities in the bracing air (you're 3,400 feet up) include an 18-hole championship golf course, one indoor and two outdoor pools, tennis courts, a lake beach, and a health club. You can also go horseback riding or rent bicycles, canoes, paddleboats, and fishing boats. A variety of activities such as children's game days and weekly family bingo are offered in the community room. During the winter, you may choose to try out the resort's four ski slopes, which have a 425-foot vertical drop. Ski equipment rentals are available.

INNS AND BED-AND-BREAKFASTS

■ **4½ Street Inn**. Expensive. 4½ Street between Chestnut and Hickory Streets (828-526-4464; www.4andahalfstinn.com). This beautiful inn occupies a fully restored 100-year-old home on 1.3 acres five blocks from town. The inn has a hot tub, a wraparound porch, gardens, and a sun deck. Its 10 guest rooms have private baths; some have fireplaces. Guests are warmly welcomed with afternoon refreshments and home-baked cookies. In the evening, the hosts serve wine and hors d'oeuvres. Room rates include a gourmet breakfast, a morning paper, and fluffy robes. Bicycles are available for a trek into town. The bird feeders in the backyard provide great entertainment during breakfast.

- *Kelsey & Hutchinson Lodge*. Expensive/Moderate. 450 Spring Street (888-245-9058 or 828-526-4746; www.k-hlodge.com). Located on three beautiful acres overlooking downtown Highlands, this lodge is within an easy walk of restaurants and shops. It offers 33 rooms, many with a fireplace, a whirlpool, and a porch or balcony. Children are welcome here. The hosts will gladly help plan recreational activities. Room rates include continental breakfast and an evening hospitality hour.

- *Skyline Lodge and Cabins*. Expensive/Moderate. Flat Mountain Road (828-526-2790; www.highlandsinfo.com/skyline.htm). Located atop 4,100-foot Flat Mountain, this lodge has 50 guest rooms and several two- and three-bedroom cabins on 50 private acres. The wide variety of recreational facilities here includes a sauna, a steam room, a swimming pool, and tennis courts. Hiking trails on the grounds lead to a 45-foot waterfall. A full-service restaurant is open on the weekends in season. Rooms are available May through the first week of November. The cabins remain open year-round.

- *Highlands Inn*. Moderate. Main Street (800-694-6955 or 828-526-9380; www.highlandsinfo.com/lodgings/highinn.htm). Located at the corner of Main and Fourth, the Highlands Inn has been a cornerstone of this town since 1880. Listed on the National Register of Historic Places, it attracts a loyal crowd of guests with its rocking chairs on the veranda and its flags extending from the second-floor railing. Each room has a private bath and is beautifully decorated with period furniture. An extended continental breakfast is included in the room rate.

- *Old Edwards Inn*. Moderate. Main Street (888-526-9319 or 828-526-9319). Located at the corner of Main and Fourth across the street from the Highlands Inn, the Old Edwards Inn has been offering "21 good rooms for ladies and gentlemen" since 1878. The ambiance here is elegant country. The rooms all have private baths and are light and airy. Guests enjoy the hand stenciling on the walls and the pretty coverlets on the antique pencil-post and canopy beds. Room rates include an extended continental breakfast.

Places to Eat

- **The Log Cabin.** Expensive. 130 Log Cabin Lane (828-526-3380). This cabin was built in 1924 as a summer home for a family from Anderson, South Carolina. Most of the furniture was done by Tiger Mountain Woodworks, located in Highlands. The menu features appetizers such as Texas quail and smoked trout pâté, entrées from the grill like New Zealand lamb chops and fried frog legs, seafood specialties such as North Carolina trout and barbecued shrimp, and a variety of pasta dishes. The freshly made desserts include such goodies as coconut cake, "Snicker Doodle Pie," warm pear cake, and the famous "Brickle Basket," filled with a variety of surprises.

- **Ristorante Paoletti.** Expensive. Main Street (828-526-4906; www.paoletti.com). This is fine dining Italian-style. Ristorante Paoletti offers homemade pastas, seafood, and prime cuts of meat in an intimate setting in downtown Highlands. The highlights include veal chops, chicken with prosciutto and mozzarella, and Colorado lamb. The wine list is extensive. The restaurant is open for dinner Monday through Saturday.

- **Central House Restaurant.** Expensive/Moderate. Main Street (828-526-9319). Central House Restaurant is located at the Old Edwards Inn. Soups, salads, and sandwiches make up most of the lunch menu. For dinner, seafood entrées like snapper, blackened catfish, and crab-stuffed North Carolina trout are featured. Chicken and steak entrées are also available. Breakfast is served to guests of the inn only. Lunch and dinner are served daily to the public. The restaurant is closed from New Year's to Valentine's Day.

- **Lakeside Restaurant**. Expensive/Moderate. Smallwood Avenue overlooking Lake Harris (828-526-9419). This place, which bills itself as "a casual restaurant with serious cuisine," comes highly recommended by local residents. Fresh seafood, beef, veal, lamb, chicken, and pasta dishes are on the menu. The portions are generous and delicious. Daily specials are offered, as is a good wine list. Between June and October, Lakeside serves lunch daily and dinner Monday through Saturday. During April, May, and November, the restaurant is closed Sunday and Monday. Reservations for dinner are strongly recommended.

- **Nick's**. Expensive/Moderate. N.C. 28 at Satulah Road (828-526-2706). This is where you'll find the locals. The decor is casual—calico curtains and bright copper pots. The lunch menu features steak, club, and fish sandwiches. The dinner offerings include lobster crepes, lamb chops, steak, and shrimp. Nick's is open for lunch and dinner Thursday through Tuesday.

FRANKLIN
by Sue Clark

The town of Franklin is the center of a thriving gem-mining industry. No wonder they call the place the "Jewel of the Southeast."

In the latter part of the 19th century, the Cowee Valley, just north of Franklin, was found to contain a high occurrence of corundum—rubies and sapphires, for those of us who don't know our quartz from our carbonite. Several commercial mining companies began digging exploratory mines. Rubies were found in all the gravel beds, but not in quantities sufficient to support extensive mining operations.

Commercial mining ended around the turn of the 20th century. All the better for us, since the Cowee Valley has continued to yield hundreds of rubies, sapphires, and other gemstones. Visitors can enjoy the chance to unearth one of these treasures. The predominant business in Franklin is accommodating all these rock hounds. Several gem shops will sell you raw stones or cut and mount those you find at one of the many gem mines catering to tourists.

The other "jewel" in Franklin's crown is location. Just outside town, you can visit the beautiful Nantahala National Forest and Nantahala Gorge, which offer many recreational opportunities.

When you visit Franklin, notice the large, grass-covered mound at the bottom of the hill on U.S. 64 Business. This is all that remains of an 18th-century Cherokee village called Nikwasi. Many archaeologists have asked permission to excavate it, but in the end, Franklin officials have always decided to leave things just as they are.

JUST THE FACTS

Franklin is located at the junction of U.S. 64, U.S. 23/ U.S. 441, and N.C. 28.

The Macon County Airport has one lighted runway; call 828-524-5529 for information.

The Franklin Area Chamber of Commerce is located at 425 Porter Street; call 888-510-GEMS or 828-524-3161.

The two local papers are the *Franklin Press*, published twice weekly, and the *Macon County News*, published weekly.

Things to Do

MUSEUMS AND SCIENCE CENTERS

■ *Franklin Gem and Mineral Museum*, at 25 Phillips Street, is housed in the old city jail, built in the 1850s and used until 1972. The displays include a wide range of mineral specimens, fossils, and Indian artifacts. One room contains samples from all over North Carolina, while another has specimens from every other state in the union. One of the most interesting displays contains rocks under florescent light that continue to glow after the light has been switched off. The museum was established and is maintained by volunteers of the Gem and Mineral Society of Franklin. It is open Monday through Saturday from 10 A.M. to 4 P.M. from May through October. Admission is free. Call 828-369-7831 for information.

▪ *Scottish Tartans Museum and Heritage Center*, at 86 East Main Street, celebrates the Scottish heritage of the North Carolina mountains. Displays document the evolution of the kilt and the influence of the Scots on Appalachian culture. If you are of Scottish descent, you can find your family tartan in the Tartan Room. The gift shop sells items from Scotland and handmade Appalachian crafts. The museum is open Monday through Saturday from 10 A.M. to 5 P.M. and Sunday from 1 P.M. to 5 P.M. A modest admission fee is charged. Call 828-524-7472 for information.

▪ *Ruby City Gems and Minerals*, at 130 East Main Street, isn't strictly a museum. It's also a lapidary shop that sells raw and cut gemstones, lapidary equipment and supplies, and mineral samples such as geodes and amethyst crystals. The museum, located on the lower level, displays hundreds of mineral samples in well-lighted glass cases. The main attraction is a sapphire specimen that weighs 382 pounds. The shop and museum are open Monday through Saturday from 9 A.M. to 5 P.M. from April through December. Admission is free, though donations are accepted. Call 828-524-3967 for information.

SPECIAL SHOPPING

▪ *MACO Crafts, Inc.*, is located at 2846 Georgia Highway (U.S. 441) three miles south of Franklin. One of the largest craft cooperatives in the Appalachian Mountains, it displays the work of about 250 members. A vast array of decorative and utilitarian items is for sale here. You'll find pottery, baskets, embroidered aprons, stained glass, candleholders, wreaths, dolls, and Christmas decorations. Some of the exquisite creations by master quilters go for up to $1,800. You can also purchase from a large selection of fabrics and quilting supplies. The shop is open Monday through Saturday form 9 A.M. to 5:30 P.M. and Sunday from 1 P.M. to 5:30 P.M. from May to November; it is open Monday through Saturday from 10 A.M. to 5 P.M. and Sunday from 1 P.M. to 5 P.M. the rest of the year. Call 828-524-7878 for more information.

RECREATION

■ Franklin's main attraction is gem mining.

According to an Indian legend, rubies appeared in the Cowee Valley because the beautiful daughter of a tribal chief fell in love with the son of her father's archenemy. When the father found out, he was so enraged that he ordered the lovers put to death on the spot. The couple's love was so strong that their blood ran together into the earth and hardened into precious stones.

When you go mining for rubies and crystals, you'll pay for three or four buckets of rock and soil from the mine. Then, sitting at the edge of a flume line (a trough with gently flowing water), you'll rinse the soil from the rocks a scoop at a time and pick out the raw stones. Keep in mind that raw, uncut stones bear little resemblance to what you see in the jeweler's window. The mine operators will help you learn what to look for. Some mines enrich—or "salt"—the dirt with gravel known to contain some stones. If you've got children with you, choose one of these mines, where you'll have a better chance of keeping the kids' interest. You aren't likely to find large, gem-quality rubies, but you will have a lot of fun finding small, pretty stones to take away as souvenirs of your trip.

The Franklin Area Chamber of Commerce can provide you a complete list of local gem mines. I can personally recommend **Mason Mountain Mine** (828-524-4570) and **Rose Creek Mine and Campground** (828-524-3225).

■ **Rafting** in the Nantahala Gorge, about 20 miles north of Franklin, will appeal to those who like thrills and outdoor excitement—and to those who like getting soaked by cold mountain water. Several companies offer guided raft trips down the Nantahala River, which features class II and class III rapids. Don't let that intimidate you. Safety equipment is issued, and the guides tell you everything you need to do, so it's fun for even those with no rafting experience. The trips last about four hours and don't require special clothing except for something dry to change

Whitewater rafting the Nantahala Gorge
COURTESY OF NANTAHALA OUTDOOR CENTER

into when the trip is done. Children who weigh at least 60 pounds may participate. Raft trips operate from April through October. For a complete list of the companies that operate on U.S. 19 between Bryson City and Andrews, call 828-524-3161.

SEASONAL EVENTS

■ *Macon County Gemboree* is held twice each year, in late July and mid-October. Rock hounds gather from all over to display and sell gem and mineral specimens. Call 828-524-3161 for information.

Places to Stay

INNS AND BED-AND-BREAKFASTS

■ *Blaine House Bed-and-Breakfast and Cottage*. Expensive/Moderate. 661 Harrison Avenue (888-349-4230 or 828-349-4230; www.intertekweb.com/blainebb). Blaine House reflects the grace and serenity of homes of yesteryear. This 1910 home has been restored to its original state; lovers of fine things will appreciate the beautiful oak floors. The four guest rooms have private baths. The cottage offers one bedroom with a full bath, a spacious living and dining room, a full kitchen, and a balcony. Room rates in the main house include a gourmet breakfast.

■ *Hummingbird Lodge*. Expensive/Moderate. 1101 Hickory Knoll Ridge Road (828-369-0430; www.bbonline.com/NC/hummingbird). A true mountain retreat, this lodge is an all-log structure with wonderfully appointed decorations, large fireplaces, and quilted comforters on the beds. Peace, solitude, and a relaxing ambiance are the order of the day here. Each of the three guest rooms is decorated with a different North Carolina theme. All have private baths. Room rates include a full gourmet country breakfast. Evening wine and hors d'oeuvres are included on Friday and Saturday.

- **The Snow Hill Inn**. Expensive/Moderate. 531 Snow Hill Road (828-369-2100; www.bbonline.com/nc/snowhill). The Snow Hill Inn is an elegantly restored 1914 schoolhouse. Guests can relax on the shaded front porch or in the gazebo, enjoy the 14 acres of quiet seclusion, and play croquet or badminton on the lawn. Room rates include a full breakfast served in the dining room, where the main attraction is watching the birds at the feeders.

- **Heritage Inn**. Moderate. 43 Heritage Hollow Drive (888-524-4150 or 828-524-4150; www.intertekweb.com/heritage). Southern hospitality and country charm await you at this tin-roofed inn. The six comfortable rooms are decorated with antiques, collectibles, quilts, and a country flavor. Each has its own entrance, bath, and porch. Rooms with kitchenettes are available, as is a fully furnished one-bedroom apartment. Rates include a full homemade breakfast. Restaurants and antique and craft shops are within walking distance.

- **High Country Haven**. Moderate. 29 Bates Branch Road (888-815-4783 or 828-524-4783; www.highcountryhaven.com). This bed-and-breakfast is located in the headmaster's house of what was once the Morrison Industrial Girls' School. The home is surrounded by lovely landscaped grounds and is beautifully decorated with charming antiques. It has a covered greenhouse with a hot tub, a gracious parlor, and four beautifully appointed rooms, all with private baths. Room rates include a full country breakfast and evening dessert in the dining room. High Country Haven also offers three private apartments located at the rear of the guest house in what was originally the school's dormitory. And that's not all. The inn's campground, open from May through October, offers RV and tent sites; two camper cabins and two on-site campers are even available for rent.

Places to Eat

- **Patriccio's**. Expensive/Moderate. 801 Highlands Road (828-524-9229).

Italian fare made of the freshest possible ingredients, a small and intimate setting, and superb service add up to a wonderful evening. The menu here runs the gamut from antipasto to veal piccata to lasagna. Desserts made daily help bring the evening to a sumptuous close. Dinner is served Monday through Saturday.

- **The Frog & Owl Kitchen.** Moderate. 46 East Main Street (828-349-4112). Located in the heart of Franklin's downtown shopping district, the Frog & Owl Kitchen is the perfect place to stop and take stock of your day's explorations. The menu includes raspberry citrus salad, lentil bean salad, a pesto chicken sandwich, a lamb burger, and mountain trout. A wine shop is on the premises, as is a deli, where gourmet pastas and salads are available for takeout. Desserts and breads are baked fresh every day. Lunch is offered Monday through Saturday.

- **The Gazebo Creekside Café.** Inexpensive. 44 Heritage Hollow (828-524-8783). This lovely restored gazebo, located along a babbling creek, is a relaxing retreat in the middle of Franklin. The menu includes a wide variety of soups, salads, and sandwiches. For a cool drink, try a smoothie or a shake. Desserts include turtle cheesecake and Key lime pie, but my favorite is the chunky apple pie—à la mode, of course. Lunch is served daily and dinner Tuesday through Friday.

Nearby

- **Wayah Bald** is a massive stone outcrop in Nantahala National Forest at an elevation of more than a mile. Its "baldness" is in dramatic contrast to the lush forest that surrounds it. You can see Wayah Bald from downtown Franklin, but the trip to experience it up close takes about an hour. Take U.S. 64 West to S.R. 1310, then turn right on S.R. 69, which will lead you deep into the forest, where you'll see wildflowers and streams cascading down hillsides. You can park close to the summit, then walk about a quarter-mile on a paved trail for a spectacular view from the top.

- **Dillsboro** is about 20 miles north of Franklin on U.S. 441. The drive takes you through a picturesque mountain valley to a lovely little town on a hillside.

Dillsboro has several shops selling antiques, crafts, toys, and gifts. **Dogwood Crafters** (828-586-2248), located on Webster Street, is a craft cooperative carrying the work of many artisans. The nine shops comprising **Riverwood Shops** (828-586-6996), located across the railroad tracks on River Road, offer hammered pewter, leatherwork, weavings, and more.

Many people come to Dillsboro for an excursion aboard the **Great Smoky Mountains Railroad**. One of the excursions that departs from Dillsboro travels along the Tuckasegee River. This three-hour ride visits the setting of the escape scene at the beginning of the movie *The Fugitive*, starring Harrison Ford. The railway was hired by the film company to stage a train derailment with actual, full-size trains. They had only one shot at it, and it went perfectly. The remains of the wreck are featured on the excursion, which also includes the 836-foot-long Cowee Tunnel. Other excursions depart from Bryson City and Andrews. One of the Bryson City trips crosses Fontana Lake on a trestle 791 feet long and 179 feet high. Great Smoky Mountains Railroad also offers raft-and-rail trips, special excursions such as a "Santa Train" in December, and dinner excursions. Call 800-872-4681 for more information.

If you'll be staying overnight in Dillsboro, consider the **Squire Watkins Inn** (828-586-5244), just off U.S. 441. For a terrific meal, try the **Jarrett House** (828-586-0265), located on Main Street. This regional landmark opened as a hotel in 1882. Famous for its family-style meals, the restaurant specializes in fried chicken, country ham, and mountain trout. Each meal comes with bowls of vegetables, slaw, stewed apples, and hot biscuits. And be sure to try the vinegar pie.

■ The **John C. Campbell Folk School** is about 60 miles west of Franklin in Brasstown. The school was founded in 1925 to preserve and teach traditional Appalachian crafts. During the Depression, it provided economic opportunities for farm families by selling their high-quality woodcarvings.

Week-long courses are offered year-round today. They include pottery, weaving, basketry, woodcarving, bookbinding, Appalachian dancing, and newer crafts such as jewelry making and kaleidoscope making. Students come back year after year and often sign up for several courses at a time. The craft shop sells a variety of pottery, weavings, decorative ironwork, split-oak baskets, and beautiful work by some of the original Brasstown carvers. The shop is open Monday through Saturday from 8 A.M. to 5 P.M. and Sunday from 1 P.M. to 5 P.M. Call 828-837-2775 for more information.

The Great Smoky Mountains

Great Smoky Mountains National Park

Cherokee

Maggie Valley

Waynesville

By Sue Clark

$\mathcal{T}$raveling west from Asheville, you'll find the Blue Ridge Mountains in your rearview mirror and the Great Smoky Mountains ahead of you. This mountain range gets its name from the persistent haze that veils the rounded summits. These ancient mountains exude serenity while cloaking a rugged wilderness that, in many areas, remains untouched by modern hands.

Legend says the haze comes from a time when the Cherokees had been smoking the peace pipe with their enemies. Though the meeting continued for seven days, they all continued to quarrel. The Great Spirit, becoming annoyed, turned the men into grayish white flowers called Indian pipes and made smoke over the mountains to remind all men that they should live together in peace.

The scientific explanation is less interesting. It states that the haze is caused by an excess of oxygen and humidity created by the thick forestation. This oxygen and humidity mix with a microscopic mist of rosin-scented organic compounds called terpenes.

The Smokies area is a naturalist's paradise. They are home to more than 1,000 varieties of flowering plants and hundreds of species of mosses and trees. The Smokies contain the largest stand of old-growth hardwoods in North America. The diversity of plants and animals is unmatched anywhere in the country.

Fortunately, much of this magnificent wilderness has been incorporated into the National Park system to ensure that its wild beauty will be preserved. However, tourism has indeed intruded. Even so, these mountains are considered by many—this author included—to be the most beautiful part of North Carolina.

Scenic view along the Blue Ridge Parkway
COURTESY OF ASHEVILLE CONVENTION AND VISITORS BUREAU
(ALSO USED IN THE BACKGROUND OF PAGE 527)

GREAT SMOKY MOUNTAINS NATIONAL PARK

by Sue Clark

The Grand Canyon receives over 5 million visitors each year, Yosemite over 4 million, and Yellowstone over 3 million. But it is Great Smoky Mountains National Park that has more visitors than any other National Park—over 10 million each year. The park encompasses more than a half-million acres along 70 miles of the North Carolina–Tennessee border. It contains some of the oldest mountains on earth. Within the park are 16 peaks more than 6,000 feet high—and only one road cuts among them. Between the park entrances at Cherokee, North Carolina, and Gatlinburg, Tennessee, Newfound Gap Road twists and turns, revealing one spectacular view after another. During fall color season, this road is so congested that the crossing can take twice as long as it does during other times.

Great Smoky Mountains National Park was established by an act of Congress in 1926, but that was easy part. Raising the money to buy the property was difficult, and negotiations were complex. Within the designated boundaries of the park, 85 percent of the property was owned by 18 timber companies and the rest in tiny parcels by nearly 6,000 homesteaders. Years of state appropriations and private contributions netted only $5 million—half the necessary funds. John D. Rockefeller, Jr., matched that amount, and the park finally opened to the public in 1934.

Natural beauty is not the only thing preserved here. More than 75 historic structures are maintained by the park. These include the log cabins, barns, mills, and stables of some of the families that settled in the mountains in the 19th century.

Ways to explore the park seem endless. Those with only a little time can drive Newfound Gap Road, but they'll miss much of the park. A smaller road leads up to Clingmans Dome, the highest peak in the park, at 6,634 feet. Those who make the half-mile walk up to the observation tower will be rewarded with a stunning view of the Smokies. Those who enjoy hiking or horseback riding will appreciate the more than 800 miles of trails. Back-country camping is also a great way to explore these majestic and rugged mountains. Regardless of your preference for exploration, Great Smoky Mountains National Park will leave an impression on you that will last a lifetime.

The park's busiest months are June, July, August, and October. At these times, the campgrounds are full and the roads accessing the park are crowded. It can get cool here even in summer, so remember to bring a jacket or sweater. Also note that the park gets 50 to 80 inches of rain annually, so rain gear should be part of your preparations. And one other word of warning: There are bears in this part of the country, and none of them is named Yogi. If you see one, enjoy watching it from a distance, but *never* attempt to feed it or entice it for a closer view.

JUST THE FACTS

Great Smoky Mountains National Park is 50 miles west of Asheville on U.S. 19. The North Carolina entrance is at the town of Cherokee. The Tennessee entrance is at Gatlinburg. Three visitor centers offer maps, guidebooks, museum displays, weather and road information, schedules of park activities (including ranger-guided walks and talks), and calendars of special events. The centers are open every day except Christmas. For information, contact Great Smoky Mountains National Park, 107 Park Headquarters Road, Gatlinburg, Tenn. 37738 (865-436-1200).

Be sure to pick up a copy of *Smokies Guide* at one of the visitor centers. The official newspaper of the park, it is packed with information to make your visit the best possible.

Things to Do

MUSEUMS AND SCIENCE CENTERS

- The **Mountain Farm Museum** is located at the North Carolina entrance to the park. It consists of buildings typical of those found in the area around 1900. Corn is ground here every day, and the meal is available for purchase at the water-powered Mingus Mill, located a half-mile north of the farmstead.

- **Cades Cove,** on the Tennessee side of the park, is the site of a re-created pioneer mill community. Visitors can enjoy several cabins, a church, and a mill. They can also drive the 11-mile one-way loop around the settlements and adjacent pastures, or stroll among the buildings and observe life as it was for the early settlers. Park rangers lead a 30-minute guided walking tour daily during the summer. A small bookstore offers material about the area and its history. After dark, old-fashioned hayrides delight the kids.

RECREATION

As with most outdoor recreation, information is the key to a great time. The park's visitor centers and the rangers who staff them are the best source for up-to-date information on recreational opportunities.

■ **Hiking** is almost a religion at Great Smoky Mountains National Park. An endless variety of trails serves hikers of every taste and ability. The grandfather of them all, of course, is the **Appalachian Trail**, which zig-zags for 70 miles through the park on the crests of the mountains between Davenport Gap, near the eastern boundary, and Fontana Dam, in the southwest.

If you're a serious hiker, you'll need serious maps, which are available at the visitor centers. *The Smokies Hiking Map and Guide* includes an up-to-date hiking map and information on back-country campsites. Another reliable source is *Hiking Trails of the Smokies*, which describes every hike in the park.

■ **Camping** is also very popular in the park.

A permit—available from the visitor centers—is required for back-country camping. Back-country camping is free but is allowed only at designated campsites along the trails. If you wish to camp in the shelters along the Appalachian Trail, reservations are required. For more information, call the back-country office at 865-436-1231.

The park also offers 10 developed campgrounds with water but no showers, no electricity, and no trailer hookups. A fee is charged for the use of these campgrounds. Information and reservations can be made by calling 800-365-CAMP.

The campsites close in November and reopen in mid-March.

■ Those who enjoy **picnicking** will appreciate the 10 picnic areas in the park. Each has tables and fire grates. Please be aware of current fire conditions, and be conscientious about any outdoor cooking. The same for trash, as no one wants any four-footed guests crashing their party.

■ **Horseback riding** is offered through several licensed concession stables. Call 865-436-1200 for information.

- **Fishing** for brown and rainbow trout is popular in park streams all year long. You must have either a North Carolina or a Tennessee fishing license, both of which are honored throughout the park regardless of which side of the border you are on. Please check with the visitors centers for regulations regarding size and catch limits.

- **Naturalist programs** are offered by rangers from May to October at developed campgrounds and at the visitor centers. Some are talks, some involve short walks, and some are geared for children. Topics include wildflowers, hardwood trees, animal habitats, and pioneer life. For a special treat, consider one of the walks offered at sunset or twilight. Call 865-436-1200 for more information.

> Please be aware of the rules of the park and be considerate of the visitors who will come after you. Park regulations prohibit littering, defacing natural features, picking wildflowers, digging up plants, feeding wildlife, and letting pets run loose.

Places to Stay

INNS AND BED-AND-BREAKFASTS

- **LeConte Lodge**. Inexpensive. On top of Mount LeConte (865-429-5704). The only overnight facility inside the park, this lodge is accessible by a half-day hike. The premises are definitely rustic and the meals plain. Reservations are required. The lodge is open from late March through late November.

Oconaluftee Indian Village
COURTESY OF THE NORTH CAROLINA DIVISION OF TOURISM,
FILM AND SPORTS DEVELOPMENT

CHEROKEE
by Sue Clark

*T*he town of Cherokee is the largest community in the Qualla Boundary, the almost 56,000 acres of reservation land held in trust for the Eastern Band of the Cherokee Nation. The Cherokees are one of the Five Civilized Tribes of Muskogean-speaking people. They were the first Indians to have a written language, created by Sequoyah in 1821. At one time, they were an extremely powerful nation, controlling a territory of 135,000 square miles that stretched from the Ohio River southward into parts of present-day Georgia and Alabama. The forced removal of the Cherokees to the Oklahoma territory has come to be called the "Trail of

Tears." Several hundred Cherokees remained in the mountains during the removal. In 1866, they were finally granted the legal right to remain in their homeland. About 8,200 members of the Eastern Band reside in communities throughout the Qualla Boundary.

The town of Cherokee is undergoing some profound changes. Survival for the Native Americans used to depend on stereotypical tourist attractions that bore little resemblance to authentic Cherokee heritage. Ironically, the arrival of a large casino has pumped sorely needed revenue into the tribe. That revenue has been put to use improving the attractions that showcase the rich history and heritage of the Cherokee people.

JUST THE FACTS

Cherokee is located 48 miles west of Asheville at the intersection of U.S. 19 and U.S. 441. Just three miles north of Cherokee is the southern entrance to Great Smoky Mountains National Park.

The Cherokee Travel and Promotion Visitor Center is located where U.S. 19 and U.S. 441 merge. For information, call 800-438-1601 or 828-497-9195, or visit their website at www.cherokee-nc.com.

The *Cherokee One Feather* is a weekly newspaper available throughout town.

Things to Do

HISTORIC PLACES, GARDENS, AND TOURS

▪ *Oconaluftee Indian Village*, located on Drama Road a half-mile north of U.S. 441, is a re-creation of a Cherokee village as it was 250 years ago. Here, you can watch Cherokees creating tools and decorations, carving weapons and cooking utensils, grinding corn, cooking, finger-weaving, making baskets and beadwork, and burning out dugout canoes. Cherokee guides escort visitors on a two-hour journey into the past. Visitors are welcome to linger, take pictures, and ask questions. One of the highlights of the tour is the seven-sided council house. Surrounding the village is a beautiful botanical garden with paths leading past mossy rocks, trickling water, flower gardens, and vegetable gardens. The village is open daily from 9 A.M. to 5:30 P.M. from May 15 through October 25. Admission is charged. For more information, call 828-497-2315, or visit their website at www.oconalufteevillage.com.

MUSEUMS AND SCIENCE CENTERS

■ The *Museum of the Cherokee Indian*, located on U.S. 441 North, was totally renovated in 1998. Its state-of-the-art exhibits trace the history of the Cherokees, honor outstanding individuals, and show examples of traditional arts and crafts. Artifacts and relics are presented in real-life settings of the time period. A seven-minute, three-screen, multisensory film presents the Cherokee creation story. In the exhibit halls, you can view maps of the Trail of Tears and read newspaper accounts of the removal. At the display on Sequoyah's syllabary, you can listen to audio samplings of the language. The museum's gift shop carries books and souvenirs. The museum is open daily from 9 A.M. to 5 P.M. from September to May and from 9 A.M. to 8 P.M. from June through August. Admission is charged. Call 828-497-3481 for more information.

SPECIAL SHOPPING

■ *Qualla Arts and Crafts Mutual, Inc.*, located on U.S. 441 North, was organized by Native American craftsmen in 1946. It has grown to become the most successful Indian-owned and -operated craft cooperative in the United States. You'll find handmade Cherokee baskets, beadwork, pottery, woodcarvings, masks, and dolls. Another room displays crafts made by Indians of other tribes. The cooperative is open daily from 8 A.M. to 6 P.M. during the spring and fall, from 8 A.M. until 8 P.M. in the summer, and from 8 A.M. until 4:30 P.M. in the winter. Call 828-497-3103 for more information.

RECREATION

- **Harrah's Cherokee Casino**, located on U.S. 441, has brought a great deal of revenue to the Eastern Band of the Cherokee Indians. The size of three football fields, the casino features 2,300 video gaming machines, three restaurants, a gift shop, and even a day-care facility. Neon lightning bolts flash across the ceiling whenever someone wins a jackpot over $1,000; the sound of thunder means the jackpot's even bigger. The 1,500-seat Cherokee Pavilion provides live entertainment. The casino is where the action is 24 hours a day, seven days a week. Call 800-HARRAHS for more information.

- **Fishing** is popular around Cherokee, since the streams and ponds on the reservation are stocked and managed by the Cherokee Fish and Game Management. While you don't need a state fishing license, you must purchase a tribal fishing permit, available at convenience stores, campground offices, and other locations throughout town. Call 828-497-5201 for more information.

SEASONAL EVENTS

- **Unto These Hills** is performed at the 2,800-seat Mountainside Theater on U.S. 441. This play by Kermit Hunter is the most popular outdoor drama in the state. It uses words and music to tell the story of the Trail of Tears. Performances are staged Monday through Saturday from mid-June to late August. Shows begin at 8:45 P.M. until the end of July and at 8:30 P.M thereafter. Admission is charged. For more information, call 828-497-2111, or visit their website at www.untothesehills.com.

Places to Stay

The town of Cherokee has a number of motels, cabins, and lodges, many of them along the Oconaluftee River. And the arrival of the casino has brought many of the major chain hotels.

To reach the following lodgings—which are more in keeping with the nature of this book—you will have to head up U.S. 19 to Bryson City.

INNS AND BED-AND-BREAKFASTS

■ **Hemlock Inn**. Deluxe/Expensive. Off U.S. 19 east of Bryson City (828-488-2885). This is a lovely one-level inn on a Great Smoky Mountains hilltop. If you sit in a rocker on the porch, all you'll hear is the songs of the birds. The inn offers 21 rooms and four cottages furnished country-style. You can enjoy a fire in the hearth of the big family room. Breakfast and dinner, served in the dining room, include home-baked bread and homemade desserts.

■ **Fryemont Inn**. Moderate. Fryemont Road in Bryson City (828-488-2159). The Fryemont, an old-fashioned country inn built by timber baron Amos Frye, opened in 1923. The hardwood floors gleam in front of the field-stone hearth in the lobby. The inn's 44 rooms feature chestnut paneling, private baths, four-poster beds, simple furnishings, and special touches such as a basket with herbal bath granules in the bathroom. The inn has a tennis court and a swimming pool. The dining room has a bandstand for weekend entertainment. The inn is open from April through October.

■ **Randolph House**. Moderate. Fryemont Road in Bryson City (828-488-3472). Randolph House is the 1895 mansion that timber magnate Amos Fry built for himself. The seven cozy guest rooms are furnished with antiques, some dating to the 1850s. The sitting room is filled with overstuffed chairs that invite guests to while away a quiet evening after dinner. And what a dinner! Gourmet dining is the norm here. The menu includes such items as trout, flounder, prime rib, and stuffed Cornish game hens. Then there's the selection of homemade desserts. And let's not forget breakfast, which is equally sumptuous. Room rates include these two wonderfully prepared meals. The inn is open from mid-April through October.

Places to Eat

■ **The Chestnut Tree**. Moderate/Inexpensive. U.S. 19 South in the Holiday Inn Cherokee (828-497-9181). This is about the fanciest restaurant you'll find in Cherokee. It features mountain trout, steak, chicken, and a good selection of sandwiches. It is open for breakfast and dinner Monday through Saturday and for all three meals on Sunday.

■ **Grandma's Pancake and Steak**. Inexpensive. U.S. 19/U.S. 441 (828-497-9801). Grandma's is a casual family restaurant where you can get great country breakfasts any time of the day and steak, shrimp, and chicken entrées for lunch and dinner. It is open for breakfast and lunch Monday through Thursday and for all three meals on Friday, Saturday, and Sunday.

■ **Tee Pee Restaurant**. Inexpensive. U.S. 441 North (828-497-5141). Though the selection here is standard, the food is a cut above most places in Cherokee. The specialty is mountain trout. Buffets are offered for each meal, but only at certain times; diners can order from the menu at any time. Breakfast, lunch, and dinner are served daily.

Nearby

■ **Fontana Village**, located about 50 miles west of Cherokee on N.C. 28 North, is a resort community that grew from the housing units occupied by the workers who built Fontana Dam in the 1940s. The dam is the highest in the eastern United States and the largest facility of the Tennessee Valley Authority. Upon the dam's completion in 1945, the housing development was sold to private owners, who turned it into a family resort village.

The village has an inn with 94 rooms (some of which have fireplaces) and 250 rustic cottages equipped with kitchens. A restaurant, a buffet house, and a village café all serve meals to those who choose not to cook. Recreational activities include miniature golf, swimming, boating, fishing, hiking, horseback riding, archery, and badminton. A playground, craft classes, and other organized activities are available for children. The mountains that surround Fontana Lake make a magnificent setting for an extended family vacation. The village is open year-round. For more information, call 800-849-2258 or 828-498-2211, or visit their website at www.fontanavillage.com.

▪ *Joyce Kilmer Memorial Forest* contains one of the last stands of virgin forest on the East Coast. The forest is left completely to nature's control; no plants or trees, living or dead, may be cut or removed. The result is a magnificent forest containing more than 100 species of trees, many specimens of which are over 300 years old. A two-mile recreation trail loops through the forest and the adjoining 14,000-acre Slickrock Wilderness Area. Fittingly, the forest is named for the author of the well-known poem "Trees." Joyce Kilmer was still a young man when he was killed in France during World War I. To reach the forest named in his honor, take U.S. 129 North from Robbinsville and follow the signs. For information, contact the Cheoah Ranger Station at 828-479-6431.

▪ For overnight accommodations in the area, try *Snowbird Mountain Lodge* (828-479-3433), located at 275 Santeetlah Road. This rustic mountain inn, built of chestnut logs and native stone, offers an excellent view of the Snowbird range from its terrace.

The Trail of Tears

The facts are staggering: some 14,000 Cherokees were forced to leave their ancestral home with whatever they could carry; they walked to the Oklahoma territory in the dead of winter; no exceptions were made for the elderly, the sick, the pregnant, or the very young; approximately 20 percent died on the way.

In one of the most shameful episodes in this nation's history, the United States government decided to break numerous treaties with the Cherokees of the Blue Ridge and Great Smoky Mountains. In 1828, President Andrew Jackson put through Congress the Indian Removal Act, which commanded that all Indians be led west of the Mississippi River. Cherokee land was confiscated when gold was discovered in the Appalachians. The 1835 Treaty of New Echota provided the Cherokees $5 million and land in what is now Oklahoma in exchange for their 7 million acres in the East. But by May 1838, only 2,000 of the 16,000 Cherokees had moved voluntarily. General Winfield Scott and a force of 7,000 men were sent to evict the remaining Indians. The tragedy that transpired eventually came to be called the Trail of Tears.

First, stockades were built to hold the Indians. Then small squads armed with rifles and bayonets were sent out to round up every Cherokee they could find. No time was allotted for packing—men were seized in the fields and women and children from their homes. The soldiers prodded and drove the Indians to the stockades. Behind the soldiers came bands of looters, who pillaged and burned the Cherokees' former homes.

By October 1838, the removal was set to begin. The 1,200-mile trek took six months through the teeth of the winter. The average distance covered was 10 miles a day. The Cherokees stopped only to bury those who died along the way—of disease, starvation, and exhaustion.

The numbers are indeed staggering, but they do little to explain man's cruelty to man. When greed intercedes, there seems no end to the damage one people can inflict upon another.

MAGGIE VALLEY

by Sue Clark

$\mathcal{M}$ aggie Valley, a resort community at the base of the Balsam Mountains, was named for the daughter of the town's first postmaster. It is four miles from the Blue Ridge Parkway and 16 miles from Cherokee and the entrance to Great Smoky Mountains National Park. Maggie Valley has a permanent population of about 200, but that number swells in the summer, when tourists stay in the many motels along U.S. 19 (Main Street in town) and visit Ghost Town in the Sky and the Stompin' Ground. Cataloochee Ski Area is the big attraction during the winter.

JUST THE FACTS

Maggie Valley is on U.S. 19 about 30 miles west of Asheville.

The Maggie Valley Chamber of Commerce is on the south side of Main Street; call 828-926-1686 for information.

The newspaper that covers this area is Waynesville's *Enterprise Mountaineer*, which also puts out a tabloid of regional activities and advertising called *Adventure in the Smokies*.

Things to Do

RECREATION

■ At the top of the mountain, accessed by a chairlift or an inclined tram, is **Ghost Town in the Sky**, a facsimile of an Old West town. The town includes a general store, dancing girls in the Silver Dollar Saloon, and an occasional bank robbery or gunfight in the street. The 20 carnival-type rides and live shows by musicians and Indian dancers draw thousands of tourists each year. Ghost Town in the Sky is on U.S. 19 at the west end of town. It is open daily from May through October. An admission fee is charged except for children under three. Call 828-926-1140 for more information.

- The wooden stage of the **Stompin' Ground** comes alive with professional clogging teams dancing to Appalachian music provided by fiddlers, guitar strummers, and banjo pickers. This is a great place to experience the folk dancing unique to the Appalachians. The audience is encouraged to participate, so don't be afraid to try your hand at clogging, line dancing, or even waltzing. The Stompin' Ground opens at 8 P.M. from May through October. An admission fee is charged. It is located on U.S. 19. Call 828-926-1288 for more information.

- Built in 1961, **Cataloochee Ski Area** was the first ski resort in North Carolina. It was so successful that it spawned a new industry. Now, ski areas dot the North Carolina mountains from here to the Virginia border. Cataloochee's lodge and restaurant have a friendly atmosphere where families are welcome. The ski area has nine slopes and a vertical drop of 740 feet. Ski instruction and equipment rental are available. Cataloochee is located at 1080 Ski Lodge Road. Call 800-768-0285 or 828-926-0285 for more information.

SEASONAL EVENTS

- **Folkmoot USA** is a 10-day cultural event in July that features traditional dance groups from all over the world. It is hosted in several western North Carolina cities. Folkmoot's Maggie Valley performances are held at the Stompin' Ground. For information and a calendar of performances, call 828-926-1686.

Places To Stay

RESORTS, HOTELS, AND MOTELS

▪ **Cataloochee Ranch**. Deluxe. U.S. 19 (800-868-1401 or 828-926-1401). Located atop a mountain overlooking Maggie Valley, this is a special place with spectacular views. The lodge is rustic but well appointed. The staff is attentive to every detail. The seven cabins and two lodges contain 22 units with pine paneling and quilts on the beds. Horseback riding is the main activity here, but hiking trails and trout fishing are also offered. Rocking on the front porch and sitting before the fireplace in the lodge are also popular ways to spend time at Cataloochee Ranch. Generous country-style breakfasts and dinners, served from April through November, are included in the room rate. The ranch is open year-round.

▪ **Maggie Valley Resort and Country Club**. Deluxe/Expensive. On Moody Farm Road a half-mile west of the intersection of U.S. 19 and U.S. 276 (800-438-3861 or 828-926-1616). Located in a lush setting with a mountain backdrop, Maggie Valley Resort offers 64 luxurious rooms, 11 private villas, a golf course, tennis courts, and an outdoor pool. Breakfast and lunch, served in the resort's restaurant, are included in the room rate, as are golf privileges.

INNS AND BED-AND-BREAKFASTS

▪ **Jonathan Creek Inn and Villas**. Expensive/Moderate. 4324 Soco Road (800-577-7812 or 828-926-1232). At first glance, this may look like many of the motels in Maggie Valley, but look deeper. The 42 spacious, comfortable rooms here have back doors that open on to Jonathan Creek. All rooms have refrigerators and coffee makers; some have whirlpools, hot tubs, fireplaces, and wet bars. The three villas are an option for those desiring even more privacy. The beautifully landscaped grounds include several garden areas, hammocks, a picnic area, and a gazebo. The inn has an indoor pool.

- **Smoky Shadows Lodge**. Moderate/Inexpensive. On Fietop Road off U.S. 19 near the ski area (828-926-0001). The 12 guest rooms at this primitive-style lodge have chestnut paneling and ceilings of log beams. A separate cabin sleeps six. The long porch that extends across the back of the building offers a magnificent view. The country-gourmet meals, not included in the room rate, don't leave anyone hungry. Smoky Shadows is open year-round.

Places to Eat

- **Maggie Valley Resort and Country Club**. Expensive/Moderate. On Moody Farm Road a half-mile west of the intersection of U.S. 19 and U.S. 276 (828-926-1616). This is as fine a dining experience as you'll find in Maggie Valley. The restaurant has a sweeping view of the mountains; one whole wall of the dining room is a window. The menu features regional specialties such as mountain trout and well-prepared standard fare like prime rib, New York strip steak, and chicken. The restaurant is open daily for breakfast and dinner. Lunch is served in the pub, which is located in the clubhouse.

- **J. Arthur's Restaurant**. Moderate/Inexpensive. Soco Road (828-926-1817). The big, rambling, ranchlike building that houses J. Arthur's welcome families who flock here after a day of touring. Prime rib and steak are the specialties, but you'll find some surprises, too—such as "Gorgonzola Cheese Salad." Kids can satisfy their appetites with a range of hamburgers and sandwiches. The restaurant is open for dinner daily in the summer and Wednesday through Saturday in the winter.

WAYNESVILLE

by Sue Clark

Waynesville is an ideal mountain town. It doesn't have a manufactured tourist destination or a large business district. What Waynesville offers is a chance to get away from it all and still be close enough to visit the area's attractions. The downtown area boasts a wonderful selection of retail shops, galleries, and restaurants. The streets are lined with shade trees and comfortable benches.

Waynesville plays host to a variety of street festivals in the summer and fall. The wide range of entertainment at these outdoor celebrations includes parades, dance exhibitions, and craft displays. Thanks to plenty of charm and just the right amount of activity, Waynesville may become one of your favorite mountain destinations.

JUST THE FACTS

Waynesville is located at the intersection of U.S. 74 and U.S. 276 west of Asheville.

The Haywood County Chamber of Commerce, at 73 Walnut Street, is the place to go for information about the town. Call 800-334-9036 or 828-456-3021.

Waynesville's newspaper, the *Enterprise Mountaineer*, is published three times a week. The paper puts out a tabloid of regional activities and advertising called *Adventure in the Smokies*.

Things to Do

MUSEUMS AND SCIENCE CENTERS

- The **Museum of North Carolina Handicrafts**, at 49 Shelton Street, houses a fascinating collection of pottery, porcelain, baskets, woodcarvings, and turned bowls. Other treasures include hand-carved dulcimers, quilts, and a collection of Cherokee crafts and artifacts. The museum's gift shop sells a variety of crafts. An admission fee is charged. The hours are seasonal, so call before you visit; the number is 828-452-1551.

SEASONAL EVENTS

▪ *Smoky Mountain Fall Days* is a series of festivals held nearly every day during September and October in the towns of Waynesville, Maggie Valley, Canton, and Clyde. Festivities include the *Smoky Mountain Folk Festival*, the *High Country Quilt Show*, and the *Church Street Arts and Crafts Show*. For more information, call 800-334-9036 or 828-926-7538, or visit their website at www.smokymountains.net\html\fall.

▪ *Folkmoot USA*, held during July, is a 10-day festival featuring international dance performances by guest groups from all over the world. Many of the performances are in Waynesville. This festival is over 15 years old and is one of the finest gatherings of international dancers in the country. Call 828-452-2997 for more information.

Places to Stay

INNS AND BED-AND-BREAKFASTS

▪ *The Swag Country Inn*. Deluxe. On Hemphill Road off N.C. 276 (828-926-0430). The Swag has earned a reputation as one of the most exclusive inns in the mountains. The drive to the top of its private mountain is breathtaking. The rustic inn is made of hand-hewn logs taken from original Appalachian structures. The inn has a private entrance to Great Smoky Mountains National Park, an indoor racquetball court, a spring-fed swimming pond, and 250 acres of secluded land to explore. Special programs are offered throughout the summer. The Swag is open from May through mid-November.

• **Balsam Mountain Inn**. Expensive. On Seven Springs Drive off U.S. 23/U.S. 74, a half-mile from the Blue Ridge Parkway (828-456-9498; www.balsaminn.com). Opened in 1908 to serve the highest railway depot east of the Rockies, this restored National Historic Place offers beautiful mountain views from its two-tiered porch. The inn has 50 luxurious rooms with private baths, a 2,000-volume library, a card-and-puzzle room, and a spacious lobby with two fireplaces. You won't find telephones in the rooms, and there isn't a single television in the entire inn. Room rates include a full country breakfast. The inn's restaurant serves breakfast and dinner Monday through Saturday and all three meals on Sunday.

• **Waynesville Country Club Inn**. Expensive. Country Club Road (828-452-2258). This is one of Waynesville's most elegant lodgings. The three-story 1920s fieldstone inn is set against densely wooded mountains. Its 92 luxurious guest rooms offer views of the mountains or the 27-hole golf course. Amenities include tennis courts and a heated outdoor pool. The wood-paneled dining room is open for all three meals. In-season rates include breakfast and dinner.

• **Mountain Creek Bed-and-Breakfast**. Moderate. 146 Chestnut Walk (800-557-9766; www.bbonline.com/nc/mcbb). Finally, a bed-and-breakfast that's not filled with Victorian lace and antiques. The proprietors call the decor "retro 50s," and it's a refreshing and comfortable change of pace. A former corporate-retreat lodge, the main house is situated above a rock-lined pond that makes for a beautiful view from the wraparound porch and the window-lined den. The renovated pool house includes a Jacuzzi suite. The innkeepers are outdoor enthusiasts who will help organize hikes and bike trips. Room rates include a gourmet breakfast prepared by a truly talented cook. Guests can arrange for an equally delicious special dinner.

• **Ten Oaks**. Moderate. 224 Love Lane (800-563-2925; www.bbonline.com/nc/tenoaks). This charming bed-and-breakfast has three guest rooms and two suites, each with its own sitting area, fireplace, and private bath. The large front porch is perfect for rocking and taking in the mountain view. Room rates include breakfast and afternoon refreshments.

Places to Eat

- **Lomo Grill** and **Lomo's Bakery and Café**. Expensive/Moderate. 44 Church Street (828-452-5222). Lomo Grill features authentic Italian and Mediterranean cuisine. The finest meats are grilled in a wood-burning oven. The dining room's romantic ambiance complements the award-winning food and one of the finest wine cellars in the area. Dinner is served Monday through Saturday. Lomo's Bakery and Café is patterned in the French style. Its delicious right-out-of-the-oven goodies include breads, pastries, and gourmet cookies. You can also enjoy specialty sandwiches, vegetarian entrées, homemade soups, unique quiches, and beautifully prepared salads. Lunch is offered Monday through Saturday.

- **Michael's**. Expensive/Moderate. North Haywood Street (828-452-2620). This is one of those rare places where you can come dressed up or casual and still be treated to an elegant dinner and superb service. The front of the building features a beautiful bentwood bar and long, graceful windows. The dining room has white columns and mahogany furnishings. Upstairs is where large receptions are held. The menu selections include smoked trout, seafood pasta, apple-glazed pork tenderloin, and filet mignon. Entrées are served with fresh vegetables in season and tasty breads. Desserts include Michael's famous "White Chocolate Crème Brûlée." Dinner is served Tuesday through Saturday.

- **Bogart's**. Moderate/Inexpensive. 303 South Main Street (828-452-1313). This casual restaurant and tavern really hits its groove at night, when it gets pretty lively. The rustic interior is highlighted by stained-glass windows. Diners may choose from a good selection of burgers and sandwiches, as well as rainbow trout, stir-fried chicken, and sirloin tips. Lunch and dinner are served daily.

- **Mast Candy Barrel**. Inexpensive. 55 North Main Street (828-452-0075). Okay, so it's not technically a restaurant, but anything that can satisfy my sweet tooth deserves mention. The old-fashioned soda fountain draws as many customers looking for nostalgia as it does people in search of a cold drink. After enjoying their favorite malt or float, they head to the candy bins for a selection they haven't seen since childhood. Mast Candy Barrel is open seven days a week.

- **Whitman's Bakery and Sandwich Shoppe**. Inexpensive. 18 North Main Street (828-456-8271). This bakery has been serving downtown shoppers delectable goodies since 1945. The name *Whitman* (my maiden name) drew me in, but the aroma held me. The items I sampled were fresh, delicious, and deserving of such a fine name; let me personally recommend the butter cookies with the pastel centers. Sandwiches are prepared to order by the friendly, inviting staff. Lunch is offered Tuesday through Saturday.

Appendix

The following pages contain a collection of key facts and phone numbers that should help answer travel queries and make it easier to plan a North Carolina vacation.

STATE AGENCIES

North Carolina Division of Tourism, Film, and Sports Development
301 North Wilmington Street
Raleigh, N.C. 27601
(800-VISIT-NC or 919-733-4171; www.visitnc.com)

This should be your first contact for information about North Carolina. The tourism office provides state maps and several useful publications. It publishes a full-color booklet of over 150 pages listing accommodations, campgrounds, events around the state, and state parks and historic sites. The booklet also contains a map. If you stop by the Raleigh office, you can pick up free brochures for many attractions statewide.

Coastal Management Division
2728 Capitol Boulevard
Raleigh, N.C. 27604
(919-733-2293; www.dcm2.enr.state.nc.us)

Historic Sites Section
North Carolina Division of Archives and History
532 North Wilmington Street
Raleigh, N.C. 27604
(919-733-7862; www.ah.dcr.state.nc.us/sections/hs)

North Carolina Aquariums
417 North Blount Street
Raleigh, N.C. 27601
(919-733-2290; www.ncaquariums.com)

North Carolina Department of Transportation
1 South Wilmington Street
Raleigh, N.C. 27601
(919-733-2520; www.dot.state.nc.us)

North Carolina Division of Forest Resources
512 North Salisbury Street
Raleigh, N.C. 27604
(919-733-2162; www.dfr.state.nc.us)

North Carolina Division of Parks and Recreation
512 North Salisbury Street
Raleigh, N.C. 27604
(919-733-4181; www.ncsparks.net)

North Carolina Wildlife Resources Commission
512 North Salisbury Street
Raleigh, N.C. 27604
(919-733-7291; www.state.nc.us/wildlife)

GENERAL SOURCES

Blue Ridge Parkway
Superintendent
199 Hemphill Knob Road
Asheville, N.C. 28803
(828-271-4779; www.blueridgeparkway.org)

Cape Hatteras National Seashore
Superintendent
Route 1, Box 675
Manteo, N.C. 27954
(252-473-2113; www.nps.gov/caha)

Cape Lookout National Seashore
Superintendent
131 Charles Street
Harkers Island, N.C. 28531
(252-728-2250; www.nps.gov/calo)

Cherokee Visitors Center
P.O. Box 460
Main Street
Cherokee, N.C. 28719
(800-438-1601 or 828-497-9195; www.cherokee-NC.com)

Great Smoky Mountains National Park
Superintendent
107 Park Headquarters Road
Gatlinburg, Tenn. 37738
(865-436-5615 or 865-436-1200; www.nps.gov/grsm)

National Forests in North Carolina
Superintendent
160 Zillicoa Street
Asheville, N.C. 28802
(828-257-4200; www.cs.unca.edu/nfsnc)

North Carolina Association of RV Parks and Campgrounds
893 U.S. 70 West
Suite 202
Garner, N.C. 27529
(919-779-5709; www.gocampingamerica.com)

North Carolina Bed-and-Breakfast and Inns Association
P.O. Box 1077
Asheville, N.C. 28802
(800-849-5392; www.ncbbi.org)

North Carolina High Country Host
1700 Blowing Rock Road
Boone, N.C. 28607
(800-438-7500 or 828-264-1299; www.highcountryhost.com)

North Carolina Ski Areas Association
940 Ski Mountain Road
Blowing Rock, N.C. 28605
(828-295-7828; www.appskimtn.com)

Smoky Mountain Host of North Carolina
4437 Georgia Road
Franklin, N.C. 28734
(800-432-HOST; www.smokymtnhost.com)

Travel Council of North Carolina
4101 Lake Boone Trail
Suite 201
Raleigh, N.C. 27607
(919-787-5181, ext. 242; www.nctravel.org)

WELCOME CENTERS

I-26
P.O. Box 249
Columbus, N.C. 28722
(828-894-2120)

I-77 North
P.O. Box 1066
Dobson, N.C. 27017
(336-320-2181)

I-40 West
P.O. Box 809
Waynesville, N.C. 28785
(828-627-6206)

I-77 South
P.O. Box 410724
Charlotte, N.C. 28241-0724
(704-588-2660)

I-85 North
P.O. Box 156
Norlina, N.C. 27563
(252-456-3236)

I-95 North
P.O. Box 52
Roanoke Rapids, N.C. 27870
(252-537-9836)

I-85 South
P.O. Box 830
Kings Mountain, N.C. 28086
(704-937-7861)

I-95 South
P.O. Box 518
Rowland, N.C. 28383
(910-422-8314)

STATE HISTORIC SITES

Alamance Battleground
5803 N.C. 62 South
Burlington, N.C. 27215
(336-227-4785; www.ah.dcr.state.nc.us/sections/hs/alamance/
alamanc.htm)

Aycock Birthplace
264 Governor Aycock Road
Fremont, N.C. 27830
(919-242-5581; www.ah.dcr.state.nc.us/sections/hs/aycock/aycock.htm)

Bennett Place
4409 Bennett Memorial Road
Durham, N.C. 27705
(919-383-4345; www.ah.dcr.state.nc.us/sections/hs/bennett/bennett.htm)

Bentonville Battleground
5466 Harper House Road
Four Oaks, N.C. 27524
(910-594-0789; www.ah.dcr.state.nc.us/sections/hs/bentonvi/
bentonvi.htm)

Brunswick Town
8884 St. Philips Road SE
Winnabow, N.C. 28479
(910-371-6613; www.ah.dcr.state.nc.us/hsbrunswic/brunswic.htm)

Charlotte Hawkins Brown Memorial
6136 Burlington Road
Sedalia, N.C. 27342
(336-449-6515; www.ah.dcr.state.nc.us/hs/chb/chb.htm)

CSS *Neuse* (and Governor Caswell Memorial)
2612 W. Vernon Avenue (U.S. 70 Business)
P. O. Box 3043
Kinston, N.C. 28502
(252-522-2091; www.ah.dcr.state.nc.us/sections/hs/neuse/neuse.htm)

Duke Homestead
2828 Duke Homestead Road
Durham, N.C. 27705
(919-477-5498; www.ah.dcr.state.nc.us/sections/hs/duke.duke.htm)

Elizabeth II
1 Festival Park
Manteo, N.C. 27954
(252-475-1500; www.roanokeisland.com)

Fort Dobbs
438 Fort Dobbs Road
Statesville, N.C. 28625
(704-873-5866; www.ah.dcr.state.nc.us/hs/dobbs/dobbs.htm)

Fort Fisher
P.O. Box 169
Kure Beach, N.C. 28449
(910-458-5538; www.ah.dcr.state.nc.us/sections/hs/fisher/fisher.htm)

Historic Bath
207 Carteret Street (N.C. 92)
Bath, N.C. 27808
(252-923-3971); www.ah.dcr.state.nc.us/sections/hs/bath/bath.htm)

Historic Edenton
P.O. Box 474
Edenton, N.C. 27932
(252-482-2637); www.ah.dcr.state.nc.us/sections/hs/iredell/iredell.htm)

Historic Halifax
25 St. Davids Street
Halifax, N.C. 27839
(252-583-7191); www.ah.dcr.state.nc.us/sections/hs/halifax/halifax.htm)

Historic Stagville
5825 Old Oxford Highway
Bahama, N.C. 27503
(919-620-0120); www.ah.dcr.state.nc.us/sections/hs/stagville/default.htm)

Horne Creek Living History Farm
320 Hauser Rd.
Pinnacle, N.C. 27043
(336-325-2298; www.ah.dcr.state.nc.us/sections/hs/horne/horne.htm)

House in the Horseshoe
324 Alston Road
Sanford, N.C. 27330
(910-947-2051; www.ah.dcr.state.nc.us/sections/hs/horsesho/
horsesho.htm)

North Carolina State Capitol
1 East Edenton Street
Raleigh, N.C. 27601-2807
(919-733-4994; www.ah.dcr.state.nc.us/sections/capitol)

North Carolina Transportation Museum
411 South Salisbury Avenue
Spencer, N.C. 28159
(704-636-2889; www.nctrans.org)

Polk Memorial
308 South Polk Street
Pineville, N.C. 28134
(704-889-7145; www.ah.dcr.state.nc.us/sections/hs/polk/polk.htm)

Reed Gold Mine
9621 Reed Mine Road
Stanfield, N.C. 28163
(704-721-4653; www.itpi.dpi.state.nc.us/reed)

Somerset Place
2572 Lake Shore Road
Creswell, N.C. 27928
(252-797-4560;www.ah.dcr.state.nc.us/sections/hs/somerset/
somerset.htm)

Thomas Wolfe Memorial
52 North Market Street
Asheville, N.C. 28801
(828-253-8304; www.wolfememorial.home.att.net)

Town Creek Indian Mound
509 Town Creek Mound Road
Mount Gilead, N.C. 27306
(910-439-6802); www.ah.dcr.state.nc.us/sections/hs/town/town.htm)

Tryon Palace
610 Pollock Street
New Bern, N.C. 28562
(252-514-4900; www.tryonpalace.org)

Vance Birthplace
911 Reems Creek Road
Weaverville, N.C. 28787
(828-645-6706; www.ah.dcr.state.nc.us/sections/hs/vance/vance.htm)

OUTDOOR RECREATION

For most of the following, more complete information is provided in the text of this book; the index will tell you exactly where. This is intended as a quick-reference telephone list.

National Recreational Areas

Blue Ridge Parkway
(828-271-4779)

Cape Hatteras National Seashore
(252-473-2113)

Cape Lookout National Seashore
(252-728-2250)

Croatan National Forest
(252-638-5628)

Great Smoky Mountains
   National Park
(465-436-1200)

Nantahala National Forest
(828-257-4200)

Pisgah National Forest
(828-877-3265)

Uwharrie National Forest
(910-576-6391)

State Parks and Recreational Areas

Boone's Cave
(704-982-4402)

Carolina Beach
(910-458-8206)

Cliffs of the Neuse
(919-778-6234)

Crowders Mountain
(704-853-5375)

Duke Power
(704-528-6350)

Eno River
(919-383-1686)

Falls Lake
(919-676-1027)

Fort Fisher
(910-458-5798)

Fort Macon
(252-726-3775)

Goose Creek
(252-923-2191)

Hammocks Beach
(910-326-4881)

Hanging Rock
(336-593-8480)

Jockey's Ridge
(252-441-7132)

Jones Lake
(910-588-4550)

Jordan Lake
(919-362-0586)

Kerr Lake
(252-438-7791)

Lake James
(828-652-5047)

Lake Waccamaw
(910-646-4748)

Lumber River
(910-628-9844)

Medoc Mountain
(252-586-6588 or 252-445-2280)

Merchants Millpond
(252-357-1191)

Morrow Mountain
(704-982-4402)

Mount Mitchell
(828-675-4611)

New River
(336-982-2587)

Pettigrew
(252-797-4475)

Pilot Mountain
(336-325-2355)

Raven Rock
(910-893-4888)

Singletary Lake
(910-669-2928)

South Mountains
(828-433-4772)

Weymouth Woods
(910-692-2167)

Stone Mountain
(336-957-8185)

William B. Umstead
(919-571-4170)

Theodore Roosevelt
(252-726-3775)

FISHING AND HUNTING

You can get a fishing or hunting permit from any license agent, of which there are many. Look for them at hardware, sporting-goods, and K-mart stores. Some licenses expire June 30, while others expire one year from the date of purchase.

For further information, contact the North Carolina Wildlife Resources Commission.

Resident fishing license—$15
Resident fishing license (including trout)—$20
    Daily permit—$5
    Trout license—$10
Nonresident fishing license—$30
    Daily permit—$10
    Three-day permit—$15
    Trout license—$10
Saltwater recreational fishing does not require a license.

Resident sportsman license—$40
    Hunting license—$15
    Big-game permit—$10
    Trapping license—$25
Nonresident sportsman license—$40
    Six-day hunting license—$25
    Big-game permit—$40

BICYCLING

To help cyclists find safe and interesting places to ride, the Bicycle Program of the North Carolina Department of Transportation has identified primary and secondary roads that are relatively safe for cycling because of low traffic volume and good roadway conditions. Various routes encompassing over 3,000 miles have been mapped. Others will be available in the future.

Sample routes:

Mountains-to-Sea—700 miles from Murphy to Manteo
Piedmont Spur—200-mile east-west route
Carolina Connection—200-mile north-south route
Ports of Call—300 miles in the coastal area
Cape Fear Run—160 miles from Raleigh to the Cape Fear area
Ocracoke Option—175 miles from the Wilson area to the Cedar Island ferry
Southern Highlands—120 miles from the Blue Ridge Parkway to Lincolnton

Map and tour routes are available for selected areas. To order one or more of these free guides, contact the Bicycle Program, North Carolina Department of Transportation, 1552 Mail Service Center, Raleigh, N.C. 27699-1552 (919-733-2804).

AID FOR HANDICAPPED TRAVELERS

Access North Carolina is an excellent travel guide for disabled persons. It provides accessibility information for virtually every tourist attraction in the state. It evaluates parking lots, entrances, interior and exterior sites, water fountains, and restrooms and also mentions special tours and access for blind and deaf persons.

It is available at no charge from the North Carolina Division of Tourism, Film, and Sports Development.

HOTEL/MOTEL TOLL-FREE NUMBERS

These numbers may be called from anywhere in the continental United States. Consult your local telephone directory for regional listings.

Best Western International
(800-528-1234)

Hyatt Corporation
(800-228-9000)

Comfort Inns
(800-228-5150)

Marriott Hotels
(800-228-9290)

Courtyard by Marriott
(800-321-2211)

Quality Inns
(800-228-5151)

Days Inn
(800-325-2525)

Radisson Hotel Corporation
(800-333-3333)

Econo Lodges of America
(800-446-6900)

Ramada Inns
(800-228-2828)

Hampton Inn
(800-426-6900)

Red Roof Inns
(800-843-7663)

Hilton Hotel Corporation
(800-445-8667)

Renaissance Hotels and Resorts
(800-468-3571)

Holiday Inns, Inc.
(800-465-4329)

Sheraton Hotels and Inns
(800-325-3535)

Howard Johnson
(800-446-4656)

CAR RENTAL TOLL-FREE NUMBERS

Avis Reservations Center
(800-831-2847)

Budget Rent-A-Car
(800-527-0700)

Dollar Rent-a-Car
(800-800-4000)

Thrifty Car Rental
(800-367-2277)

Hertz Corporation
(800-654-3131)

U-Haul Equipment Rental
(800-468-4285)

National Car Rental
(800-227-7368)

Index